T0333808

JAMES HOGG

Contributions to
Annuals and Gift-Books

THE STIRLING / SOUTH CAROLINA RESEARCH EDITION OF
THE COLLECTED WORKS OF JAMES HOGG
GENERAL EDITORS – DOUGLAS S. MACK AND GILLIAN HUGHES

THE STIRLING / SOUTH CAROLINA RESEARCH EDITION OF
THE COLLECTED WORKS OF JAMES HOGG
GENERAL EDITORS – DOUGLAS S. MACK AND GILLIAN HUGHES

Volumes are numbered in the order of their publication in
the Stirling / South Carolina Research Edition

JAMES HOGG

Contributions to Annuals and Gift-Books

Edited by
Janette Currie and Gillian Hughes

EDINBURGH UNIVERSITY PRESS
2006

© Edinburgh University Press, 2006

Edinburgh University Press
22 George Square
Edinburgh
EH8 9LF

Typeset at the University of Stirling
Printed by MPG Books Ltd, Bodmin, Cornwall

ISBN 0 7486 1527 X

A CIP record for this book is available
from the British Library

The Stirling / South Carolina Research Edition of

The Collected Works of James Hogg

The Aims of the Edition

James Hogg lived from 1770 till 1835. He was regarded by his contemporaries as one of the leading writers of the day, but the nature
of his fame was influenced by the fact that, as a young man, he had
been a self-educated shepherd. The second edition (1813) of his
poem *The Queen's Wake* contains an 'Advertisement' which begins as
follows.

>THE *Publisher having been favoured with letters from gentlemen in vari-*
>*ous parts of the United Kingdom respecting the Author of the* QUEEN'S
>WAKE, *and most of them expressing doubts of his being a Scotch Shep-*
>*herd; he takes this opportunity of assuring the Public, that* THE QUEEN'S
>WAKE *is really and truly the production of* JAMES HOGG, *a* common

> shepherd, *bred among the mountains of Ettrick Forest, who went to service when only seven years of age; and since that period has never received any education whatever.*

His contemporaries tended to regard the Scotch Shepherd as a man of powerful and original talent, but it was felt that his lack of education caused his work to be marred by frequent failures in discretion, in expression, and in knowledge of the world. Worst of all was Hogg's lack of what was called 'delicacy', a failing which caused him to deal in his writings with subjects (such as prostitution) which were felt to be unsuitable for mention in polite literature.

A posthumous collected edition of Hogg was published in the late 1830s. As was perhaps natural in the circumstances, the publishers (Blackie & Son of Glasgow) took pains to smooth away what they took to be the rough edges of Hogg's writing, and to remove his numerous 'indelicacies'. This process was taken even further in the 1860s, when the Rev. Thomas Thomson prepared a revised edition of Hogg's *Works* for publication by Blackie. These Blackie editions present a comparatively bland and lifeless version of Hogg's writings. It was in this version that Hogg was read by the Victorians, and he gradually came to be regarded as a minor figure, of no great importance or interest.

Hogg is thus a major writer whose true stature was not recognised in his own lifetime because his social origins led to his being smothered in genteel condescension; and whose true stature was obscured after his death, because of a lack of adequate editions. The poet Douglas Dunn wrote of Hogg in the *Glasgow Herald* in September 1988: 'I can't help but think that in almost any other country of Europe a complete, modern edition of a comparable author would have been available long ago'. The Stirling / South Carolina Edition of James Hogg seeks to fill the gap identified by Douglas Dunn. When completed the edition will run to thirty-four volumes, and it will cover Hogg's prose, his poetry, his letters, and his plays.

General Editors' Acknowledgements

Editing Hogg's *Contributions to Annuals and Gift-Books* has proved to be a particularly complex task, not least because it has required the investigation of his dealings with a large number of different publishers and editors. In its early stages work on this volume was greatly assisted by the appointment of Dr Gillian Hughes to a James Hogg Research Fellowship funded by the University of Stirling, and by the appointment of Dr Janette Currie to a post-doctoral Modern Humanities Research Association Research Fellowship at the University of Stirling. We are grateful for support from the University of Stirling's Department of English Studies, which made it possible for Dr Currie to undertake research at the American Antiquarian Society, Worcester, Massachussets. Dr Hughes's research for the present volume was facilitated by a period of study in New Haven during October 2001, made possible by the award of a Frederick A. & Marion S. Pottle visiting research fellowship. Generous grants made by the Carnegie Trust for the Universities of Scotland allowed Dr Currie to undertake extended research at the Library of Congress, Washington D.C.; and allowed Dr Hughes to examine Hogg letters, manuscripts, and artefacts in New Zealand. We are also grateful for the support of the University of South Carolina, and for assistance from the Association for Scottish Literary Studies and the James Hogg Society. In addition, we record with gratitude the fact that in its later stages the work of Dr Hughes and Dr Currie on the present volume has been sustained by a major Research Grant, awarded in 2002 by the United Kingdom's Arts and Humanities Research Board in support of the research of the Stirling / South Carolina Edition of James Hogg. Douglas Mack was General Editor for this volume.

Volume Editors' Acknowledgements

We are indebted to our exemplary General Editor, Douglas Mack, for his courteous generosity in guiding us through the various complexities thrown up in the preparation of this volume. We wish to thank the following institutions and individuals for permission to cite manuscript materials in their care: the Alexander Turnbull Library, Wellington, New Zealand; the Beinecke Rare Book and Manuscript Library, Yale University; the Brotherton Collection, University of Leeds Library; the Fales Manuscript Collection, Fales Library & Special Collections, New York University; the Huntington Library, San Marino, California; the Historical Society of Pennsylvania, Philadelphia (HSP); courtesy of the Lilly Library, Indiana University, Bloomington, IN; National Archives of Scotland; the Trustees of Sir Francis Ogilvy, of Inverquharity, Bart.; the Trustees of the National Library of Scotland; the National Portrait Gallery; the Master and Fellows of Trinity College Cambridge; James Hogg Collection, Special Collections, University of Otago Library, Dunedin, New Zealand; Rare Books & Special Collections, Thomas Cooper Library, University of South Carolina; and Stirling University Library. Hogg's letter to A. A. Watts of 17 April 1827 is published with permission of the Princeton University Library. Every effort has been made to trace copyright holders, but if any have been inadvertently overlooked the publisher will be pleased to make the necessary acknowledgement at the first opportunity.

With regard to the illustrations in this volume, we record with gratitude that those from *Friendship's Offering*, *The Musical Bijou*, and *The Amulet* have been reproduced from copies owned by Dr Gillian Hughes; that from *Forget Me Not* has been reproduced by permission of Glasgow University Library, Department of Special Collections; those for 'Katie Cheyne' and 'The Shepherd Boy's Song' have been reproduced by permission of the Trustees of the National Library of Scotland; and Wilkie's 'Pitlessie Fair' and 'A Scene from Ramsay's Gentle Shepherd' are reproduced courtesy of the Trustees of the National Galleries of Scotland.

We have been assisted greatly by librarians, and particular thanks are due to: the British Library; Helen Beardsley of Stirling University Library; Joanne Chaison of the American Antiquarian Society Library; Jocelyn Chalmers of the Alexander Turnbull Library (Wellington); Donald Kerr of the Special Collections of the University of Otago Library; Sheila Mackenzie of the National Library of Scotland; Marilyn Morton of Sheffield Hallam University Library; and Margot O'Donnell of Glasgow University Library.

We thank Peter Garside for permission to reproduce and quote material from his S/SC edition of *A Queer Book*; Suzanne Gilbert for help in the preparation of this volume; Penny Fielding of the University of Edinburgh for checking the manuscript of 'Play up my Love' / 'The Shepherd Boy's Song' while she was in Philadelphia; Tom Hubbard of BOSLIT at the National Library of Scotland for information and for translation of foreign annuals; Lindsay Reid, a research midwife at Glasgow University, who provided interesting information on nineteenth-century midwifery practices; Vanessa Warne of Queen's University, Kingston, Ontario for sharing her knowledge of *The Keepsake*; and Harry Hootman and Patrick Scott of the University of South Carolina for drawing our attention to the item in this volume from *The May Flower*. We are grateful to the late Jill Rubenstein for checking this item for us, and to Mark Weinstein for checking the two items in the Huntington Library. We thank Tom Richardson for loaning his manuscript fragment from the *Young Lady's Sabbath Companion*, and for permission to make use of it in this volume. For help in the preparation of this volume, Gillian Hughes expresses personal thanks to Richard Jackson, to Meiko O'Halloran, and to Hogg's descendants, Chris Gilkison, Liz Milne, and David Parr. Janette Currie expresses personal thanks to her family, to Mardi Stewart, and to Jane Stewart.

Contents

Illustrations and Musical Settings

Some of Hogg's contributions to annuals were accompanied by illustrations or musical settings. These are reproduced in the present volume, and are listed below. The Introductory and Textual Notes contain additional illustrations at pp. 327–28.

Introduction
Janette Currie

1. The Annuals: A Brief Survey

In the section entitled 'Literary Chit-Chat and Varieties' in the *Edinburgh Literary Journal* of 16 May 1829, a short note suggested that James Hogg—song-writer, poet, novelist, and regular contributor to literary periodicals—was about to take a different turn in his writing career: 'It has been proposed to Mr. Hogg to take the Editorship of a new ANNUAL for Scotland, similar to those which have been so fashionable in England of late years' (p. 387). In the event, Hogg did not take up the editorial challenge: nevertheless the seriousness of this proposition reveals the strength of Hogg's engagement with the new publishing phenomenon represented by the annuals. Between November 1824 and the middle of the nineteenth century over sixty poems and around twenty prose tales by 'The Author of *The Queen's Wake*', 'James Hogg', or 'The Ettrick Shepherd' were published in annuals.[1] Alongside of these, in 1832 he wrote and had printed a juvenile gift-book entitled *A Father's New Year's Gift*, and shortly before his death in 1835 he projected and had almost completed a drawing-room book for women entitled *The Young Lady's Sabbath Companion*. Before discussing in detail Hogg's contributions to and involvement with the annuals, it may be useful to summarise the history of the annual from its inception in 1822 to its demise as a literary force in the 1860s.

The concept of the literary miscellany was not new in 1822. Indeed, around 1816 Hogg had projected such an enterprise. He describes this in his 'Memoir of the Author's Life':

> I took it into my head that I would collect a poem from every living author in Britain, and publish them in a neat and elegant volume, by which I calculated I might make my fortune. I either applied personally, or by letter, to Southey, Wilson, Wordsworth, Lloyd, Morehead, Pringle, Paterson, and several others; all of whom sent me very ingenious and beautiful poems.[2]

Likewise, the giving of gift-books containing quotations of poetry and moral instruction at the end of the year to one's patron, goddaughter, or godson was a custom that had been practised in Britain since at least the sixteenth century. In the autumn of 1822, this private and personal custom was combined with the literary miscellany format and developed into the commercial enterprise that became a publishing phenomenon of the first half of the nineteenth century. In the late autumn of 1822, Rudolph Ackermann, a London publisher and dealer in fine art, published *Forget Me Not: A Christmas and New Year's Present for 1823*. Anne Renier writes that this first annual 'combined two popular forms of publication, the pocket diary and almanac familiar in England and its German counterpart *Das Taschenbuch*'. The first *Forget Me Not* had 'twelve copper engravings of the months [...] accompanied by verses or "poetical illustrations" by William Combe', as well as 'stories and poems reflecting the taste for romantic gloom in the vein of the German school of writers [...] including Burger'. These were followed by 'genealogical tables of the sovereigns of Europe, lists of ambassadors at the principal courts of Europe, analysis of the [...] census of 1821', and finally 'a historical chronicle for 1822'.[3]

The following year Ackermann changed the format of the *Forget Me Not* and omitted the functional material. In this year two more annuals appeared, both of which followed Ackermann's first formula: *The Graces,* named after a popular ladies' pocket-book, and *Friendship's Offering*. In 1825, Alaric A. Watts replaced George Croly as the editor of *The Graces* and followed Ackermann's new pattern as was signalled in a new title: *Literary Souvenir; or, Cabinet of Poetry and Romance*. In 1826, T. K. Hervey took over the editorship of *Friendship's Offering* and raised the quality of the literary contributions.[4] Thereafter, Renier writes, these three annuals 'established the type which attained its greatest popularity during the 1820s: poems, verses and stories, essays and sketches, embellished with plates by the first artists and engravers'.[5]

From 1825 sales of annuals soared rapidly. In the preface to the *Forget Me Not* for 1825, the editor Frederic Shoberl noted of the previous year's edition that 'a very large impression was exhausted before the arrival of that season for which it is more particularly destined; and, for upwards of a week before Christmas, the publisher was unable to execute orders which he was continually receiving' (pp. i–ii). The production costs of an annual were extensive, but these were often offset by the high demand as Shoberl noted in the preface to the *Forget Me Not* for 1832: 'the heavy expense attendant on what are characteristically denominated "The Annuals" cannot be reimbursed but by a very extensive circulation' (p. 3). The *Literary Souvenir* for 1827 cost 'approximately £2,620 to publish' but 'more than eight thousand copies were sold at prices varying from 8s.6d. to 12s (depending on when an order was placed or a sale made)', thus offsetting the initial outlay.[6] S. C. Hall, editor of the *Amulet; or, Christian and Literary Remembrancer* from 1826 to 1836 estimated that the accumulated proceeds for the sale of all the annuals published for the year 1829 amounted to £90,000:

	£
Authors and Editors	6,000
Painters for Pictures or Copyrights	3,000
Engravers	12,000
Copper-plate Printers	5,000
Letter-press Printers	5,000
Paper Manufacturers	6,000
Book-binders	9,000
Silk Manufacturers and Leather Sellers	500
Advertisements	2,000
Incidental Expenses	1,500
	50,000
Publisher's Profits	10,000
Retail Bookseller's Profits	30,000
	90,000[7]

From the above table it can be discerned that the largest outlay for the publishers was on the visual appearance of the annual. The first annuals were covered in embossed paper enclosed within slip covers, but as annuals became a desirable commodity, objects to own and to be seen to own, they moved away from their pocket-book origins entirely and were issued in octavo and sometimes in quarto, and were encased in silk, velvet, or embossed leather. Annuals would often appear in the same year in different formats. For example, Paley records that the *Keepsake* was issued in two sizes: 'the silk-bound gilt-edged' edition 'measured only seven and a quarter by four and three-quarter inches' and was sold at a guinea; and a 'luxury, large paper volume' that 'measured nine and three-eighth by six' was available by special order for £2 12s 6d.[8] Often the engravings of the annuals were sold separately. For example, the *Amulet* for 1831 advertised 'a few set of proofs of the Illustrations to the "Amulet" [...] Proofs unlettered (set in a portfolio) £2 10s; lettered (ditto) £1 10s' (p. 361). Moreover, as Gillian Hughes notes below in 'Hogg, Art, and the Annuals', advances in technology in the early nineteenth century meant that engravings could be mass-produced. Thus, prints of the engravings of paintings by John Martin such as *The Fall of Nineveh* and *Balshaazar's Feast* were promoted in the advertisements in the *Forget Me Not* for 1830.

On the surface, then, the annuals can be identified homogeneously as mass-produced highly decorative gift-books. Owing to the lucrative potential of the annuals, however, editors and publishers adopted different and often contradictory strategies to keep ahead of their rivals. For example, the editorial policy of the *Keepsake* for 1828 was to engage 'Authors of prime celebrity—and persons distinguished by rank or fashion, or station'[9] on their lists. This was in contrast to the policy adopted in the following year by Alaric A. Watts, the editor of *Literary Souvenir*, who noted in the preface to the number for 1829 that in choosing the literary contributions he had been 'influenced less by the importance of the name than the intrinsic value of the article' (p. xi); S. C. Hall, the editor of the *Amulet* adopted a pious, semi-religious tone when he claimed that it was his intention 'to blend religious instruction with literary amusement and a taste for the fine arts' (1828, pp. 5–6), while the editor of *Winter's Wreath* for 1829, in contrast, stated (p. iii) that in this annual 'the introduction of religious topics has been carefully avoided' because 'their discussion appears unsuited to a work of elegant amusement'.

The relatively short Christmas season became extended as annuals were published as early as the end of October to steal a march on their rivals. This early printing also enabled the annuals to reach further than Britain (for example to India, Canada, and the United States of America) in time for the Christmas market. Letitia E. Landon attempted to establish an Easter annual, and there was also a small selection of summer annuals, for example, *The White Rose of York: A Midsummer Annual*, edited by George Hogarth (London: John Murray, 1834). Thomas Hood successfully introduced the *Comic Annual* in 1830, and in 1828 'juvenile annuals' were introduced with *The Christmas Box: An Annual Present for Children*, edited by T. Crofton Croker. This was followed by a number of imitators, and thereafter annuals for children became an acceptable part of the Christmas season. Overall, by 1832 there were sixty-three different annuals vying for contributions from established and beginning writers, each one paradoxically claiming a uniqueness while dressing appropriately to the form.

During their peak of popularity from the late 1820s to the early 1830s, the annuals boasted contributions not only from Hogg but also from John Clare ('the Northamptonshire peasant'), S. T. Coleridge, Sir Walter Scott, Allan Cunningham, John Galt, Mary Shelley, and Letitia Landon ('L.E.L.'). The annuals of the mid-1830s included contributions by Tennyson and Ruskin, and later annuals included contributions from Dickens. Publishers also employed established authors and poets to edit their annuals. For example, Letitia Landon, the London-based poetess, edited five different annuals between 1832 and 1839 and 'in nearly every case, she was called upon to write the entire copy text'.[10] Celebrity, it was discovered, could sell. The energetic pursuit of celebrity authors began in earnest early in 1828 when Frederic Mansel Reynolds (who replaced William Harris Ainsworth, the editor of the first issue of the *Keepsake*), and the *Keepsake's* proprietor Charles Heath embarked on a campaign to sign the most prestigious names. They personally visited Scott, Southey, Coleridge, and Wordsworth, enticing each of them with large amounts of money in exchange for a contribution for the *Keepsake*. Scott, for example, was offered '£800 to edit the *Keepsake* and £400 to contribute 70 to 100 pages', both of which he declined, agreeing instead to sell an article for £500. Wordsworth agreed terms of 'a hundred guineas for twelve pages of verse'.[11] According to its preface, the production cost for this annual was 'the enormous sum of *eleven thousand guineas*' (1829, p. iii) which was recouped through the elevated price of the annual of one guinea or more (see p. xv above for a detailed breakdown). Marketing strategies notwithstanding, the pursuit of celebrity and of maintaining the very best quality in every part of the annual: silk binding, gilt edging, engravings from paintings by celebrated artists and literary contributions from distinguished authors, together with the relatively short season, meant that many annuals did not survive. By the middle of the 1830s high production costs, declining sales, and fierce competition led to a sharp decline in the number of annuals.

In the preface to the *Forget Me Not* for 1842, Frederic Shoberl put the decline in sales of the annuals to a combination of 'fashion, caprice, [and] the positive demerits of some of those new competitors which started each succeeding year in the race of imitation, and mostly broke down in their first course' (p. 4). Certainly, both the *Anniversary* for 1829 and the *Scottish Annual* for 1836 were aborted after the first number, but others such as the *Gem* (1829–32) and the *Amulet* (1826–36) managed longer runs. Annuals with most numbers, such as the *Keepsake* (1828–57), *Forget Me Not* (1823–47), and *Friendship's Offering* (1824–44) appear to have survived by adapting to suit changes in public taste. For example, in 1835, *Forget Me Not* was presented as 'an old friend with a new face' (p. 3) and was published for the first time in a larger format, with silk bindings and with fewer contributors. Some annuals not only changed their format but also their character. Alaric A. Watts declared in the preface to what would have been the *Literary Souvenir* for 1835 that it was 'separating itself from the class of publications with which it has so long associated; laying aside their livery, and adopting a new form, and, to a certain extent, a new character'. This change was desirable, Watts argued, because 'the inconvenience of appending elaborate tales, written for the purpose, to engravings from the most celebrated pictures of the day, has been admitted on all hands' (pp. iii–iv).

The new title *The Cabinet of Modern Art* reveals the change of emphasis from literature to art. Unfortunately, the adaptability of the annuals did not prevent a decline of their popularity, and as the rise of the annual was swift so was its demise. According to A. Bose, 'the number of English Annuals, rising from nine in 1825 and 1826 to forty-three in 1830, fell to eleven in 1850, and after 1860 the species virtually died out'.[12]

While British annuals were in decline in the late 1830s, elsewhere the annuals were just reaching their peak of popularity. Alongside their European counterparts, the *Canadian Forget Me Not* was issued in 1837, and both the *Bengal Annual* and the *Australian Souvenir* were published in the late 1830s. British gift-books and annuals had sold well in America, and in December 1825 the first American annual, the *Atlantic Souvenir*, was published by the Philadelphia company of Carey and Lea.[13] Thereafter, sales of American annuals and gift-books soared. In the thirty years of their popularity, 'nearly every American writer of reputation' contributed.[14] For example, several of Nathaniel Hawthorne's *Twice Told Tales* first appeared as unsigned contributions in the *Token*, and there are contributions from Emerson, Poe, and Longfellow in the *Gift* for 1845. While some British writers contributed to foreign annuals it was more often the case that their work was 'selected' from British annuals and reprinted without their authority or knowledge.[15] Several of Hogg's contributions to British annuals were reprinted in America. For example, he contributed his prose dialogue 'What is Sin' to *Ackermann's Juvenile Forget Me Not* for 1830, and it was reprinted in Boston in *Youth's Keepsake: A Christmas and New Year's Gift for Young People* for 1836.[16] Moreover, as with British annuals an author's original work was often posthumously published. 'Song' by 'the late James Hogg, the Ettrick Shepherd', for example, appears as 'never before published' in the American annual the *May Flower* for 1846, at p. 147.[17] As Ralph Thompson rightly points out 'the American phase is in its own right important' (Thompson, p. 1), and this is true of all the different national permutations of annuals and gift-books. The international popularity of the genre highlights the overall importance of the phenomenon of the annuals.

2. Hogg's Contributions to the Annuals

Hogg's first known contribution to an annual was a poem, entitled 'Invocation to the Queen of the Fairies', that appeared in the first number of the *Literary Souvenir* (for 1825: published November 1824). The poem also forms the beginning of 'Book Sixth' of Hogg's epic poem *Queen Hynde* (published December 1824).[18] In contrast to the negative reviews of *Queen Hynde*,[19] 'Invocation to the Queen of the Fairies' was well received. The *Literary Gazette* of 13 November 1824 commented on the quality of all the contributions to the *Literary Souvenir* but singled out Hogg's for special mention: 'We are at a loss whom to station fore-most. Stand forth, however, James Hogg, for thy verse is chivalrous, imaginative, and gallant'. Hogg's poem was reprinted in full in this review,[20] and in view of its reception it is not surprising to find that in 1826 and 1827 Hogg contributed exclusively to Watts's annual.

In 1827 contributions by Hogg were solicited by Rudolph Ackermann, who sent him a copy of the most recent *Forget Me Not*. It appears to have been common practice for editors and publishers to send presentation copies of their annuals when seeking contributions for the next year, as Thomas Pringle, the editor of *Friendship's Offering*, and S. C. Hall, the editor of the *Amulet*, also introduced Hogg to their annuals in this way. Allan Cunningham, the editor of the ill-fated *Anniversary*, used a letter of 6 March 1828 to approach Hogg for contributions in his capacity as a friend: 'I want your help a little, and I know you wish me very well and that you will assist me', he wrote.[21] And in the Preface to the only number of the annual to be published he boasted: 'This volume, as it stands, will prove that I have friends, and good ones; men whose names would lend lustre to any undertaking' (p. xiv).

Friendship aside, money was the major incentive to publish in the annuals. Hogg's letter to Hall of 15 March [1829] gives an insight into why Hogg so readily acceded to requests for contributions: 'the writing for these miscellaneous works is become a kind of business now and I find it one that suits me who have only a spare day now and then very well'.[22] From 1827, Hogg, in common with many other farmers in Britain, suffered large losses both in his stock in the severe weather conditions of drought and storm, and financially in the depressed markets. Indeed, from 1827 owing to the uncertain economic climate he was in constant fear of losing

Mount-Benger, the farm in Ettrick that he had leased from the Duke of Buccleuch. In January of that year he wrote to Scott about his precarious tenancy:

> I have received word from his Grace's curators either to pay up my arrears at Whitsunday or give up my farm; as I cannot do the former without disposing of great part of my stock, so I think the latter is my only and best resource, as in spite of all my exertions (and I can do no more for it) I am continuing to lose at the rate a hundred a year.[23]

Moreover, in the publishing business the devastating financial crash of the winter of 1826 and the unsettling agitation in the early 1830s that preceded the Reform Act of 1832 provoked an air of caution and many publishers refrained from speculating in large issues of new poetry and prose. The surviving correspondence between William Blackwood and Hogg for this period reveals that Blackwood's hesitation to publish various works offered to him by Hogg was a direct result of the unstable economy. For example, in March 1826 while Blackwood thought favourably of Hogg's suggestion that a collection of his 'Select Scottish Tales' could be republished, he declined to take up the offer because 'at present [...] every thing is so dull and flat, and there is such a scarcity of money, that it would not be desirable to commence any new speculation'. And in June 1831, Blackwood was cautious about publishing Hogg's collection of ballads that came to be entitled *A Queer Book*:

> Our trade never was in such a state as it is in just now. This cursed Reform agitation has completely put a stop to the Sale of Books in London and every where else. It would be ruin therefore to attempt to publish your Ballads till business gets into a more healthy state. I was never so out of spirits in my life, for we have no orders almost at all, and Longman & Co and every publisher is in the same state. Maga is the only thing that keeps us alive.[24]

Paradoxically, during this period annuals were at their peak of popularity. It was also the most productive time for Hogg's involvement with the genre, as he published some thirty-three poems and short stories in eight different annuals in the years 1828 to 1830. Indeed, he complained to an unidentified correspondent in November 1828 that he was so 'confounded by the number of annuals that if take me book sworn at this moment I do not know which is your's and which I have wrote for and which not!'[25] Writing for the annuals, then, as

P. D. Garside has noted, 'considerably extended Hogg's options in placing his poetry' at a time when publishers were cautious about speculating in new publications of poetry and prose.[26]

Hogg could never demand the outlandish sums that were offered to Scott or Wordsworth, and the promise of lucrative rewards from editors keen to have his name on their list did not mean that actual payments were always high. Cunningham, for example, had concluded his appeal to Hogg for contributions to the *Anniversary* with the promise that 'if I succeed I trust money will be more plentiful'.[27] The income from literary contributions to the annuals was not as regular or dependable as might have been expected from such a successful venture, and Hogg's relationship with his editors was often strained because of delayed payments for his published work. In a satirical poem entitled 'The Miser's Grave', published in *Blackwood's Edinburgh Magazine* in the number for June 1831, Hogg describes the editors of the different annuals to which he contributed, and implies that he was not well paid. The poem is a dialogue between two grave-diggers, 'Teddy' and 'Gabriel', who discuss the miserly person that the grave is for: 'what could the man mean | To be a miser' asks Teddy, and Gabriel replies that by way of explanation he will write 'a Poem on't, or Play':

> The title will secure a ready market
> Into the Annuals. Pringle has applied.
> I don't like Pringle, he's too finical,
> And so pragmatical about his slaves.
> I'll try the German Shovel-board. *He* pays.
> Or Hall—But then his wife's the devil there!
> And Watts is ruin'd by false self-conceit.
> The MISER'S GRAVE! 'Tis grand!
> (vol. 29, 915–918, pp. 915–16)

Of the four editors listed, 'the German Shovel-board' (whom I take to be Frederic Shoberl), is singled out as an editor who 'pays'. Not surprisingly, *Forget Me Not* contains the largest number of Hogg's original contributions and also the largest number of his prose contributions.

Annuals were fashionable and were prominently displayed on parlour and drawing-room tables. They provided an evening's entertainment as the stories and songs were read or sung in the parlour or drawing-room in the mixed company of family and friends. Kathryn Ledbetter has described how, because of their public performance appeal, 'readers expected [literary annuals] to maintain

strict notions of propriety in language, art, and the degree of emo-
tion expressed, for they were read by the entire family'. Thus, among
the subjects that were considered suitable for inclusion in these family entertainments, she noted, were 'religion (Christianity), married
life, mild social concerns, moral lessons, and medieval romance',
while those 'not acceptable were politics, current events, radical social
opinions, hints at sexuality [...] crude or hard language, and extreme
negative emotions (grief and sorrow were the noble exceptions)'.[28]

When writing for the annuals Hogg often found these restraints
insurmountable and at times his contributions were returned as unsuitable, or they were carefully edited to suit the vogue for decorum.[29] Thomas Pringle, the editor of *Friendship's Offering*, for example, made it a rule 'to admit not a single expression which would
call up a blush in the cheek of the most delicate female if reading
aloud to a mixt company'. The surviving correspondence between
Pringle and Hogg reveals that Pringle rejected at least two unidentified contributions: a 'strange wild ballad', and a short story that was
deemed unsuitable as 'its humour [...] was *too broad*' for *Friendship's
Offering*.[30]

The epigraph that headed *Friendship's Offering* exemplified the majority of the annuals:

> This is Affection's Tribute, Friendship's Offering;
> Whose silent eloquence, more rich than words,
> Tells of the Giver's faith and truth in absence,
> And says—Forget me not!

The large number of biographical and personal poems that Hogg
contributed to the annuals, including *Friendship's Offering*, reflects the
nostalgic nature of the annuals. There are poems about his widowed mother-in-law; about Margaret, his wife; for and about his
wife's niece, Mary Gray; and for his daughter, Harriet.[31] They also
reflect the family-oriented audience, as there is nothing offensive or
erotic in them. As well as being promoted as fireside entertainment
the majority of the poems and tales in the annuals offered instruction and moral guidance. The most successful of Hogg's contributions to the annuals were those which attained the ideal of combining all or most of these three elements: 'Seeking the Houdy', 'The
Cameronian Preacher's Tale', 'Scottish Haymakers', and 'The Poachers' are amongst the finest of the form. In these tales Hogg remi-
nisces about a bucolic Border landscape and instructs the moral that
the Scottish peasants are valuable members of society whose rustic
ways are worth preserving. These tales, taken together with poems

such as 'The Minstrel Boy' and 'A Boy's Song', which paint an idealised rural childhood, evoke nostalgia for the passing of early nineteenth-century Scottish rural society. However, Hogg's nostalgia was
subtly imbued with political potency, and ought to be read in context with his essay 'On the Changes in the Habits, Amusements,
and Condition of the Scottish Peasantry', published in the *Quarterly
Journal of Agriculture* around this time.[32] In his essay and through his
nostalgic literary contributions to the annuals Hogg criticises the
rapid movement from a rural, village culture and economy to a dis-
parate urbanisation that was well under way in Scotland by the 1830s.

As noted above, the highly competitive world of the annuals forced
editors to adopt different strategies in an attempt to attract customers. In writing for an annual, therefore, as well as adhering to the
conventions of the genre of 'the annual' as Christmas gift, the tone
of particular annuals also had to be taken into consideration. For
example, as P. D. Garside notes, 'A Lay of the Martyrs' was 'well
suited for *The Amulet*, whose devout female readership would have
identified with the Covenanters' plight'.[33] The serious tone of the
Amulet can be contrasted with the eclectic nature of *Forget Me Not*, and
as noted above, it is no surprise that the latter annual contained the
largest number of original prose contributions by Hogg. Overall,
then, Hogg's contributions to the annuals were not the easy, offhand productions from the factory of 'the Ettrick Shepherd' that his
letter to Hall above appears to indicate but were carefully constructed
or chosen with individual annuals in mind.[34]

3. Hogg's Contributions to Juvenile Annuals

Hogg's description of Hall's wife, Anna Maria, an editor in her own
right of the *Juvenile Forget Me Not*, reveals the tensions he often found
writing within the constraints of the unique genre that comprised
juvenile annuals. In March 1830 Hogg sent Hall some poems and
stories for the *Amulet*, and he also included in the same package
some items for Mrs Hall. In a letter to Hogg of 2 April 1830 Mrs
Hall duly accepted 'the Prayer' for her 'Juvenile' as 'all that I can
wish', but she rejected the 'tale' that Hogg had sent, and was explicit
as to her reasons:

the tale you intended for me also, is interesting and powerfully written—but surely my dear Sir, you would not wish my
young readers to credit supernatural appearances?—I could
not take it upon my conscience to send the little darlings trem-
blingly to bed after perusing the very perfection of Ghost Sto-

ries from your pen—I find it most singularly perplexing—
that the first tale you sent me was one of Seduction—Your
Second (a thing by the way of extraordinary spirit and
beauty)—was a wanderer from fairy land—Now, when all
the sparkling—glittering—airy beings are buried under their
own green moss, and blue hare bells—it would be downright
sacrilege to fill the heads of our nurselings with their by-gone
exploits—Your last is a Ghost Story! which kept even me
awake half the night—it is a downright destruction of peace
for you to write them so well—pray pray, write me a simple
tale something about your own pure and innocent Scottish
children—without love—or ghosts—or fairies—I remember
reading what you once wrote about sheep dogs—Any thing
about *them* would be invaluable or any anecdotes you could
embody about birds or beasts—their habits and manners—
natural history is to me the sweetest study in the world—[35]

Hogg's juvenile tale was not rejected on the grounds of impropriety
as discussed above but because of prevailing ideas concerning the
intellectual capacity of children. Writing in the 1880s, Alexander
Watts noted in relation to the editorial decisions made by his mother
(who edited the *New Year's Gift and Juvenile Souvenir*) that

young people were much younger people then than they are
now; they believed more readily, and they reasoned less. It
was needful, therefore, in them to cultivate the reason [...]
She excluded, therefore, from the subjects of her little book
all apocryphal personages, giants and fairies, in all of which
children of that age were quite capable of believing to their
prejudice, and not to their profit.[36]

A survey of the stories published in both the *Juvenile Forget Me Not*
and the *New Year's Gift and Juvenile Souvenir* reveals how far removed
from the acceptable tales Hogg's ghost stories were. For example, in
Mary Jane MacKenzie's 'A Ghost Story' in the *Juvenile Forget Me Not*
for 1836 (pp. 154–63), the mother of one of a group of children
who delight and terrify each other by telling ghost stories agrees to
'lay aside her credulity' if the children can relate a ghost story that
cannot be 'in any way accounted for' (p. 157). This they cannot do,
and the instructive moral in the conclusion of the tale is that 'the
discovery of truth is the grand object for which our faculties were
given us' (p. 163). In contrast to Hogg's tales where the supernatural often points a moral, the supernatural elements in 'A Ghost Story'
are dismissed and replaced with a rational explanation.

In the early nineteenth century there were two schools of thought on what was suitable reading material for children. Mrs Hall and Mrs Watts followed such moral legislators as Mrs Trimmer, whose periodical the *Guardian of Education* was inaugurated in 1802 'for the purpose of examining [...] contemporary children's books. Each one that came her way was minutely scrutinized for undue appeal to the imagination'.[37] At the same time there were publishers such as Benjamin Tabart, whose *Juvenile Library* produced a series of fairy tales and legends designed to stimulate a child's imagination. In the world of the juvenile annuals, however, there was no room for Hogg's 'ghosts' or 'fairies'. Hogg replied to Mrs Hall by sending a replacement tale, entitled, 'A Letter to the Ettrick Shepherd'. And in his frustration at having to write in a style that would suit his female editor, Hogg sent the tale as written by a widow named 'Alice Brand'.[38] He wrote:

> I sent you a very good tale and one of those with which I delight to harrow up the little souls of my own family I say it is a *very good* tale and *exactly* fit for children and no body else; and your letter to me occassioned me writing one of the best poems ever dropped from my pen in ridicule of your's and the modern system of education [...] As I think shame to put my name to such mere common place things as you seem to want I have sent you a letter from an English Widow[39]

Despite Hogg's complaints against the 'modern system of education' his replacement tale still did not suit Mrs Hall's juvenile annual, and it was eventually published in the *Amulet* for 1836.[40]

But this is not to say that Hogg's writing for children consisted only of ghost stories, fairy tales, or sensational stories. In his prayers, hymns, and prose dialogues created specifically for children, Hogg writes from a child's perspective and in simple, unaffected language. For example, in 'A Child's Prayer' (published in *Ackermann's Juvenile Forget Me Not* for 1830), the depiction of the Crucifixion conveys the complexities of the Christian message in unsentimental terms, and in a tone that does not moralise or speak down to children:

> That thou should'st send thine only son
>   From regions of the sky
> And for this sinful race of mine
>   A dreadful death to die
>
> I cannot frame! But teach me Lord
>   With grateful heart to bow

And be that reverenced and adored
Which none concievest but thou   (p. 233, below)

4. Hogg and Gift-Books

Hogg actively promoted and participated in the new publishing phenomenon. In December 1831, when the annuals were at their peak
of popularity, Hogg visited London in an attempt to find a publisher
for a proposed collected edition of his prose works. James Cochrane,
who in the event only published one volume of the projected collection[41] before being declared bankrupt in April that year, was also
involved in preparing a juvenile gift-book by Hogg for publication.
As with his poetry for the juvenile annuals, Hogg's *A Father's New
Year's Gift* was intended to instruct rather than entertain, and it therefore does not contain any secular poetry or prose tales. This gift-
book consists of four prayers and five poems following a chronological daily pattern, and is clearly designed as a practical assistant
for parental religious guidance. The serious nature of Hogg's undertaking is signalled in the short, personal note of dedication to his
own children that prefaces the gift-book. Hogg tells them that he
sends it as a 'New Year's Present, in hopes that I shall hear you
recite them all beautifully and impressively on your knees before
your Maker on my return'.

An article in the *Literary Gazette* by John Mackay Wilson published during Hogg's stay in London re-presented him to an audience that was all too familiar with the comic, boozy figure of the
'Ettrick Shepherd' of the *Noctes Ambrosianae* series of *Blackwood's Edinburgh Magazine*:

> They who can judge of him aright must see him, as I have
> seen him, imploring the blessing of Heaven upon his hospita-
> ble board; or with his family class around him—holding an
> infant school in the wilderness! [...] —with his son by his side,
> one young daughter between his knees, and the third clinging
> round his neck [...] as they strive who shall repeat to him
> most perfectly their Sabbath-school tasks, and obtain during
> the week the reward of their preparation, in the fond caress
> and proud kiss of the father who bends over them in love.[42]

During his time in London, it might be suggested, Hogg found
that he was all too closely identified with the Shepherd of the *Noctes*,
and therefore deliberately set out to attempt to shake off the negative aspects of his Blackwoodian persona. *A Father's New Year's Gift*
can be seen as one product of this plan. Likewise, one of the last

literary projects Hogg was working on before his death in November 1835 was a devotional 'drawing-room' book for women. In June 1835 Hogg outlined this plan to James Cochrane, who had resumed business following his bankruptcy in 1832:

> I have ready for the press a small religious work "The Young Lady's Sabbath Companion." It is a thing that must not be above five shillings nor below 2/6 but as I want it a drawing-room and cabinet book I should like that it were elegant. [...] It consists of three parts "Sacred Hymns" "Religious poems" and "Prose lessons, prayers &c."[43]

Cochrane replied favourably to Hogg's proposal and wrote by return that he would 'be most happy to publish [...] the title is a good one & I will lose no time in getting it out in the finest style—suitable for the Drawing Room & Cabinet of every young lady in Britain.'[44] Within a few months Hogg sent part of the manuscript to Cochrane with explicit instructions:

> The sheets are marked by the alphabet and I send you precisely the half of the work so that you can print it accordingly. It consists of three parts of equal length "Sacred Hymns" "Religious poems" and "lessons on life death and immortality in prose with prayers &c [...] ".[45]

The work remained incomplete, and was evidently never published. However, a fragment of Hogg's manuscript seems to have survived (see p. 269). Taken together with his successfully published prayers and hymns, *A Father's New Year's Gift* and the unpublished *Young Lady's Sabbath Companion* reveal another side to the multi-faceted James Hogg: a man who was seriously committed to the moral and spiritual education of young people.

5. Reception of the Annuals

The annuals were initially perceived as a successful, short-lived publishing phenomenon.[46] During the economic slump of 1825–26 thousands of annuals were sold, while at the same time established publishers such as Constable & Co. crashed. The *New Monthly Magazine* was among the many periodicals which applauded the timely publication of the annuals:

> It is pleasing to witness these little annual assemblages of poetical names, put forth in a brotherly way to the world, as gifts for lovers to each other, or parents to their children, or friends to friends.[47]

From 1826, between the months of September and January, column after column in the monthly periodicals and weekly papers discussed the annuals. There were lengthy descriptions of the outward presentation: the binding, gilt-edging, and quality of the paper; the illustrations and 'embellishments' were minutely detailed; the contributors and engravers were listed. With the annuals at times containing up to a hundred different contributions only those engravings and literary contributions deemed exceptionally good or particularly bad were singled out and discussed at length. And examples of the 'best' contributions were reprinted in full, or liberally quoted.[48]

At the same time as the annuals were portrayed as being 'beyond criticism',[49] they were, paradoxically, subjected to increasingly hostile remarks. *Blackwood's Edinburgh Magazine*, for example, in its number for January 1826, personified the annuals for 1826 as 'four young maidens, all beautiful as angels', and criticism was therefore considered ungentlemanly conduct.[50] However, in the concluding paragraphs of their earlier review of the *Literary Souvenir* for the previous year, *Blackwood's* had proposed that 'all our good Poets, yes, one and all of them, should contribute to the next volume'. The review asks sarcastically: 'what difficulty is there in writing a beautiful poem of fifty lines, long or short metre, any summer morning before breakfast?' And to prove that composing poetry for an annual was not difficult they presume, ironically, to offer advice to poets:

> Suppose you breakfast at nine—or half past nine. Well then, up with you at five—and before the bell rings, there is your poem. Lay it aside for a week—correct it over your egg any sunshining morning—into the form of a letter with it—and off she goes to the tune of Alaric A. Watts, Esq. Leeds. Nothing can be more easy and simple than this process,—and by and by down comes, or up goes to you your beautiful large paper copy of the Souvenir.[51]

In 1828, the *Quarterly Review* objected in stronger terms to the uneven quality of contributions to the annuals:

> Are the classics of our age to continue to see their beautiful fragments doled out year after year in the midst of such miserable and mawkish trash as fills at least nineteen pages out of every twenty in the best of the gaudy duodecimos now before us?[52]

And in the same year the *Literary Gazette* for 18 October 1828 went further, complaining (p. 659):

we are really exceedingly fatigued with those floods of mediocrity, and worse than mediocrity, in metrical composition,
which are making a perfect insect-humming swamp of all the
low and meadow lands around the base of our present English Parnassus. The few who do sing on the brow of the hill
are delightful; but the multitude of buzzers in the valleys are a
wearisome tribe, and their superabundance about these *Annual* periods particularly distressing. Indeed the country is
somewhat in the condition of companies in which we have
sometimes been, where everybody *was obliged to sing*, whether
they could or not.

The above articles are just three of the many which frequently insisted, and with increasing impatience, that annuals should only include contributions from professional, established authors. Such
requests were clearly to ensure an evenness of quality in the finished annual. However, in keeping with most, if not all of the critics,
the *Literary Gazette* stopped short of denouncing the 'agreeable mis-
cellanies' as a whole. The article concludes (p. 663):

in all the opinions we offer upon the publications of its class,
we speak comparatively of the merits and demerits of their
component parts, explicitly and impartially to the best of our
judgment: at the same time we wish it to be understood, that
we consider the least successful of them to be well deserving
of popular favour.

As their numbers increased, some periodicals openly decried the
uncritical reception of all the annuals.[53] *Fraser's Magazine* for December 1830, for example, prior to a long article on 'The Annuals',
admitted they were 'not outrageous admirers of these Annuals'. They
stated that while they would 'preserve two or three of them' if they
could, they would 'put an extinguisher on the rest [...] without hesitation.'[54] A hoax 'New Annual', announced in the *Edinburgh Literary
Journal* for 17 December 1831, is described as being got up or put
together, 'printed and composed by Steam' (pp. 353–54). This small
article criticises mutual 'puffing' or overly praising inferior compositions, while at the same time it attacks the new form of writing to
illustrated plates through an ironic play on 'steam'.

As annuals came to be seen as legitimate objects for literary criticism so the periodicals changed their opinion entirely. For example,
in November 1828 the *New Monthly Magazine* claimed that annuals
were to be encouraged because of the positive effects on the readers, 'whom their very elegancies will entice to read, and study, to

the displacement of some frivolous luxury, or childish bauble, and in whom they will awaken thought, and infuse a taste for mental gratification'.[55] By 1831, the same periodical claimed annuals were a bad influence on literature: although they support established writers, no new writers had achieved fame through their pages. Moreover, annuals 'have entirely destroyed the demand for single volumes of poetry or tales, [...]. We decidedly think that their general influence is adverse to a high order of poetry'. Annuals, in the same review, are said to be detrimental to art as 'too great a supply is needed of merely pretty and second-rate pictures, to give proper encouragement to first-rate works.' The review concludes that annuals 'elevate taste, but deteriorate art'.[56]

William Makepeace Thackeray was a vociferous and amusing critic of the annuals, consistently accusing them of being detrimental to literature. In articles in *Fraser's Magazine*,[57] in *The Times*,[58] and also within his own fiction,[59] Thackeray denounced both the literature and the art of the annuals. Out of all of her belongings, it is the glittering gilt-edged 'Keepsakes and Books of Beauty' that are most prized and rescued from the bailiffs who descend on Becky Sharp in *Vanity Fair*, while in *The Newcomes*, Rosey Mackenzie pronounces ineffectually on the display of annuals in Mrs Newcome's drawing-room where 'she thought the prints very sweet and pretty: she thought the poetry very pretty and sweet'. In his criticism on the annuals, Thackeray was more acerbic.

> Miss Landon, Miss Mitford, or my Lady Blessington, writes a song upon the opposite page [to an engraving], about water-lily, chilly, stilly, shivering beside a streamlet, plighted, blighted, love-benighted, falsehood sharper than a gimlet, lost affection, recollection, cut connexion, tears in torrents, true-love token, spoken, broken, sighing, dying, girl of Florence, and so on. The poetry is quite worthy of the picture, and a little sham sentiment is employed to illustrate a little sham art.[60]

Consistently, Thackeray's denunciations were couched in parodic, biting sarcasm, which, according to Donald Hawes, was 'probably more damaging than any previous more extensive abuse'.[61]

Typically, the annuals were seen as being good for the publishing industry because they generated sales, but as bad for literature because they encouraged mediocre writing and bad editing. The main problem that most of the critics appeared to have with the annuals, and one that Thackeray consistently complained of, was that they were offering a different kind of literature: one that was written to order. 'Sham sentiment' appeared to have replaced inspired genius.

Thackeray notwithstanding, there remained those who defended annuals. For example, Glennis Stephenson notes that Christian Isobel Jonhstone, the editor of *Tait's Edinburgh Magazine*, presented the annuals as a philanthopic endeavour that had 'caught something of the grave, earnest, and thoughtful spirit of the age'.[62] Stephenson notes that in the introduction to her 1837 review of 'The Books of the Season', Johnstone revised her former criticism of the annuals as 'toys of literature', and found that although 'the writing of the Annuals, taken as a whole, is certainly not flattering to the national vanity [...] still, independently of art, these ephemeral productions have excellent uses'. Among the many 'uses' Johnstone claims for the annuals are 'a new branch of exportable manufacture'; the 'development of refined taste', and finally, they are 'concerned to expose oppression, wherever it is found'.[63] As Stephenson notes, Johnstone's criticism was social rather than literary,[64] but her championing of the annuals from the late 1830s to the mid-1840s (when the number of British annuals had dwindled to around ten), countered Thackeray, and helped to ensure that the annuals did not die out entirely.

As late as 1858, in an anonymous article in *The Bookseller* entitled 'The Annuals of Former Days', annuals are celebrated for 'diffusing a taste for elegant pursuits among the middle classes' and as being a more effective 'means of affording profitable employment [...] than any other order of publication whatsoever'. High praise is also directed towards the literary merits of the annuals:

> On the wings of these painted humming-birds the fame of the poet and the painter was wafted faster and farther than it could have been through the ordinary channels of publication; and the public will find in their pages a body of more beautiful poetry, of the fugitive class, than in any other original English publication.[65]

More recently, literary critics have formed two distinct camps: those who ignore the forty or so years of the annuals through silent omission, or those, like Jerome McGann and Daniel Riess, who highlight the importance of the annuals. McGann and Riess claim that the annuals and *Blackwood's Edinburgh Magazine* 'inaugurated an important shift in the way literature, especially poetry, essay, and short fiction, would be written for the rest of the century.'[66]

Hogg was a professional writer who grasped as early as 1824 the 'important shift' that literature was taking. He did not display the contempt for annuals of many of his contemporaries but openly accepted the new and wider opportunities that the annuals gave to him to display his writing talents.[67] In a letter of March 1833 to Shoberl, Hogg notes with disappointment that:

the rage for Annuals is over for there are none of these things about which mankind are so newfangled ever stand the test. If Mr Ackerman [*sic*] could have kept the ground to himself he would have been playing a sure card but an overstocked market and often of such vapid lady stuff must pall the public.[68]

The consistently high quality of the prose and poetry that Hogg contributed to annuals clearly demonstrates the importance that he placed on this new publishing phenomenon, and serves to highlight his acute awareness of the shifting trends of the literary marketplace.

6. The Critical Reception of Hogg's Contributions to the Annuals

As noted in section 2 above, Hogg's first contribution to an annual was 'Invocation to the Queen of the Fairies'. Appearing in the *Literary Souvenir* for 1825, this poem (as we have seen) was very favourably reviewed in the *Literary Gazette*. Thereafter, Hogg's contributions were regularly singled out for praise. For example, within the *Noctes Ambrosianæ* series in the November and December 1828 numbers of *Blackwood's Edinburgh Magazine*, 'Christopher North' and the 'Ettrick Shepherd' focus on Hogg's contributions in their review of the annuals for 1829. North asks 'Have you seen any of the Annuals, James?', to which the 'Shepherd' replies 'No ane. But I've contributed to severals o' them'. Thereafter they debate the merits of all of Hogg's contributions to the annuals for the coming year:

NORTH.
I see you have, my dear Shepherd, and that most potently and effectively, to the Anniversary, and the Forget-me-Not [...]

SHEPHERD.
[...] Is the Anniversary gude?

NORTH.
If any of the others be better, their Editors must have made a wonderful improvement on them since the last show of Christmas roses. [...] Your Carle of Invertime, is one of your most beautiful effusions, and its spirit reminds one of Kilmeny

and Mary Lee. But your prose Tale of Death and Judgment is one of the most powerful things you ever did, James—and I will back it against all the other prose compositions in all the other Annuals—Cameronian against the field.

Speaking of the contributions to the *Forget Me Not*, 'North' declares to the 'Shepherd', 'Your Eastern Apologue is admirable'. At another point the 'Shepherd' is coaxed into a song, the text of which is printed as 'John Nicholson's Daughter'.[69] 'Bravo!' applauds 'North', 'You have sent that song to our friend Pringle's Friendship's Offering—haven't you James?'—to which the 'Shepherd' replies: 'I hae—and anither as gude, or better'.[70]

In 'Monologue or Soliloquy on the Annuals', one of *Blackwood's Edinburgh Magazine*'s numerous reviews of the annuals for the forthcoming year, the entire text of 'A Bard's Address to his Youngest Daughter' is reprinted under a glowing introduction:

> It delights us to see the Ettrick Shepherd in Mr Pringle's 'Friendship's Offering'. The Shepherd's heart is as warm as his genius is bright; and no purer happiness to him than to add a string to the harp in the hand of a dear companion of old, to hang on it a garland of sweet wild flowers from the Forest. Prettier daisies are no where to be seen than those that dance on the greensward before the door of Mount Benger—and is not the beauty of the prettiest of them all made 'still more beauteous' by as fine a gush of parental poetry as ever flowed from the holiest recesses of nature in a father's bosom?[71]

The *Edinburgh Literary Journal* also wrote positively about Hogg's contributions to the annuals. In its first number (for 15 November 1828) 'The Cameronian Preacher's Tale' is described (p. 5) as

> a story of strange and supernatural interest [...] told with all that unadorned strength of narrative, and clear intuitive perception of the best mode of treating those incidents that bear upon the superstitious part of our nature, which unquestionably make the Ettrick Shepherd the best inditer of a ghost story extant.

The tale is considered by the *Edinburgh Literary Journal* to be one of only two 'worthy of mention' in the *Anniversary*.[72] In the same article, Hogg's 'Eastern Apologues' from the *Forget Me Not* is described as the 'best' tale out of the hundred or so contributions for that year (p. 6). A year later, in the *Edinburgh Literary Journal* for 17 October

1829, the *Amulet* is deemed to rank 'high among the Annuals', and from the *Amulet* the article singled out for praise is '"A Tale of Pentland", by the Ettrick Shepherd, full of graphic power and strong interest, like nearly all Hogg's tales'. Hogg's poem 'A Lay of the Martyrs' is also singled out for favourable comment (pp. 275–76). In the number for 13 November 1830 Hogg's contributions to the *Amulet* are again praised highly above others (p. 304):

> The poetry of the *Amulet* is very good. Its chief attraction is 'A Cameronian Ballad' by James Hogg, which is not only the best poem in the volume, but strikes us as the *best* poem which has this season appeared in any of the Annuals. It is powerful, pathetic, and original. Hogg himself never wrote any thing finer. We rejoice to see the Shepherd, instead of falling off as life advances on him, only coming forth with a more varied and vigorous imagination.

Indeed, the ballad was reprinted in full the following week, in the *Edinburgh Literary Journal* for 20 November 1830 (pp. 318–19), which declared (p. 318) that 'it possesses a strength of pathos, and a high poetical and national feeling, in every respect worthy of the Ettrick Shepherd, or of the best of our living poets.'

Among the laudatory comments on Hogg's contributions to annuals that appeared in the *Edinburgh Literary Journal*, there was one, very slight note of caution against Hogg's tale entitled 'Seeking the Houdy'. In the number for 31 October 1829 this tale was considered 'humorous and talented, but almost a little too homely, we should have thought, for an Annual' (p. 301). However, the criticism was directed at Shoberl, the editor of *Forget Me Not*, rather than at Hogg. Overall, Hogg's contributions to the annuals were perceived by the critics of two of the major Scottish periodicals of the time as displaying his best work.

This is not to say that the Scottish periodicals were adopting a particularly nationalistic or partial stance by promoting Hogg's contributions. In London periodicals, too, Hogg's contributions were often praised above others. The *New Monthly Magazine* declared that '"The Castle [*sic*] of Invertime" by Hogg is a fair specimen of the Shepherd's talent', and 'The Cameronian Preacher's Tale' was considered 'good'.[73] The *Gentleman's Magazine* thought 'Superstition and Grace' 'among the best pieces' from the *Bijou* for 1829. Like the *Edinburgh Literary Journal*, this periodical found merit in 'A Lay of the Martyrs' ('a beautiful simple ballad of the Covenant times'), and 'The Song of Oberon' from the *Musical Bijou* for 1830 is described as 'pretty, and was worthy of being united to [...] music'.[74] In the midst of a lengthy satirical review of the annuals as a whole in *Fraser's Magazine*, Hogg's contribution to the *Amulet* for 1835 is mentioned in favourable terms: O'doherty interjects into the conversation that 'the piety of Hogg in his "Hymn to the Redeemer" is peculiarly edifying'.[75] Finally, the *Literary Gazette* for 7 November 1835 praised Hogg's work for the *Amulet*, mentioning him among those who 'have filled up the measure of verse with productions of great merit, variety, and interest' (p. 708).

Hogg's contributions to juvenile annuals and his own gift-book, *A Father's New Year's Gift* received less critical notice. The *Edinburgh Literary Journal* for 29 October 1831 reprinted the text of 'The Shepherd Boy's Song' from *Ackerman's Juvenile Forget-Me-Not*, and declared (p. 251) that they were:

> much pleased with some simple verses by the Bard of Ettrick, illustrative of an engraving representing a shepherd boy teaching his sister to play upon his flute–the best picture in the volume. It is delightful to hear the patriarch of Yarrow accommodating himself to the tastes and thoughts of childhood. Blessings on his frosty pow!

The *Edinburgh Spectator* of 15 February 1832 pointed out that although 'this is not exactly the season for new year's gifts', *A Father's New Year's Gift*, would 'never be unacceptable to little masters and misses'. They considered the gift-book as a whole contained 'some pretty little hymns and short prayers for young folks'.[76] In its number for 4 February 1832, the *Athenaeum* (p. 78) prefaced their comments on Hogg's gift-book with a personal notice connecting his acceptance into London society:

> Mr Hogg has grown into our affections since we have had the pleasure of knowing him; even at the dinner he almost won us back to good-humour, by the confidence with which he trusted to his impulses, and laughed and talked as men only dare laugh and talk whose worst thoughts can but excite a good-humoured smile.

It is because of this, Hogg's affability, that the 'stitched sixpenny trifle' is noticed and given due praise. 'The home recollections with which it is graced–they will work upon the young heart as powerfully as either the prayers or the hymns.' The 'shortest' piece, 'Evening Prayer for Week Days', is reprinted in full as 'its universal sympathy, is worthy the honour of selection'.

Many of Hogg's contributions to annuals have never been republished or noticed since their first publication. In the late twentieth century, however, David Groves republished several of Hogg's contributions, including three short stories: 'Eastern Apologues', 'Seeking the Houdy', and 'Scottish Haymakers'.[77] In his introduction to the tales Groves suggests 'Eastern Apologues' 'be read as a satirical allegory of Hogg's volatile relations with his embattled Edinburgh publisher William Blackwood [...] and especially his editors John Wilson and J. G. Lockhart'. Groves notes that 'although only a simple story, "Eastern Apologues" illuminates Hogg's conception of art', and the tale overall 'finds a compromise between the innocence of imagination, and the experience of social realities'. The tale demonstrates 'Hogg's maturest writing'.[78] Groves presents 'Seeking the Houdy' as 'a clever metaphor for Hogg's predicament as a writer trying to appeal to the respectable women readers of the *Forget Me Not*.'[79] In 'Scottish Haymakers', according to Groves, 'through the figure of Monsieur Alexandre Hogg is expressing his reservations about art and the aesthetic temperament', and overall 'in this sketch he [Hogg] achieves profundity through simple, understated brushwork'.[80]

In the final version of his autobiography Hogg claimed, 'having been so much discouraged by the failure of "Queen Hynde," I gave up all thoughts of ever writing another long poem, but continued for six years to write fairy tales, ghost stories, songs, and poems for periodicals of every description'.[81] The welcome change from the negative and hostile reception given to his epic poem of December 1824 to the continual stream of consistently positive critical reviews that his contributions to annuals attracted, earned for Hogg, at the end of his long literary career, the plaudits from his peers he always felt he had deserved.

Notes

1. Annuals were published for the Christmas market in the late autumn prior to the year named on their titlepages. Thus Hogg's poem 'Invocation to the Queen of the Fairies' appeared in November 1824 in the *Literary Souvenir* for 1825. See the present volume's 'Listing of Hogg Texts in Annuals and Gift-Books' for a comprehensive listing of all known Hogg attributions and contributions. The principal sources for information on the annuals are: Frederick W. Faxon, *Literary Annuals and Gift Books: A Bibliography 1823–1903* (Boston: Boston Book Co., 1912; repr. Pinner: Private Libraries Association, 1973); Andrew Boyle, *An Index to the Annuals*

(Worcester: Andrew Boyle Booksellers, 1967); and Anne Renier, *Friendship's Offering: An Essay on the Annuals and Gift Books of the Nineteenth Century* (London: Private Libraries Association, 1964; repr. 1973).

2. Quoted from the 1832 version of Hogg's autobiographical 'Memoir of the Author's Life', which appeared in his *Altrive Tales* (London: Cochrane, 1832): see the relevant volume of the Stirling / South Carolina Research Edition of the Collected Works of James Hogg (hereafter S/SC Edition), *Altrive Tales*, ed. by Gillian Hughes (S/SC, 2003), p. 39 (hereafter quoted as 'Memoir'). When the scheme for a poetic miscellany fell through Hogg wrote a book of parodies, *The Poetic Mirror* (Edinburgh: Ballantyne; London: Longman, 1816): see 'Memoir', pp. 40–41. Hogg planned to publish his poetic miscellany bi-annually. I am grateful to Douglas Mack for drawing my attention to this point.

3. Renier, pp. 5–6.

4. For more detailed information on the inception of the annuals, see 'The Annuals of Former days', published in the first number of the *Bookseller*, 29 November 1858, pp. 493–99. This article is continued in no. 2 (24 December 1858), pp. 585–89.

5. Renier, pp. 6–7. See the advertisement for the *Keepsake* for 1829 in the *Athenaeum*, 22 October 1828, p. 830.

6. Quoted in Morton D. Paley, 'Coleridge and the Annuals', *Huntington Library Quarterly*, 57 (1994), 1–24 (p. 2).

7. Quoted in the *Bookseller*, 29 November 1858, pp. 493–99 (p. 493).

8. See Paley, p. 1, and Peter J. Manning, 'Wordsworth in the *Keepsake*, 1829', in *Literature in the Marketplace: Nineteenth-Century British Publishing and Reading Practices*, ed. by John O. Jordan and Robert L. Patten (Cambridge: Cambridge University Press, 1995), p. 45.

9. Reynolds to Worsdworth, quoted in Manning, pp. 44–73 (pp. 51–52).

10. Glennis Stephenson, *Letitia Landon: The Woman behind L.E.L.* (Manchester: Manchester University Press, 1995), p. 156.

11. Manning, pp. 48–49.

12. 'The Verse of the English Annuals', *Review of English Studies*, n.s. 4 (1953), 38–51 (p. 38).

13. The following discussion is indebted to Ralph Thompson's introduction to *American Literary Annuals and Gift Books 1825–1865* (1936; repr. Hamden, Conn.: Archon Books, 1967). Thompson's notes are the result of his survey of over 300 different American annuals and gift-books out of over a thousand that were published in the period.

14. Thompson, p. 23.

15. Thompson lists 'Mary Anne Browne, Felicia Hemans, Mrs Amelia Opie, James Montgomery, R. Shelton Mckenzie [...] and perhaps a few others', as regular contributors to American annuals. He adds, interestingly, 'Mrs Sigourney appealed to Worsdworth for a contribution to her *Religious Souvenir* for 1839, but apparently did not get it' (p. 23).

16. *Indices to American Literary Annuals and Gift Books 1825–1865*, compiled by E. Bruce Kirkham and John W. Fink (New Haven, Conn.: Research Publications, 1975), supplies indices to Thompson's collection, and was helpful in tracing the treatment of Hogg in some of the American annuals and gift-

books. All known printings of works by Hogg in the annuals and gift-books, including printings that were unauthorised, are included in the present volume's 'Listing of Hogg Texts in Annuals and Gift-Books'.

17. What little is known of the history of this 'Song' is discussed in the Introductory and Textual Notes of the present volume (see pp. 340–41).

18. See the *Literary Souvenir* for 1825, pp. 122–26; and *Queen Hynde* (London: Longman; Edinburgh: Blackwood, 1824; some copies are dated 1825), pp. 361–66.

19. Suzanne Gilbert and Douglas S. Mack discuss the reception of *Queen Hynde* in the 'Introduction' of their S/SC edition of the poem (1998).

20. The reviewer of the *Literary Gazette* did not appear to notice that 'Invocation to the Queen of the Fairies' was derived from *Queen Hynde*. The latter poem was extensively reviewed in the number for 25 December 1824, 817–19.

21. See NLS, MS 8887, fols. 36–37 and NLS, MS 2245, fols 114–15.

22. Fales Library & Special Collections, New York University, MS 89: 20.

23. NLS, MS 3904, fol. 31.

24. Blackwood to Hogg, 25 March 1826 (NLS, MS 30,309, pp. 163–65); Blackwood to Hogg, 25 June 1831 (NLS, MS 30,312, pp. 201–02). See also Blackwood to Hogg, 23 September 1826 (NLS, MS 30,309, pp. 385–87).

25. Brotherton Library, University of Leeds, BC Miscellaneous Letters PRI (Pringle Album).

26. Hogg, *A Queer Book*, ed. by P. D. Garside (S/SC, 1995), p. xii.

27. NLS, MS 2245, fols. 114–15.

28. Kathryn Ledbetter, '"BeGemmed and BeAmuletted": Tennyson and those "Vapid" Gift Books', *Victorian Poetry*, 34 (1996), 235–45 (p. 236).

29. Hogg was aware that his work in the annuals was open to censorship, as he encouraged editors to refine his work prior to publication. For example, Thomas Roscoe, the editor of *Remembrance*, thanked Hogg for allowing him the liberty of editing his contributions to suit the public taste: see NLS, MS 2245, fol. 323.

30. For further details see Gillian Hughes's discussion of Pringle's aversion to 'indelicacy' in the Introductory and Textual Notes to *Friendship's Offering* on pp. 309–11 below.

31. For a more detailed discussion on Hogg's relationship's with the editors and publishers see Gillian Hughes's Introductory and Textual Notes to each annual, and for a discussion on the specificity of Pringle's request to Hogg for short pieces of a biographical nature see pp. 309–11. See also the Introductory and Textual Notes to 'An Aged Widow's Own Words'; to 'A Scots Luve Sang'; to 'Verses to a Beloved Young Friend', to 'Ballad'; and to 'A Bard's Address to his Youngest Daughter' (pp. 290, 311–16).

32. *Quarterly Journal of Agriculture*, 3 (1831–32), 256–63.

33. *A Queer Book*, ed. Garside, p. 239

34. P. D. Garside has noted that the annuals gave Hogg 'the challenge of writing in different contexts and for a new and extensive readership': see *A Queer Book*, ed. Garside, p. xii.

35. James Hogg Collection, Special Collections, University of Otago Library: in a copy of the *Juvenile Forget Me Not* for 1831. See also Gillian Hughes's

Introductory and Textual Notes in the present volume, pp. 348–49.

36. Alexander Watts, *Alaric Watts: A Narrative of his Life*, 2 vols (London: Richard Bentley, 1884), I, 312–13.

37. See Marjory Moon, *Benjamin Tabart's Juvenile Library: A Bibliography of Books for Children Published Written Edited and Sold by Mr. Tabart 1801–1820* (Winchester: St Paul's Bibliographies, 1990), p. 3.

38. Andrew Boyle attributes this tale to an author named 'Alice Brand', and not to James Hogg in *An Index to the Annuals* (Worcester: Andrew Boyle Booksellers, 1967), p. 38.

39. See the Introductory and Textual Notes to 'A Letter to the Ettrick Shepherd', below. See also the Introductory and Textual Notes to the *Juvenile Forget Me Not* for further discussion of Hogg's relationship with Mrs Hall.

40. Hogg was apparently suspicious that his work would be published without his knowledge, and in his correspondence with editors he often repeated his requests to have all unpublished material returned to him. The example of S. C. Hall's treatment of Coleridge tends to suggest that Hogg was wise to do so. Coleridge's 'Fragments of a Journey Over the Brocken' was published in the *Amulet* for 1829, and the manuscript had been sent along with a few poems to Hall in 1827. According to H. J. Jackson and J. R. de J. Jackson, 'Hall unscrupulously kept copies of the mss and printed them later without offering payment to the author, and apparently without allowing him to correct proofs': see *The Collected Works of Samuel Taylor Coleridge*, ed. by Kathleen Coburn (London: Routledge; Princeton: Princeton University Press, 1971–), XI: *Shorter Works and Fragments*, ed. by H. J. Jackson and J. R. de J. Jackson, 2 vols (1995), II, p. 1472. For a full discussion of Hogg's dealings with the Halls see the present volume's Introductory and Textual Notes to the *Amulet* and the *Juvenile Forget Me Not*.

41. The volume was *Altrive Tales: Collected among the Peasantry of Scotland and from Foreign Adventurers* (London: Cochrane, 1832).

42. *Literary Gazette*, 25 February 1832, pp. 121–23 (p. 123).

43. Hogg to James Cochrane, 15 June 1835 (Beinecke Rare Book & Manuscript Library, Yale University, James Hogg Collection, Gen MSS 61, Box 1, Folder 6).

44. NLS, MS 2245, fols 262–63.

45. Beinecke Rare Book & Manuscript Library, Yale University, James Hogg Collection, Gen MSS 61, Box 1, Folder 6. This letter is undated, but it was written some time in 1835, between June and Hogg's death in November.

46. See, for example, the essay entitled 'Christmas Gifts' in *Blackwood's* for January 1826, where the reviewer claims 'it would be rash to assert that the state of mankind—nay even of Europe, will be widely, deeply, or permanently affected by the publication of these annual periodicals. In half a century they may even be generally forgotten—but who cares, if they are all perused or looked at with pleasure now?': *Blackwood's Edinburgh Magazine*, 19 (1826), 80–90 (p. 81).

47. *New Monthly Magazine*, 18 (1826), 447.

48. In 'Wordsworth in the *Keepsake*, 1829' (p. 59), Manning has noted that these uncritical descriptions placed the reviewers in a new role: 'less as

arbiters of praise or blame than as allies in publicity'.

49. Manning, p. 59.

50. 'Christmas Gifts', *Blackwood's Edinburgh Magazine*, 19 (1826), 80–90 (p. 80). The four annuals were the *Literary Souvenir*, the *Amulet*, *Forget Me Not*, and *Friendship's Offering.*

51. '*The Literary Souvenir*', *Blackwood's Edinburgh Magazine*, 17 (1825), 94–101 (p. 100).

52. *Quarterly Review*, 37 (1828), 84–102, p. 99; quoted in Faxon, p. xxii.

53. For example, see a short article entitled 'Literary Criticism', in the *Edinburgh Literary Journal* for 15 November 1828, pp. 2–3.

54. *Fraser's Magazine*, 2 (1830), 543–54 (pp. 544–45). Interestingly, Hogg contributed to all but the last of the small number of annuals *Fraser's* regarded as worthy of preserving: *Friendship's Offering*, the *Amulet*, the *Literary Souvenir*, and *Hood's Comic Annual.*

55. *New Monthly Magazine*, 23 (1828), 461–69 (p. 469).

56. *New Monthly Magazine*, 32 (1831), 455–61 (p. 455).

57. Thackeray's articles appeared as 'A Word on the Annuals' (December 1837) and 'Our Annual Execution' (January 1839). These were reprinted in a collective selection of his criticism on the annuals entitled, *Our Annual Execution* (Philadelphia: H. W. Fisher, 1902).

58. See 'The Annuals', in *The Times*, 2 November 1838.

59. See, for example, *Pendennis* Chapter XXXI.

60. Quoted in Donald Hawes, 'Thackeray and the Annuals', *Ariel*, 7 (1976), 3–31 (p. 17).

61. Hawes, p. 17.

62. Quoted in Stephenson, *Letitia Landon: The Woman behind L.E.L.*, p. 130.

63. Quoted in Stephenson, pp. 129–31.

64. Stephenson, p. 131.

65. The author notes that 'the *Athenaeum*, the *Spectator*, the *Examiner*, and the *Art Journal*, and several of our most trustworthy critical periodicals have, to a very late date, protested against the injustice of which these works have been the objects': see the *Bookseller* for 29 November 1858, 493–99 (p. 493).

66. See Letitia Elizabeth Landon, *Selected Writings*, ed. by Jerome McGann and Daniel Riess (Ontario: Broadview, 1997), pp. 11–33 (p. 17). Some new websites that highlight the importance of literary annuals are located within Laura Mandell's *Poetess Project* at Miami University, Ohio: *Forget Me Not: A Hypertextual Archive of Ackermann's 19th-Century Annual* ed. by Katherine D. Harris; *The Bijou; or, Annual of Literature and the Arts for 1828*, ed. by Laura Mandell; *Index of British Annuals and Giftbooks*, ed. by Harry Hootman. These can all be found at http://www.orgs.muohio.edu.

67. For examples of how authors complained bitterly about the annuals while at the same time contributing to them, see the articles by Kathryn Ledbetter and Peter J. Manning, to which reference has already been made.

68. NLS, MS 1809, fol. 85.

69. The song is a reprinting of Hogg's poem 'Auld Joe Nicholson's Bonny Nannie'. See the Introductory and Textual Notes to this poem.

70. The conversations are in *Blackwood's Edinburgh Magazine*, 24 (1828), 640–76

(pp. 672–73), and 677–708 (p. 688). They appear in the series entitled 'Noctes Ambrosianæ' (nos XXXIX and XL).

71. 'Monologue or Soliloquy on the Annuals', *Blackwood's Edinburgh Magazine*, 26 (1829), 948–76 (pp. 969–70).

72. 'A Tale of the Times of the Martyrs' by Edward Irving is the other tale that is singled out for praise.

73. *New Monthly Magazine*, 23 (1828), 466–67.

74. *Gentleman's Magazine*, 98 (1828), 545; 99 (1829), 353; 99 (1829), 535.

75. *Fraser's Magazine*, 10 (1834), 602–23 (p. 608).

76. Noted by David Groves in *Notes & Queries*, n.s. 35 (1988), 312–13.

77. James Hogg, *Tales of Love and Mystery*, ed. by David Groves (Edinburgh: Canongate, 1985).

78. *Tales of Love and Mystery*, pp. 17–18.

79. *Tales of Love and Mystery*, pp. 21–24 (p. 21).

80. *Tales of Love and Mystery*, pp. 27–29 (p. 28).

81. See 'Memoir', p. 58. However, during this period Hogg published, or had near completion, several important volumes. These were: a collection of rural tales entitled *The Shepherd's Calendar* (1829); a revised and annotated collection of his *Songs* (1831); and a volume of new and revised poetry, *A Queer Book* (1832).

Hogg, Art, and the Annuals

Gillian Hughes

The same elite condescension that has diminished the literary importance of the annuals has also led to their art-work being seriously undervalued, both in itself and in its social and cultural significance. Access to original paintings is now possible through the great institutional galleries of Britain's capital and provincial cities, while the media that bombard each one of us with a plethora of images enable the free circulation of copies of art-works of the present and of past generations. It was not so at the end of the eighteenth century, and a child like James Hogg could quite easily grow up starved of pictures: his experience in the farm-houses of the Borders would probably be limited to the cheap woodcuts adorning chapbooks or pasted onto walls, and a very occasional book illustration.[1] Original paintings hung in upper-class social venues and the homes of the wealthy (to which an Ettrick Shepherd would not often have access), while fine engravings were purchases generally beyond the means of a working man. A taste for painting would therefore seem an unlikely quality for a peasant-poet almost totally lacking in formal education to possess, and yet Hogg certainly seems to have developed such a taste.

During the years between his removal to Edinburgh in 1810 and his marriage in 1820 Hogg seized on the chances provided by metropolitan life for artistic as well as literary self-education. Hogg's essay-periodical *The Spy* of 1810–11 gives some indication of what these may have been: for example, John Knox's panorama of Loch Lomond from the top of Ben Lomond was on public exhibition in Edinburgh in 1810, while Hogg regrets in the issue for 17 November 1810 that 'Neither the theatre, nor exhibition of paintings is yet open [...]'. The Edinburgh Theatre opened for the season almost immediately afterwards, and in giving an acccount of the first performance Hogg specifically mentions the 'new decorations', created under the supervision of the Scottish artist Alexander Nasmyth (1758–1840) which included a dropscene of 'a fine view of St Bernard's Well, seen through pillars'.[2] The exhibition of paintings was the fourth held by the Associated Society of Artists, a body of professional Scottish painters who joined together to show their own work to the public and to counteract the aristocratic art-lovers of Edinburgh, who were intent on displaying their Old Masters to one another and inclined to despise modern practitioners. This particular exhibition was held in Raeburn's premises at 16 York Place from 8 April 1811, and was strongly supported also by the Nasmyth family. Hogg's interest in the artists of this professional body was clearly maintained in the succeeding years, for the catalogue of the Edinburgh Exhibition of Paintings for 1813 lists a 'Portrait of the Ettrick Shepherd' by W. S. Watson (on public display only weeks after the publication of *The Queen's Wake* on 30 January). Portraits of Hogg by William Nicholson (1781–1844) featured in the exhibitions of 1815 and 1816.[3] The movement towards a modern Scottish art represented in these exhibitions clearly found its inspiration and parallel in the Scottish literary tradition of Burns and Scott to which Hogg also belonged: the catalogues frequently quote tags of poems in referring to paintings with literary subjects, while portraits include those of the city's notable literary men. No wonder then that Hogg when introduced to David Wilkie at Bowhill in 1817 should have greeted him so enthusiastically with the words 'Thank God for it. I did not know that you were so young a man!', seeing him as a former pupil of Nasmyth and the culmination of a well-known school of native Scottish (and literary) painting. The three sketches Hogg wrote to accompany a Wilkie engraving for *The Amulet* are another tribute to an admired Scottish painter.[4] An early advertisement for the fifth or subscription edition of Hogg's *The Queen's Wake*, in the *Edinburgh Evening Courant* of 26 May 1817 advertises the work as a luxury product, to cost two guineas in quarto, elegantly printed, and 'ornamented with engravings from designs by Scottish artists'; illustrations for which Hogg presumably intended to draw on his contacts among Scottish painters.[5]

Towards the end of this period of his life Hogg became a member of the Dilettanti Society of Edinburgh, the object of which was 'the diffusion of a love for the Fine Arts, and the cultivation of a friendly intercourse with each other'. The members dined together four times a year, but also held weekly or fortnightly meetings in Young's Tavern at 209 High Street, when the drinks were restricted to the relatively inexpensive Edinburgh ale and whisky toddy. Among the painter-members of the Dilettanti were Henry Raeburn, Alexander Nasmyth, Hugh Williams, John Schetky, the Rev. John Thomson of Duddingston, and William Allan, while the literary members included Scott, John Ballantyne, Hogg himself, John Gibson Lockhart, and John Wilson. Hogg's friend David Bridges, Junior, was the Secretary, a clothier known for the collection of paintings in the basement of his High Street shop and nicknamed 'Director-General of the Fine Arts for Scotland'.[6] The Dilettanti Society is appropriately commemorated in a fine painting by William Allan, with Hogg one of the most significant figures in it.[7] The few printed notices of the Dilettanti that have survived also suggest that Hogg was an active and important member: at the meeting of 28 January 1819, for example, he proposed the admission of two new members, one proposal being made in conjunction with the Secretary. A sarcastic notice of the Society in *Blackwood's Edinburgh Magazine* for August 1818 rejoices that the members' 'powers of taste are no longer confined, as of old, to deciding on the merits of Davy Bridges' bowls of punch, or Jamie Hogg's pitchers of toddy'.[8] One of Hogg's social outings with fellow-member Alexander Nasmyth is commemorated in 'Scottish Haymakers', written by Hogg for the *Forget Me Not*.[9]

Hogg's marriage in April 1820 settled him at Altrive Lake in Yarrow rather than in Edinburgh, and presumably diminished his involvement with the Dilettanti to that of a country member visiting the metropolis only at intervals. However, important paintings would still be open to his inspection when the now-celebrated Ettrick Shepherd was received as a guest at Bowhill, Floors Castle, Abbotsford, and other Scottish country mansions. One indication of Hogg's continuing interest in painting is the fact that he mixed with many artists during his London visit from January to March 1832. A ticket to admit 'James Hogg, Esq[r.] and Party' to the private view of the Ninth Exhibition of the Society of British Artists at Suffolk Street, Pall Mall, on 23 March 1832 has survived, and Hogg dined in company with artists such as John Martin, William Brockeden, and George Cruikshank.[10]

The 1820s were also years of technical innovation in the printing-trade that would democratize painting, bringing good-quality copies within the budget of many middle-class families. Iain Bain explains exactly why the production of good-quality engravings had been so labour intensive, and consequently expensive.[11] The surface of a copper plate was prepared for engraving by applying an acid-resisting ground to it, and then a reduced-scale drawing of the original painting was applied to the plate and passed through the rolling press, transferring the pencil lines to the prepared surface. The engraver would then follow the pencil lines with a variety of needles to bare the surface of the metal below according to the drawing. After that a raised border of wax would be built up around the edge of the plate to contain the acid applied subsequently to it. The longer the lines were exposed to the acid the deeper they became, so successive applications of acid were made and the finer lines were protected against it for subsequent exposures. Certain areas of the plate might also be finished with the graver after this etching with acid was completed. The engraver was a highly-skilled craftsman engaged in a laborious process, and would be paid accordingly: Bain records that the engraver Charles Warren spent thirteen weeks on a single plate to illustrate Scott's *The Lady of the Lake*, commenting that the fifty guineas he was paid for it, though a large sum, was nevertheless 'a modest enough reward for the close and exacting labour of thirteen weeks'. The plate would then be handed to a specialist printer, for the actual printing was also an exacting business: the plate would need to be carefully charged with ink and wiped with various cloths to ensure that the ink was all removed from the surface but stayed in all the engraved lines, for the heavy press pushed the damp paper into the lines of the plate where it picked up the ink. Unfortunately, the copper plate would soon become abraded by the wiping cloths of the printers, fine work being destroyed perhaps within the taking of only a hundred impressions, when the plate would need to go back to the engraver again for expensive restoration-work.

In 1819, however, Jacob Perkins took out a patent for a long-life steel plate, from which thousands of impressions could be made without deterioration during the printing process. This meant that the high initial costs of producing the plate could in theory be spread over a large edition, drastically reducing the cost of producing each individual print. It was no accident that Rudolph Ackermann (1764–1834), the originator of the annual in Britain, was a fine-art publisher: he understood that a high-quality article could be sold at a remarkably low price, but only if there were exceptionally large sales to justify the initial investment. Naturally enough the producers of the annuals tended, in order to stimulate sales, to emphasise what a bargain the purchasers were getting: the 'Preface' to the *Forget Me Not* for 1832, for example, says that the annuals prove

> [...] the truth of the paradox, that a part is more valuable than the whole—inasmuch as sets of their engravings are regularly sold at a higher rate than the entire volumes from which they have been separated. It is well known also that single proof impressions of particular plates have obtained a price superior to that of the complete work.[12]

The middle-class purchasers of the annuals were gaining access to a world of art previously beyond their reach. Paintings from private collections were seen by thousands of people in the form of engravings in the annuals. For example, Christine Alexander explains that various annuals were prized possessions of the Brontë children in their remote Yorkshire parsonage, and that ten engravings from *Friendship's Offering* for 1829, the *Literary Souvenir* for 1830, and the *Forget Me Not* for 1831 were painstakingly copied by Charlotte, Branwell, and Emily. She explains that until the Brontës went to London their experience of great art had been second-hand, that although they knew of leading artists they had never seen their works except in the form of books and engravings.[13] To that family as to many others of similar means the annuals therefore performed an invaluable service. Some artists, too, were helped by the increased publicity given to their work through engravings. The work of John Martin (1789–1854), for example, was rejected by the establishment Royal Academy and he showed no paintings there from 1824 until 1837, his income chiefly deriving not from sales of his paintings but from sales of prints of them. He set up his own printing shop, and William Feaver demonstrates that 'in dealings with Ackermann, Colnaghi, and provincial printsellers (notably in Manchester and Liverpool), he made nearly £3,000 between June 1826 and December 1827 from *Belshazzar* and *Joshua*. The price varied from 10 guineas for an unlettered proof of *The Deluge* to one guinea for a run-of-the-mill impression'. Martin was also one of the most popular artists of the annuals: his *Marius Curtius*, for example, was engraved for the *Forget Me Not* for 1829, which sold ten thousand copies.[14] The development of the steel-plate had effectively created a middle-class art market through the mass production of engravings sold separately and in the bargain package of the annuals. Within the annuals this was reinforced by technological developments in book-binding: as Eleanore Jamieson indicates, the invention of the fly-embossing press of the mid-1820s, and of the Imperial Arming Press of 1832 meant that bindings could be mechanically embossed or gold-blocked, reducing the cost per item of a luxury binding.[15] A mid-Victorian writer about the annuals claims that the wide circulation of prints in the annuals, by raising public awareness of art, eventually created a new market for paintings among the wealthy citizens of the country's industrial cities, and was thus indirectly responsible for the creation of many provincial art-collections:

> Previous to the appearance of the Annuals, there were few, if any, collectors in Manchester, Birmingham, Liverpool, or Leeds, and there is now scarcely a gentleman of wealth in any one of these cities who has not a gallery of modern works of art [...].[16]

Hogg's establishment at Altrive after his marriage was very much the type of modest but aspiring middle-class home to which the engravings and annuals most appealed: Mrs Parr in recording his purchase of wallpaper in September 1825, for example, remarks that 'It is possible this was an innovation in the district!'.[17] Hogg's simple library in the eastern wing of the house contained 'a round table [...] in the centre of the floor, covered with engravings and annuals', and we know that there were 'some good pictures hanging on the wall, among which was an excellent portrait of one of his children—a likeness of his early dog Hector—and two of Martin's well-known engravings, one of them being the Fall of Nineveh'.[18] Engravings of the sort that featured in the annuals, therefore, clearly appealed to James Hogg and became part of the furniture of his house, but what was the nature of their appeal?

That the engravings of a Romantic artist like John Martin (a key artist for the annuals) appealed significantly to the denizens of the rapidly-expanding industrial cities of the North of England appears to be highly significant in this context: one of the problems of the age was to cope mentally and socially with rapid social change and the expansion of the city, and this was also an important though understated aspect of the literary work of James Hogg.

One aspect of Hogg's writing in the annuals as elsewhere was the preservation and reinterpretation of the rural peasant society and landscape of his childhood and youth for a middle-class urban readership. In tales such as 'Seeking the Houdy', for example, Hogg sounds an elegaic note for the birthing customs of his youth, as well as relating a fine supernatural tale, while 'The Cameronian Preacher's Tale' evokes a firmly-led and firmly-grounded religious community in which God's justice over-rules human mistakes and moral error. A poem like 'St Mary of the Lows' resolves the past conflicts of Hogg's native society within a tranquil, organic rural landscape. Hogg was well aware, however, that such resolutions were the result of selection and arrangement, and explores this by analogy to the painting of Alexander Nasmyth in 'Scottish Haymakers'. As Nasmyth remarks to his artist son, 'It is amazing how little makes a good picture; and frequently the less that is taken in the better'. Duncan Macmillan elaborates Hogg's insight by saying, 'The formality of the composition gives harmony and stability to a real view. He was prepared to edit but not to depart from the essentials of the scene in front of him'. Nasmyth also viewed Edinburgh in similar harmonious terms, as an organic whole, where a splendid natural landscape, buildings created by man, and busy citizens cooperate to form a unity.[19] The engraving that Hogg's tale in fact accompanied was from a painting by 'W. Kidd', but Hogg's writing is nevertheless partly a tribute to Nasmyth's vision and partly a Romantic disruption of it—the party of friends from the city admire the rosy country girls at their haymaking and the picture they make in the landscape setting, but their presence soon dissolves the harmony they admire. Monsieur Alexandre's ventriloquism may amuse the rest of the walking-party, but it delays the haymakers' work, drives one countryman insane, and persuades the local inn-keeper and his family that they have had the devil among them. The story ends in the opposite mood to its peaceful, even idyllic, opening, with injury and even, it is hinted, eventual death.

Hogg's tribute to Wilkie in the annuals is less ambiguous, reflecting the contemporary praise of him as the Scottish Teniers. Hogg was invited by S. C. Hall to write some letterpress to accompany one of Wilkie's domestic scenes, 'The Dorty Bairn', engraved from a painting 'in the possession of Sir Willoughby Gordon, Bart.'. Hall was clearly expecting a sentimental or moral poem or tale from the way he describes the engraving:

> It represents a little girl who has quarrelled with her bread & butter—her mother is saying "look at your pretty face" and showing her a looking glass. Can you be good enough to write for me, a few lines to accompany this plate—I should far prefer them in the dialect of your country.[20]

Hogg does indeed obey this instruction in the first of his three sketches, also giving a glimpse of his personal life as he did in several other annuals contributions (readers clearly enjoyed this then as now), but the real subject of his article is an appreciation of David Wilkie as the premier Scottish artist of the time. Each section provides a snapshot scene of Scottish life, described as if captured on canvas by Wilkie, and the three together demonstrate the range of his genius: the domestic interior of the engraving is succeeded by the bustle of a country fair such as the one depicted by Wilkie in his *Pitlessie Fair*, and this in turn by an acute and insightful interpretation by Wilkie of a well-known scene from an influential work of Scottish literature, Allan Ramsay's *The Gentle Shepherd*. Hogg's contribution emphasises the closeness of the native traditions of Scottish painting and of Scottish literature, where Wilkie's art is inspired by Scottish rural life and Scottish writing, and then Hogg's own writing is inspired by Wilkie's art and his native landscape viewed as through Wilkie's eyes.

So far as can be determined now, Hogg was never invited to write a tale or poem for the annuals to accompany a John Martin engraving, though Martin was a favourite artist in such works and (although he seems to have been primarily interested in the Scottish tradition of painting) Hogg responded powerfully to the Romantic iconoclasm of Martin's work. Hogg owned Martin engravings (see above), and he reported enthusiastically to his wife on his meeting with 'Martin, the sublime painter' in London in January 1832. During this London visit Hogg persuaded Martin to paint a scene from his own visionary poem, 'Kilmeny', suggesting that the artist's daughter Isabella should be the model for Kilmeny awakening in the land of thought. Martin, however, preferred a slightly later passage where Kilmeny is seated on 'a mountain green' and views both 'an endless whirl of glory and light' and a distant representation of a Scottish landscape. Martin's watercolour was shown at the exhibition of the Society of British Artists in the spring of 1833.[21]

Hogg and Martin were both well-versed in the apocalyptic tradition of Biblical and Calvinistic literature, and both were interested in its adaptation to the cultural circumstances of their own times and their own countries, just as William Blake could see Jerusalem built among the dark Satanic mills. William Feaver explains that Martin had been brought up in the Tyne valley where the proximity of the ancient Roman monument of Hadrian's Wall and his pious mother's tendency to relate all experience to Biblical precedent had laid the groundwork for his subsequent artistic vision. In his paintings Martin combined well-known British landscapes, recent industrial and technological developments, and imaginative reconstructions of the ancient civilisations retrieved by contemporary archaeologists in such artefacts as the sculpted head of Rameses II (brought to the British Museum in 1818), or the Elgin Marbles.[22] An implicit parallel was thus drawn between the collapse of newly-retrieved ancient cities and the anxieties created by the rapidly-developing cities of early nineteenth-century Britain, of which Edinburgh was not the least.

The proliferation of Edinburgh's monuments, and the new estates laid out to the north of Queen Street were easily related to the panoramic grandeurs of Martin's depicted Babylon or Nineveh, while episodes like the great Edinburgh fire of 1824 in which a large section of the old buildings around the Parliament Square were destroyed in an inferno lasting several days echoed the fall of Sodom or Gomorrah. Feaver indeed states that in Martin's 1852 painting of *The Great Day of his Wrath* 'Edinburgh collapses, with Calton Hill,

Arthur's Seat, and the Castle Rock falling together upon the valley between them'.[23]

Hogg probably shared Martin's sense of living in a modern apocalypse after the Napoleonic Wars—Napoleon could all too easily be seen as the Antichrist, and the burning of Moscow as an episode from the Latter Days. For Hogg's generation (as for subsequent ones up to the outbreak of another European war almost a hundred years later in 1914) the Napoleonic conflict was envisaged as the war to end wars, or as Hogg remarked in his *Lay Sermons*, 'After the campaigns of Buonaparte, and the slaughter of so many millions among the most civilised nations on the face of the earth, and which ended so completely in smoke, I really thought there would never be any more wars in Europe [...]'.[24] Hogg's sense of imminent apocalypse is also revealed in his self-mocking account of his early reading as a shepherd of 'Bishop Burnet's Theory of the Conflagration of the Earth':

> All the day I was pondering on the grand millennium, and the reign of the saints; and all the night dreaming of new heavens and a new earth—the stars in horror, and the world in flames!
> (*Memoir*, p. 16)

Martin's paintings were discussed in both *Blackwood's Edinburgh Magazine* and the *Edinburgh Review* and frequently displayed in major British cities (presumably to stimulate sales of the profitable mezzotints and engravings). The twenty-first edition of the catalogue accompanying the public exhibition of Martin's *Belshazzar's Feast*, for instance, reveals that the picture was then on show 'at the Hall of the Calton Company, Waterloo Bridge, Edinburgh' in 1822, where Hogg may well have seen it while he was in town for the visit of that modern feasting Belshazzar George IV.[25]

Although Hogg did not directly write to a specific Martin engraving for the annuals, several of his contributions reflect Martin's influence or allude to his painting. In 'Eastern Apologues', for example, an oriental despot named Sadac is made to realise the limitations of his power and his capacity for happiness by an aged songwriter and sage named Ismael, who is in turn instructed by him in the rules of practical politics. The story of Sadac comes originally from James Ridley's *Tales of the Genii* (1762), and concerns the conflict between an unjust Sultan and a Persian noble, Sadak, whom he tricks into volunteering to search for the Waters of Oblivion. Martin's Romantic painting *Sadak in Search of the Waters of Oblivion* (1812) depicts Sadak struggling in exhaustion on the brink of a rocky ledge,

with the Waters of Oblivion before him and an immense abyss below. The painting was engraved for the *Keepsake* of 1828, where it
appeared with a poem now known to be by Shelley, entitled 'Sadac
the Wanderer'.[26] The theme of Hogg's tale of painful self-discovery
in an oriental setting is clearly related to this rather lurid painting
with its hellish, or perhaps industrial, flaming reds and ochres. Hogg's
relation of Biblical prophecy to contemporary archaeology in 'The
Judgment of Idumea' is also characteristic of Martin's artistic vision,
although no exact equivalent in paint by Martin to Hogg's reinterpretation of Isaiah 34 has been found.

The engravings in the annuals, therefore, were not irrelevant embellishments or meaningless decoration but an exciting new opportunity for middle-class families of limited means to gain access to
paintings and to possess their own copies of them. Hogg's earlier
self-education in the visual arts had prepared him to share in this
opportunity, and he responded to it both as a purchaser and as a
writer. His work for the annuals explores his own reactions to those
artists who meant most to him—notably Nasmyth, Wilkie, and Martin—and therefore adds a new dimension to our understanding of
his life and work.

Notes

1. In his *Memoir*, designed as an account of his literary life, Hogg in describing his want of formal education is explicit about his lack of access even to
books in the traditional farmhouses in which he served—see 'Memoir of
the Author's Life' in *Altrive Tales*, ed. by Gillian Hughes (S/SC, 2003), pp.
11–78 (pp. 14–16). This is hereafter referred to as *Memoir*. Valuable information on the circulation of prints is provided by Sheila O'Connell, *The
Popular Print in England 1550–1850* (London: British Museum, 1999).

2. See nos. 12, 13, and 15, in *The Spy*, ed. by Gillian Hughes (Edinburgh:
Edinburgh University Press, 2000), pp. 118, 131, 157–58 and notes. See
also 'Scottish Drama', *Edinburgh Annual Register for 1809*, 2. 2 (Edinburgh,
1811), 385–401 (pp. 386–87) and the *Edinburgh Evening Courant* for 1 November 1810. The closeness of writing, theatre, and painting during this
time is more fully discussed in Gillian Hughes, 'James Hogg and the
Theatre', *Studies in Hogg and his World*, 15 (2004), 53–66.

3. Some account of the rise of an organisation representing contemporary
Scottish painters is given in the National Gallery of Scotland leaflet 'Early
Victorian Draughtsmen and the Rise of the Scottish Academy' (HMSO,
1980), and in Duncan Macmillan, *Painting in Scotland: The Golden Age* (Oxford: Phaidon Press, 1986), pp. 134–36. Information on the Edinburgh
exhibitions of these years, and the Hogg portraits shown at them is drawn
from the surviving exhibition catalogues, in particular *Fourth Annual Exhi-*

bition of Paintings &c. in Scotland by the Associated Society of Artists (Edinburgh: Oliver & Boyd, 1811); *Sixth Annual Exhibition of Paintings, &c. in Scotland, by the Associated Artists* (Edinburgh: Oliver & Boyd, 1813); *Catalogue of the Edinburgh Exhibition of Paintings for 1815* (Edinburgh: Oliver & Boyd, 1815); and *Catalogue of the Edinburgh Exhibition of Paintings for 1816* (Edinburgh: Oliver & Boyd, 1816). The catalogue of the 1813 Exhibition gives the opening date as 5 April 1813, while an advertisement in the *Edinburgh Evening Courant* of 30 January 1813 describes *The Queen's Wake* as 'This day is published [...]'. As paintings were normally entered for exhibition some days previous to the opening (to allow time for hanging and the production of the catalogue), Watson's portrait must have been finished within a period of two months from the publication of *The Queen's Wake*, if it was not begun before it.

4. J. G. Lockhart, *The Life of Sir Walter Scott, Bart.*, 7 vols (Edinburgh: Cadell; London: Murray and Whittaker, 1837–38), IV, 98. See his three sketches entitled 'The Dorty Wean', 'The History of an Auld Naig', and 'David Wilkie' in the present volume, pp. 181–85 and notes.

5. For a detailed account of the efforts made by Hogg to include engravings in the subscription edition of *The Queen's Wake* and their obvious importance to him see Meiko O'Halloran, 'Hogg, Mary, Queen of Scots, and the Illustrations to *The Queen's Wake*' in *The Queen's Wake*, ed. by Douglas S. Mack (S/SC, 2004), pp. lxxxvii–cxiii (pp. lxxxvii–lxxxix). As O'Halloran notes (p. xci), Hogg even specified that Edinburgh's leading engraver, William Home Lizars (1788–1859) should be employed on the work.

6. See James Nasmyth, *An Autobiography*, ed. by Samuel Smiles (London: Murray, 1883), pp. 35–36. David Bridges and his shop are also vividly portrayed in Lockhart's *Peter's Letters to his Kinsfolk*, 3 vols (Edinburgh: Blackwood; London: Cadell and Davies, 1819), II, 230–33, and by Robert Chambers in his *Walks in Edinburgh* (Edinburgh: W. Hunter, 1825), pp. 71–78. The printed 'Regulations of the Society of Dilettanti' (NLS, MS 5406, fol. 18), are supplemented by information gleaned from five printed papers of the Dilettanti in NLS, MS APS.3.83.7.1.

7. This picture, now entitled *The Celebration of the Birthday of James Hogg*, hangs in the Scottish National Portrait Gallery in Edinburgh and is dated 1823 or possibly 1825. It is described as a meeting of the Dilettanti Society by James Nasmyth in his *Autobiography* (p. 35), who mentions the detail that his father Alexander Nasmyth is 'represented as illustrating some subject he is describing, by drawing it on the part of the table before him, with his finger dipped in toddy', and adds that it was sold to a Mr Horrocks of Preston in Lancashire. The background may represent the Society's meeting-place at Young's tavern on the High Street.

8. The printed summons of the members to the meeting of 28 January 1819 is in NLS, MS APS.3.83.7.1. The irreverent account of the socialities of the Society is given in 'Letter to the Committee of Dilettanti, Occasioned by their Report on the Plans for the Repair of St Giles' Church, Edinburgh', *Blackwood's Edinburgh Magazine*, 3 (August 1818), 524–27 (p. 525). The writer declares that he regards the society 'with great affection and some respect', having been induced to join by hearing that 'there was an excel-

lent hot supper in the wind every Thursday evening, at the moderate expense of one shilling a head' and that the landlord, Bill Young, kept a good store of potable rum and whisky.

9. For 'Scottish Haymakers' see pp. 78–84 and notes below.

10. I am grateful to Hogg's New Zealand descendants Chris Gilkison, Liz Milne, and David Parr for much useful information about their famous ancestor: the ticket for the private view of the exhibition of the Society of British Artists forms part of a family scrapbook compiled by Hogg's eldest daughter, Jessie Phillips Hogg. John Martin and George Cruikshank are referred to by Hogg in *A Series of Lay Sermons*, ed. by Gillian Hughes with Douglas S. Mack (S/SC, 1997), p. 33. Hogg's letter to Brockedon of 15 March 1832 (National Portrait Gallery, NPG 2515, p. 119D) refers to him as 'one with whom I have had too short aquaintance', and offers him a copy of each of the volumes of the *Altrive Tales* collection as they are published as a return for a presentation copy of Brockedon's own *Illustrations of Passages of the Alps* (1827–29), which included a hundred engravings from Brockedon's own drawings.

11. The technical explanation which follows is essentially a summary of the excellent detailed description in Iain Bain's essay 'Gift Book and Annual Illustrations: Some Notes on their Production', in Frederick W. Faxon, *Literary Annuals and Gift Books: A Bibliography 1823–1903*, repr. with supplementary essays by Eleanore Jamieson and Iain Bain (Pinner, Middlesex: Private Libraries Association, 1973), pp. 19–25. The quotation is from p. 22.

12. See the Preface to the *Forget Me Not* for 1832, pp. 3–6 (pp. 4–5).

13. See Christine Alexander, 'The Influence of the Visual Arts on the Brontës', in Christine Alexander and Jane Sellars, *The Art of the Brontës* (Cambridge: Cambridge University Press, 1995), 9–35 (pp. 15, 24).

14. William Feaver, *The Art of John Martin* (Oxford: Clarendon Press, 1975), pp. 130, 84, 102. Meiko O'Halloran has rightly pointed out to me that this argument requires some qualification, in that various Martin works were exhibited before these dates at the Royal Academy, such as 'Sadac in Search of the Waters of Oblivion' in 1812, and that in 1820 his name was even proposed for membership. However his paintings attracted little interest there and no votes succeeded his nomination. Feaver's statement in his *Oxford DNB* biography that Martin 'was never accepted as a serious painter by the art establishment as constituted by the Royal Academy' is not on balance unreasonable.

15. See Eleanore Jamieson, 'The Binding Styles of the Gift Books and Annuals', in Faxon, *Literary Annuals and Gift Books*, pp. 7–17.

16. 'The Annuals of Former Days', in *The Bookseller*, 29 November and 24 December 1858, pp. 493–95 and 585–89 (p. 494).

17. Norah Parr, *James Hogg at Home: Being the Domestic Life and Letters of the Ettrick Shepherd* (Dollar: Douglas S. Mack, 1980), p. 72.

18. 'A Visit to the Ettrick Shepherd. By an American Tourist', *American Monthly Magazine*, 3 (1834), 85–91 (p. 88), and also 'Life of the Ettrick Shepherd', in *The Works of the Ettrick Shepherd: Poems and Life*, ed. by Thomas Thomson, centenary edition (London and Glasgow, [1872]), pp. ix–lxxi (p. li).

19. Duncan Macmillan's excellent account of both Nasmyth's landscapes and Edinburgh paintings is to be found in his *Painting in Scotland: The Golden Age*, pp. 144–46.

20. The engraving (reproduced in the present edition at p. 180) is to be seen in *The Amulet* for 1830, where it is accompanied by 'The Dorty Bairn: A Fable' by the Rev. William Wilkie on pp. 101–02. S. C. Hall's letter to Hogg of 25 June [1829] is in NLS, MS 2245, fols 148–49.

21. See Hogg's letter to his wife of 10 January 1832, in Mrs Garden, *Memorials of James Hogg, the Ettrick Shepherd* (Paisley and London, n.d.), pp. 247–48. Martin's letter to Hogg of 29 May 1833 (in NLS, MS 2245, fols 222–23) refers to Hogg's admiration of the painter's daughter whom he wished to be her father's model for an illustration to 'Kilmeny' and outlines the passage illustrated. A notice of the 1833 exhibition of the Society of British Artists in the *Athenaeum* of 13 April 1833 (pp. 233–34) notices in 'the Water-colour Room' 'an illustration of Hogg's "Kilmeny", by MARTIN, in which the landscape is admirable, "Little peaceful heavens in the bosom of earth" '. For further information about Hogg's social contact with Martin in London and Martin's water-colour illustration of 'Kilmeny' see Meiko O'Halloran, 'Hogg, Mary, Queen of Scots, and the Illustrations to *The Queen's Wake*, in *The Queen's Wake* (S/SC, 2004), pp. lxxxvii–cxiii (pp. c–civ).

22. See Feaver, *The Art of John Martin*, pp. 1–6, 39–40.

23. Feaver, p. 6.

24. James Hogg, *A Series of Lay Sermons* (S/SC, 1997), p. 41. In Thomas Hardy's *The Dynasts* (1904–08), one example of the far-reaching impact of the conflict, political events of the Napoleonic Wars alternate with scenes affecting ordinary folk and events are observed by supernatural intelligences of various descriptions.

25. See *A Description of The Picture, Belshazzar's Feast Painted by Mr. J. Martin*, 21st edn (London: Printed for the Proprietors, 1822). R. P. Gillies, in his *Memoirs of a Literary Veteran*, 3 vols (London, 1851), III, 71 mentions meeting Hogg by chance on the lawn of Melville Castle during George IV's Edinburgh visit, and that Hogg was accompanied by Croly, who had been introduced to him by Blackwood.

26. Feaver, pp. 16–17.

Literary Souvenir

Invocation

to the

Queen of the Fairies

By James Hogg

No Muse was ever invoked by me,
But a harp uncouth of olden key;
And with her have I ranged the border green,
The Grampians stern, and the starry sheen;
With my gray plaid flapping around the strings,   5
And my ragged coat with its waving wings.
But ay my heart beat quick and high,
When an air of heaven in passing by
Breathed on the mellow chords, and then
I knew it was no earthly strain;   10
But a rapt note borne upon the wind
From some blest land of unbodied kind;
But whence it flew, or whether it came
From the sounding rock, or the solar beam,
Or the seraph choir, as passing away   15
O'er the bridge of the sky in the showery day,
When the cloudy curtain pervaded the east,
And the sunbeam kissed its watery breast;
In vain I looked to the cloud over head;
To the echoing mountain, dark and dread;   20
To the sun-fawn fleet, and aërial bow;
I knew not whence were the strains till now.

They were from thee, thou radiant dame,
O'er Fancy's region that reign'st supreme!
Thou lovely thing of beauty so bright,   25
Of everlasting new delight;
Of foible, of freak, of gambol and glee;
    Of all that teases,
    And all that pleases,
All that we fret at, yet love to see.   30
In petulance, pity, and passions refined,
Thou emblem extreme of the female mind!

Thou seest thyself, and smil'st to see
A shepherd kneel on his sward to thee;
But sure thou wilt come, with thy tuneful train,   35
To assist in his last and lingering strain.
O come from thy halls of the emerald bright,
Thy bowers of the green and the mellow light,
That shrink from the blaze of the summer noon,
And ope to the light of the modest moon;   40
I long to hail the enchanting mien
Of my loved Muse, my Fairy Queen,
Her rokelay of green with its sparry hue,
Its warp of the moonbeam and weft of the dew;
The smile where a thousand witcheries play,   45
And the eye that steals the soul away;
The strains that tell they were never mundane,
And the bells of her palfrey's flowing mane;
Ere now have I heard their tinklings light,
And seen my Queen at the noon of the night   50
Pass by with her train in the still moonlight.

Then she, who raised old Edmund's lay
Above the strains of the olden day;
And waked the Bard of Avon's theme
To the visions of a midnight dream;   55
And even the harp that rang abroad
O'er all the paradise of God,
And the sons of the morning with it drew,
By her was remodelled and strung anew.
Come thou to my bower deep in the dell,–   60
Thou Queen of the land 'twixt heaven and hell,–
That land of a thousand gilded domes,
The richest region that Fancy roams!

I have sought for thee in the blue harebell,
And deep in the foxglove's silken cell,   65
For I feared thou hadst drank of its potion deep,
And the breeze of this world had rocked thee asleep.
Then into the wild rose I cast mine eye,
And trembled because the prickles were nigh,
And deemed the specks on the foliage green   70
Might be the blood of my Fairy Queen;
Then gazing, wondered if blood could be

In an immortal thing like thee!
I have opened the woodbine's velvet vest,
And sought in the lily's snowy breast;   75
At gloaming lain on the dewy lea
And looked to a twinkling star for thee,
That nightly mounted the orient sheen,
Streaming with purple, and glowing with green,
And thought, as I eyed its changing sphere,   80
My Fairy Queen might sojourn there.

   Then would I sigh and turn me around,
And lay my ear to the hollow ground,
To the little air-springs of central birth
That bring low murmurs out of the earth;   85
And there would I listen in breathless way
Till I heard the worm creep through the clay,
And the mole deep grubbing in darkness drear,
That little blackamoor pioneer;
Nought cheered me, on which the daylight shone,   90
For the children of darkness moved alone;
Yet neither in field nor on flowery heath,
In heaven above nor in earth beneath,
In star nor moon nor midnight wind,
His elvish Queen could her Minstrel find.   95

   But now have I found thee, thou vagrant thing,
Though where I neither may say nor sing;
But it was in a home so passing fair
That an angel of light might have lingered there;
It was in a place never wet by the dew,   100
Where the sun never shone, and the wind never blew,
Where the ruddy cheek of youth ne'er lay,
And never was kissed by the breeze of day;
As sweet as the woodland airs of even,
And pure as the star of the western heaven;   105
As fair as the dawn of the sunny east,
And soft as the down of the solan's breast.

   Yes, now have I found thee, and thee will I keep,
Though spirits yell on the midnight steep,
Though the earth should quake when nature is still,   110
And the thunders growl in the breast of the hill;

Though the moon should scowl thro' her pall of gray,
And the stars fling blood on the Milky Way;
Since now I have found thee I'll hold thee fast
Till thou garnish my song,– it is the last: 115
Then a maiden's gift that song shall be,
And I'll call it a Queen for the sake of thee.

ALTRIVE LAKE
Oct. 6, 1824

Love's Jubilee

By James Hogg

FIRST SPIRIT

Lovely Spirit, where dost thou fly
With such impatience in thine eye?–
Behold the hues of the closing day
Are mingled still with the gloaming gray;
And thine own sweet star of the welkin sheen,   5
The star of love, is but faintly seen!
See how she hangs like a diamond dim
By the walks of the holy Seraphim,
While the fays in the middle vales of blue
Have but half distilled their freight of dew.   10
It is too early in the night
For a spirit so lovely and so bright
To be tracing the walks of this world beneath,
Unhallowed by sin, and mildewed by death;
Where madness and folly are ever rife,   15
And snares that beleaguer mortal life.–
I know thee well, sweet Spirit of Love,
And I know thy mission from above;
Thou comest with every grace refined
To endow the earthly virgin's mind;   20
A record of her virtues to keep,
And all her thoughts awake and asleep.
Bright Spirit, thou hast a charge of care!
Come tarry with me in this woodland fair,
I will teach thee more in one hour of joy   25

Than all thou hast learned since thou left'st the sky.
Come tarry with me, let the maidens be,
'Till the hour of dreaming and phantasy;
And then will I seek with thee to share
The task of fanning their foreheads fair,   30
And scaring the little fays of sin
That tickle the downy dimpling chin;
That prank with the damask vein of the cheek,
And whisper words it were wrong to speak.
From all these foes thy wards shall be free,   35
If thou wilt go woo in the wood with me;
Till yon twin stars hang balanced even,
Like ear-rings on the cheeks of heaven!

SECOND SPIRIT

And who art thou, that with shameless brow,
Darest here such license to avow?   40
If aright I judge from what I've heard,
This courtesy might well be spared;
For of all the spirits beneath the sun
Thou art the one that I most would shun!
Art thou not he of guardian fame,   45
That watchest over the sex supreme?
Say, Spirit, was the charge not given
To thee, before the throne of heaven,
To guard the youth of this vale from sin,
From follies without and foibles within?   50
If so, thou hast honour of thy trade!
A glorious guardian hast thou made!
To the dole and the danger of mine and me,–
My malison light on it and thee!
Go woo with thee!–by this heavenly mind   55
I had rather go woo with a mortal hind!

FIRST SPIRIT

Sweet Spirit, sure thou could'st never opine
That my charge could be as pure as thine?
Something for sex thou should'st allow;
Yet have I done what spirit might do,   60
And more will I still, if thou wilt go rest
With me on the wild thyme's fragrant breast,
By form of an angel never prest!

I will spread thee a couch of the violet blue,
Of our own heaven's cerulean hue;   65
The sweetest flowers shall round thee be strewed,
And I'll pillow thy head on the gossamer's shroud;
And there, 'neath the green leaves closely furled,
I will cool thy cheek with the dew of the world;
I will bind thy locks with the sweet wood-reef,   70
And fan thy brow with the wabron leaf;
I will press thy heaving heart to mine,
And try to mix with our love divine
An earthly joy, a mortal bliss;
I will woo thee and woo thee for a kiss,   75
As a thing above all gifts to prize,
And I'll swear 'tis the odour of Paradise!
In earthly love, when ardent and chaste,
There's a joy which angels scarce may taste;
Then come to the bower I have framed for thee;   80
We'll let the youth of the vale go free,
And this eve shall be LOVE's JUBILEE!

SECOND SPIRIT

I will not, I dare not such hazard run,
My virgin race may be all undone.
The breeze is chill,—it is wearing late,   85
Away thou guardian profligate!

FIRST SPIRIT

Sweet spirit, why that quivering lip,
Which an angel of light might love to sip?
And why doth thy radiance come and go,
Like the hues of thine own celestial bow?   90
And why dost thou look to the ground and sigh,
And away from the green-wood turn thine eye?
Are these the symptoms, may I divine,
Of an earthly love, and is it mine?

SECOND SPIRIT

Ah, no! it is something about my head,   95
Some qualm of languor or of dread.
That breeze is surely in a glow,
And yet it is chill—what shall I do?

Wilt thou not go?—ah! haste away
Unto thy charge; thou art worse than they. 100

FIRST SPIRIT

I will not, cannot leave thee so;
I must woo thee whether thou wilt or no;
Let us hide from the star-beam and the gale,—
Why dost thou tremble and look so pale?

SECOND SPIRIT

Oh, my dear maidens of beauty so bright, 105
What will become of you all to-night!
For I fear me this eve of wizard spell
May be, by shade, by bower, and dell,
An eve to dream of—not to tell!

FIRST SPIRIT

I will charge the little elves of sin 110
To keep their silken cells within,—
In the night-flower's breast, the witch-bell blue,
Or wrapt in the daisy's silver flue;
And not to warp, on any pretence,
The thoughts or the dreams of innocence. 115
There shall not one of them dare to sip
The dew of love from the fervid lip,
Till the sleeping virgin, pale and wan,
Shrink back, as if from the kiss of man.
There shall no elfin, unreproved, 120
Take the dear form of the youth beloved;
Or whisper of love within the ear
A word for maiden unmeet to hear.
From man's deep wiles thy sex I'll guard,
If a smile from thine eye be my reward; 125
For all beside we must let them be,
And this eve shall be LOVE's JUBILEE!

The guardian angel of virgin fame,
In one sweet dale which I may not name,
Was won for that dear eve, to prove 130
The thrilling enjoyments of earthly love:

And if by matron the truth was said,
There was ne'er such an eve since the stars were
    made,
For young delight, and for moments bright,
And all that could virtuous love requite;   135
For all was holy, and pure, and chaste,
As the angels that wooed in their home of rest.
The welkin glowed with a rosy blue,
And its star of love had a brighter hue;
The green wood strains with joy were rife,   140
And its breeze was a balm of heavenly life.
Ay, 'twas an eve—by bower and dell—
An eve to dream of—not to tell:
For ever hallowed may it be,
That eve of LOVE's HIGH JUBILEE!   145

ALTRIVE LAKE
Candlemas-day, 1825

The Border Chronicler

By James Hogg

Charlie Dinmont

As I was sauntering about Prince's-street a few months ago, I es-
pied, at a distance, some one walking along, at whom all the passers-
by turned round and gazed; indeed, the person or persons seemed
to be moving on in the midst of a considerable crowd of people, all
of whom expressed, by their looks, no small degree of interest. I
hastened forward, and soon discovered the object of their curiosity.
He was a tall, herculean countryman, rather coarsely and singularly dressed. He had huge topped boots, all of one colour; steel
spurs; a rough coat of Galashiels grey; a good oak staff under his
arm; and immense whiskers that curled over his cheek. "How silly
these people are," said I to myself, "thus to interest themselves in
everything of country extraction. Certainly, if I may judge from appearances, yon farmer is a very clownish and ignorant fellow." I
have heard it remarked, that "the multitude are never wrong." Of
this I shall not pretend to judge; but I had not overtaken this man,

and walked by his side half a minute, before I discovered that there was something original about him; his very manner of walking the streets had somewhat of novelty in it. When any well-dressed or beautiful woman met him, he looked her full in the face, with a sort of good-natured familiarity, as if he had wished to address her with—"How's a' w'ye the day, my bonnie lassie?"—while she in return could scarcely maintain the gravity of her deportment till fairly past him. At length, a little spruce old man, with a powdered wig, was pushed against him by the crowd,—"Tak care, callant!" said he, "ye'll ding wee fock owre if ye stite that way;" and then, turning his face up to the sun, and laughing at his own jest, he strode on.

It struck me that I had somewhere seen such a figure before, though I could not remember in what place, and I therefore kept close by him, in hopes of finding an opportunity of introducing myself. Soon afterwards he stepped into an auction room, and sauntered some time in the front shop. He took some papers and prospectuses from the counter, and pretended to be reading their contents, but was all the while looking out at the corner of his eye at the clerk, as if he were a fellow of whom he had some jealousy, or with whom he wanted to pick a quarrel; but perhaps he only suspected that the man was angry with him, or might not quite understand what was his business there. At length, seeing some gentlemen pass up the staircase, he ventured up likewise, but with a considerable degree of caution. The sale was over, at which he appeared disappointed, looking always around as if he wished to see the auctioneer. A tall, spare gentleman now made up to him, and accosted him instantly with some common-place observations about the weather, and the books at which they were looking. I drew near, and, affecting to read, listened to the following curious conversation between them:

"What news from the country? How are matters going on there?"

"How do ye ken that I come frae the country, lad?"

"Oh! quite well; we know a countryman at first sight, from his very appearance."

"Appearance!—what do you mean by his appearance?" Here the farmer looked at his clothes on both sides, and all around, to see if there was anything particularly wrong in them.

"Though not easily to be defined, yet there is always something materially different in the manner, air, and make."

"Make! yes, thank God, there is some little odds there. I doubt aye that you town bodies get nae feck o' meat!"

"Rather doubt that the greater part of us get far too much, friend."

"It disna kythe on ye, man! for deil hae me, if there is na a hantle o' ye just like reested kippers. But ye war speering about the news? Indeed, honest man, they were never so ill i' my day, nor my father's afore me. I hae heard him say that things gat a sair slump at the end o' the 'Merican war; but nothing ava like this. The hauf o' the farmers are maistly ruined already; but the weather's turned unco guid,–the braxy has na been ill this year,–Candlemas-day turned out foul, an' we would fain hope that things are gaun to turn a wee better wi' us."

"Do not you hope any such thing. The vain and foolish hopes of the farmers have ruined them! Young man, you must look farther than a change of the weather, before you begin again to cherish such ridiculous and extravagant expectations. We are a ruined nation,–a nation on the very verge of bankruptcy, and its attendants, anarchy and confusion; and, instead of things growing better, to every reflecting person it is as plain as that two and two make four, that they will yet be many degrees worse."

"I am unco vexed to hear that, man; for I cam just into Edinbroch to tak twa or three farms, trowing that things could na be waur wi' us. The sheep stocks are comed to hauf naething, an' there's plenty o' land out. There's my Lord Hickathrift, Sir Duncan M'Grip o' the Hungrey-hall, an' Mr. Screwhimup the laird o' Bareboddam, have a' sequestered their tenants, an' warned them away, an' now they canna get a single bode for their land; they daurna stock it theirsels, an' by this time, I trow, they'll gie ane a farm for a sma matter. Now, sir, if ye binna gayan sure o' what ye're saying, I like unco ill to gang hame wanting a farm or twa; for to tell the truth, there's a bit bonny lassie that I hae an ee to,–I downa bide to want her muckle langer;– I canna bring her in ower the head o' my auld mither an' my titties,– an' unless we get a mailen o' our ain we'll be obligated to pit off. I hae a gay pickle siller, she has mair, an' my uncle Dan, he's to be caution for the lave. Ye'll, may be, ken him?–a hantle o' fock ken him."

"I do not, at this moment, recollect. Pray, sir, may I ask your name?"

"I'm Charlie Dinmont o' the Waker-cleuch; I leeve just a wee bit off the hee-road, as ye gang to the Cauld-staine kirk, where Dr. Christoff, the original-sin man, preaches, ye ken; an' if ever ye gang by that way, ye'll find a prime road to the right, through Drowncow, along the Pikestane-brae, an' out owre the mids o' Hobblequamoss, till ye come in sight o' a lang theeket-house wi' three chimleys,– that's ours; an' my mither an' titties will be happy to see you; an' I'll tak in hand to make ye fatter than ye're just now in eight days, though I sude pit ye i' the kirn!"

"You are very kind,–very kind indeed, sir; but–"

"Come, nane o' your buts; ye had better do't, ye hae muckle need on't: we hae aye plenty o' meat, sic as it is, about the Waker-cleuch, an' we hae whiles something to drink too;–for, d'ye ken, our herd keeps a bit 'ewie wi' the crooket horn,' in his ben-end, that gies mair milk, an' straunger milk, an' heartsomer milk, than a' the ewes o' Dead-for-cauld. I count mysel muckle behadden t'ye for your advice about the farms; an' if I war sure that ye warna for some of them yoursel, I wad mak na ill use o' it, for I hae great hopes that ye'll may be prove wrang in your calculations."

"I wish that there were but a bare possibility of it; no one would rejoice more heartily than I. But whoever considers the state of our finances, and the enormous load of debt under which the nation is groaning, must soon perceive that neither private nor public credit can longer be maintained. We are duped, cheated, and ruined!"

"Hout, man! I dinna like these sweeping halesale remarks; we hae studden some dowrer striffles than ony that are facing us just now. D'ye ken I hae thought a great deal about that national debt; an' there was ae year I had very near comprehendit it. I countit,–an' I reckoned,–an' I addit,–an' I multiplied, till I had a grit lang raw o' nothings, that gaed amaist across the slate; but when I cam to subtract, it didna answer ava;–it was aye nothing fra nothing, an' we's no mention the remainder. Weel, sir, I thought it was a' owre wi' us, as ye say; but instead o' that, things gaed aye just on as weel as ever, an' rather better, an' I saw that I had never fathomed it in the least; sae I am now resolved never to puzzle my harns more about the cause o' ony thing, but just stand by the effects. If ony body war to speer at ye, how the cauld moon could gar the sea rise an' fa?–how a wee bit clippit thing, that gangs harling athwart the lift, sud heeze up the great ocean fra its very marl-pits?–Lord! ye wad think the thing impossible! Aha! look at the effect, lad! I can lippen til her that she'll keep her time wi' the tide to a second. But the thing that has convinced me maist ava is the staine stairs in this New Town o' Edinbroch; od! ye wad think they're hanging i' the air. An' tak me beuk-sworn, I canna comprehend how they stand, an' yet I can trust to them, an' gang up an' down them as freely as I war on the solid yird. I was aince a wee concerned about the na-tional debt, till I saw the staine stairs o' Edinbroch; but they hae satisfied me that a man should nae count a' things absurd that he canna comprehend. Now, sir, I rede you do the same. Wad ye but just look upon the nation as a great staircase, an' the *debt* neither more nor less than the stair that bears a man up or down, precisely as he behaves an' manages himsel, I'll lay thee a guinea thou turns a third fatter. Look at me; I think, for a' the warld, you an' I standing thegither, are exactly like cause an' effect!"

About this time I went forward and shook honest Charlie by the hand, reminding him of our having once met before. I soon drew him into a conversation about Border tales and Border manners, and at length he took me by the hand, and without asking my leave, trailed me down stairs into the street, and there, instead of placing his arm within mine, put it round my shoulder, impelling me on at no ordinary pace. "Aha, man, but I is glad I ha' met wi' thee!" said he, "for hadna thou sae many poetical flights in thy head, thou's the man could give ane a sound advice anent the times. Whatten a lang, doure, grumbling chap is he yon?"

"He is a radical Whig," said I, "and the most discontented, ill-boding person in this city; you need not regard his surmises; but I think you have hit him down for once about the national debt and the stone stairs of Edinbro'." He laughed at this remark till he made the street echo, and every person turn round and gaze who was in the division. By this time we had reached the door of a tavern, at the east end of Rose-street, and into that Charlie hurried me as fast as possible, without waiting to ask my consent, or to hear any remonstrances.

"I hae waggled up an' down on them hard free-stains," said he, "till I'se like to swairf wi' baith hunger an' drouth, but we shall vanquish them baith or we twa part." I began to expostulate, and declare off, talking of engagements elsewhere; Charlie regarded all that I said the same as if I had not been speaking, and, in the very midst of my excuses, was ordering a cold round of beef, with which he had had some former acquaintance, cold mutton-pies, and cockamers, as he called them; I said I was engaged to dinner and could *not* eat.

"Never mind! never mind!" said he, "tak the less, man,—tak the less; I'll, may be, mak up for your deficiencies. Deil a hair the waur you'll be o' a snack; for me, I tak my dinners as weel again when I get something to eat an' drink on a forenoon. Whenever I get a hard booze my auld mither gars me aye eat a saut herring next day, some strang ewe milk cheese, an' twa or three brandered legs o' a fowl, made as hot as fire wi' pepper, to sharpen my appetite a wee; an' then she'll say (for she has maistly aye ae address to me on sic occasions);" here he mimicked the voice of an old woman, " 'Now Charlie, my man, how is thy sharping-stane gaun to fit?–is the stomach o' thee getting ony bit edge yet?'

"'Troth, no, mither, it is as blunt as a bittle!'

"'Dear Charlie, man, does thou no ken thysel a bit hungrier for a' thou hast eaten?'

"'I really canna say that I do, mither; I am no' ae straw hungrier than when I began.'

"'Ha, ha, ha! that is, indeed, very hard, Charlie, poor man!–I'm unco wae for thee–ha, ha, ha!'"

I had before this time agreed to join Charlie in his meal, and confess that it did my heart good to see with what zest he enjoyed it; neither did he spare the liquor in washing it down;–he mimicked everybody with great effect, and appeared in reality the Mathews of the Border. We talked about farms, and various other subjects; but ever and anon his conversation manifested a prejudice against all town people. Whenever he touched upon their character it was apparently with a degree of prejudice for which I could not account; and these sentiments, from a man so shrewd, convinced me that there is something radically wrong in the ideas of the country people, relating to their town neighbours, which must have been handed down, by father to son, from the ages of chivalry. I rallied Charlie, as bitterly as I could, on his false and exaggerated calculations; but he hemmed, shook his head, and remained apparently incredulous.

Town and Country Apparitions

"After a', man," said Charlie Dinmont, in a tone which seemed only half in earnest, "after a', man, how can it be that they're as upright an' conscientious men i' the city as thou hauds them up to be?–how can there be ony conscience, or fear o' God, wi' focks that hae neither deils, ghosts, nor bogles amang them? Ay, thou may'st laugh the fill o' thee; but, in truth an' verity, I think the want o' deils, ghosts, an' bogles, are the greatest want that a community can be subjected to. They are the greatest of a' checks on human crimes; an' I marvel that there are none o' them at Edinbroch, where heinous wickedness is so abundant."

"I believe that there are very many of them in Edinbro', Charlie," said I, striking in with his whimsical humour, "but here it is impossible to distinguish them. I am well assured that ghosts of hapless females, who have fallen a prey to the selfish voluptuousness of the other sex, roam these streets every night, and to a certain hour in the morning."

"Lord preserve us!–do you think sae?" said Charlie.

"I am quite certain of it," returned I, "having frequently seen them myself moving about, after midnight, with a melancholy and desponding air: but their forms throw no shadows on the pavement; their footsteps make no noise, not so much as the falling of a leaf; and, whenever they chance to look one in the face, their eyes have that dead stillness in them, that white moveless opacity, that denotes them, at first sight, to be only the ghosts of what they were."

"That's perfectly awsome, an' dreadful, an' terrible!" said he, "thou gars a' my flesh creep to hear thee! but I hae no doubt o' the circumstance, not ae grain;–poor undone, misfortunate beings! kicked out of a' rational happiness here, an' out o' heaven hereafter! O! man, I had aye some hopes that creatures like these might be made without answerable souls; but it seems my hopes have been ill-foundit. Is it not a terrible thing to think that they should come back to linger and lament round the altars on which they sacrificed heaven an' earth at the same instant! I canna think of ony state sae dreadfu' an' hopeless as a spirit o' that kind."

"There are sights to be seen here every night, Charlie," said I, "that cannot fail of impressing every serious heart with the deepest awe, and would be enough to drive the inhabitants of a whole glen out of their senses."

"Thou never said a truer word, man, a' the days o' thy pilgrimage here on earth," said he; "for I hae seen sights in it mysel, that, wi' a little change o' scene, wad hae freezed the blood. Consider for ane instant, a countryman setting hame his sweetheart on a Sunday evening, after saying o' questions, reading lang skreeds o' sermons, an' hearing prayers. Weel; the twa chop on;–the rood grows aye eirier an' darker, an' they cling aye closer thegither; hardly daring to talk above their breath, till, just at the corner o' a dark pine wood, they perceive a glimmering light shining from behind the trees across their path;–they stand still–hesitate, but dare not speak, an' their hearts beat as they would burst their tenements; at length the maid ventures to whisper, 'What can yon be?' 'God only kens!' says the other; when, at that instant, there issues from behind the corner, a hideous figure wrapped up in sack-cloth; his head swathed in a white napkin with a cowl over it. This demon carries a dark lantern in its horrid paw, that only tends to make darkness visible, an' hideousness ten times more hideous; an' just as the couple are ready to sink into the earth, the horrid apparition cries out aloud–'Past *twall o' clock!!!*' "

Here I could not help bursting into a fit of laughter, at the humourous manner in which he had exaggerated the picture; but he went on, adding, "Eh! what think ye o' the effect there, sir?—as I am an honest man, I saw sic a sight the last night, an' could na help thinking that if I had been at the Gird-wood corner, it was as muckle as my seven senses were worth."

"I am a believer in apparitions myself," said I, "and in the existence of fairies and witches; at least I believe that these last did exist, and am never quite sure that the greater part of the women are not still witches to this day; and I am even so antiquated in my notions, as to believe in the existence of the devil likewise, and also in that of innumerable spirits, both good and evil;—what say you to all these, Charlie?"

"I believe in them a' as sternly as I believe the gospel," said he; "I canna but say that we wad be muckle the better of a new deil now, for the auld ane is rather beginning to lose his effect. I notice that the bits o' prime weel-bred minister lads think it shame now to bring him forward, an' seem rather inclined to mak a laughing-stock o' him. But I wadna wonder should he play them a smirl by-and-by, though he is rather in the back ground just now. But wha wadna believe in spirits?—what a cauldrife, insignificant, matter-o'-fact world this wad be without hoards o' spirits bustling amang us?—it makes a man of nae importance at a' when neither good nor ill spirits are looking after him, an' counteracting ane another on his account. But weel may I believe in such interferences! for I hae mysel seen some o' the grandest instances o' them that ever fell to the lot o' man to recount; an' there was ane o' them na farther gane than the last Hempton market, at Carlisle, whilk I'll tell thee."

Gillanbye's Ghost

"I was gaun across to Annandale at that time, to see Willie Byrrell an' John Church, an twa or three friends; an' so I leaves Carlisle with a dozen o' Scotsmen, an' three ministers amang them, an' we takes the near road across the Solway sands at the mouth of the Esk. Several o' them pretended to ken the fords; but there was a whisper o' high tides rase amang them, an' we resolved to hae a guide on horseback. When we called at the guide's house he was gane across wi' a party, and the wife doubted whether he would get back that night, before the advance of the tide. We asked if there was danger; and she answered, that unless we were very expeditious there certainly would be danger; so with that we spurred into the level sand, and kept always shouting out, hoping we should meet the guide on his return. The water soon began to deepen; and we were fairly at a stand, for it was very near pitch dark. I'll never forget that night! So as we were standing deliberating, ane o' the ministers o' the gospel says, 'Na, na, sirs, we'll no venture in wanting a guide, for there is just the deil's dozen o' us, an' something will befal one or more of us before we get o'er.'

"'Count again, honest man!' said a stranger gentleman, whom never ane o' us had seen till that moment. Now I was as sure that that man, an' his black horse, rase out of the earth, as that I am flesh and blood; for there were thirteen o' us a' the way, an' no man could approach us, on that light-coloured plain o' sand, without having been seen. 'Count again, honest man!' said he. I counted, an' sundry of us counted, an' in verity there were fourteen. From that time forth, my tongue an' the roof o' my mouth grew as dry as a whistle, an' I keepit near the hinder end o' the troop. 'Wha's this?' said one. 'Where came he from?' whispered another; an' ilka body was muttering something. But there was a Mr. Little, who was hauf drunk, he rides up to him, an' he says, 'Whae the deil are you, sir?—an' where did ye cam fra?—for, as I'm a sinner, I never saw you till this moment.'

"'I came from the market, sir,' says the stranger, 'where I have had a busy, busy day, and am hastening across to Scotland:—do you ford the river?'

"'We proposed as much,' said Little, 'but are rather grown eiry about finding the track.'

"'I have crossed it at all seasons, and at all weathers,' said the stranger; 'but I have not time to trifle,—if you want to cross follow me; if not, good night.'

"'Have wi' ye!' says Little; 'I like a chap that cries *follow me*, better than ane that cries *lead on*, at sic a time as this. Have with thee, I say;—at any rate thou's have to drown first,—that's ay some comfort.'

"'I should have brought my hogs to a bad market then,' said the stranger.

"'An' thysel to nae good ane,' said Little. 'But pray now, hast thou done muckle business at the Hempton to-day?'

"'A little, a little,' said he; 'but I intend doing more before the turn of the night. I have a grand scheme in view to-night, and hope to effect it.'

"'Ay; but dinna thou count afore the point, guid man,' says Little, 'for may be thou may'st be mista'en. I's wager thou's a dealer in bacon; I sees by thy face an' thy way o' riding.'

"'Yes, I sometimes deal a little in the flesh,' said the stranger, 'but rather more in the spirit,—the former is a vile drudgery, but in the latter I take delight.'

"'Ay, ay! an' so thou's a smuggler then?' says Little. 'Confound thee! an' I did'na find a strang reekit saur about thee a' this time, an' coudna ken what it was. But, lad, where art thou leading us, for dost thou ken my beast is up to the thrapple, an' snorting like a whale.'

"'Only a deep step or two,' cried the stranger, who was riding on with all the ease imaginable; 'only a deep step or two;—come on, fine footing here.' Some time before this, we had all stopped, except Little, owing to the depth of the tide; but more on account of a figure which approached us, on a white horse, with the swiftness of the wind, calling on us to turn back. We thought it ane going to cross in our company, an' paid little attention to him for a space. Which made him ride still faster, an' call the louder. At length we did pause, all in a body, as we were like to be swamped, an' then we heard him calling these words—

"'Stop! stop!—for the sake of heaven and your own souls, stop! Do you know where you are going?—or whom you are following?'

"Some of our party hearing this vehement interrogatory were stunned, an' involuntarily answered—'No, we do not.'

"'I wot that is true!' said he, 'for you are going direct into the middle of the crooked swamp, into which man never went and escaped; and, in the second place, you are following old Gillanbye, or rather the devil in his likeness.'

"'I was almost petrified, for I had heard of the ghost of that old wretch leading people into jeopardies and death: and the moment our preserver uttered these words, I looked after our hellish guide, who at the same instant left us with a loud guffaw of a laugh, an' scoured, at a light gallop, across the tide, till he vanished in the dark. In the meantime, Little and his horse were swamped: for he was so busy talking to the devil, whom he took for a bacon-dealer and smuggler, that he never heard our preserver calling after us.

"'There is only a deep step or two,' says the deil; 'come on, fine footing here!' Those were the last words that I heard him say; and poor Little, who saw him riding with such ease, spurred on after him, but in half a second he was over the head. He was riding a good black mare; an' loth, loth was she to take the tide after the deil's horse; for she baith snorted an' reared on end; but her rider clapped the spurs in her side, an' plunge she went ower the head!— she gave two or three flounders, as if struggling in a bog, then down both of them went, an' the billows came up with the bursts o' their parting breath. 'Ha! ha! ha!' quo' the deil; an' away he flew across the Solway, as if he had been riding for a broose.

"'Little's down!' cried ane; 'Come on! come on! an' let us save Little,' cried every body at ance; an' we were a' rushing in after him, but the figure on the white horse stopped us again, held up his hand, an' charged us, in God's name, to keep back. 'All Cumberland cannot save him,' said he, 'for by this time he is five fathoms deep in quicksands. That swamp will suck a thing of half the weight of that poor fellow and his horse down in three seconds, never more to be seen. Turn, and follow me; there is only one possible path to Scotland to-night, by which I will lead you.'

"We did as he commanded us, without a murmur, or without one gainsaying. It was manifest that he had saved all our lives, and the scenes which we had witnessed made so deep an impression on our minds, that we rode after him scarcely uttering a word. He kept galloping considerably a-head of us; but his white horse appeared so conspicuous through the gloom, that we followed him with whip and spur, and always kept him in view. Whether it was an inlet of the firth, or the mouth of the river Eden, that we crossed, I do not know, but we rode on in deep water for a considerable while, and all of us believed that we had crossed the beds of the Esk to the Scottish side.

"However, none asked any questions. In a short time we came upon the high road, on which he said,—'You are safe now on the high road for Annandale; keep together in a body, and see that you fall not out by the way,'—saying which, he rode gently on before us; but on reaching the top of the first declivity, we lost him, and never saw or heard of him any more.

"We rode on, and rode on, expecting to come upon Graitney; till at length we thought we must have passed it, and should arrive at Annan; but, ere ever we kend, we found ourselves in the middle of Langtown, on the Border. There we heard that there had been a terrible tide in the firth, that came running up breast high, like the dam of a river broken open; that several persons had been lost, and others in great jeopardy; an' that it was suspected that either the deil, or the ghost of old Gillanbye, had been acting as a guide that night.

"I am perfectly assured that it was the devil, who would have led us into the crookit swamp; how else could he have galloped across that, an' the broad firth? And I am as well convinced that the man on the white horse was an angel of mercy sent to save us; and who, indeed, took us by the only path by which any of us could have reached our homes that night.

" 'Od! sir, I wadna hae exchanged my feelings o' gratitude to heaven that night, for a' the cauldrife dogmas of a' the heartless philosophers that ever drew the breath o' life.

"Now, sir, this is but one o' many, many instances that I could relate to you of the interference of Providence, by means out o' the common course o' nature to preserve life; an' that gars me believe baith in good an' ill spirits. I dinna believe in a' the hallanshaker spirits that are supposed to haunt every eiry spot through the hale country; I dinna believe that a ghost wad arise frae the dead, an' stand up in its winding-sheet, like a bog-stalker, merely to fright a body out o' his judgment that was half crazed afore. But if there is human life or innocence to preserve, or guilt and murder to bring to light, an' no earthly hand to help, I'll trust to an over-ruling Providence yet, be the means as incomprehensible as they may.

"Didst thou ever hear the story of the White Lady of Glen-Tress?"

"I think I have printed an edition of that story myself, Charlie."

"Deil ma care! thou'lt be none the waur o' hearing my way o' it. It is an excellent story, soon told, and very pat to the purpose."

The White Lady of Glen-Tress

"In my grandfather's days, the house of Glen-tress was a farm-house, which had long been in the possession of a family of the name of Tait; a douss, decent, pious family they were, an' suffered muckle for religion's sake. At length they fell back in the warld; and then their farm was taken frae them, an' laid into that of Colquhar: but the family was sae respectable an' weel likit, that the new tenant wadna turn them out, but keepit them as his shepherds. John Tait, the elder brother, had a wife an' seven children, an' his brother lived with him; an' they remained in the old farm-house, in which their fathers had lived for generations, an' in which they had always been devout worshippers o' the Almighty.

"Weel, it sae happened that one fine summer's evening, after the sun had gone down, a' the family were assembled, save one little maid. They had taken their supper, an' the goodman had reached down the bible to begin family worship. He had taken it down, an' laid aside his bonnet; he had not begun the psalm, but sat waiting till little Mary should come in. She soon came in, breathless with haste, and said:—

" 'Come a' out, sirs!—haste ye!—come a' out, an' see wha's coming!'

" 'Wha's coming here at this time o' night, bairn?' said her mother.

" 'The grandest lady that ever was seen in this warld!' said the child; 'she's as bonny as an angel, an' a' clad in white!—she was close on me ere ever I ken'd, an' she bade me tell you to come all to her directly. Haste ye, an' come away!–I tell you she's coming!– she's coming!'

"'We had better defer the worship till we see what she wants,' said John; an' with that he went out, wi' the big bible under his arm. The moment he had passed the threshold, he saw a figure, as white as a meteor, coming towards him, an' beckoning him, with an air of impatience, to meet her. He answered this singular summons, an' this brought the whole family out to the green. They every one saw her coming to meet John Tait, an', at that time, they two did not appear to be more than ten or twelve yards asunder; they viewed her for a moment, in silence, when the attention of all was taken off by a tremendous crash, which was followed by a scream from the family group. John started, an' looked round; and behold the house was fallen in, an' the dust from the rubbish was rising, like a cloud, to heaven! With a palpitating heart, an' a head 'mazed with aston- ishment, he perceived that he an' his numerous family had been miraculously saved from instantaneous death. He turned to address his splendid guest, but she was gone, once an' for ever! By no one but themselves had this benevolent apparition been observed.

"Now wha will venture to deny the interference of a kind Provi- dence there, in saving an amiable an' devout family from momen- tary destruction?–an' who wadna rather hae heard poor Johnny Tait express his gratitude to his Maker an' Preserver that night, than a moral harangue fra ane that attributes ilka thing, baith in salvation an' providence, to our ain doings? Ay! poor Johnny Tait didna miss the prayers that night, though he had e'en to sing his psalm, an' kneel to his God, in the shieling ahind the kie."

––––––––––––

I have a great many more of Charlie's instances noted down, which shall be forthcoming in the next volume of the *Literary Souvenir* ; although it is probable they may not prove as interesting and con- genial to the enlightened and polished part of the community as they did to me.

ALTRIVE LAKE
April 17, 1825.

Stanzas for Music

By the Ettrick Shepherd

I.

My sweet little cherub, how calm thou'rt reposing!
Thy suffering is over, thy mild eye is closing;
This world hath proved to thee a step-dame unfriendly;
But rest thee, my babe, there's a spirit within thee.
A mystery thou art, though unblest and unshrieven—   5
A thing of the earth, and a radiance of Heaven;
A flower of the one, thou art fading and dying—
A spark of the other, thou'rt mounting and flying.

II.

Farewell my sweet baby, too early we sever;
I may come to thee, but to me thou shalt never.   10
Some angel of mercy shall lead and restore thee,
A pure living flame, to the mansions of glory.
The moralist's boast may sound prouder and prouder,
The hypocrite's prayer rise louder and louder;
But I'll trust my babe, in her trial of danger,   15
To the mercy of Him that was laid in the manger.

The Bijou

An Aged Widow's Own Words

Versified by James Hogg, the Ettrick Shepherd

O IS he gane my good auld man?
  And am I left forlorn?
And is that manly heart at rest,
  The kindest e'er was born?

We've sojourned here through hope and fear   5
  For fifty years and three,
And ne'er in all that happy time,
  Said he harsh word to me.

And mony a braw and boardly son
  And daughters in their prime,   10
His trembling hand laid in the grave,
  Lang, lang afore the time.

I dinna greet the day to see
  That he to them has gane,
But O 'tis fearfu' thus to be   15
  Left in a world alane.

Wi' a poor worn and broken heart,
  Whose race of joy is run,
And scarce has little opening left,
  For aught aneath the sun.   20

My life nor death I winna crave,
  Nor fret nor yet despond,
But a' my hope is in the grave
  And the dear hame beyond.

Ane Waefu' Scots Pastoral*

By James Hogg, the Ettrick Shepherd

1.

O MOOR-COCK, moor-cock, dinna craw
    Sae crouse on wing of mottled feather,
Nor spread that boardly breast sae braw
    Upon thy height of Highland heather;
For that's a brewing on the sea   5
    Will mar thy pride afore the even,
And hap thy teemfu' mate and thee
    Deep frae the glowing light o' heaven.

2.

Thy voice gars a' the echos blair
    From viewless dens of rock and river;   10
Like some wild spirit of the air
    Thou mak'st its billows quake and quiver,
Proud of the mate thou lovest best;
    But o'er her hame nae mair thou'lt craw,
Her grave maun be her lowly nest,   15
    Her winding-sheet the wreathe o' snaw.

3.

Thou lawless black-cock dinna spread
    That speckled fan so bright of hue,
Why all that pride of evil deed
    Pruning thy wing of glossy blue,   20
In wooing of a silly dame,
    Who knows full well thy love's a flam,
And that for her 'tis much the same,
    As raven's for the sickly lamb?

* These verses were written on the evening of the 23rd of April, 1827, about the time the great storm of snow was at the height. Next morning many of the snow wreathes on the hills of Ettrick Forest were from twelve to twenty feet deep, and many thousands of lambs, singing birds, and moor game perished. All those of the latter that had begun incubation were literally destroyed.

4.

Begone thou heartless libertine,   25
   And locker in thy sheltered glade;
For soon that motely love of thine,
   And thou shall both be lowly laid;
Yet I will miss thee in the glen
   When August winds breathe o'er the fell,   30
As mounting from thy braken den,
   Or skimmering o'er the heather bell.

5.

The laverock lilts within the lift,
   The mavis touts upon the tree;
The blackbird hardly makes a shift   35
   To strain one note of melody;
For ay he cowers his sooty wing
   An' points his yellow bill on high,
And fears he has foreflown the spring
   Misled by winter's courtesy.   40

6.

For the sand-lark I needs must wail
   Sae ruefully he pours his pain,
And as he sits and wags his tail,
   And whews upon his cauldrife stane,
He sees the lapper on the stream,   45
   And Yarrow's banks sae sternly piled,
That Sandy* thinks he's in a dream,
   Or landed in some polar wild.

7.

The curlew's neb's a weary length,
   The pease-weep's crest is like a tree,   50
The chirping wagtail scarce has strength
   To turn his white cheek to the lee,
Their necks are lang, their shanks are sma'
   Through perfect downright consternation,
An' ay they cower by holt an' ha'   55
   Like thriftless weavers in starvation.

* SANDY or SANDY-LAVEROCK is the local name in Ettrick for the
sand piper.

8.

The shilfu clars amang the firs,
　　The yellow yorline in the thorn,
But a' the simmer's harbingers
　　Are buried ere the break of morn,　　　　　　60
The lambs lie smothered in the dean,
　　The ewes stand bleating loud an' lang,
While the poor shepherd dights his een,
　　And thinks the world is a' gane wrang.

MOUNT BENGER
April 24th, 1827

Woman

By the Ettrick Shepherd

AYE, now I've lit upon a theme
Unbounded, thrilling, and supreme,
So let me try my mountain lore
In the delirious theme once more;
For what is Bard, with all his art,　　　　　　5
Who scorns to take the fair one's part,
And never hath in life perceived
(What once I sparingly believed)
That Woman's fair and lovely breast
Was framed the sanctuary blest,　　　　　　10
The home, all other homes above,
Of virtuous and of faithful love?
Sweet sex! I fear with all my zeal
I ne'er can laud you as I feel:
If nature's glowing hand imbue　　　　　　15
Thy early bloom with beauty's dew,
Stamp in thine eye the 'witching wile,
And light with love thy opening smile,
Ere prudence rises to thine aid,
A thousand snares for thee are laid;　　　　　　20
While still to revel, wrong or right,
Among these snares is thy delight.

'Tis thus that thousands wreck'd, and hurl'd
From virtue's paths, traverse the world,
Regardless of creation's scorn,   25
Unblest, unfavoured, and forlorn.
Oh! take not one degraded mind,
For model of dear womankind.
But let us rise in our compare
To beauties of the earth and air,   30
With their reverses—range the sea,
The wood, the waste, the galaxy,
And rather urge a parable
'Twixt rays of heaven and shades of hell,
Than Woman's fair and virtuous fame   35
Should suffer but in thought or aim,
Or from her sacred temples fall
The smallest flower celestial.
Take Woman as her God hath made her,
And not as mankind may degrade her,   40
Else as well may you take the storm
In all its hideousness, to form
An estimate of nature's cheer,
And glories of the bounteous year:
As well compare the summer flower   45
With dark December's chilling shower,
Or summer morning, pearled with dew,
With winter's wan and deadly hue;
The purple ocean, calm and glowing,
With ocean when the tempest's blowing,   50
Then say with proud discourtesy,
"This is the earth, and that the sea;
And this is Woman—what you will
Please you to say, she's Woman still;
And will be Woman, more or less   55
A being prone to perverseness.
Hath it not flowed from sage's tongue,
And hath not moral poet sung,
That men to war or business take,
But Woman is at heart a rake?"   60
Injurious Bard, such thing to say,
Degraded be thy shameless lay,
Such ruinous principle to own,
And damning dogma to lay down;

'Tis false:—woe to the blighted name   65
That would attach promiscuous blame
To all the gentle, fair, and wise,
And only view to generalize.
For me, I'm Woman's slave confest—
Without her, hopeless and unblest;   70
And so are all, gainsay who can,
For what would be the life of man,
.   If left in desert or in isle,
Unlighted up by beauty's smile:
Even though he boasted monarch's name,   75
And o'er his own sex reigned supreme
With thousands bending to his sway,
If lovely Woman were away,
What were his life?—What could it be?—
A vapour on a shoreless sea;   80
A troubled cloud in darkness toss'd,
Amongst the waste of waters lost;
A ship deserted in the gale,
Without a steersman or a sail,
A star, or beacon-light before,   85
Or hope of haven evermore;
A thing without a human tie,
Unlov'd to live, unwept to die.
Then let us own through nature's reign
Woman the light of her domain;   90
And if to maiden love not given,
The dearest bliss below the heaven,
At least due homage let us pay,
In rev'rence of a parent's sway,
To that dear sex whose favour still   95
Our guerdon is in good or ill—
A motive that can never cloy,
Our glory, honour, and our joy;
And humbly on our bended knee
Acknowledge her supremacy.   100

Superstition and Grace

An Unearthly Ballad
By the Ettrick Shepherd

There was an auld carle won'd under yon shaw,
His cheek was the clay, and his hair was the snaw;
His brow was as glazed as a winter night,
But mingled with lines of immortal light;
And forth from his livid lips there flew 5
A flame of a lurid murky hue.
But there was a mystery him within
That roused up the twangs and terrors of sin;
And there was a gleide in that auld carle's ee,
That the saint and the sinner baith trembled to see. 10

But, oh! when the moor gat her coverlet gray,
When the gloaming had flaughted the night and the day,
When the craws had flown to the greenwood shaw,
And the kid blett over the Lammer law;
When the dew had laid the valley asteep, 15
And the gowan had fauldit her buds to sleep;
When naething was heard but the merlin's maen,
Oh then that gyre carle was never his lane.
A bonny wee baby sae meek and mild,
Then walked with him in the dowy wild; 20
But, oh! nae pen that ever grew
Could describe that baby's heavenly hue:
Yet all the barmings of sturt and strife,
And weary wailings of morteel life,
Would soon have been hushed to endless peace 25
At ae blink of that baby's face.

Her brow sae fair and her ee sae meek,
And the pale rose-bloom upon her cheek;
Her locks, and the bend of her sweet ee-bree,
And her smile might have wakened the dead to see. 30
Her snood befringed wi' many a gem
Was stown frae the rainbow's brightest hem;
And her rail, mair white than the snowy drift,
Was never woven aneath the lift;
It threw sic a light on the hill and the gair 35

That it showed the wild deer to her lair;
And the brown bird of the moorland fell
Upraised his head from the heather bell,
For he thought that his dawning of love and mirth,
Instead of the heaven was springing from earth;   40
And the fairies waken'd frae their beds of dew,
And they sang a hymn, and that hymn was new.
Oh! Ladies list—for never again
Shalt thou hear sic a wild unearthly strain.
For they sang the night-breeze in a swoon,   45
And they sang the goud locks frae the moon:
They sang the redbreast frae the wood,
And the laverock out o' the marled cloud;
The capperkyle frae the bosky brae,
And the seraphs down frae the milky way;   50
And some wee feres of bloodless birth
Came out o' the worm-holes o' the earth,
And swoof'd sae lightly round the lea,
That they wadna kythe to mortal ee;
While the eldrich sang it rase sae shrill   55
That the waesome tod yooled on the hill:
Oh! Ladies list—for the choral band
Thus hymned the song of the Fairy-land.

Song of the Fairies

Sing! sing! How shall we sing
Round the babe of the Spirits' King?   60
How shall we sing our last adieu,
Baby of life when we sing to you?
Now the little night-burdie may cheip i' the wa',
The plover may whew and the cock may craw;
For the bairny's sleep is sweet and sure,   65
And the maiden's rest is blest and pure,
Through all the links of the Lammer-muir:
Sin our bonny baby was sent frae heaven,
She comes o'ernight with the dew of even;
And when the day-sky buds frae the main,   70
She swaws wi' the dew to heaven again;
But the light shall dawn, and the howlet flee,
The dead shall quake, when the day shall be,
That she shall smile in the gladsome noon,
And sleep and sleep in the light of the moon.   75

Then shall our hallelues wake anew,
With harp and viol and ayril true.
    But well-a-day!
    How shall we say
Our earthly adieu ere we pass away?   80
How shall we hallow this last adieu,
Baby of life when we sing to you?
    Ring! ring!
    Dance and sing,
And on the green broom your garlands hing;   85
Hallow the hopes of this ray of grace,
For sweet is the smile of our baby's face;
And every ghaist of gysand hew
Has melted away in the breeze she drew;
The kelpie may dern in dread and dool,   90
Deep in the howe of his eiry pool;
Gil-moules frae hind the hallan may flee,
Through by the threshold, and through by the key,
And the mermaid moote in the safron sea:
But we are left in the greenwood glen,   95
Because we love the children of men,
Sweetly to sing, and never to rue,
Till now that we hymn our last adieu;
Baby of life we sing it to you!
    Sing! sing!   100
    How shall we sing
Round the babe of the Spirits' King?
Hither the breezes of elfland bring,
Then fairies away—away on the wing!
We now maun flit to a land of bliss,   105
To a land of holy silentness;
To a land where the night-wind never blew,
But thy fair spring shall ever be new;
When the moon shall wake nae mair to wane,
And the cloud and the rainbow baith are gane,   110
In bowers aboon the break o' the day,
We'll sing to our baby for ever and ay.

Then the carle beheld them swoof alang,
And heard the words of their fareweel sang.
They seem'd to ling asklent the wind,   115
And left a pathway of light behind;

But he heard them singing as they flew,
'Baby of life, adieu! adieu!
Baby of grace we sing to you!'

Then the carle he kneeled to that seraph young,   120
And named her with a tremulous tongue;
And the light of God shone on his face
As he looked to Heaven and named her GRACE;
And he barred the day of sorrow and pain
Ever to thrall the world again: 125
Then he clasped his hands and wept full sore,
When he bade her adieu for evermore.

Oh! never was baby's smile so meek
When she felt the tear drop on her cheek;
And never was baby's look so wae   130
When she saw the stern auld carle gae;
But a' his eeless and elfin train,
And a' his ghaists and gyes were gane:
The gleids that gleamed in the darksome shaw,
And his fairies had flown the last of a'.   135
Then the poor auld carle was blithe to flee
Away frae the queen isle of the sea,
And never mair seeks the walks of men,
Unless in the disk of the gloaming glen.*

MOUNT BENGER
May 7th, 1828

* An edition of this ballad was published long ago by some other
name. It is now so entirely altered that only a few lines of the original
remain.

                                                          J. H.

Forget Me Not

The Sky Lark

A Song

By the Ettrick Shepherd

Bird of the wilderness,
  Blithesome and cumberless,
Light be thy matin o'er moorland and lea!
  Emblem of happiness,
  Bless'd is thy dwelling place,   5
O to abide in the desart with thee!

  Wild is thy lay and loud
  Far in the downy cloud,
Love gives it energy, love gave it birth.
  Where on thy dewy wing   10
  Where art thou journeying?
Thy lay is in heaven, thy love is on earth.

  O'er fell and fountain sheen,
  O'er moor and mountain green,
O'er the red streamer that heralds the day;   15
  Over the cloudlet dim,
  Over the rainbow's rim,
Musical cherubim hie thee away!

  Then when the gloaming comes,
  Low in the heather blooms,   20
Sweet will thy welcome and bed of love be!
  Emblem of happiness!
  Bless'd is thy dwelling place!
O to abide in the desart with thee.

ALTRIVE LAKE
April 2d 1827

The Descent of Love

By the Ettrick Shepherd

[Manuscript Version]

Ah youthful love! thy votarist,
Though oft he turns into a jest
Thy freaks or foibles, adventine,
Yet will he worship at thy shrine,
And eulogise thee morn and even   5
As the best earliest gift of heaven.
  Thou blushing thing of pain and bliss!
Child of a happier sphere than this!
Wert thou a nursling of the sky
Fostered in Paradise on high,   10
To thrill the radiant breasts above?
No—angels know not youthful love;
Their's is a flame without compend,
An holy ardor without end:
But our's a joy, supreme, intense,   15
A short and splendid recompense
For an esteem, unbroke, unmoved,
Which man immortal might have proved.
Art thou not then O virtuous love
The dearest gift of heaven above!   20
  Blest be thy native home on earth,
The place that owned thy mystic birth,
When far beneath the golden morn
Was thy seraphic being born.
Where Euphrates and Tygris strands   25
Join 'mid the sweet Arabian lands;
When that great river rolling blue
Mirrored the earliest flowers that grew,
When scarce had bud begun to blow,
Or blossom decked the world below,   30
Then was the shade of tiny tree
The bed of thy nativity.
  While the first pair of human frame
Lay weeping their immortal blame,
By deep remorse and sorrow tossed   35
For all their gifts and glory lost;
Even then, when grief was at the full,

And no redress their pains to lull,
Thy cherub form from heaven descended,
In all the rays of beauty blended,   40
And their repentant breasts above
Thou wov'st the holy ties of love;
While by a mystic art unnamed
Of thy fair self the bonds were framed,
And ne'er did heavenly art entwine   45
A wreath so cheering and divine.
   Full soon the pair thy presence own'd;
They found their hearts to nature bound
By tie, not proved, nor understood,
A band of kindred and of blood,   50
And in delight without alloy
Their hearts rejoiced in nature's joy.
The river flowed more silvery bright,
The flowers were glowing with delight,
The young twin roses had begun   55
Their homage to the morning sun,
In odours breathed from bosoms meek,
And made obeisance cheek to cheek.
   In a new world they seemed to move,
A world of pathos and of love,   60
Where all was decked in glories new;
The sunbeam kissed the morning dew;
The fields were robed in deeper green;
The blue of heaven was more serene;
The birds sang sweeter in the grove   65
Hailing the natal morn of love,
Not even from Eden's sacred tree
Was ever poured such melody.
   But of all extacies refined
The greatest still remained behind,   70
A new delight, refined, subdued,
When eye met eye with love imbued;
When he with raptures scarce terrene
First turned his view on nature's queen,
On that dear form whose softened charms   75
Besought protection in his arms;
Whose every look, and smile, and sigh,
Bespoke a chastened courtesy.
He saw her eye of deeper blue,

Her cheek grown rosier in its hue,   80
While her fair bosom's gentle swell
With hallowed heavings rose and fell;
Then was thy heavenly being bless'd
With earthly home of holy rest,
And woman's breast was found to be   85
The tabernacle meet for thee!

ALTRIVE LAKE BY SELKIRK
April 2d 1827

The Descent of Love

By the Ettrick Shepherd

[Published Version]

AH youthful Love! thy votarist,
Though oft he turns into a jest
Thy freaks or foibles, yet will join
In humble worship at thy shrine,
And eulogise thee morn and even   5
As the best, earliest gift of Heaven.

Thou blushing thing of pain and bliss!
Child of a happier sphere than this!
Wert thou a nursling of the sky,
Foster'd in Paradise on high,   10
To thrill the radiant breasts above?
No—angels feel not youthful love;
Their's is a flame we cannot know,
A holy ardour free from wo;
But our's a joy, supreme, intense,   15
A short and splendid recompense
For an esteem, unbroke, unmoved,
Which man immortal might have proved.
Art thou not then, O virtuous love,
The dearest gift of Heaven above?   20

Blest be thy native home on earth,
The place that own'd thy mystic birth,
When far beneath the golden morn
Was thy seraphic being born.

Where Euphrates and Tigris' strands 25
Join 'mid the sweet Assyrian lands;
Where that great river rolling blue
Mirror'd the earliest flowers that grew,
When scarce had bud begun to blow,
Or blossom deck'd the world below, 30
Then was the shade of tiny tree
The bed of thy nativity.

While the first pair of human frame
Lay weeping their immortal blame,
By deep remorse and sorrow tost, 35
For all their gifts and glory lost;
Even then, when grief was at the full,
And no redress their pains to lull,
Thy cherub form from heaven descended,
In all the rays of beauty blended, 40
And their repentant breasts above
Thou wov'st the holy ties of love;
While by a mystic art unnamed
Of thy fair self the bonds were framed,
And ne'er did heavenly art entwine 45
A wreath so cheering and divine.

Full soon the pair thy presence own'd;
They found their hearts to nature bound
By tie, not proved, nor understood,
A bond of kindred and of blood, 50
And in delight without alloy
Their hearts rejoiced in nature's joy.
The river flow'd more silvery bright,
The flowers were glowing with delight,
The young twin roses had begun 55
Their homage to the morning sun,
In odours breathed from bosoms meek,
And made obeisance cheek to cheek.

In a blest world they seem'd to move,
A world of pathos and of love, 60
Where all was deck'd in glories new;
The sunbeam kiss'd the morning dew;
The fields were robed in deeper green;
The blue of heaven was more serene;

The birds sang sweeter in the grove,   65
Hailing the natal morn of love;
Not even from Eden's sacred tree
Was ever pour'd such melody.

But of all ecstacies refined
The greatest still remain'd behind,   70
A new delight thrill'd and subdued,
When eye met eye with love imbued;
When he with raptures scarce terrene
First turn'd his view on nature's queen,
On that dear form whose soften'd charms   75
Besought protection in his arms;
Whose every look, and smile, and sigh,
Bespoke a chasten'd courtesy.
He saw her eye of deeper blue,
Her cheek grown rosier in its hue,   80
While her fair bosom's gentle swell
With hallow'd heavings rose and fell;
Then was thy heavenly being blest
With earthly home of holy rest,
And woman's breast was form'd to be   85
The tabernacle meet for thee!

St. Mary of the Lows

By James Hogg, the Ettrick Shepherd

O lone St. Mary of the waves,
  In ruin lies thine ancient aisle,
While o'er thy green and lowly graves
  The moorcocks bay and plovers wail;
  But mountain-spirits on the gale   5
Oft o'er thee sound the requiem dread,
  And warrior shades and spectres pale
Still linger by the quiet dead.

Yes, many a chief of ancient days
  Sleeps in thy cold and hallow'd soil,   10
Hearts that would thread the forest maze
  Alike for spousal or for spoil,

That wist not, ween'd not, to recoil
Before the might of mortal foe,
   But thirsted for the border-broil,   15
The shout, the clang, the overthrow.

Here lie those who, o'er flood and field,
   Were hunted as the osprey's brood,
Who braved the power of man, and seal'd
   Their testimonies with their blood: 20
   But long as waves that wilder'd flood
Their sacred memory shall be dear,
   And all the virtuous and the good
O'er their low graves shall drop the tear.

Here sleeps the last of all the race   25
   Of these old heroes of the hill,
Stern as the storm in heart and face;
   Gainsay'd in faith or principle,
   Then would the fire of heaven fill
The orbit of his faded eye,   30
   Yet all within was kindness still,
Benevolence and simplicity.

GRIEVE, thou shalt hold a sacred cell
   In hearts with sin and sorrow tost,
While thousands, with their funeral-knell,   35
   Roll down the tide of darkness lost;
   For thou wert Truth's and Honour's boast,
Firm champion of Religion's sway—
   Who knew thee best revered thee most,
Thou emblem of a former day!   40

Here lie old forest bowmen good;
   Ranger and stalker sleep together,
Who for the red-deer's stately brood
   Watch'd, in despite of want and weather,
   Beneath the hoary hills of heather: 45
Even Scotts, and Kerrs, and Pringles, blended
   In peaceful slumbers, rest together,
Whose fathers there to death contended!

Here lie the peaceful, simple race,
  The first old tenants of the wild,   50
Who stored the mountains of the chace
    With flocks and herds—whose manners mild
    Changed the baronial castles, piled
In every glen, into the cot,
    And the rude mountaineer beguiled,   55
Indignant, to his peaceful lot.

Here rural beauty low reposes,
  The blushing cheek and beaming eye,
The dimpling smile, the lip of roses,
    Attractors of the burning sigh,   60
    And love's delicious pangs that lie
Enswathed in pleasure's mellow mine:
  Maid, lover, parent, low and high,
Are mingled in thy lonely shrine.

And here lies one—here I must turn   65
  From all the noble and sublime,
And o'er thy new but sacred urn
    Shed the heath-flower and mountain-thyme,
    And floods of sorrow, while I chime
Above thy dust one requiem.   70
  Love was thine error, not thy crime,
Thou mildest, sweetest, mortal gem!

For ever hallowed be thy bed,
  Beneath the dark and hoary steep;
Thy breast may flowerets overspread,   75
    And angels of the morning weep
    In sighs of heaven above thy sleep,
And tear-drops of embalming dew;
  Thy vesper-hymn be from the deep,
Thy matin from the æther blue!   80

I dare not of that holy shade
  That's pass'd away one thought allow,
Not even a dream that might degrade
  The mercy before which I bow:

Eternal God, what is it now?   85
Thus asks my heart, but the reply
  I aim not, wish not, to foreknow;
'Tis veiled within eternity.

But O, this earthly flesh and heart
  Still cling to the dear form beneath,   90
As when I saw its soul depart,
  As when I saw it calm in death:
  The dead rose and funereal wreath
Above the breast of virgin snow,
  Far lovelier than in life and breath,   95
I saw it then and see it now.

That her fair form shall e'er decay
  One thought I may not entertain;
As she was on her dying day,
  To me she ever will remain: 100
  When Time's last shiver o'er his reign
Shall close this scene of sin and sorrow,
  How calm, how lovely, how serene,
That form shall rise upon the morrow!

Frail man! of all the arrows wounding   105
  Thy mortal heart, there is but one
Whose poisoned dart is so astounding
  That bear it, cure it, there can none.
  It is the thought of beauty won
To love in most supreme degree,   110
  And by the hapless flame undone,
Cut off from nature and from thee.

Farewell, dear shade! this heart is broke
  By pang which no allayment knows;
Uprending feelings have awoke   115
  Which never more can know repose.
  O, lone St. Mary of the Lows,
Thou hold'st a treasure in thy breast,
  That, where unfading beauty glows,
Must smile in everlasting rest.   120

Eastern Apologues

By James Hogg
the Ettrick Shepherd

The Divinity of Song

As Sadac, the son of Azor, was sitting at the door of his pavilion in the cool of the day, he saw a man approaching, who soon riveted his whole attention. The man was lame, for he had lost a limb; and that limb was replaced by an awkward and unpolished piece of sycamore-wood. When he came nigher, Sadac perceived that he had also lost an arm and one of his eyes; and yet that man, as he came halting along, was singing a strain of so much mirth and gaiety, that he not only appeared to possess a share of happiness, but to be happiness itself personified.

Now Sadac, the son of Azor, was prince of Cathema, and governor over all that country, from the confines of Persia to the great desert of Amerabia; and when he saw this mutilated man of mirth passing by, he called to him to come; but the man regarded him only with a slight glance and a nod, and skipped away over his crutch, singing his song with increased vigour and glee.

Then Sadac called his servants, and said unto them, "Go, bring that cripple back unto me; for what is he, or what is his father's house, that he should despise the order of Sadac, prince of Cathema?"

And the servants followed the lame man; and the first that overtook him strove to detain him, but he struck the servant of Sadac on the head with his crutch until he fell down, and then the lame man went on singing: and the second and the third came up, and, lo! he did unto them even as he had done to the first; and the men were greatly astonied, and they rose up and returned to their master; and the cripple went on his way, singing as before.

And Sadac was very wroth with the men; and he said, "Why have ye not detained him and brought him back?" But they answered and said, "Lo! he struck us on the head and on the hands, and we had no power to stand before him, but fell down as dead men." And they said, "Perhaps he is an angel sent from Mahomed;" but Sadac laughed them to scorn.

And he sent out other servants, who were more in number, and mightier than the first; and he said unto them, "Bring back the man;" and they brought him. And Sadac communed with him, and said unto him, "Why didst thou not come when I called thee? How daredst thou disobey the command of thy prince and ruler?"

"Because I was then singing to myself a song," said the lame man; "and rather than have stopped short in my song, without finishing it, I would that thy head had been struck off and mine to boot."

And Sadac said, "Thou shalt surely suffer death for speaking in this manner to the son of Azor, thy prince, and also for lifting up thine hand against the messengers that he sent unto thee."

And the lame man said, "If my life will oblige my prince, I shall be exceedingly happy to give it up to him. It is but half a life; for I have given up one half of my body for him and his family already, and the poor remainder is at his service whenever he shall see meet to require it. I will give him up my life, but not my song."

And Sadac said, "Was it that wild and foolish strain which thou wert singing as thou passedst along, and which made thee caper as with ecstasy, and extend thy voice unto strains of happy delirium? Now, by the life of Mahomed! thou shalt sing it before thou stirrest from that spot."

"Nay, that I shall never do at the behest of mortal man," said the cripple. "My prince may take my life, for it is his right; but my song is mine own, and in it he has neither right nor portion."

And Sadac said, "How can that be?"

And the lame man said, "Because it is the child of the soul, and over the soul of man and its lineage thou hast neither power nor dominion. Knowest thou not that the gift of song is an emanation from the Deity? that it is a ray of paradise, enlightening and endowing the immortal part of man with the qualification of angels? that it enriches the soul with a measure of the capabilities of those seraphs who hymn their everlasting hallelujas around the throne of heaven? O thou divine and hallowed gift! what are all the gratifications of sense; what is might or dominion; what are thrones, principalities, and powers, compared with thee, thou sublime intellectual radiance, that connectest man with the hosts above? It was thy holy flame that poured from the mouths of Moses, of David, of Isaiah, and of Mahomed; therefore, hallowed be thy essence, and may no human ruler ever claim dominion over thee!"

And Sadac was greatly astonished, and he gazed upon the lame and mutilated figure as on some superior being; and he thought within himself, "Why did it not please God and our prophet to endow me, Sadac, the son of Azor, with the gift of song?"

And he said unto the lame man, "What is thy name?" And he answered, "Ismael, the son of Berar, thy servant." And Sadac said, "Verily thou art wise as thou hast proved thyself valiant; come within the cover of my tent, and sit thee down here on my left hand, that I may converse with thee about many things:" and the man did as Sadac had commanded him.

The Beauty of Women

And Sadac said unto Ismael, the son of Berar, "Wherein consists thy great happiness?—for of all the men whom these eyes have ever beheld thou appearest to me to be the most perfectly happy. I have been in search of it all the days of my life—and, oh, how eagerly I have pursued it!—but evermore has it fled from my grasp, and left me the more unhappy on every new enjoyment. So often hath disappointment sickened my soul, that I have resolved again and again to change conditions with the first happy man whom I should meet; and were it possible for me to part with my limb, my arm, and mine eye, I would pleasantly change conditions with poor Ismael, the son of Berar: I would resign to him all my power and all my dominions, with all the riches of Cathema, all my wives, and all my concubines, save one, and with her would I traverse different lands, and try if happiness would follow, for overtaken it will not be."

And Ismael, the son of Berar, laughed exceedingly, until he even fell backward upon his seat by reason of his laughter, it was so great, and he said, "O Sadac, thou son of Azor, great art thou in power, and great is accounted thy wisdom, but there is folly with thee, for thou hast been seeking happiness where it is not to be found. But long, long will it be, before the poor son of Berar exchange conditions with thee!"

And he said furthermore: "After the siege of Bahara, which belonged to Persia, when all the fields and vineyards were laid waste and abandoned, an ox that had been left alive found his way into them; and he gloated over the riches and fertility of the soil, and he consumed, and ate up, and devoured, of all the good and pleasant things, until he was so encumbered with his own fatness that he found it impossible to make his escape from the enclosures; and his soul sickened within him even to loathing, so that he yearned for the liberty of the forest, to browze again on its leaves and dry herbage. But to the forest he could not win, for he was involved in labyrinths of luxury, and the smallest fence could he not surmount, even though but a few feet in height; so that there was he condemned to wallow on in luxury and discontent.

"And the ox observed that every day a wild goat came from the forest which skirted the desert; and the goat was lean and haggard in his appearance, and he skipped lightly over the fences, and browzed greedily on such herbs as he liked for a short space of time; and he would gambol among the flowers, and butt down the young vines and olives as with disdain, and then, bounding over the fences, escape again into the forest.

"And the ox languished exceedingly, and greatly did he envy the goat, whom before he had held in derision; and he watched his approach, and waylaid him, and tried to bring him into conversation, which he at last effected; for the goat fled not from this overgrown victim of luxury.

"And the ox said, 'Why liest thou not still in these rich pastures and among the vineyards, to feed on all the delicacies of the earth? Why shouldst thou remain so lean, when the fat of the land is before thee?' The goat returned him no answer, but fell a-skipping and dancing round the ox in all the madness of frolic; and he leaped upon the highest walls, vanishing beyond them; so that the ox thought the madcap had gone off to the forest. Then would he appear again, running upon the walls, and bounding over every impediment, until the ox became greatly chagrined; but yet he wished in his heart to change places with that bearded mountebank. Then he called unto him again, and said, 'Tell me, I pray thee, why thou wilt not remain amongst these luxuries?' And the goat said, 'Because it suits not with my nature and delight to feed myself fat, so as to be coveted for a prey by man, and likewise render myself incapable of escaping from his hand.'

"And the ox groaned in spirit, for he perceived that the hint applied to him; and he said, 'Lo, I will exchange places with thee; remain thou here, and eat, and drink, and rejoice; and conduct me hence, that I may go into the desert in thy stead.' But the wild goat refused, and said, 'It lists me not to do so with thee; for were I to remain here I should surely die, and wert thou banished to the desert, after thy feasting and luxury, thou wouldst pine away and die also, even by a death the most tedious and deplorable. Therefore, since thou hast not been able to discern this truth, that a moderate portion of the good things of this life is better than unrestrained luxury and unlimited fulness, in that labyrinth of sloth and sensual gratification must thou remain until thou perish.' And while he yet spoke, a band of forayers appeared, and they said one to another, 'Behold, what a prey!' And they bent their bows, and took their javelins in their hands, and rushed upon the twain; but the wild goat skipped over the wall, and ere they could let fly their arrows he had bounded away to the forest. But the unwieldy ox became their victim, and fell dead, uttering many grievous and repentant groans, and pierced with a thousand wounds."

And Sadac, the son of Azor, was grieved in spirit, and his countenance fell, and he hung down his head, and laid his hand upon his breast, and sighed very deeply, and he said, "Thy story hath made me sad; nevertheless tell me wherein thy great happiness consisteth, and peradventure I may find means of sharing it with thee; for, of all men I ever beheld thou seemest to me to have the least cause of rejoicing, since thou hast lost a limb, an eye, and a hand, and moreover thou art poor, and hast none of the enjoyments of life."

And Ismael said, "O my prince, it is because thou hast not learned to discern wherein the enjoyment of life consists. Thou hast not learned, like thy servant, to be pleased with mankind as they are, and with events as they occur; and, when evil befalleth thee, to be thankful that it is not worse. When I lost one of my limbs, fighting in the camp of thy father, I thanked Allah that I had not lost them both. When I lost an eye, fighting in my own cause, I conquered my inveterate enemy, and rejoicing said, 'I shall see the clearer with the eye that is left.' And when I lost an arm, fighting under thee in the great battle of Bahara, in which the pride of Persia sank before our might, the men who bound up my wound said unto me, 'Ismael, thou art sorely wounded and lame besides; retire thou into the tent.' But I refused, and said, 'I have one hand left, and with it will I fight for my prince until I fall, or the battle be gained.' We conquered, and I rejoiced. I know of no man who has more reason to be thankful to God and our prophet than poor Ismael, the son of Berar."

"I cannot for my life perceive wherein it consists," said Sadac, "unless it be in deprivations, which are contrary in their nature to happiness. Tell me one of the chief enjoyments of the heart."

And Ismael said, "The highest enjoyment of which my frail nature is capable has been in the endearments of one beloved object—in the society of Abra, my beloved wife, my only spouse, and the darling of my heart. She has proved to me the light of my soul, my crown of rejoicing, my stay and comfort in affliction, and the affectionate sharer in all my joys and sorrows. Ismael, the son of Berar, has had no earthly felicity that can be compared with the love and society of that beautiful, blessed, and divine, creature."

And Sadac marvelled exceedingly, and he said, "I have thirty and six wives, and seventy and two concubines, the most beautiful women in the world. They are all pure and without blemish; arrayed in the silken gauze of Cashmere, covered over with jewels and perfumes, and all ready to bestow their smiles and favours on the son of Azor; yet, instead of being my chief joy, from them proceed my greatest earthly plagues and torments. O Ismael, bring thy

Abra before me, that I may look upon that beauty which is sufficient to confer such happiness on the possessor."

But Ismael said, "Shouldst thou covet and take her from me, thy servant's chief happiness in this world would be extinct."

But Sadac swore unto him, that though he admired her ever so much, yet would he not deprive him of what he held so dear. "For I have sufficiency of female beauty already," added he; "which when thou seest thou shalt acknowledge." And he led the lame Ismael away to the apartments of the women, and caused every one of them, amounting to more than a hundred, to pass by before him, and to unveil themselves. They were all beautiful as roses, for they were from beyond the river, and fair of complexion. And Sadac said, "Thou seest how lovely they are; wouldst thou not exchange thine Abra for any of these?"

And Ismael answered and said, "No, prince; I would not exchange my Abra for any of these, nor for all, beautiful though they are, which I deny not, though thou shouldst add the wealth of Cathema to boot."

And Sadac marvelled greatly, and said, "O Ismael, let me see this wonder of my dominions, whose beauty, single and alone, can ravish and delight a man, and render him completely happy from year to year." And Ismael did as his prince and ruler commanded, and he brought his wife, and she stood before Sadac the son of Azor. And Sadac said, "Is this thy wife, even thy beloved Abra?"

And Ismael said, "It is."

And Sadac lost all power, and fell from his seat down upon the floor of his pavilion; but it was not with love for the wife of Ismael, but with laughter at the style of her beauty. For the woman was old and homely in the extreme, with a broad brown face, and gray eyes of a heavy and mild lustre. And the servants of Sadac tried to lift him up and to set him on his seat, but they could not, for he had no power either to rise or to support himself thereon; and they said one to another, "What shall we do for Sadac, the son of Azor, our lord?"

And Sadac laughed seven days and seven nights at the beauty of Abra, the wife of Ismael.

And it came to pass after these days that he called Ismael unto him, and said, "O Ismael, son of Berar, how hast thou mocked me by asserting thy happiness with thy Abra, in derision of all the beauty in my harem, collected from the great river Euphrates even to the borders of Media for my pleasure and happiness, which all that beauty has yet failed to produce! But, trust me, Ismael, should we change conditions, thou shalt keep thy Abra for me; for I would as soon think of taking to my embrace the great snake of the desert. If happiness is not to be found with beauty, how is it to be found with woman? Therefore, Ismael, dare not thou any more to mock thy prince."

And Ismael said, "Far be it from me to mock my prince, or to tell him any word that is not downright truth. I agree with him, that without beauty there can be no happiness with woman; but of female beauty there are many kinds and degrees; as many as in the whole range of nature besides. There is one beauty of the flowers of the field, another of the storms of heaven, and another of the sun shining in all his glory and strength. So in woman there is one beauty of the skin, and another of the soul; but the one is as superior to the other, as the sun shining in his glory and strength is to the short-lived and fading flowers of the valley. These perish and decay, and fall down in the dust, and are succeeded by others. What striking emblems of the beauty of women, of that beauty of the skin which alone is admired by the son of Azor! But the beauties of virtue, mercy, and benevolence, and all the other glorious qualifications of the soul, have no decay, but continue to advance onward and onward in strength and splendour through time and eternity. Thou, O Sadac, seekest only for selfish gratification, deeming that there happiness is to be found. How certain the event that thou wert to be disappointed! So shall all those be who expect to find true happiness in the pleasures of sense and the vanities of time. But I have sought and found a union of souls that began in youth, has strengthened with age, and will continue to improve and brighten for ever and ever."

And Sadac went home into his house heavy and concerned, and he said unto himself, "I would instantly go in search of that union of souls if I wist what it was."

Maxims of Sadac, the Son of Azor

And Sadac gave unto Ismael a house near to the palace, and a maiden to wait on Abra; and Ismael became a favourite counsellor to his master, who conferred many benefits on him, and conversed with him daily; and the latter days of the old soldier and son of song glided on in happiness. But the nobles of the land envied him exceedingly, and they consulted together and said, "We must banish this fantastic old man from about our court, else our dignity shall depart from us, and the mean and the vile shall have the dominion." And one said after this manner, and another after that; but at last it was agreed that out of his own mouth they would condemn him, by reason of the freedom of his expressions. So they forced him into argument, and drove him to wrath by their wrangling, and he uttered words unadvisedly against the divinity of the prophet.

Then they rejoiced in heart, and gnashing with their teeth, as in great wrath, they seized him and carried him before the tribunal of Sadac to receive sentence of death; for there were not wanting abundance of witnesses, who said, "He hath blasphemed God and his prophet Mahomed." And Sadac was exceedingly grieved for his friend, for he perceived that there had been a conspiracy against him, and he devised how to save him out of their hands.

And he said unto them, "O ye nobles and men of Cathema, I perceive the truth of your accusation, and believe that this man's heart is not right as it ought to be with the Lord and with Mahomed his prophet. But, know ye not, O men, and believe ye not, that our holy prophet has all power under God to punish the transgressors of his law and the unbelievers in his doctrine?" And they said, "We know and believe it."

Then said he unto them, "Perceive ye not, also, that our prophet hath vindicated his cause in the eyes of all men? for, lo! hath he not punished this man already for his errors and unbelief as never man was punished before? Hath he not first deprived him of a limb, then of an eye, and latterly of an arm? And since it is so that our supreme prophet hath taken up the vindication of his own cause, it would be unmeet for man to intermeddle between the aggressor and his righteous judge. The cause now lies between them, and let us leave the culprit to the terrible chastisement which the injured Mahomed shall see meet to inflict. I will punish injustice and offences committed against men; but with those committed against God I dare not to interfere. He can punish if he will; but if he sees meet to bear with the offences and contumely of an erring creature, well may I."

And the men said, "Our prince hath spoken that which is just and right;" and they went to their houses, and Ismael, the son of Berar, also went unto his house.

And Sadac sent for him afterwards, and said unto him: "O son of Berar, beware how thou again venturest out of thy proper sphere; for as a lamb is among young leopards, or a roe among the cubs of the lion, so is a poor man entering the ranks of the great. Is it not better for thee to be at the head of those of thy own degree—to thrill them with thy songs, to astonish them with thy adventures, and to tell unto them tales that instruct in the beauty of virtue, than to mingle with the nobles of the land, who abhor every excellence in humble life, and among whom thou wilt find thyself like the buffalo among wild oxen, every one having his horn in thy side? Thou art brave in spirit, brilliant in imagination, and intelligent in the virtues of the soul of man; but of the rules of life thou knowest no more than a babe at the breast; yet it is by these that society is directed, and in these can I be thy monitor. Fear thy God, and reverence all his statutes. Honour and obey thy ruler, for a good ruler is the greatest blessing bestowed on a nation; know thy place, and pay deference to all who are above thee in rank and learning, for self-conceit is the mark of Cain stamped on those of low origin. Love all who depend on thee for comfort; do good as far as thou art able; and wish well to the whole human race. These, O Ismael, are the rules of Sadac, the son of Azor; and in the name of the most merciful God and his prophet he strives to observe them."

And Ismael grew in favour with his prince until the day of his death, and those are his songs that are chanted through all the coasts of Arabia unto this day.

Seeking the Houdy

By the Ettrick Shepherd

THERE was a shepherd on the lands of Meggat-dale, who once set out riding with might and main, under cloud of night, for that most important and necessary personage in a remote and mountainous country, called by a different name in every country of the world, excepting perhaps Egypt and England; but by the Highlanders most expressively termed *bean-glhuine*, or *te the toctor*.

The mare that Robin rode was a black one, with a white face like a cow. She had a great big belly, a switch tail, and a back, Robin said, as sharp as a knife; but perhaps this part of the description was rather exaggerated. However, she was laziness itself personified, and the worst thing of all, her foal was closed in at home; for Robin had wiled the mare and foal into the bire with a piece of bread, which he did not give her after all, but put in his pocket in case of farther necessity: he then whipped a hair halter on the mare's head, and the straw sunks on her back, these being the only equipment within his reach; and it having cost Robin a great deal of trouble to get the foal into the bire, he now eyed him with an exulting, and at the same time a malicious, look. "Ye mischievous rascal," said he, "I think I have you now; stand you there an' chack flees till I come back to teach you better manners."

Robin then hurried out the mare to the side of the kail-yard dike, and calling out to Jean his wife not to be in ower grit a hurry, and to exercise all the patience she was mistress of, he flew on the yaud's back, and off he went at full gallop.

The hair halter that Robin rode with had a wooden snibbelt upon the end of it, as all hair halters had erewhile, when there were no other bridles in Meggat, saving branks and hair halters annexed; consequently with the further end of this halter one could hit an exceeding hard stroke. Indeed, I never saw any thing in my life that hurt so sore as a hair halter and wooden snibbelt at the end of it; and I may here mention, as an instance of its efficacy, that there was once a boy at Hartwood mines, near Selkirk, who killed with a snibbelt two Highland soldiers, who came to press his horses in *the forty-five*.

Well, to this halter and snibbelt Robin had trusted for a rod, there being no wood in Meggat-dale, not so much as a tree; and a more unlucky and dangerous goad he could scarcely have possessed, and that the black mare, with a white face like a cow, felt to her experience. Robin galloped by the light of the full moon down by the Butt-haugh and Glengaber-foot about as fast as a good horse walks; still he was galloping, and could make no more of it, although he was every now and then lending the yaud a yerk on the flank with the snibbelt. But when he came to Henderland, to which place the mare was accustomed to go every week to meet the eggler, then Robin and the mare split in their opinions. Robin thought it the most natural and reasonable thing in the world that the mare should push on to the Sandbed, about eight miles further, to bring home the wise woman to his beloved wife's assistance. The mare thought exactly the reverse, being inwardly convinced that the most natural and reasonable path she could take was the one straight home again to her foal; and without any farther ceremony, save giving a few switches with her long ill-shapen tail, she set herself with all her might to dispute the point with Robin.

Then there was such a battle commenced as never was fought at the foot of Henderland-bank at midnight either before or since. O my beloved and respected editor and readers! I wish I could make you understand the humour of this battle as well as I do. The branks were two sticks hung by a headsteel, which, when one drew the halter hard, nipped the beast's nose most terribly; but then they were all made in one way, and could only turn the beast to the near side. Now the black mare did not, or could not, resist this agency of the branks; she turned round as often as Robin liked, but not one step farther would she proceed on the road to Sandbed. So roundabout and roundabout the two went; and the mare, by a very clever expedient, contrived at every circle to work twice her own length nearer home. Saint Sampson! how Robin did lay on with the halter and snibbelt whenever he got her head round towards the way he wanted her to go! No—round she came again! He cursed her, he flattered her, he reminded her of the precarious state of her mistress, who had so often filled her manger; but all would not do: she thought only of the precarious state of her foal, closed in an old void smearing-house.

Robin at last fell upon a new stratagem, which was this, that as the mare wheeled round whenever her head reached the right point, he hit her a yerk with the wooden snibbelt on the near cheek, to stop that millstone motion of hers. This occasioned some furious plunges, but no advancement the right way, till at length he hit her such a pernicious blow somewhere near about the ear, that he brought her smack to the earth in a moment; and so much was he irritated, that he laid on her when down, and nodding like ane falling asleep. After two or three prolonged groans, she rose again, and, thus candidly admonished, made no further resistance for the present, but moved on apace to the time of the halter and the snibbelt. On reaching a ravine called Capper Cleuch, the mare, coming again in some degree to her senses, perceived that she was not where she ought to have been, at least where it was her interest, and the interest of her foal, that she should have been; and, raising her white face, she uttered a tremendous neigh. The hills to the left are there steep and rocky; and the night being calm and frosty, first one fine echo neighed out of the hill, then another, and then another. "There are plenty of foals here," thought the old mare; and neighing again even louder than before, she was again answered in the same way; and, perceiving an old crabbed thorn-tree among the rocks, in the direction whence the echo proceeded, it struck her obtuse head that it was her great lubber of a foal standing on very perilous ground; and off she set at a right angle from the road, or rather a left one, with her utmost speed, braying as she went, while every scream was returned by her shaggy colt with interest. It was in vain that Robin pulled by the hair halter, and smote her on the cheek with the wooden snibbelt: away she ran, through long heath and large stones, with a tremendous and uncultivated rapidity, neighing as she flew. "Wo! ye jaud! Hap-wo! chywooo!" shouted Robin; "Hap-wo! hap-wo! Devil confound the beast, for I'm gone!"

Nothing would stay her velocity till she stabled herself against a rock over which she could not win, and then Robin lost no time in throwing himself from her back. Many and bitter were the epithets he there bestowed on his old mare, and grievous was the lamentation he made for his wife, as endeavouring to lead back the mare from the rocky hill into the miserable track of a road. No; the plague o' one foot would the mare move in that direction! She held out her long nose, with her white muslin face, straight up to heaven, as if contemplating the moon. She weened that her foal was up among the crags, and put on a resolution not to leave him a second time for any man's pleasure. After all, Robin confessed that he had some excuse for her, for the shadow of the old thorn was so like a colt, that he could scarcely reason himself out of the belief that it was one.

Robin was now hardly set indeed, for the mare would not lead a step; and when he came back to her side to leather her with the snibbelt, she only galloped round him and round him, and neighed. "O plague on you for a beast that ever you were foaled!" exclaimed Robin; "I shall lose a dearly beloved wife, and perhaps a couple of babies at least, and all owing to your stupidity and obstinacy! I could soon run on foot to the Sandbed, but then I cannot carry the midwife home on my back; and could I once get you there, you would not be long in bringing us both home again. Plague on you for a beast, if I winna knock your brains out!"

Robin now attacked the mare's white face with the snibbelt, yerk for yerk, so potently, that the mare soon grew madly crazed, and came plunging and floundering from the hill at a great rate. Robin thus found out a secret not before known in this country, on which he acted till the day of his death; namely, "that the best way to make a horse spring forward is to strike it on the face."

Once more on the path, Robin again mounted, sparing neither the mare nor the halter; while the mare, at every five or six paces, entertained him with a bray so loud, with its accompanying nicker, that every one made the hills ring again.

There is scarcely any thing a man likes worse than this constant neighing of the steed he rides upon, especially by night. It makes him start as from a reverie, and puts his whole frame in commotion. Robin did not like it more than other men. It caused him inadvertently to utter some imprecations on the mare, that he confessed he should not have uttered; but it also caused him to say some short prayers for preservation; and to which of these agencies he owed the following singular adventure he never could divine.

Robin had got only about half a mile farther on his road, when his mare ceased her braying, and all at once stood stone-still, cocking her large ears, and looking exceedingly frightened. "Oho, madam! what's the matter now?" said Robin; "is this another stratagem to mar my journey, for all the haste that you see me in? Get on, my fine yaud, get on! There is nothing uncanny there."

Robin coaxed thus, as well to keep up his own spirits, as to encourage his mare; for the truth is, that his hair began to stand on end with affright. The mare would neither ride, lead, nor drive, one step further; but there she stood, staring, snuffing the wind, and snorting so loud, that it was frightsome to hear as well as to see her. This was the worst dilemma of all. What was our forlorn shepherd to do now? He averred that the mare *would not* go on either by force or art; but I am greatly deceived, if by this time he durst for his life have gone on, even though the mare could have been induced to proceed. He took the next natural expedient, which was that of shouting out as loud as he could bellow, "Hilloa! who's there? Be ye devils, be ye witches, or be ye Christian creatures, rise an' shaw yoursels. I say, hilloa! who's there?"

Robin was at this time standing hanging by the mare's hair halter with both his hands, for she was capering and flinging up her white face with such violence, that she sometimes made him bob off the ground; when, behold! at his last call, a being like a woman rose from among some deep heather bushes about twenty yards before him. She was like an elderly female, dressed in a coarse country garb, tall and erect; and there she stood for a space, with her pale face, on which the moon shone full, turned straight towards Robin. He then heard her muttering something to herself; and, with a half-stifled laugh, she stooped down, and lifted something from among the heath, which Robin thought resembled a baby. "There the gipsy yaud has been murdering that poor bairn!" thought Robin to himself: "it was nae wonder my auld yaud was frighted! she kens what's what, for as contrarysome as she is. And murderess though the hizzy be, it is out o' my power to pursue her wi' this positive auld hack, for no another foot nearer her will she move."

Robin never thought but that the mysterious being was to fly from him, or at least go off the road to one side; but in place of that she rolled her baby, or bundle, or whatever it was, deliberately up in a blanket, fastened it between her shoulders, and came straight up to the place where Robin stood hanging by his mare's head. The mare was perfectly mad. She reared, snorted, and whisked her long ill-shaped tail; but Robin held her, for he was a strong young man, and the hair halter must have been proportionably so, else it never could have stood the exercise of that eventful night.

Though I have heard Robin tell the story oftener than once when I was a boy, there was always a confusion here which I never understood. This may be accounted for, in some measure, by supposing that Robin was himself in such perplexity and confusion, that he neither knew well what passed, nor remembered it afterwards. As far as I recollect, the following was the dialogue that passed between the two.

"Wha's this?"

"What need ye speer, goodman? kend fo'k, gin it war daylight."

"I think I'm a wee bit at a loss. I dinna ken ye."

"May be no, for ye never saw me afore. An' yet it is a queer thing for a father no to ken his ain daughter."

"Ay, that wad be a queer thing indeed. But where are you gaun at this time o' the night?"

"Where am I gaun? where but up to the Craigyrigg, to get part o' my ain blithemeat. But where are you riding at sic a rate?"

"Why, I'm just riding my whole might for the houdy: an' that's very true, I hae little need to stand claverin here wi' you."

"Ha, ha, ha, ha! daddy Robin! It is four hours sin' ye came frae hame, an' ye're no won three miles yet. Why, man, afore ye get to the Sandbed an' hame again, your daughter will be ready for spaining."

"Daughter! what's a' this about a daughter? Has my dear Jean really a daughter?"

"You may be sure she has, else I could not have been here."

"An' has she only ane? for, od! ye maun ken wifie that I expectit twa at the fewest. But I dinna understand you. I wish ye may be canny enough, for my white-faced yaud seems to jalouse otherwise."

"Ye dinna ken me, Robin, but ye will ken me. I am Helen Grieve. I was weel brought up, and married to a respectable farmer's son; but he turned out a villain, and, among other qualifications, was a notorious thief; so that I have been reduced to this that you see, to travel the country with a pack, and lend women a helping-hand in their hour o' need. An', Robin, when you and I meet here again, you may be preparing for another world."

"I dinna comprehend ye at a', wifie. No; a' that I can do, I canna comprehend ye. But I understand thus far. It seems ye are a houdy, or a meedwife, as the grit fo'ks will ca' you. Now that's the very thing I want at present, for your helping hand may be needfu' yonder. Come on ahint me, and we'll soon be hame."

I must give the expedition home in Robin's own words.

"Weel, I forces my yaud into the Cleuch-brae, contrary as she was, wi' her white face, for she had learned by this time to take a wee care o' the timmer snibbelt. I was on her back in a jiffey; an', to say truth, the kerling wi' the pale round face, and the bit lang bundle on her back, wasna slack; for she was on ahint me, bundle an' a', ere ever I kend I was on mysel. But, Gude forgie us! sickan a voyage as we gat! I declare my yaud gae a snore that gart a' the hills ring, an' the verra fire flew frae her snirls. Out o' the Cleuch-brae she sprang, as there hadna been a bane or a joint within her hide, but her hale carcass made o' steel springs; an' ower bush, ower breer, ower stock, an' ower stane she flew, I declare, an' so be it, faster than ever an eagle flew through the firmament of the heavens.

"I kend then that I had either a witch or a mermaid on ahint me; but how was I now to get quit o' her? The hair halter had lost a' power, an' I had no other shift left, than to fix by instinct on the mane wi' baith hands, an' cry out to the mare to stop. 'Wo ye auld viper o' the pit! wo, ye beast o' Bashan!' I cries in outer desperation; but ay the louder I cried, the faster did the glyde flee. She snored, an' she grained, an' she reirdit baith ahint an' afore; an' on she dashed, regardless of a' danger.

"I soon lost sight o' the ground—off gaed my bonnet, an' away i' the wind—off gaed my plaid, an' away i' the wind; an' there was I sitting lootching forret, cleaving the wind like an arrow out of a bow, an' my een rinning pouring like streams of water from the south. At length we came to the Birk-bush Linn! and alangst the very verge of that awsome precipice there was my dementit beast scouring like a fiery dragon. 'Lord preserve me!' cried I loud out; an' I hadna weel said the word, till my mare gae a tremendous plunge ower something, I never kend what it was, and then down she came on her nose. No rider could stand this concussion, an' I declare, an' so be it, the meedwife lost her haud, and ower the precipice she flew head foremost. I just gat ae glisk o' her as she was gaun ower the top o' the birk-bush like a shot stern, an' I heard her gie a waw like a cat; an' that was the last sight I saw o' her.

"I was then hanging by the mane an' the right hough; an', during the moment that my mare took to gather hersel' up, I recovered my seat, but only on the top o' the shoulder, for I couldna win to the right place. The mare flew on as madly as ever; and frae the shoulder I came on to the neck, an' forret, an' forret, piecemeal, till, just as I came to my ain door, I had gotten a grip o' baith the lugs. The foal gae a screed of a nicher; on which the glyde threw up her white face wi' sic a vengeance, that she gart me play at pitch-an'-toss up in the air. The foal nichered, an' the mare nichered, an' out came the kimmers; an' I declare, an' so be it, there was I lying in the gutter senseless, wanting the plaid, an' wanting the bonnet, an' nae meedwife at a'; an' that's the truth, sir, I declare, an' so be it.

"Then they carried me in, an' they washed me, an' they bathed me, an' at last I came to mysel'; an', to be sure, I had gotten a bonny doughter, an' a' things war gaun on *as weel as could be expectit.* 'What hae ye made o' your plaid, Robin?' says ane. 'Whare's your bonnet, Robin?' says another. 'But, gudeness guide us! what's come o' the houdy, Robin? Whare's the meedwife, Robin?' cried they a' at aince. I trow this question gart me glower as I had seen a ghaist. 'Och! huh!' cried the wives, an' held up their hands; 'something has happened! something has happened! We see by his looks!–Robin! what has happened? Whare's the meedwife?'

"'Haud your tongue, Janet Reive; an' haud ye your tongue too, Eppie Dickson,' says I, 'an' dinna speer that question at me again; for the houdy is where the Lord will, an' where my white-faced yaud was pleased to pit her, and that's in the howe o' the Birk-bush Linn. Gin she be a human creature, she's a' dashed to pieces: but an she be nae a human creature she may gang where she like for me; an' that's true, I declare, an' so be it.'"

Now it must strike every reader, as it did me at first and for many years afterwards, that this mysterious nocturnal wanderer gave a most confused and unintelligible account of herself. She was Robin's daughter; her name was Helen Grieve; she was married to such and such a man; and had now become a pedlar, and acted occasionally as a midwife: and finally, when they two met there again, it would be time for Robin to be preparing for another state of existence. Now, in the first place, Robin never had a daughter till that very hour and instant when the woman rose out of the heather-bush and accosted him. All the rest appeared to him like a confused dream, of which he had no comprehension, save that he could never again be prevailed on to pass that way alone by night; for he had an impression that at some time or other he should meet with her again.

But by far the most curious part of this story is yet to come, and it shall be related in few words. Robin went with some others, as soon as it was day, to the Birk-bush Linn, but there was neither body nor blood to be seen, nor any appearance of a person having been killed or hurt. Robin's daughter was christened by the name of Helen, after her maternal grandmother, so that her name was actually Helen Grieve: and from the time that Robin first saw his daughter, there never was a day on which some of her looks did not bring the mysterious midwife to his mind. Thus far the story had proceeded when I heard it related; for I lived twelve months in the family, and the girl was then only about seven years of age. But, strange to relate, the midwife's short history of herself has turned out the exact history of this once lovely girl's life; and Robin, a few days before his death, met her at the Kirk Cleuch, with a bundle on her back, and recognized his old friend in every lineament and article of attire. He related this to his wife as a secret, but added, that "he did not know whether it was his *real* daughter whom he met or not."

Many are the traditions remaining in the country, relative to the seeking of midwives, or houdies, as they are universally denominated all over the south of Scotland; and strange adventures are related as having happened in these precipitate excursions, which were proverbially certain to happen by night. Indeed it would appear, that there hardly ever was a midwife brought, but some incident occurred indicative of the fate or fortunes of the little forthcoming stranger; but, amongst them all, I have selected this as the most remarkable.

I am exceedingly grieved at the discontinuance of midwifery, that primitive and original calling, in this primitive and original country; for never were there such merry groups in Scotland as the midwives and their kimmers in former days, and never was there such store of capital stories and gossip circulated as on these occasions. But those days are over! and alack, and wo is me! no future old shepherd shall tell another tale of SEEKING THE HOUDY!

A Sea Story

By the Ettrick Shepherd

So lately as forty years ago, and upward time out of mind, the woollen manufactures of Scotland were principally supplied from the cottages and from the kitchens of the farmers. Over the whole of the lowland districts the *muckle wheel* was plied early and late. The old women carded, and the young ones span; and a more graceful employment for a handsome young woman never existed, as she flew backward and forward over the floor. Many cottagers depended solely on the sale of this yarn for their bread. The goodman's earnings were laid out in the purchase of wool, which his wife and daugh-

ters spun into yarn; and for this commodity there was always a certain demand and ready money; for the country swarmed with yarn-
merchants, and among them there was a good deal of rivalry; so
that there was little danger of the holder not making the most of it.

Among other itinerants was one John Robson, a very old man,
but a great favourite with the wives. He had plenty of money, plenty
of long prayers and graces, and plenty of long romantic stories of
battles and perils by land and water; and with those advantages,
John contrived to get the best bargains all over the country, and was
sure of a snug lodging when night overtook him. Among his stories
there was one which I heard him tell twice or thrice over, and which
I remember very well, save that I do not recollect the place from
whence the vessel sailed on her voyage homeward to the Clyde; but
I think it was from some port in Spain. I shall tell it in John's own
words, or, at least, in his own peculiar way.

"We were sailing and sailing as sweetly afore a gentle breeze as
ever rippled the sea, when, ae morning after break o' day, we saw
something floating lightly o'er and o'er the waves, like a buoy; and
when it was pointed out to the captain, he had some curiosity to see
what it was, and made us luff to come up with it. And what was it
but a boy, sitting crying in a wicker basket! We were a' terribly
astonished how the creature was preserved; for the basket was just
like another basket; the water gaed through and through it as fast
as it likit; but the lightness o't keepit it afloat. We hauled in the poor
object without a moment's delay, or the least hesitation, and then
he cried for his creel, until we were obliged to bring it on board
likewise.

"As soon as we got time to look at him, we didna like him unco
weel. He was a creature about four feet lang, wi' an auld withered
face, like a fairy, or some o' thae half-earthly half-hellish beings. We
gae him different kinds o' meat, and he eatit like mad, and seemed
hardly ever to be satisfied. He spoke very readily, and very prettily
too, but it was in a language that no ane o' us could understand a
word of; sae we could neither learn what he was nor wha he was.

"But I think he hadna been ten minutes aboard, when we heard a
kind o' crash in the rigging o' the top-gallant, and at the same time
the ship gae a rock like a cradle. 'What the devil's that?' cried the
captain. Every man declared his ignorance of the matter, for at that
time we felt no difference of the breeze on deck, and saw not the
slightest symptoms of an approaching gale; and while we were all
standing gazing to see if we could discern from whence the shock
proceeded, we heard a kind of moaning in the shrouds, like a wind

wi' a voice in it; and in a few minutes crash went the upper shrouds a second time, and reel went the ship with double violence.

"The captain was now terribly alarmed at a thing sae contrair to a' that he had ever seen before; however, he commanded us to reef with all expedition, as there seemed a kind o' whirlwind descending on us. Never will I forget that morning; for, without the least prelude or appearance of a storm, the wind came on us thud after thud, and aye the last the loudest, till we were soon in the middle of sic a turmoil as e'e o' man never saw. The wind daddit us, and cuffed us, whiles on the ae side and whiles on the other, till at one time I really believed the ship was whirled up in the air. The beam wappit about backward and forward, knocking a' down that came before it; the rigging crashed, and the jib-sail went to tatters. All was utter confusion; and we were sometimes running in one direction, and instantly again in another. The waves o' the sea werena rowing away before the gale wi' full sweep, but they were boiling and clashing against each other. The thunder roared, the fire flashed, and the hailstanes rattled; and there were we towering to the cludds, and then down with a dive into the channels o' the ocean. We gaed sae deep at ae time that I heard our keel play rusk against the gravel and sludge in the bottom.

"In short, as the hurricane had an unnatural beginning, so there wasna ae natural thing in it, and it was the greatest miracle that I ever saw how we escapit a' wi' life; but what need I say that? for our time hadna been come, nor the number o' our days fulfilled. At length there comes an auld man astern and he says: 'Captain M'Nicol, it strikes me that there's an Achan in the camp, a Jonah on shipboard; and it is better that he share the lot o' the prophet than that we should a' perish. Take an auld foggie's word for it, captain, this is nae natural convulsion of the elements, and it is my confirmed opinion that the creature we took out o' the weltering waves, sailing in a creel forsooth, is either a murderer, or a deil, or at the very least a water-kelpie.'

"The words gaed to the captain's heart, for, as he held on with both hands, he spake not a word, but stared wildly round him. There is no doubt that the whole of the circumstances taken together struck him as having a most ominous appearance, but yet he was mair awis than I could hae expectit. At length he said, 'What the deil shall we do? As it is, we must now go to the bottom in a few minutes, or perhaps seconds, for the sea is going on like a boiling cauldron.'

"'Just pop the imp overboard into his native element,' said the old man, 'unless you wish every soul on board to perish. There's nae fear o' him; he'll haud away ower the waves like a toom barrel.'

"'It is a fearsome and a cowardly thing,' said I, 'to throw a poor little fellow, wham we saved from a watery grave already, into these merciless waves. Let us trust in Providence, and try to weather the gale. The Almighty can save or destroy us, as seemeth good to him; for, are not the winds and waves at his control, and what influence can a poor object like that have on them?'

"The captain was puzzled how to act, for the confusion on board had stupified him, and from the commencement of the hurricane he appeared to me as scarcely himself. But at that moment there was a great hubbub before the mast, and a mixed body of marines and sailors came rushing abaft to the captain, crying out–'We have caught the devil, sir! we have caught the devil! This little fellow here, sir, is the devil.'

"'How, the devil?' said the captain.

"'O, sir,' said one, 'him was running and jumping like a cat on all fours through the rigging in the midst of the fire of lightning, and screaming and laughing for joy.'

"'And please your honour,' said another, 'I seed him sitting like a monkey with a tail on the top-gallant-mast, chuckling and making faces, and waving the storm to come on.'

"'Over the side with him! over with him! over with him!' shouted fifty voices at once; and, in spite of my efforts and some others who opposed it, they bore him to the very gunnel, while the creature fought and jabbered in a way that utterly astounded them, making many of them to lie senseless on deck; and he kept repeating one word, 'Batta, batta,' or some such sound, until one said that he was calling for his basket. 'Bring him his basket; keep nothing belonging to him,' cried the captain: and this was the only acquiescence he manifested in the horrid alternative. As soon as the creature got hold of his large basket he held by it like grim death, and overboard he and it were both plunged. The ship, for all the damage she had sustained, must then have been running at a terrible speed, for I only saw him once with his creel gaun skreeving ower the rigging of a wave behind us, as swift as the wind. He was then struggling with his basket; and when he reached the verge of the wave, he uttered a rending unearthly scream, dived into the gulf beyond, and was seen no more.

"The people stood and gazed on one another as if astonished at what they had done. But we had soon greater reason for astonishment, for in one minute afterward the storm began to abate, and in five or six minutes more it was as lovely an afternoon as it had been a morning: we saw all around us, and the main ocean appeared never to have been agitated. And what was more curious, though not more wonderful, the rigging and sails, that during the height of the turmoil seemed to be tattered to pieces and flapping about our ears, we found now all standing in state and form: so that the whole repairs did not take above two hours, when we again held on our course. But the strangest part of all was, if true, that we were carried in a retrograde direction more than a hundred miles, which I never could believe, although it was affirmed both by the captain and boat-swain. I said, if such a thing had taken place we must have been whirled up out of the sea and borne through the air, and that I once had a feeling of the sort as if we were. So superstitious are seamen, and so terribly were all the latent sparks inherent in their nature aroused that morning, that ere night it was talked of and believed through the whole ship, that we had been heaved out of the sea, and borne a hundred miles through the air!

"Now, I ken you are a' thinking that auld John Robson's story is dune,—and perhaps it's mair than time it were dune; but sae far frae that, it is little mair than beginning yet. For, ye see, the next morn-ing, about the second watch, the man at the mast-head bawled out— 'A sail! a sail! Helm-a-lee, you lubber!—ahoy!—smack she goes!' with some other incoherent exclamations of horror. All hurried before the mast, and Lieutenant Jones, being on duty, was there himself the very first; but, perceiving nothing, he shouted to the look-out man, inquiring what was the matter. 'We are struck, sir; there's a sail down,' was the reply. The lieutenant swore the man was raving, for there was no shock; however, he put about ship, and lay-to. But all was quiet; there was neither voice heard nor wreck seen; and when the man was examined, he affirmed that he saw a light vessel com-ing full sail a-head on an angle of six, and that she ran her ledges right against our prow and went down; that he perceived one man on board, and felt a slight shock. It was noted that Captain M'Nicol looked wistful and pale, but all on board besides only laughed at the story. He was heard muttering to himself—'So, then, it seems, we are not to get past this same latitude—this cursed spot!'

"But, behold, about the break of day it became apparent that the ship was water-logged. She ran deep before, refused the helm, and appeared to be fast sinking. All was now commotion and dismay; for, the hold being searched, there was no water found, and the pumps were soon drawn dry. Then there was such heaving of stuff out of the forecastle, and such searching; but all to no purpose, the leak could not be found; and in the mean time the ship continued to sink deeper and deeper: the crew became unmanageable, and had already cut the fastenings of the long-boat, when one of the searchers set his head out of the forecastle, and cried, 'O Lord! come an' see what's here!' There were soon plenty to rush to the spot, and behold! there lay what they called 'the deil's basket,' the very individual machine which they had lifted from the waves, with a wretched human creature in it, and committed to the waves again! And as the group stared upon one another in utter consternation, they were startled by an unearthly chatter of a laugh behind them, and, on turning round, there was the creature itself sitting on a cask, with a countenance of stern and fearless defiance. The whole of the crew now fled from the face of the creature; but it pointed always downward to the cask on which it was sitting, and made signs and motions, as if it wished to have the cask to itself, or to have it examined. None, however, durst venture near it; but they began to think, from its signs and its gestures, that it wanted a word of the captain. When they told him, he became like one beside himself, and cried out to shoot it—to throw it overboard; and then to put out the long-boat, and let him escape. Lieutenant Jones and the boatswain opposed this, and proffered to accompany him to this strange visitant, as, perchance, it might be a mean of saving his Majesty's ship; and then, half by force, they led him away to the concealed corner where the wretch was sitting on its cask. Now this cask had never been seen by any of us before. It had been covered up with lumber and trunks, ever so deep, in its corner, till uncovered that night in the search for a leak that existed not. The creature jabbered, and spoke, and pointed to the cask, while its eyes had a strange gleam of exultation, and still it beckoned the captain to approach. When, at last, he was forced near it, it sprang from its seat, and whispered only one word, or rather a name, in his ear, and then again took its place on the cask, shaking its head at him in a menacing manner.

"The horror of the captain was now quite unspeakable. So much was he overwhelmed with terror, that his officers wondered how so brave a man could be so much affected. He was completely in a state of derangement; and, indeed, an indefinable terror and confusion reigned on board. The ship grovelled and wallowed in the waves like an unwieldy hulk, and the seamen and marines were running about without order. Jones did all that a brave officer could to preserve subordination; for he ran about swearing terribly, belabouring some, and knocking down others. As for the captain, all his orders were about *the evil one*, or the *ghost*, as he now called it, which no one would face. This new appellation was unfortunate. The sailors were not so much afraid to face the devil; they were brought up in the knowledge that he was their enemy, and a cunning and dangerous one, whom it was their duty to contend with. But the idea of being haunted by a ghost had an implication that shook their very souls. The captain at first took shelter in the cabin; but the feeling of confinement shocked him, and terror lest the being should enter the companion-door between him and the open air, and cut off his retreat, shook his nerves, and from thence he flew to the top of the round-house, where, in a voice that trembled with agitation, he ordered both boats to be put out, and the ship to be set on fire. 'Over with the boats, over with the boats!' now resounded from one part of the crew, and 'No, no!' from another; and, in the midst of this confusion, out comes the creature from the forecastle, carrying its cask and a hatchet, as if with intent to have it broken up; and, with its gleaming eyes fixed steadily on the captain, it made straight toward him. The crew fled from before it, some into the shrouds, and some into one place, and some another; but the captain, with a maniac yell of the most dreadful horror, jumped on deck, threw himself overboard, and disappeared.

"The creature then uttered an eldrich laugh, flew to seek its basket, and with that in both its hands jumped overboard after our unfortunate captain. The yawl was put out and manned by the boatswain and other two; but ere ever they could get free of the ship (for they were not over-fond of their employment), those on board saw the demoniac creature pick up Captain M'Nicol and drag him into the infernal basket, and away it went with the twain, like a blown-up buoy before the wind. We heard a few broken, short cries from the sufferer, and that was all. They were soon out of sight, and never more seen or heard of either on sea or land.

"The moment that the captain and his persecutor left the ship, she hove. She did not rise gradually to her former draught, but came up at one spring, which I both saw and felt, and can therefore bear testimony to its truth. But the most curious thing of all was this, which I cannot attest, not understanding these things; but it seems that we were carried a great way south by the hurricane, and on the intervening day having been sailing the same ground ower again, so happened that this last catastrophe befel us on the very same spot with the first; and of this the captain was doubtless aware when he said, 'So then, it seems, we are not to get past this latitude–this cursed spot!'

"What had been transacted there on former days was only left to conjecture; and that you may all conjecture as well as any on board,

I must tell you that as soon as we got our vessel again into sailing trim, the first thing that we did was to open the cask about which our hellish visitant had made so much ado. This was done on deck before a hundred witnesses, and all that it contained was the body of a young woman, which was disembowelled, cut in twain, and stuffed into a barrel of pickle. And it appeared further, that the woman had been murdered by the cutting of her throat; and this is all that I know for certain. I did hear afterwards, but that was long after I had come to Ayrshire, that once, on a former voyage, Captain M'Nicol having had two handsome young foreigners aboard, who were coming to Liverpool, the young man disappeared, and it was certain the captain took possession of his mistress. But, as to whether this was her body, or not her body, I cannot tell. There is little doubt that some great and crying sin had been committed at or near to that spot on the high seas at which our captain met a fate so terrible. And it ought to be a warning to a' you young fo'ks wha hae the warld afore ye never to do ony dauring deed o' wickedness in hopes that it will remain in darkness. If ye will think but o' the chances that it has to come to light, and what shame and ruin would be attendant thereon, it will amaist restrain ye, if ye be nae perfect slaves to your own vicious inclinations. But at ony rate, ye may aye depend on this —that there is a day coming when every foul deed done in the flesh shall be laid open and exposed to the derision of men and angels."

A Love Ballad

By the Ettrick Shepherd

The drowsy postman o' the night
　　The beetle sounds his eiry horn
The lambs last bleat is on the height
　　It takes its dewy bed till morn
The harper rail has bumb'd his strings　　　　5
　　An' labours at his uncouth strain
While every note the blackbird sings
　　I'm fear'd may be his last Amen

O what can ail my bonny Jane
　　Wha wont to be sae true to me　　　　　10
That thus she lets me sit my lane
　　An' strain my een outower the lea

The blackbird's note 'tis now sae late
    Has died away and a' is still
He cowers him down beside his mate   15
    An' has o' dear delight his fill

But I may sit my lane till morn
    There's not a sound from tower or tree
Except the rail's amang the corn
    An' he has lost his love like me   20
Poor bird! His note down in the dell
    Is grown a craik of black despair
I'm wae for him an' for mysel
    For O my loss is ten times mair

For his is but a motely quean   25
    Of lacker limb and tawny hue
But sic a flower as my dear Jane
    For love ne'er brush'd the e'ening dew
Hush colley! Hush! what's that I hear?
    A smother'd laugh ayont the wa'   30
There's a sweet pawkie listener near
    The dearest sight I ever saw

"Ha cunning Jane! An' are you here
    Ye've come the wrang way ower the knowe
Some other wooer lad I fear   35
    Has rowed you in his plaid till now"
"An' what for no? I just thought right
    To come an' tell you to gang hame
I canna come to court the night
    Sae ye may gang the gate ye came"   40

"Provoking elf! Come ower the dike
    An' woo till daylight ope her ee"
"Na thank you lad. Befa' what like
    The wa shall stand 'tween you an' me
I thought it hard that you should sit   45
    An' fret a' night sae gruff an' glum
Sae I came ower on lightsome fit
    To tell you that I coudna come"

Outower the dike I lap I flew
    An' ere that she gat time to chide   50
I had her seated on the dew
    An' closely press'd unto my side
But O the tut's the taunts the scorn
    That I endured were hard to bear
Yet never till the break of morn   55
    Did she propose to leave me mair

This world has muckle grief an' gloom
    Atween the cradle an' the grave
Yet there are little fields of bloom
    So sweet the heart no more can crave   60
Some little tints of loveliness
    Beyond what angels can enjoy
Of youthful love they cannot guess
    Though their's is bliss without alloy

And there's a joy without a sting   65
    With a dear lassie by your side
A virtuous lovely loving thing
    Whom you intend to make your bride
It is a bliss befa' what may
    That makes man's happiness supreme   70
It winna sing it winna say
    'Tis sic a pure elysian dream

Maggy o' Buccleuch

By the Ettrick Shepherd

AIR –Days of Yore

O CAM' ye through the forests green,
    By Yarrow's mountains wild an blue;
O saw ye beauty's rural queen,
    The bonny Maggy o' Buccleuch!
For Maggy is the bonniest flower   5
    On Yarrow braes that ever grew,
That ever graced a vernal bower,
    Or frae the gowan brushed the dew.

But O! it's no her comely face,
    Nor blink o' joy that's in her ee,   10
Nor her enchanting form o' grace,
    That maks the lassie dear to me;
Na, na, it's no the cherry lip,
    The rosy cheek an lily chin,
Which the wild bee wad like to sip—   15
    'Tis the sweet soul that dwells within.

I hae been up the cauldrife north,
    'Mang hills an dells o' frozen brine,
As far as reels the rowin earth,
    An far ayont the burning line;   20
But a' the lasses e'er I saw,
    For modest mien an lovely hue,
There was na ane amang them a'
    Like bonny Maggy o' Buccleuch.

The Battle of the Boyne

By the Ettrick Shepherd

This random sketch alludes to the death of the Reverend George Walker, rector of Donnochmore, the hero who defended Londonderry, with a few half-starved militia, against the whole regular and well appointed army of King James, who lost ten thousand men in his fruitless attempt. Walker afterwards fell at the battle of the Boyne, near to King William's right hand. He was certainly a man unequalled in bravery and resolution, as every one who has read the account of that notable siege will admit. The hint concerning his tenets is taken from an account of his Life, in a pamphlet printed in Dublin in 1700.

SCENE—*A field of battle. Alarums in the distance. The Rev.* GEORGE WALKER *mortally wounded, supported by his son,* JOHN.

    John. My father, thou art dying. Turn thy thoughts
To that momentous change. Thy wound is mortal:
Thou know'st it, or shouldst know it. Yet thou seem'st
Blithe as a bridegroom on the tiptoe verge
Of Hope's dilated height, gazing enrapt   5
On the delirious joys so long deferred.
O my loved lord and father! let me say,
This gaiety ill suits the door of death.

Walker. What, John, art turned confessor? Thanks,
 good boy,
For this kind admonition. For my part,   10
I think not of my death, save as a speck
Of darkness mid a day of joyful light.
The victory's our's, boy! Think of that award!
Our brutal deadly enemies dispersed
Like chaff before the wind. Look but to that,   15
And what's an old man's life? The tyrant's arm
Is broke for ever. That cold-hearted bigot,
Who trampled on the necks of free-born men,
And gloried in their blood—where is he now?
Flying like traitor-coward, as he is,   20
From out his last red hold, like hunted fox,
Or ravening wolf. Boy, that man was a fiend,
Who o'er God's heritage long time hath shed
Death, pestilence, and famine, by his breath.
I've crossed him somewhat, playing my small part   25
To his confusion, and I yield my life
In the good cause with joy. What then is death?
One passing pang—no more—I leave yourself
And five bold brothers in my humble stead:
And I must be immortal here on earth   30
As well as in the heavens—if that, indeed,
There be such place for souls of mortal men—
Ay—if such thing as after-life there be—
There it is dark—well—I shall know it soon.
 John. My father, do I hear these doubtful words   35
From thy revered and consecrated lips,
Even in the view of Time's fast gaining shore
And ocean of Eternity beyond!
Thou doubt'st not of a glorious life hereafter!
It cannot be! Tell me thou rav'st through pain,   40
And ease my soul of this oppressive load.
 Walker. Why, John, I've thought, and thought, and
 preached, and prayed,
And doubted: thought, and preached, and prayed, again,
And all that I have reached is a resolve
To take my chance with others—and I'll do it!   45
I neither do believe nor disbelieve—
I DO NOT KNOW.
 John. To hear the champion of the cause of Christ

Speak thus amazes me. The man whose deeds
Make mankind stare and wonder! he who taught   50
The path of life through Jesus, till the young
Shed tears of love, and old men trembling leaned
Their heads upon their hands and inly groaned!
How's this, my father? I am all amazement!
    Walker. Boy, pester me no farther, for my time   55
Draws near a close. I taught the way through Christ,
Because no other surely led to peace,
To virtue, and to happiness on earth,
Which must to everlasting glory lead,
If such the lot of erring man can be.   60
But when I 'thought me of the human millions
Swept off by famine, pestilence, and sword,
From Adam down to this—the serf, the savage,
The infidel, the sage—men of all casts,
Tenets, beliefs, strewed o'er the world's wide face,   65
From age to age, like carrion—why, I doubted;
Though zealous to believe, I doubted sore.
Don't teaze me, boy! I cannot help it now!
In his infinite mercy who created
This frame and all its energies I trust.   70
Farewell! A darkness settles o'er the field—
God shield King William! Round his sacred head
And his good consort's may the grace of Heaven
Be shed abundantly! Boy, where's thy hand?
Pray let me feel it: kneel beside me here,   75
And pray for me—I love to hear thy voice—
It sounds like a renewal of my own,
And of my young belief—Oh, it is sweet!
   John. (Kneeling and bowing over his father.) O thou
      Almighty Father, who presid'st
O'er all the destinies of mortal men,   80
Look here in pity! on thy servant look!
Who, bathed in blood, stood in the breach for thee,
And the pure renovation of thy church,
When those in office basely turned their backs,
And now lays down his life in that great cause!   85
One look of mercy, gracious God, bestow!
For though thy throne of glory's in the heavens,
In light ineffable, yet thou art here,
Surveying this red field, and taking note

Of all who fought and bled for right or wrong,   90
Their motives and advisement. God of mercy!
While the benevolent spirit of my father
With frail humanity holds intercourse,
Open his eyes to view the only path
From earth to heaven, through that mystic bond   95
Which never can be cancelled—God with man!
Before his soul pass o'er that awful bourn
From whence there's no revert, no disannulment
Of bygone edicts, O unseal the valves
Laid open to the walks of grace and glory   100
By forfeiture divine, by deodand,
Which men or angels could not comprehend!
Sun of the soul! bright polar star of hope!
And prostrate human nature's adoration!
What would creation be without thy light!   105
What would the heaven and all its treasures be,
Its blest society, euphonies, and joys,
Without *thy* glories, O Redeeming Love!
    And what eternity? Ah! there the soul,
Standing on reason's farthest, loftiest verge,   110
And gazing onward o'er a gulf profound,
Quakes at the dim perspective—darkness there
Brooding for ever—ages after ages
In millions of blue billows rolling on
Far, far away, into the void obscure,   115
Unfathomed by the darkling soul's proud scale,
By plummet or by line!
    Where shall the trembling spirit turn? Where fly?
Ah, the retreat is palpable and near!
To thy most blessed word, thou God of truth,   120
Where life and immortality appear
Blazoned in living light. Unto that spring,
Opened in David's house, O lead my father,
To bathe in light divine, and pass to thee
Believing and rejoicing!
                He is gone!   125
That ardent noble spirit, who ne'er knew
Dissimulation, interest, or alarm
At aught save at dishonour! Brave, brave father,
And kind as brave!—my model thou shalt be
In all my perils through this world below!   130

Scottish Haymakers

By the Ettrick Shepherd

THERE is no employment in Scotland so sweet as working in a hay-field on a fine summer day. Indeed it is only on a fine summer day that the youths and maidens of this northern clime can work at the hay. But then the scent of the new hay, which of all others in the world is the most delicious and healthful, the handsome dress of the girls, which is uniformly the same, consisting of a snow-white bedgown and white or red striped petticoat, the dress that Wilkie is so fond of, and certainly the most lovely and becoming dress that ever was or ever will be worn by woman; and then the rosy flush of healthful exercise on the cheeks of the maidens, with their merry jibes and smiles of innocent delight! Well do I know, from long and well tried experience, that it is impossible for any man with the true feelings of a man to work with them or even to stand and look on—both of which I have done a thousand times, first as a servant, and afterwards as a master—I say it is impossible to be among them and not to be in love with some one or other of them.

But this simple prologue was merely meant to introduce a singular adventure I met with a good many years ago. Mr. Terry, the player, his father and brother-in-law, the two celebrated Naesmiths, and some others, among whom was Monsieur Alexandre, the most wonderful ventriloquist that I believe ever was born, and I think Grieve and Scott, but at this distance of time I am uncertain, were of the party. However, we met by appointment; and, as the weather was remarkably fine, agreed to take a walk into the country and dine at "The Hunter's Tryste," a little, neat, cleanly, well-kept inn, about two miles to the southward of Edinburgh. We left the city by the hills of Braid, and there went into a hay-field. The scene certainly was quite delightful, what with the scent of the hay, the beauty of the day, and the rural group of haymakers. Some were working hard, some wooing, and some towzling as we call it, when Alexander Naesmith, who was always on the look-out for any striking scene of nature, called to his son—"Come here, Peter, and look at this scene. Did you ever see aught equal to this? Look at those happy haymakers on the foreground; that fine old ash tree and the castle between us and the clear blue sky. I declare I have hardly ever seen such a landscape! And if you had not been a perfect stump as you are, you would have noticed it before me. If you had I would have set ten times more value on it."

W. Adde. pinx.t

Pub.d by Ackermann & C.o London.

Jn.o Wr.ht scultp.

"Oh! I saw it well enough," said Peter, "and have been taking a peep at it this while past, but I hae some other thing to think of and look at just now. Do you see that girl standing there with the hay-rake in her hand?"

"Ay now, Peter, that's some sense," said the veteran artist. "I excuse you for not looking at the scene I was sketching. Do you know, man, that is the only sensible speech I ever heard you make in my life."

There were three men and a very handsome girl loading an immense cart of hay. We walked on, and at length this moving haystack overtook us. I remember it well, with a black horse in the shafts and a fine light grey one in the traces. We made very slow progress; for Naesmith would never cease either sketching or stopping us to admire the scenery of nature, and I remember he made a remark to me that day which I think neither he nor his most ingenious son, now no more, ever attended much to; for they have often drawn most extensive vistas the truest to nature of any thing I ever saw in my uncultivated judgment, which can only discern what is accordant with nature by looking on nature itself: but, if a hundred years hence the pictures of the Naesmiths are not held invaluable, I am no judge of true natural scenery. But I have forgot myself. The remark that he made to me was this: "It is amazing how little makes a good picture; and frequently the less that is taken in the better." Some of the ladies of the family seem to have improved greatly on this hint.

But to return to my story. We made such slow progress on account of Naesmith, that up came the great cart-load of hay on one side of us, with a great burly Lothian peasant sitting upon the hay, lashing on his team, and whistling his tune. We walked on, side by side, for a while, I think about half a mile, when, all at once, a child began to cry in the middle of the cart-load of hay. I declare I was cheated myself; for, though I was walking alongside of Alexandre, I thought there was a child among the hay; for it cried with a kind of half smothered breath, that I am sure there never was such a deception practised in this world. Peter Naesmith was leaning on the cart-shaft at the time, and conversing with the driver about the beautiful girl he had seen in the hay-field. But Peter was rather deaf, and, not hearing the screaming of the child, looked up in astonishment, when the driver of the cart began to stare around him like a man bereaved of his senses.

"What is the meaning of this?" said Terry. "You are smothering a child among your hay."

The poor fellow, rough and burly as was his outer man, was so much appalled at the idea of taking infant life, that he exclaimed in a half-articulate voice: "I wonder how they could fork a bairn up to me frae the meadow, an' me never ken!" And without taking time to descend to loose his cart-ropes, he cut them through the middle, and turned off his hay, roll after roll, with the utmost expedition; and still the child kept crying almost under his hands and feet. He was even obliged to set his feet on each side of the cart for fear of trampling the poor infant to death. At length, when he had turned the greater part of the hay off upon the road, the child fell a-crying most bitterly amongst the hay, on which the poor fellow, (his name was Sandy Burnet), jumped off the cart in the greatest trepidation. "Od! I hae thrawn the poor thing ower!" exclaimed he. "I's warrant it's killed"—and he began to shake out the hay with the greatest caution. I and one of my companions went forward to assist him. "Stand back! stand back!" cried he. "Ye'll maybe tramp its life out. I'll look for't mysel'." But, after he had shaken out the whole of the hay, no child was to be found. I never saw looks of such amazement as Sandy Burnet's then were. He seemed to have lost all comprehension of every thing in this world. I was obliged myself to go on to the brow of the hill and call on some of the haymakers to come and load the cart again.

Mr. Scott and I stripped off our coats, and assisted; and, as we were busy loading the cart, I said to Sandy, seeing him always turning the hay over and over for fear of running the fork through a child, "What can hae become o' the creature, Sandy?—for you must be sensible that there was a bairn among this hay."

"The Lord kens, sir," said Sandy.

"Think ye the lasses are a' safe enough an' to be trusted?" said I.

"For ony thing that I ken, sir."

"Then where could the bairn come frae?"

"The Lord kens, sir. That there was a bairn, or the semblance o' ane, naebody can doubt; but I'm thinking it was a fairy, an' that I'm hauntit."

"Did you ever murder any bairns, Sandy?"

"Oh no! I wadna murder a bairn for the hale world."

"But were ye ever the cause o' any lasses murdering their bairns?"

"Not that I ken o'."

"Then where could the bairn come frae?—for you are sensible that there is or was a bairn amang your hay. It is rather a bad-looking job, Sandy, and I wish you were quit of it."

"I wish the same, sir. But there can be nae doubt that the creature among the hay was either a fairy or the ghaist of a bairn, for the hay was a' forkit off the swathe on the meadow. An' how could ony body fork up a bairn, an' neither him nor me ken?"

We got the cart loaded once more, knitted the ropes firmly, and set out; but we had not proceeded a hundred yards before the child fell a-crying again among the hay with more vehemence and with more choaking screams than ever. "Gudeness have a care o' us! Heard ever ony leevin the like o' that! I declare the creature's there again!" cried Sandy, and, flinging himself from the cart with a summerset, he ran off, and never once looked over his shoulder as long as he was in our sight. We were very sorry to hear afterwards that he fled all the way to the highlands of Perthshire, where he still lives in a deranged state of mind.

We dined at "The Hunter's Tryste," and spent the afternoon in hilarity: but such a night of fun as Monsieur Alexandre made us I never witnessed and never shall again. On the stage, where I had often seen him, his powers were extraordinary, and altogether un-equalled; that was allowed by every one: but the effect there was not to be compared with that which he produced in a private party. The family at the inn consisted of the landlord, his wife, and her daughter, who was the landlord's step-daughter, a very pretty girl, and dressed like a lady; but, I am sure that family never spent an afternoon of such astonishment and terror from the day they were united until death parted them—though they may be all living yet, for any thing that I know, for I have never been there since. But Alexandre made people of all ages and sexes speak from every part of the house, from under the beds, from the basin-stands, and from the garret, where a dreadful quarrel took place. And then he placed a bottle on the top of the clock, and made a child scream out of it, and declare that the mistress had corked it in there to murder it. The young lady ran, opened the bottle, and looked into it, and then, losing all power with amazement, she let it fall from her hand and smashed it to pieces. He made a bee buz round my head and face until I struck at it several times and had nearly felled myself. Then there was a drunken man came to the door, and insisted in a rough obstreperous manner on being let in to shoot Mr. Hogg; on which the landlord ran to the door and bolted it, and ordered the man to go about his business for there was no room in the house, and there he should not enter on any account. We all heard the voice of the man going round and round the house, grumbling, swearing, and threatening, and all the while Alexandre was just standing with his back to us at the room-door, always holding his hand to his mouth, but nothing else. The people ran to the windows to see the drunken man going by, and Miss Jane even ventured to the corner of the house to look after him; but neither drunken man nor any other man was to be seen. At length, on calling her in to serve us with some wine and toddy, we heard the drunken man's voice coming in at the top of the chimney. Such a state of amazement as Jane was in I never beheld. "But ye neednae be feared, gentlemen," said she, "for I'll defy him to win down. The door's boltit an' lockit, an' the vent o' the lumb is na sae wide as that jug."

However, down he came, and down he came, until his voice actually seemed to be coming out of the grate. Jane ran for it, saying, "He is winning down, I believe, after a'. He is surely the deil!"

Alexandre went to the chimney, and, in his own natural voice ordered the fellow to go about his business, for into our party he should not be admitted, and if he forced himself in he would shoot him through the heart. The voice then went again grumbling and swearing up the chimney. We actually heard him hurling down over the slates, and afterwards his voice dying away in the distance as he vanished into Mr. Trotter's plantations. We drank freely, and paid liberally, that afternoon; but I am sure the family never were so glad to get quit of a party in all their lives.

To prove the authenticity of this story, I may just mention that Peter Naesmith and Alexandre ran a race in going home for half a dozen of wine, and, it being down hill, Peter fell and hurt his breast very badly. I have been told that that fall ultimately occasioned his death. I hope it was not so; for, though a perfect simpleton, he was a great man in his art.

The Lord of Balloch

By the Ettrick Shepherd

The eagle has left his eiry stern,
On shaggy Nevis dark and dern;
He sailed high over the Laggan loch,
And down by the braes of Badenoch;
Then eastward, eastward, sped his way,   5
Far over the lovely links of Spey;
Till the Lord of Balloch turned his eye
To the haughty journeyer of the sky;

And he said to his henchman, Gil-na-omb,
"What brings yon eagle so far from home?"   10

Then Gillian watched his lord's dark eye,
And his voice it faltered in reply,
While he said—"My lord, who needs to care
For the way of the eagle in the air?
Perhaps he is watching Lochdorbin's men,   15
Or the track of the Gordons of the glen;
For he spies, from his stories of the wind,
That the dead are often left behind;
Or haply he knows in our forest bounds
Of some noble stag dead of his wounds."   20

"Go saddle my steed without delay!
I have marked yon eagle, day by day,
Still hovering over yon lonely dell;
There's a dread on my soul which I dare not tell.
Gillian—no mystery may I brook—   25
I like not your suspicious look;
And have noted your absence from my hand,
More than I approve or understand;
Say—have you heard no word at all
Of some one missed from her father's hall?"   30

"No, my good lord—no, not one word,
As I shall be sworn upon my sword!
And why should the eagle's yelling din
Awake suspicions your heart within?"

That lord he mounted his gallant steed,   35
But at his henchman he shook his head,
And gave him a look, as bounding away,
That filled his heart with black dismay;
So he fled to hide in the bosky burn,
For he durst not wait his lord's return.   40

The Lord of Balloch away is gone,
With beating heart, to the wild alone;
For in the dead of night he had dreamed
Of that dell o'er which the eagle screamed,
And there with the eyes of his soul had seen   45

A vision of terror and of teen;
And something whispered his mind oppressed
Of a deed that could never be redressed;
For there are spirits all scenes that scan,
And whisper them to the soul of man.   50

The eagle he sailed upon the cloud,
And he spread his wings and screamed aloud;
He durst not alight in the lonely dell,
But his rage made all the echoes yell;
For he saw the blood below his feet,   55
And he saw it red, and he knew it sweet;
Yet, though death was lovely to his eye,
The silken tartans sailed too nigh.

The Lord of Balloch rode on and on,
With a heavy gloom his heart upon;   60
Till his steed began to show demur,
For he snorted and refused the spur;
And, or for coaxing or for blow,
Further one step he would not go;
He reared aloft and he shook with fear,   65
And his snortings were terrible to hear.
The gallant steed is left behind,
And the chief proceeds with troubled mind.

But short way had that good lord gone,
Ere his heart was turned into a stone;   70
It was not for nought that the steed rebelled,
It was not for nought that the eagle yelled,
It was not for nought that the spirits of night
Presented that lord with a grievous sight,
A sight of misery and despair—   75
But I dare not tell what he found there.
For the hearts of the old would withhold belief,
And the hearts of the young would bleed with grief,
Till the very fountains of life ran dry;
Sweet sleep would forsake the virgin's eye;   80
And man, whose love she had learned to prize,
Would appear a monster in disguise,
A thing of cursed, unhallowed birth,
Unfit to reign on his Maker's earth;
The very flowers of the wildered dell   85

Would blush were I that tale to tell;
It may not be heard, it may not be sung,
It may not be lisped by a human tongue.

Ah, the clan of Lochdorbin for ever may rue
That the dream of that lord should prove so true;   90
For twenty serfs of that cursed dome,
And at their head the base Gil-na-omb,
Were hung by the neck around that dell,
To bleach in the snows and rains that fell:
A lesson to men of each degree   95
How sacred the virgin's form should be.
As for Lochdorbin's brutal chief,
He was pinioned like a common thief,
And cast into a dungeon deep,
Below the Balloch castle-keep;   100
To pine to death, there not the first,
Who had died of hunger and of thirst.
On his own flesh he strove to dine,
And to drink his blood instead of wine;
Then groaned his sickened soul away,   105
Cursing the Lord of Balloch's sway.

He is gone, extinct, and well away,
His castle a ruin unto this day;
That strength unequalled in the North,
Which has puzzled the sages of the earth;*   110
And neither shepherd nor hind can tell
The name of the chief that there did dwell;
But the abhorrence of his crime
Will never abate till the end of time.
Now all that remains of that cruel beast,   115
Who laid the Buchan and Bogie waste,
Are some shreds of bones 'neath the Balloch keep,
Still kicked about in that donjon deep,
Or haply some films of dust unshrined,
Whirled on the eddies of the wind.   120
So perish all, without remede,
That dare such vile and cruel deed!

* This magnificent and amazing castle is in the parish of Cromdale, on the Spey.

The Anniversary

The Carle of Invertime

By the Author of The Queen's Wake

Who has not heard of a Carle uncouth,
The terror of age, and the scorn of youth;
Well known in this and every clime
As the grim Gudeman of Invertime;
A stern old porter who carries the key 5
That opens the gate to a strange countree?

The Carle's old heart with joy is dancing
When down the valley he sees advancing
The lovely, the brave, the good, or the great,
To pay the sad toll of his darksome gate. 10
'Tis said nought gives such joy to him
As the freezing blood and the stiffening limb;
It has never been mine his house to scan,
So I scarce trow this of our grim Gudeman.

Wise men believe, yet I scarce know why, 15
That he grimly smiles as he shoves them by;
And cares not whither to isles of bliss
They go—or to sorrow's dark wilderness;
Or driven afar, their fate should be
To toss on the waves of a shoreless sea; 20
Or sunk in lakes of surging flame,
Burning and boiling and ever the same:
Where groups of mortals toss amain
On the sultry billow and down again.
Time from the sky shall blot out the sun, 25
Yet ne'er with this den of dool have done.
It makes me shake and it makes me shiver,
His presence forbid it should last for ever!

Sad, wise, or witty—all find to their cost
That the grim old Carle is still at his post. 30
He sits and he sees, with joy elate,
In myriads, men pour in at his gate.
Some come in gladness and joy, to close
Account with Time and sink to repose;

Some come in sorrow, they think in sooth   35
It hard to be summoned in strength and youth.
There lady and losel,—peasant and lord,
Men of the pen, the sermon, the sword;
The counsellor, leach, and the monarch sublime,
All come to the Carle of Invertime.   40

    Amongst the others, one morning came
An aged and a venerable Dame,
Stooping and palsied and pained to boot,
Moaning, and shaking from head to foot.
Slow in her pace, yet steady of mind,   45
She turned not once, nor looked behind;
Nor dreading nor daring her future fate,
She tottered along to the dismal gate.

    A gleam of light glanced in the eye
Of the grim Gudeman as the dame drew nigh;   50
Little cared he for an old gray wife,
Who hung like a link 'tween death and life;
But by the side of the eldern dame,
A Form so pure and so lovely came,
That the Carle's cold veinless heart heaved high,   55
A tear like an ice-drop came to his eye;
He vowed through his gate she should not win,
She seemed no child of sorrow and sin.
As thus he stood in his porch to mark,
His looks now light and his looks now dark,   60
He marvelled to hear so lovely a thing
Lift up her voice and gently sing
A strain, too holy, too sweet, and wild
And charming to come from an earthborn child;
It glowed with love and fervour and faith,   65
And seemed to triumph o'er time and death.

    "Great Fountain of Light, and Spirit of Might,
To work thy will has been my delight;
And here at my knee, from guiltiness free,
I bring a mild meek spirit to thee.   70
When first I went to guide her to truth,
She was in the opening blossom of youth;
When scarce on her leaf, so spotless and new,

Ripe reason had come with her dropping dew.
Where life's pure river is but a rill   75
She grew and scarce knew good from ill;
But my sisters three came soon to me,
Pure Love, true Faith, sweet Charity.
Through doubts and fears, these eighty years,
We have showed her the way to the heavenly spheres. 80
Our first stage down life's infant stream
Was all a maze and a childish dream;
And nought was there of sin or sense
But dawning beauty and innocence:
A fairy dance of sweet delight,   85
Through flowers and bowers and visions bright.
Sometimes a hymn and sometimes a prayer,
Was poured to Thee with a fervent air;
'Twas sung or said, and straight was seen
The sweet child gamboling on the green;   90
While the pure hymn, late poured to thee,
Was chanted light as a song of glee.

   "As we went down the vale of life,
With flowers the road became less rife.
By pitfall, precipice, and pool,   95
Our way was shaped by line and rule.
'Mid hours of joy and days of mirth,
And hopes and fears, high thoughts had birth,
And natural yearnings of the mind,
Of something onward undefined—   100
Which scarce the trembling soul durst scan,
Of God's most wondrous love to man—
And some far forward state of bliss,
Of beauty and of holiness;
But to all woes and evils blinded,   105
Or thoughts of death, unless reminded.
O! happy age, remembered well,
Where neither sin nor shame can dwell.
Even then thine eye, from heaven high,
Saw that her monitor was nigh;   110
At morn and even, to turn to heaven
The grateful eye, for blessings given.
And from the first prevailing tide
Of sin, and vanity and pride,

To save her, and to lead her on   115
To glories unrevealed, unknown.

"Onward we came; life's streamlet then
Entered a green and odorous glen;
Increased, and through fair flowerets rolling,
And shady bowers, seemed past controlling;   120
Flowing, 'mid roses, fast and free—
This was a trying stage for me;
The maiden's youthful heart began
To dance through scenes elysian.
To breathe in Love's ambrosial dew,   125
Moved by sensations sweet and new;
For without look or word of blame,
Her radiant blushes went and came;
Her eye, of heaven's own azure blue,
In glance and lustre brighter grew: 130
Showing fond feelings all akin
To that pure soul which lived within.

"With heart so soft and soul sincere,
Love found his way by eye and ear.
Then how I laboured, day and night,   135
To watch her ways and guide her right.
I brought cool airs from paradise
To purify her melting sighs.
I steeped my veil in heaven's own spring
And o'er her watched on silent wing;   140
And when she laid her down to rest,
I spread the veil o'er her virgin breast:
All earthly passions far did flee,
And heart and soul she turned to thee.
Throughout her life of wedded wife,   145
I weaned her soul from passion's strife;
But Oh! what fears and frequent tears
For the peril of childhood's tender years!
And when her firstborn's feeble moan
Was hushed by the soul's departing groan;   150
In that hour of maternal grief,
I pointed her way to the sole relief.
Another sweet babe there came and went—
Her gushing eyes she fixed and bent

Upon that mansion bright and sweet,   155
Where severed and kindred spirits meet.

    "She has wept for the living, and wept for the dead,
Laid low in the grave her husband's head.
She has toiled for bread with the hands of age,
And through her useful pilgrimage,   160
Has seen her race sink one by one—
All, all she loved—yet left and lone,
With cheer unchanged, with heart unshook,
On God she fixed her steadfast look.
And now with the eye of purest faith,   165
She sees beyond the vale of death,
A day that has no cloud or shower—
She has less dread of her parting hour,
Than ever had babe of its mother's breast,
When it lays its innocent head to rest.   170
Oh! Maker of Earth, dread Ruler above,
Receive her spirit, her faith approve—
A tenderer mother, a nobler wife,
Ne'er waged, 'gainst earth and its sorrows, strife;
I never can bid a form arise   175
With purer heart than her's to the skies."

    The Carle was moved with holy fear,
That lovely seraph's sweet song to hear;
He turned away and he covered his head,
For over him fell a visible dread.   180
While she gave her form to the breeze away,
That came from the vales of immortal day;
And sung her hymns far over the same,
And heavenly HOPE was the seraph's name:
The guide to a land of rest and bliss,   185
To a sinless world—how unlike this.

    To earth's blest pilgrim, old and gray,
The gate dissolved like a cloud away;
And the grim old Carle he veiled his face,
As she passed him by with a holy pace;   190
With a touch of his hand and a whisper mild,
He soothed her heart as one stills a child.
The song of faith she faintly sung,
And God's dread name was last on her tongue.

Now from the pall, bright and sublime,   195
That hangs o'er the uttermost skirts of Time,
Came righteous souls and shapes more bright,
Clothed in glory and walking in light;
Majestic beings of earthly frame,
And of heavenly radiance over the same,   200
To welcome the Pilgrim of this gross clime,
They had come from Eternity back to Time—
And they sung, while they wafted her on the road,
"Come, righteous creature, and dwell with God."

The Cameronian Preacher's Tale

By the Author of The Queen's Wake

SIT near me, my children, and come nigh, all ye who are not of my
kindred, though of my flock; for my days and hours are numbered;
death is with me dealing, and I have a sad and a wonderful story to
relate. I have preached and ye have profited; but what I am about to
say is far better than man's preaching, it is one of those terrible
sermons which God preaches to mankind, of blood unrighteously
shed, and most wondrously avenged. The like has not happened in
these our latter days. His presence is visible in it; and I reveal it that
its burthen may be removed from my soul, so that I may die in
peace; and I disclose it, that you may lay it up in your hearts and tell
it soberly to your children, that the warning memory of a dispensa-
tion so marvellous may live and not perish. Of the deed itself, some
of you have heard a whispering; and some of you know the men of
whom I am about to speak; but the mystery which covers them up
as with a cloud I shall remove; listen, therefore, my children, to a
tale of truth, and may you profit by it!

On Dryfe Water, in Annandale, lived Walter Johnstone, a man
open hearted and kindly, but proud withal and warm tempered;
and on the same water lived John Macmillan, a man of a nature
grasping and sordid, and as proud and hot tempered as the other.
They were strong men, and vain of their strength; lovers of pleasant
company, well to live in the world, extensive dealers in corn and
cattle; married too, and both of the same age—five and forty years.
They often met, yet they were not friends; nor yet were they companions, for bargain making and money seeking narroweth the heart

and shuts up generosity of soul. They were jealous, too, of one another's success in trade, and of the fame they had each acquired for feats of personal strength and agility, and skill with the sword—a weapon which all men carried, in my youth, who were above the condition of a peasant. Their mutual and growing dislike was inflamed by the whisperings of evil friends, and confirmed by the skilful manner in which they negotiated bargains over each other's heads. When they met, a short and surly greeting was exchanged, and those who knew their natures looked for a meeting between them, when the sword or some other dangerous weapon would settle for ever their claims for precedence in cunning and in strength.

They met at the fair of Longtown, and spoke, and no more—with them both it was a busy day, and mutual hatred subsided for a time, in the love of turning the penny and amassing gain. The market rose and fell, and fell and rose; and it was whispered that Macmillan, through the superior skill or good fortune of his rival, had missed some bargains which were very valuable, while some positive losses touched a nature extremely sensible of the importance of wealth. One was elated and the other depressed—but not more depressed than moody and incensed, and in this temper they were seen in the evening in the back room of a public inn, seated apart and silent, calculating losses and gains, drinking deeply, and exchanging dark looks of hatred and distrust. They had been observed, during the whole day, to watch each other's movements, and now when they were met face to face, the labours of the day over, and their natures inflamed by liquor as well as by hatred, their companions looked for personal strife between them, and wondered not a little when they saw Johnstone rise, mount his horse, and ride homewards, leaving his rival in Longtown. Soon afterwards Macmillan started up from a moody fit, drank off a large draught of brandy, threw down a half-guinea, nor waited for change—a thing uncommon with him; and men said, as his horse's feet struck fire from the pavement, that if he overtook Johnstone, there would be a living soul less in the land before sunrise.

Before sunrise next morning the horse of Walter Johnstone came with an empty saddle to his stable door. The bridle was trampled to pieces amongst its feet, and its saddle and sides were splashed over with blood as if a bleeding body had been carried across its back. The cry arose in the country, an instant search was made, and on the side of the public road was found a place where a deadly contest seemed to have happened. It was in a small green field, bordered by a wood, in the farm of Andrew Pattison. The sod was dinted deep with men's feet, and trodden down and trampled and sprinkled over with blood as thickly as it had ever been with dew. Blood drops, too, were traced to some distance, but nothing more was discovered; the body could not be found, though every field was examined and every pool dragged. His money and bills, to the amount of several thousand pounds, were gone, so was his sword—indeed nothing of him could be found on earth save his blood, and for its spilling a strict account was yet to be sought.

Suspicion instantly and naturally fell on John Macmillan, who denied all knowledge of the deed. He had arrived at his own house in due course of time, no marks of weapon or warfare were on him, he performed family worship as was his custom, and he sang the psalm as loudly and prayed as fervently as he was in the habit of doing. He was apprehended and tried, and saved by the contradictory testimony of the witnesses against him, into whose hearts the spirit of falsehood seemed to have entered in order to perplex and confound the judgment of men—or rather that man might have no hand in the punishment, but that God should bring it about in his own good time and way. "Revenge is mine, saith the Lord," which meaneth not because it is too sweet a morsel for man, as the scoffer said, but because it is too dangerous. A glance over this conflicting testimony will show how little was then known of this foul offence, and how that little was rendered doubtful and dark by the imperfections of human nature.

Two men of Longtown were examined. One said that he saw Macmillan insulting and menacing Johnstone, laying his hand on the hilt of his sword with a look dark and ominous; while the other swore that he was present at the time, but that it was Johnstone who insulted and menaced Macmillan, and laid his hand on the hilt of his sword and pointed to the road homewards. A very expert and searching examination could make no more of them; they were both respectable men with characters above suspicion. The next witnesses were of another stamp, and their testimony was circuitous and contradictory. One of them was a shepherd—a reluctant witness. His words were these: "I was frae hame on the night of the murder, in the thick of the wood, no just at the place which was bloody and trampled, but gaye and near hand it. I canna say I can just mind what I was doing; I had somebody to see I jalouse, but wha it was is naebody's business but my ain. There was maybe ane forbye myself in the wood, and maybe twa; there was ane at ony rate, and I am no sure but it was an auld acquaintance. I see nae use there can be in questioning me. I saw nought, and therefore can say nought. I canna but say that I heard something—the trampling of horses, and a rough voice saying, 'Draw and defend yourself.' Then followed the clashing of swords and half smothered sort of work, and then the sound of horses' feet was heard again, and that's a' I ken about it; only I thought the voice was Walter Johnstone's, and so thought Kate Pennie, who was with me and kens as meikle as me." The examination of Katherine Pennie, one of the Pennies of Pennieland, followed, and she declared that she had heard the evidence of Dick Purdie with surprise and anger. On that night she was not over the step of her father's door for more than five minutes, and that was to look at the sheep in the fauld; and she neither heard the clashing of swords nor the word of man or woman. And with respect to Dick Purdie, she scarcely knew him even by sight; and if all tales were true that were told of him, she would not venture into a lonely wood with him, under the cloud of night, for a gown of silk with pearls on each sleeve. The shepherd, when recalled, admitted that Kate Pennie might be right, "For after a'," said he, "it happened in the dark, when a man like me, no that gleg of the uptauk, might confound persons. Somebody was with me, I am gaye and sure, frae what took place— if it was nae Kate, I kenna wha it was, and it couldna weel be Kate either, for Kate's a douce quean, and besides is married." The judge dismissed the witnesses with some indignant words, and, turning to the prisoner, said, "John Macmillan, the prevarications of these witnesses have saved you; mark my words—saved you from man, but not from God. On the murderer, the Most High will lay his hot right hand, visibly and before men, that we may know that blood unjustly shed will be avenged. You are at liberty to depart." He left the bar and resumed his station and his pursuits as usual; nor did he appear sensible to the feeling of the country, which was strong against him.

A year passed over his head, other events happened, and the murder of Walter Johnstone began to be dismissed from men's minds. Macmillan went to the fair of Longtown, and when evening came he was seated in the little back room which I mentioned before, and in company with two men of the names of Hunter and Hope. He sat late, drank deeply, but in the midst of the carousal a knock was heard at the door, and a voice called sharply, "John Macmillan." He started up, seemed alarmed, and exclaimed, "What in Heaven's name can *he* want with me?" and opening the door hastily, went into the garden, for he seemed to dread another summons lest his companions should know the voice. As soon as he was gone, one said to the other, "If that was not the voice of Walter Johnstone, I never heard it in my life; he is either come back in the flesh or in the spirit, and in either way John Macmillan has good cause to dread him." They listened—they heard Macmillan speaking in great agitation; he was answered only by a low sound, yet he appeared to understand what was said, for his concluding words were, "Never! never! I shall rather submit to His judgment who cannot err." When he returned he was pale and shaking, and he sat down and seemed buried in thought. He spread his palms on his knees, shook his head often, then, starting up, said, "The judge was a fool and no prophet—to mortal man is not given the wisdom of God—so neighbours let us ride." They mounted their horses and rode homewards into Scotland at a brisk pace.

The night was pleasant, neither light nor dark; there were few travellers out, and the way winded with the hills and with the streams, passing through a pastoral and beautiful country. Macmillan rode close by the side of his companions, closer than was desirable or common; yet he did not speak, nor make answer when he was spoken to; but looked keenly and earnestly before and behind him, as if he expected the coming of some one, and every tree and bush seemed to alarm and startle him. Day at last dawned, and with the growing light his alarm subsided, and he began to converse with his companions, and talk with a levity which surprised them more than his silence had done before. The sun was all but risen when they approached the farm of Andrew Pattison, and here and there the top of a high tree and the summit of a hill had caught light upon them. Hope looked to Hunter silently, when they came nigh the bloody spot where it was believed the murder had been committed. Macmillan sat looking resolutely before him, as if determined not to look upon it; but his horse stopt at once, trembled violently, and then sprung aside, hurling its rider headlong to the ground. All this passed in a moment; his companions sat astonished; the horse rushed forward, leaving him on the ground, from whence he never rose in life, for his neck was broken by the fall, and with a convulsive shiver or two he expired. Then did the prediction of the judge, the warning voice and summons of the preceding night, and the spot and the time, rush upon their recollection; and they firmly believed that a murderer and robber lay dead beside them. "His horse saw something," said Hope to Hunter; "I never saw such flashing eyes in a horse's head;"—"and *he* saw something too," replied Hunter, "for the glance that he gave to the bloody spot, when his horse started, was one of terror. I never saw such a look, and I wish never to see such another again."

When John Macmillan perished, matters stood thus with his

memory. It was not only loaded with the sin of blood and the sin of robbery, with the sin of making a faithful woman a widow and her children fatherless, but with the grievous sin also of having driven a worthy family to ruin and beggary. The sum which was lost was large, the creditors were merciless; they fell upon the remaining substance of Johnstone, sweeping it wholly away; and his widow sought shelter in a miserable cottage among the Dryfesdale hills, where she supported her children by gathering and spinning wool. In a far different state and condition remained the family of John Macmillan. He died rich and unincumbered, leaving an evil name and an only child, a daughter, wedded to one whom many knew and esteemed, Joseph Howatson by name, a man sober and sedate; a member, too, of our own broken remnant of Cameronians.

Now, my dear children, the person who addresses you was then, as he is yet, God's preacher for the scattered kirk of Scotland, and his tent was pitched among the green hills of Annandale. The death of the transgressor appeared unto me the manifest judgment of God, and when my people gathered around me I rejoiced to see so great a multitude, and, standing in the midst of them, I preached in such a wise that they were deeply moved. I took for my text these words, "Hath there been evil in the land and the Lord hath not known it?" I discoursed on the wisdom of Providence in guiding the affairs of men. How he permitted our evil passions to acquire the mastery over us, and urge us to deeds of darkness; allowing us to flourish for a season, that he might strike us in the midst of our splendour in a way so visible and awful that the wildest would cry out, "Behold the finger of God." I argued the matter home to the heart; I named no names, but I saw Joseph Howatson hide his face in his hands, for he felt and saw from the eyes which were turned towards him that I alluded to the judgment of God upon his relative.

Joseph Howatson went home heavy and sad of heart, and somewhat touched with anger at God's servant for having so pointedly and publicly alluded to his family misfortune; for he believed his father-in-law was a wise and a worthy man. His way home lay along the banks of a winding and beautiful stream, and just where it entered his own lands there was a rustic gate, over which he leaned for a little space, ruminating upon earlier days, on his wedded wife, on his children, and finally his thoughts settled on his father-in-law. He thought of his kindness to himself and to many others, on his fulfilment of all domestic duties, on his constant performance of family worship, and on his general reputation for honesty and fair dealing. He then dwelt on the circumstances of Johnstone's disappearance, on the singular summons his father-in-law received in Longtown, and the catastrophe which followed on the spot and on the very day of the year that the murder was supposed to be committed. He was in sore perplexity, and said aloud, "Would to God that I knew the truth; but the doors of eternity, alas! are shut on the secret for ever." He looked up and John Macmillan stood before him—stood with all the calmness and serenity and meditative air which a grave man wears when he walks out on a sabbath eve.

"Joseph Howatson," said the apparition, "on no secret are the doors of eternity shut—of whom were you speaking?" "I was speaking," answered he, "of one who is cold and dead, and to whom you bear a strong resemblance." "I am he," said the shape; "I am John Macmillan." "God of heaven!" replied Joseph Howatson, "how can that be; did I not lay his head in the grave; see it closed over him; how, therefore, can it be? Heaven permits no such visitations." "I entreat you, my son," said the shape, "to believe what I say; the end of man is not when his body goes to dust; he exists in another state, and from that state am I permitted to come to you; waste not time, which is brief, with vain doubts, I am John Macmillan." "Father, father," said the young man, deeply agitated, "answer me, did you kill and rob Walter Johnstone?" "I did," said the Spirit, "and for that have I returned to earth; listen to me." The young man was so much overpowered by a revelation thus fearfully made, that he fell insensible on the ground; and when he recovered, the moon was shining, the dews of night were upon him, and he was alone.

Joseph Howatson imagined that he had dreamed a fearful dream; and conceiving that Divine Providence had presented the truth to his fancy, he began to consider how he could secretly make reparation to the wife and children of Johnstone for the double crime of his relative. But on more mature reflection he was impressed with the belief that a spirit had appeared to him, the spirit of his father-in-law, and that his own alarm had hindered him from learning fully the secret of his visit to earth; he therefore resolved to go to the same place next sabbath night, seek rather than avoid an interview, acquaint himself with the state of bliss or woe in which the spirit was placed, and learn if by acts of affection and restitution he could soften his sufferings or augment his happiness. He went accordingly to the little rustic gate by the side of the lonely stream; he walked up and down; hour passed after hour, but he heard nothing and saw nothing save the murmuring of the brook and the hares running among the wild clover. He had resolved to return home, when something seemed to rise from the ground, as shapeless as a cloud at first, but moving with life. It assumed a form, and the appearance of John Macmillan was once more before him. The young man was nothing daunted, but looking on the spirit, said, "I thought you just and upright and devout, and incapable of murder and robbery." The spirit seemed to dilate as it made answer. "The death of Walter Johnstone sits lightly upon me. We had crossed each other's purposes, we had lessened each other's gains, we had vowed revenge, we met on fair terms, tied our horses to a gate, and fought fairly and long; and when I slew him, I but did what he sought to do to me. I threw him over his horse, carried him far into the country, sought out a deep quagmire on the north side of the Snipe Knowe, in Crake's Moss, and having secured his bills and other perishable property, with the purpose of returning all to his family, I buried him in the moss, leaving his gold in his purse, and laying his cloak and his sword above him.

"Now listen, Joseph Howatson. In my private desk you will find a little key tied with red twine, take it and go to the house of Janet Mathieson in Dumfries, and underneath the hearthstone in my sleeping room you will get my strong-box, open it, it contains all the bills and bonds belonging to Walter Johnstone. Restore them to his widow. I would have restored them but for my untimely death. Inform her privily and covertly where she will find the body of her husband, so that she may bury him in the churchyard with his ancestors. Do these things, that I may have some assuagement of misery; neglect them, and you will become a world's wonder." The spirit vanished with these words, and was seen no more.

Joseph Howatson was sorely troubled. He had communed with a spirit, he was impressed with the belief that early death awaited him; he felt a sinking of soul and a misery of body, and he sent for me to help him with counsel, and comfort him in his unexampled sorrow. I loved him and hastened to him; I found him weak and woe-begone, and the hand of God seemed to be sore upon him. He took me out to the banks of the little stream where the shape appeared to him, and having desired me to listen without interrupting him, told me how he had seen his father-in-law's spirit, and related the revelations which it had made and the commands it had laid upon him. "And now," he said, "look upon me. I am young, and ten days ago I had a body strong and a mind buoyant, and gray hairs and the honours of old age seemed to await me. But ere three days pass I shall be as the clod of the valley, for he who converses with a spirit, a spirit shall he soon become. I have written down the strange tale I have told you and I put it into your hands, perform for me and for my wretched parent, the instructions which the grave yielded up its tenant to give; and may your days be long in the land, and may you grow gray-headed among your people." I listened to his words with wonder and with awe, and I promised to obey him in all his wishes with my best and most anxious judgment. We went home together; we spent the evening in prayer. Then he set his house in order, spoke to all his children cheerfully and with a mild voice, and falling on the neck of his wife, said, "Sarah Macmillan, you were the choice of my young heart, and you have been a wife to me kind, tender, and gentle." He looked at his children and he looked at his wife, for his heart was too full for more words, and retired to his chamber. He was found next morning kneeling by his bedside, his hands held out as if repelling some approaching object, horror stamped on every feature, and cold and dead.

Then I felt full assurance of the truth of his communications; and as soon as the amazement which his untimely death occasioned had subsided, and his wife and little ones were somewhat comforted, I proceeded to fulfil his dying request. I found the small key tied with red twine, and I went to the house of Janet Mathieson in Dumfries, and I held up the key and said, "Woman, knowest thou that?" and when she saw it she said, "Full well I know it, it belonged to a jolly man and a douce, and mony a merry hour has he whiled away wi' my servant maidens and me." And when she saw me lift the hearth-stone, open the box, and spread out the treasure which it contained, she held up her hands, "Eh! what o' gowd! what o' gowd! but half's mine, be ye saint or sinner; John Macmillan, douce man, aye said he had something there which he considered as not belonging to him but to a quiet friend; weel I wot he meant me, for I have been a quiet friend to him and his." I told her I was commissioned by his daughter to remove the property, that I was the minister of that per-secuted remnant of the true kirk called Cameronians, and she might therefore deliver it up without fear. "I ken weel enough wha ye are," said this worthless woman, "d'ye think I dinna ken a minister of the kirk; I have seen meikle o' their siller in my day, frae eighteen to fifty and aught have I caroused with divines, Cameronians, I trow, as well as those of a freer kirk. But touching this treasure, give me twenty gowden pieces, else I'se gar three stamps of my foot bring in them that will see me righted, and send you awa to the mountains bleating like a sheep shorn in winter." I gave the imperious woman twenty pieces of gold, and carried away the fatal box.

Now, when I got free of the ports of Dumfries, I mounted my little horse and rode away into the heart of the country, among the pastoral hills of Dryfesdale. I carried the box on the saddle before me, and its contents awakened a train of melancholy thoughts within me. There were the papers of Walter Johnstone, corresponding to the description which the spirit gave, and marked with his initials in red ink by the hand of the man who slew him. There were two gold watches and two purses of gold, all tied with red twine, and many bills and much money to which no marks were attached. As I rode along pondering on these things, and casting about in my own mind how and by what means I should make restitution, I was aware of a morass, broad and wide, which with all its quagmires glittered in the moonlight before me. I knew I had penetrated into the centre of Dryfesdale, but I was not well acquainted with the country; I therefore drew my bridle, and looked around to see if any house was nigh, where I could find shelter for the night. I saw a small house built of turf and thatched with heather, from the window of which a faint light glimmered. I rode up, alighted, and there I found a woman in widow's weeds, with three sweet children, spinning yarn from the wool which the shepherds shear in spring from the udders of the ewes. She welcomed me, spread bread and placed milk before me. I asked a blessing, and ate and drank, and was refreshed.

Now it happened that, as I sat with the solitary woman and her children, there came a man to the door, and with a loud yell of dismay burst it open and staggered forward crying, "There's a corse candle in Crake's Moss, and I'll be a dead man before the morning." "Preserve me! piper," said the widow, "ye're in a piteous taking; here is a holy man who will speak comfort to you, and tell you how all these are but delusions of the eye or exhalations of nature." "Delusions and exhalations, Dame Johnstone," said the piper, "d'ye think I dinna ken a corse light from an elf candle, an elf candle from a will-o'-wisp, and a will-o'-wisp from all other lights of this wide world." The name of the morass and the woman's name now flashed upon me, and I was struck with amazement and awe. I looked on the widow, and I looked on the wandering piper, and I said, "Let me look on those corse lights, for God creates nothing in vain; there is a wise purpose in all things, and a wise aim." And the piper said, "Na, na; I have nae wish to see ony mair on't, a dead light bodes the living nae gude; and I am sure if I gang near Crake's Moss it will lair me amang the hags and quags." And I said, "Foolish old man, you are equally safe every where; the hand of the Lord reaches round the earth, and strikes and protects according as it was foreordained, for nothing is hid from his eyes—come with me." And the piper looked strangely upon me and stirred not a foot; and I said, "I shall go by myself;" and the woman said, "Let me go with you, for I am sad of heart, and can look on such things without fear; for, alas! since I lost my own Walter Johnstone, pleasure is no longer pleasant: and I love to wander in lonesome places and by old churchyards." "Then," said the piper, "I darena bide my lane with the bairns; I'll go also; but O! let me strengthen my heart with ae spring on my pipes before I venture." "Play," I said, "'Clavers and his Highlandmen', it is the tune to cheer ye and keep your heart up." "Your honour's no cannie," said the old man; "that's my favourite tune." So he played it and said, "Now I am fit to look on lights of good or evil." And we walked into the open air.

All Crake's Moss seemed on fire; not illumined with one steady and uninterrupted light, but kindled up by fits like the northern sky with its wandering streamers. On a little bank which rose in the centre of the morass, the supernatural splendour seemed chiefly to settle; and having continued to shine for several minutes, the whole faded and left but one faint gleam behind. I fell on my knees, held up my hands to heaven, and said, "This is of God; behold in that fearful light the finger of the Most High. Blood has been spilt, and can be no longer concealed; the point of the mariner's needle points less surely to the north than yon living flame points to the place where man's body has found a bloody grave. Follow me," and I walked down to the edge of the moss and gazed earnestly on the spot. I knew now that I looked on the long hidden resting place of Walter Johnstone, and considered that the hand of God was manifest in the way that I had been thus led blindfold into his widow's house. I reflected for a moment on these things; I wished to right the fatherless, yet spare the feelings of the innocent; the supernatural light partly showed me the way, and the words which I now heard whispered by my companions aided in directing the rest.

"I tell ye, Dame Johnstone," said the piper, "the man's no cannie; or what's waur, he may belong to the spiritual world himself, and do us a mischief. Saw ye ever mortal man riding with ae spur and carrying a silver-headed cane for a whip, wi' sic a fleece of hair about his haffets and sic a wild ee in his head; and then he kens a' things in the heavens aboon and the earth beneath. He kenned my favourite tune 'Clavers'; I'se uphaud he's no in the body, but ane of the souls made perfect of the auld Covenanters whom Grahame or Grierson slew; we're daft to follow him." "Fool body," I heard the widow say, "I'll follow him; there's something about that man, be he in the spirit or in the flesh, which is pleasant and promising. O! could he but, by prayer or other means of lawful knowledge, tell me about my dear Walter Johnstone; thrice has he appeared to me in dream or vision with a sorrowful look, and weel ken I what that means." We had now reached the edge of the morass, and a dim and uncertain light continued to twinkle about the green knoll which rose in its middle. I turned suddenly round and said, "For a wise purpose am I come; to reveal murder; to speak consolation to the widow and the fatherless, and to soothe the perturbed spirits of those whose fierce passions ended in untimely death. Come with me; the hour is come, and I must not do my commission negligently." "I kenned it, I kenned it," said the piper, "he's just one of the auld persecuted worthies risen from his red grave to right the injured, and he'll do't discreetly; follow him, Dame, follow him." "I shall follow," said the widow, "I have that strength given me this night which will bear me through all trials which mortal flesh can endure."

When we reached the little green hillock in the centre of the morass, I looked to the north and soon distinguished the place described by my friend Joseph Howatson, where the body of Walter Johnstone was deposited. The moon shone clear, the stars aided us with their light, and some turfcutters having left their spades standing near, I ordered the piper to take a spade and dig where I placed my staff. "O dig carefully," said the widow, "do not be rude with mortal dust." We dug and came to a sword; the point was broken and the blade hacked. "It is the sword of my Walter Johnstone," said his widow, "I could swear to it among a thousand." "It is my father's sword," said a fine dark haired boy who had followed us unperceived, "it is my father's sword, and were he living who wrought this, he should na be lang in rueing it." "He is dead, my child," I said, "and beyond your reach, and vengeance is the Lord's." "O, Sir," cried his widow, in a flood of tears, "ye ken all things; tell me, is this my husband or no?" "It is the body of Walter Johnstone," I answered, "slain by one who is passed to his account, and buried here by the hand that slew him, with his gold in his purse and his watch in his pocket." So saying we uncovered the body, lifted it up, and laid it on the grass; the embalming nature of the morass had preserved it from decay, and mother and child, with tears and with cries, named his name and lamented over him. His gold watch and his money, his cloak and his dress, were untouched and entire, and we bore him to the cottage of his widow, where with clasped hands she sat at his feet and his children at his head till the day drew nigh the dawn; I then rose and said, "Woman, thy trials have been severe and manifold; a good wife, a good mother, and a good widow hast thou been, and thy reward will be where the blessed alone are admitted. It was revealed to me by a mysterious revelation that thy husband's body was where we found it; and I was commissioned by a voice, assuredly not of this world, to deliver thee this treasure, which is thy own, that thy children may be educated, and that bread and raiment may be thine." And I delivered her husband's wealth into her hands, refused gold which she offered, and mounting my horse, rode over the hills and saw her no more. But I soon heard of her, for there rose a strange sound in the land, that a Good Spirit had appeared to the widow of Walter Johnstone, had disclosed where her husband's murdered body lay, had enriched her with all his lost wealth, had prayed by her side till the blessed dawn of day, and then vanished with the morning light. I closed my lips on the secret till now; and I reveal it to you, my children, that you may know there is a God who ruleth this world by wise and invisible means, and punisheth the wicked, and cheereth the humble of heart and the lowly minded.

Such was the last sermon of the good John Farley, a man whom I knew and loved. I think I see him now, with his long white hair and his look mild, eloquent, and sagacious. He was a giver of good counsel, a sayer of wise sayings, with wit at will, learning in abundance, and a gift in sarcasm which the wildest dreaded.

Katie Cheyne

By James Hogg

Scene I

"WHAT are ye greeting for, Katie Cheyne?" "I'm greeting nane, Duncan, I wonder to hear ye." "Why, woman, ye're greeting till yere very heart's like to burst the laces of your gown—gae owre, for gude sake, else I shall greet too." "O no, Duncan Stewart, I wadna wish to see you greeting like a wean—how can I help sobbing, when I leave my mother's house for a fremit place?" "Keep up your heart, lass—your new place will grow like a hame, and fremit folk like sisters and brothers." "Weel, I trust sae; what ails that wee lamb, that it bleats so sairly, Duncan?" "It's bleating for its mother, it has lost her, poor thing." "Can lambs like other creatures better than their mothers?" "Na, Katie, nor ony half so weel either." "O they

Painted by Wᵐ Kidd.   Engraved by J.Shury.

KATIE CHEYNE.

S.Robinson,London.

are happy, happy creatures; but I maun gang—sae gude day."

"Now that young simple lassie with the light foot, the blue een, the white hand, and with sae little to say, has gone far to gaur me make a fool of myself. She maun have magic in her feet, for her light steps go dancing through my heart; and then her een!—I think blue een will be my ruin, and black anes are little better; and then her tongue, 'Can lambs like other creatures better than their mothers, Duncan?' The lassie will drive me demented. Simple soul, now she little kenned that artless words are the best of all words for winning hearts. I think I'll step on and tell her."

"Katie Cheyne, my dow, ye're no very ill to overtake." "I didna like to hurt ye wi' rinning after me, Duncan." "Did ye na, Katie?— simplicity again! weel, now I like simplicity—simplicity, saith the proverb—it's nae matter what the proverb saith—but I say this, that I love ye, Katie Cheyne—with all my heart—and with both my hands, as the daft sang says." "Men are queer creatures, Duncan Stewart, and ye are ane of the queerest of them, and I'm no sure that I understand you. Did Jane Rodan and Peg Tamson understand ye when ye vowed by more stars than the sky contains that ye loved them, and loved them alone? Duncan! Duncan!" "Hout, that was when I kenned nae better; love them, gigling hempies! I'd sooner bait a fox trap with my heart than send it sae gray a gate. But I am a man now, Katie Cheyne, and I like you, and liking you I love you, and loving you I would fain marry you. My heart's lighter with the confession." "And my heart's lighter too, Duncan Stewart—sae we may e'en let twa light hearts gang thegither. But, O Duncan, this mauna be some-time yet. We maun be richer—we maun gather mair prudence; for, alas! what is two young creatures, though their hearts be full of love, when the house is empty of plenishing?" "Now this is what I call happiness, Katie Cheyne—I am baith daft and dizzy—but we mauna wed yet, ye say, till we gather gear and plenishing—be it sae. But now, dear Katie, ye are a simple creature, and may profit by the wisdom of man. Take care of yourself in the grand house you are going to. Folk there have smooth looks and sly tongues, and never put half the heart in their words that an honest shepherd lad does, who watches his flocks amang the mountains, with the word of God in his pocket and his visible firmament above him. Be upright and faithful and just towards me—read at spare times in your bible; and beware of those creatures whose coats are of divers colours, and who run when the bell rings." "Aye, and take ye care of the ewe-milking lasses, Duncan. There will be setting on of leglins, and happing with plaids, and song singing and whispering when Katie

Cheyne's out of sight. But whenever ye see ripe lips and roguish een think on me, and on our solemn engagement, Duncan Stewart." "Solemn engagement! the lass has picked that out of some Cameronian sermon. It sounds like the kirk bell. I shall set ye in sight of your new habitation, and then farewell till the Lammas fair."

Scene II

"WEARY fa' thee, Duncan Stewart—solemn engagement! What a serious sound there is in the very words. I have leaped o'er the linn with baith een open—I have broken my head with my ain hand. To be married is nothing—a light soke is easily worn, and a light yoke is easily borne—but I am worse than wedded. I am chained up like a fox among chickens—tied like a hawk among hen birds—I am fastened by a solemn engagement, and canna be loosed till siller comes. I maun gang to kirk and market wi' an antinuptial collar round my neck, and Kate Cheyne's name painted on it—and all who run will read. I'll never can face Peg Tamson nor Nell Rodan—they'll cry, 'There gangs poor Duncan Stewart, the silly lad, that is neither single nor married.' I like nae lass half sae weel, but then it's the bondage of the solemn engagement: who would have thought such a simple creature could have picked up two such lang-nebbit, peacock-tailed words? Hoolie—Duncan, here comes thy mother."

"Duncan! son Duncan! you are speaking to yourself. No young man ever speaks to himself unless he is in love." "An what an I be, dear mither, there is nought unnatural in the situation." "Love, my son, is natural only when fixed on a proper object; you have good blood and high blood in your veins, and if you look low you will lift little. Keep your mother's house in remembrance." "I never thought a thought about it. I ken ye were a lady, for ye have ay said sae—but simple blood hauds up the poor man's roof tree, while gentle blood pulls it about his lugs." "Lugs! O that son of mine should utter that vulgar word! O that a descendant of the ancient and honourable house of Knockhoolie should speak the language of plebeian life! How will you speed in your wooing with your fair cousin of Glenpether, if you are guilty of such vulgarisms? How will a man enter with dignity upon her fair possession—seven acres of peat moss and a tower with a stone stair—who says 'Lugs?'" "O mither, mither, it is all over—all these grand visions maun vanish now—I am not my own man—I am settled—tied up—tethered—sidelangled—I am under a solemn engagement." "What! has a son of Knockhoolie wedded below his degree? O that shame should ever fall on an ancient

house—on a house whose dowry is a long descent and spotless honour—on a house that's as good as related to that of Pudinpoke, one
of the most ancient names in the south country. Duncan Stewart,
there has been Knockhoolies in Knockhoolie longer than tongue
can tell or history can reckon." "Married! mither, marrying's nought—
it's but a shoot thegither of twa foolish things, by a man mair foolish
than either. But I'm contracted, bespoke, given awa—I'm no my ain
man, I am the slave of a solemn engagement; heard ye ever sic
binding and unloosable words? And wha would have thought that a
simple quean, like Katie Cheyne, would have had such words in
her head." "Solemn engagement, my son, these are loosable words—
keep the enchantment of the law and the spell of pen and ink away
from them. But Kate Cheyne! a lassie who has never heard of her
grandfather—a creature dropped like a flower-seed in a desert—is
she decreed to give an heir to the house of Knockhoolie?" "O mither,
I am a born gowk, a predestined gomeral, and doomed to be your
sorrow. O can wit or wise words loose me. Try your hand—but be
not severe with the lassie—for she's a simple lassie. Slide cannilie
into the leeside of her good opinion, and slip this antinuptial halter
out of her hand; and then I shall gang singing with a free foot o'er
the hill to my cousin of Glenpether." "Spoken like thy mother's son.
O that ye had ever such a sense of your born dignity! O that ye
would leave off the vulgar pursuits of the quoits, and pitch the bar,
and hap step and loup, and learn to speak the language of polished
life. Learn to think much and say little, and look as if ye knew every
thing, so that the reputation of wisdom might remain with the house
of Knockhoolie."

Scene III

"WEEL, mither, what says Kate? O the simple slut! O the young
uninstructed innocent! 'Can lambs like other creatures better than
their mothers, Duncan?' She's as sweet as a handful of unpressed
curd—and as new to the world as fresh kirned butter. But solemn
engagement—What says she to the solemn engagement?" "Little,
Duncan, very little; first she put one hand to her eye and then another, and at last said, 'He made it, and he may undo it—but I must
have his ain word for it—for mithers are mithers, and may be wilfu'."
"O then, I have got this matrimonial hap-shackle off, and am free.
Losh! how light I am! I think I have wings on. Now I can flee east
and flee west—here a word and there a word—step afore the lasses
as crouse as a cock with a double kame on. I'll make them sigh at

their suppers." "Ye have reason, my son, to be lifted up of heart—ye can now act as becomes your mother's house. What colour had your cousin of Glenpether when ye stept ben, with the kind word and the well bred bow?" "Colour! just the auld colour, a kind of a dun and yellow. But ye see there was a great deal of blushing and snirting, and bits of made coughs, as if to keep down a thorough guffau. I have nae great notion of courting of ladies." "Tell me, Duncan, how you demeaned yourself, and how your cousin received you." "That's a lang story, mither, and a misrid ane. I rapped and I whistled, and who should come to the door but a dink and sonsie lass, ane Bell Macava—'Is Miss Mattie at hame,' says I. 'Deed is she,' says the lass, as nice a hussy as well could be. So ye think, mother, that Kate Cheyne will free me?" "No doubt of it, Duncan, my child.— Well, what next?" "Weel, this Bell Macava says to me—I wish ye had only seen her, mother, a queen wi spunk and smeddum, and then her tongue—says Bell, says she, 'Yes, sir, she is at hame—will ye walk into the kitchen till I inform her?' The kitchen, thinks I, is a step beneath me, howsever she gied me sic a look, sae into the kitchen went I, shoulder to shoulder with Bell Macava." "O, son Duncan, ye will break my heart—a kitchen wench—and you a son of the house of Knockhoolie." "'If you are not in a hurry, sir,' says Bell Macava, 'I have a baking of bread to put to the fire.' 'I *am* in a great hurry,' says I. 'No doubt on't,' said she, 'sir,'—she ay sirred me—'they are ay in the greatest haste have least to do.' She's a queer weel faured quean now, this Bell Macava, and has a gift at haurning bread." "Son, son, tell me what passed between you and your lady cousin, or hold your peace for ever." "O, but I maun relate baith courtships, for that ane has a natural reference to the other." "Both courtships! Have ye courted both maid and mistress." "Mither, mither, be reasonable now—if ye saw a lass—bonnie belike—skilful with her een— mischievous with her tongue—spreading out all her loveliness before ye, like Laird Dobie's peacock's tail." "How, Duncan, can ye speak so to me, one of the daughters of the house of Knockhoolie?" "Daughter! aye! but had ye been ane of its sons! Or, what would please me better, were ye as young as ye hae been, and as well faured, wi' an auld farrand tongue, and twa een that could look the lark out of the lift, and you to meet a pleasant lad, with love strong within him—ah, mither!" "My dear son—my dear son—why remind me of other days?—let all byganes be byganes." "There, now, I kenned nature wad speak, in spite of you: and was I to blame for an hour's daffin wi' bonnie Bell Macava? I am free to own—but a man canna help his nature—I have a wonderful turn for falling in love. So, says

Bell Macava to me—this was hinderend of all—says Bell, says she, 'If ye miss a kind reception up stairs, ye may come down again and give a poor body a flying bode.' 'There's my thumb on't,' says I; and I walked up stairs wi' her, hand for hand. Then ye see she opened the door of my lady cousin's room, and cried out, 'Mr. Duncan Stewart, ma'am, from Knockhoolie;' and in I gaed—my bonnet in my hand—my best plaid wrapt round me—wi' beck and wi' binge-looking this way and that way." "Duncan Stewart, are ye raving—a gray plaid, and becking and binging!—had you both your dogs with you?" "I wish they had been, poor dumb creatures; but I did my best without them. Bell Macava looked at my cousin, and my cousin at Bell Macava—that queer kind of look when, without speaking, lasses say sic a ane's a sumph, or sic a ane's a sensible fallow. Now Bell Macava's twa een said, 'He's a comical chap—he's no a' made up frae the pan and spoon.' 'Be seated, cousin Duncan,' said my cousin to me; and down she sat on the sofa, and down I clinked beside her. 'Sit still, Mattie,' says I, 'for I have some queer things to say.' 'Say away,' she says; 'what would ye say?' 'I'm no certain yet,' quoth I, 'what I am going to say; but I ken brawly what I am going to do.' And afore she either kenned or cared, I had nearly given her a hearty smack that wad ha done her heart gude."

"Ha! ha! well done, Duncan. It was a bold and downright way of beginning to woo—but the ladies of our blood love the brave and the bold—though I know such strong measures are opposed by many ladies of quality. Nevertheless *I* approve—go on; how did she take it?" "Just middling—she reddened up, called me rude, forward, country bred, till I was obliged to try my lip on her cheek again—and that sobered her." "Well, Duncan, well—but ye should not have been quite so audacious. Men never pity woman's softness, but are rude in the sight of the world." "Na, mither, na,—I threw my plaid o'er her, and under that pleasant screen e'en put it to my cousin if she could like me—me rude afore the world!—I ken better than that." "There's hope of you yet, my son—and what said the young lady?" "Young lady! nane sae young—five and thirty, faith! says she to me, 'I hate plaids.' 'Ye hate plaids,' says I, 'that's queer.' 'No sae queer either,' said she, 'for they make us do things we would never have the face to do without them.'

"'O blessings on the shepherd's plaid,' cried I, 'it haps us frae the storm—it is the canopy of kindly hearts—many a sweet soft word, many a half unwilling kiss, many a weel fulfilled vow have passed below it. The een of malice canna glance through it—the stars nor the moon either—it's a blessed happing.' 'Ye had better, as ye have na far to gang to grow daft, break into song at once,' said our cousin. 'Thank ye,' I said; and I sang sic a song—ane made on the moment— clean off loof—none of your long studied, dreigh of coming compositions. Na! na! down came the words wi' me, with a gush like a mill shelling. I have verse the natural gate, and other folk by inoculation. I sang such a song—listen now:——

The Shepherd's Plaid

My blessings on the cozie plaid,
  My blessings on the plaidie;
If I had her my plaid has happ'd,
  I'd be a joyful laddie.

Sweet cakes and wine, with gentlemen,
  All other fare surpasses,
And sack and sugar with auld wives,
  But bonnie lads with lasses.

O for a bonnie lad and lass—
  And better for a ladie,
There's nought in all the world worth
  The shepherd's cozie plaidie."

"Really, Duncan, my dear son, there is a rustic glibness about the verses—but do not give up your mind to such a common accomplishment. What said your cousin?" " 'Pray favour me with the chorus,' quoth she; 'I am fond of choruses.' 'This is the chorus,' said I, and I tried my lip; but aha—she was up—had been disciplined before. 'Off hands,' quoth my cousin, 'and sit in peace till my father comes; else I shall ring for Bell Macava to show you to your own room, where ye may cool yourself till my father comes home.' 'Do sae,' says I, 'do sae, I have no objection to the measure, if Bell bears me company:' so I offered to ring the bell, thinking there would be some fun in the change. 'Stay,' said my lady Mat, 'stay,' said she, and she laid her hand on mine—'I was going to observe,' said she, 'that Bell Macava is a superior girl.' 'I think so too,' says I, 'shall I ring for her?' 'No,' says my cousin; 'all that I was going to say is, that Bell is a good looking young woman.' 'I told her sae,' says I, 'no an hour since. She is a thrifty girl, and a hard working—she bakes bread weel,' said I. 'She has a very fine eye,' said my cousin. 'Twa of them,' said I, 'and shiners.' 'Well, then, she would make you a capital wife,' says Mattie to me. 'Would she?' said I: 'I wish ye had told me sooner, for I am in a manner disposed of; a woman has a kind of property in

me—I have come under a solemn engagement. Have ye never heard
that I am to be married to a certain saucy cousin of my ain, a great
heiress, wha has broken the hearts of three horse coupers wi' drinking her health in brandy?'

"'And who is this fair cousin of yours?' says Miss Mattie to me: 'I
never heard of such a matter.' 'That's queer again,' said I, 'for my
mother has talked of it—aye, and she can talk—she talks nought but
the wale of grand words—born gifts, born gifts—and we shouldna be
vain. But, as I said, my mother has talked, and I have talked, and
the thing's next to certain.' 'But,' said my cousin, 'name her—name
her—ye have nae many cousins, and they have all names.' 'And this
ane has a name too,' says I; 'but she's no that young, and she's no
very bonnie—but the pretty acres about her are the thing. She's rich
and ripe and disposed to be married.' 'Now,' said she, and her rage
nearly reddened her yellow complexion, 'this is some of your mother's idle dreams. She sits building palaces of the imagination. Go
and tell her from me, that, though I am *auld* and *ugly* and *rich* and
disposed to be married, I am no a fool. I'm no sae simple a bird as to
big my nest with the gowk.'

"I never loot on I heard her. 'But my cousin,' says I, 'has a waur
fault than lack of beauty—she has a fine gift at scolding, and she
rages most delightfully. I maun take her though—canna draw back.'
'Duncan Stewart,' cried she, 'begone! Never shall your cousin give
her hand to such a lump of God's unkneaded clay as you. Never
connect herself with folly, though she is *disposed* to be married. Could
I wed a clown, and see his mad mither sitting next me at my table?'
'Who was talking of your table?' says I, 'the table will be mine, and
next me shall my ain auld mother sit. But sit down, Mat, my lass—
dinna rin awa.' I trow I answered her." "You behaved very well, my
dear Duncan—very well considering. I scorn her personal insinuations. Alas! the children of this generation have not the solid qualities of those of the last. You have other cousins, Duncan, my son—
cousins with land and houses—who love your mother for her mind
and her sense of family dignity. Ye must not lay a dog in a deer's
den—you must always lay out your affections on birth and breeding." "My father was a shepherd, mother—spelt the bible as he read
it—drank hard at clipping time and lambing time, when the heather
was in blossom and the snaw was on the ground. Was he a man of
birth and breeding?" "Duncan, I doubt you are incapable of com-
prehending the feeling which influences those of ancestry and eleva-
tion of soul. I married your father for his good sense and good taste—
he never made love to low bred maidens." "An excellent apology for

all manner of marriages, mother. Bell Macava, now, is a lass of taste, and so is Jenny Steenson—and poor Kate Cheyne has the best taste of a'; but I have shaken myself free of Katie—I wrote her such a letter—ye never saw such words—it will drive her to the dictionar and grammar—neer a ane of less length than her ain words 'solemn engagement,' and all as high sounding as 'tremendous.' They were all nice, long-nebbit words, and I'm only afraid the scholarship's the thing wad tie her love to me the faster."

Scene IV

"HERE it is—here's Kate's answer—sealed nae less—I'll lay my lugs she has stood by the solemn engagement—sealed and touched down by her thimble—a thrifty lass and kindly—and folded—gosh, how it's folded—that's prudent now of Katie Cheyne; and she begins, 'Dear Duncan,'—now I canna stand this—I maun marry the lass, I think— and yet my cousin's seven acres of peat moss, a capital place for whaups and craneberries, and Bell Macava's blue een. Weel now, what says Kate? says Kate, says she, 'Dear Duncan,—Your mother's words maist broke my heart, and I was sae dull that I was obliged to go to a dance, and every body noticed my looks; and ane said, What ails ye, Katie Cheyne; and I said, I kenned what ailed me: and anither took me by the hand, and said, Lass, will ye dance? and I said, I cared na, sae I stood up; then he said, What tune will ye have? and I said, O play me a light tune, for I have a heavy heart; and sae I danced—and the ane that danced wi' me gade home wi' me, and then I got your letter—and, O Duncan, but it was fou of schoolmaster words. Ye asked for a release, and ye'se get a release; but, O man, dinna gang about the land breaking folks' hearts. So the lad that was wi' me said, Ye are sad, lass; and I said, How can I be but sad? and sae I showed him your letter—ye never saw sic spite, he laughed till the very tears stood in his een, and cried, This cowes a! a letter! it's a spell—a spell written by that uncannie dame his mother—was she ever suspected of witchcraft, Duncan?—it's as hard as the tenth of Nehemiah. Sae I said, Give me my letter; and I flew to him—ye never saw sic a touzle.' Kate Cheyne, ye will break my heart: but here comes my mother, and laughing too."

"Duncan, my own dear son, here's a release—the best of all re- leases—your foot's as free as the goshawk's, and ye may spread your wings and go where ye like." "Then, mither, I'll away to Kate Cheyne—it's time I were awa." "Truly is it, Duncan, and of that I am come to speak; she bids ye to her bridal. She is to be wedded at twelve o'clock, to a man of her own degree, Colonel Clapperton's grieve, Jock Hutcheon–Jenny Davison's Jock–like draws ay to like." "Jock Hutcheon, mother–what! lang Jock Hutcheon–that can never be! He's naebody, ye may say–lang, and black, and tinker-looking– and has thrashen me twenty times–it canna be him." "But it is him, Duncan, and glad I am of it; so get down the saddle with the plated stirrups–the silver's sore gone, still they *were* plated–and catch the horse on the common, wisp it down, and ride like your ancestors of old–cock your bonnet, and wag your arm manfully." "Mother, I'll be married too–married I shall be–married if there's a willing lass in the country side, and as muckle law in the land. Married I *shaal* be–I'm as fixed as Queensberry, as Criffil, as Skiddaw-fell–O for the names of more mountains!" "Duncan, dear Duncan, be guided; are ye mad?" "Yes, I'm mad; d'ye think the marrying fit would ever come on me unless the mad fit came afore it?" "Now then, my son, be ruled; throw not away the last child of an ancient line on name- less queans; wed in your degree. It would be a pity to see an old inheritance like mine going to the children of some lass whose kin cannot be counted." "It's easy talking, mother; will a born lady, with as muckle sense as a hen could haud in her steeked neeve, tauk Duncan Stewart? I maun marry them that will marry me. I hear the trampling of horses."

"Horses, ay, here's horses–here's your full cousin Grisel Tungtaket of Tungtaket, riding on her galloway nag away to Kate Cheyne's penny wedding, with her lang riding habit and her langer pedigree. She's a perfect princess, and come to the years of discretion–with a colour in her cheek to stand sun and rain. Take her Duncan, take her–she's lady of Tungtaket; a fair inheritance–feeds six ewes in a dropping year. Take her, Duncan, take her." "Take her! no, an she were heiress of all the sun shines on. Take her! she has a heart that wad hunger me, and a tongue that would clatter me to death. Cousins are closers, mither–cousins are closers–the mad fever fit of wedlock's more composed since ye spake. I think I may shoot owre till winter. I wadna' thought of marrying at a' if that daft hempie, Kate Cheyne, hadna put it into my head. I'll owre the hill to the Elfstane burn, and grope a dizen of trouts for our dinner, and let the bridal train ride by. I wonder if Kate will be wedded in her green gown–and if Jock Young of Yetherton will be best man?"

Friendship's Offering

Auld Joe Nicholson's Bonny Nannie

A Sang

By the Ettrick Shepherd

THE daisy is fair, the day-lily rare,
  The bud o' the rose as sweet as it's bonny;
But there ne'er was a flower, in garden or bower,
  Like auld Joe Nicholson's bonny Nannie.
     O my Nannie,   5
     My dear little Nannie,
   My sweet little niddlety-noddlety Nannie;
     There ne'er was a flower,
     In garden or bower,
  Like auld Joe Nicholson's bonny Nannie.   10

Ae day she came out wi' a rosy blush
  To milk her twa kye sae couthie an' cannie;
I cowered me down at the back o' the bush,
  To watch the air o' my bonny Nannie.
     O my Nannie, &c.   15

Her looks so gay o'er nature away,
  Frae bonny blue een sae mild an' mellow,
Saw naething sae sweet in nature's array
  Though clad in the morning's gowden yellow.
     O my Nannie, &c.   20

My heart lay beating the flowery green,
  In quaking quavering agitation;
And tears came trickling down frae my een,
  Wi' perfect love an' wi' admiration.
     O my Nannie, &c.   25

There's mony a joy in this warld below,
  And sweet the hopes that to sing were uncannie;
But of all the pleasures I ever can know,
  There's none like the love o' my dearest Nannie.

O my Nannie,   30
  My dear little Nannie,
My sweet little niddlety-noddlety Nannie;
  There ne'er was a flower,
  In garden or bower,
Like auld Joe Nicholson's bonny Nannie.   35

Ballad

By the Ettrick Shepherd

Now lock my chamber door, father,
  And say you left me sleeping;
But never tell my step-mother
  Of all this bitter weeping.
A slumber deep may ease my smart,   5
  Or partially reprieve it;
But there's a pang at my young heart
  That never more can leave it.

O let me lie and weep my fill
  O'er wounds that heal can never: 10
And, oh kind heaven, were it thy will
  To close these eyes for ever!
For how can maid's affections dear
  Recal her love mistaken?
Or how can heart of maiden bear   15
  To know that heart forsaken?

Ah, why should vows so fondly made
  Be broken ere the morrow,
To one who loved, as never maid
  Loved in this world of sorrow!   20
The look of scorn I cannot brave,
  Nor pity's eye more dreary;
A quiet sleep within the grave
  Is all for which I weary.

Farewell, ye banks of hazel green,   25
  Ye beds of primrose yellow,
Too happy has this bosom been
  Within your arbour mellow:

That happiness is fled for aye,
  And all is dark desponding,   30
Save in the opening gates of day,
  And the dear home beyond them!

Verses to a Beloved Young Friend

By the Ettrick Shepherd

OH, the last look is hard to bear
  Even of a stock or old grey stone,
Or any thing to childhood dear
  Which memory loves to dwell upon!

But fond affection never proved   5
  So thrilling, so severe a pain,
As looking on a face beloved
  We know we ne'er can see again.

Then, Mary, when with hasty gaze
  I saw thine eye bewildered roam,   10
For the last time, o'er Yarrow's braes,
  And thy dear kinsman's happy home,—

I felt a pang—it was not grief,
  But something language never bore,
From which the soul found no relief—   15
  Child of a darkling world before!

A lightning flash, a lurid gleam
  O'er billows of a darksome sea;
A momentary feverish dream
  Of time and of eternity!   20

Woe to the guileful tongue that bred
  This disappointment and this pain—
Cold-hearted villain! on his head
  A poet's malison remain!

Now thou hast left the Forest glade,   25
  By sorrows deep to thee endeared,
Where more beloved was never maid,
  Nor maiden's feelings more revered.

And O may blessings thee abide,
  Delights unbounded and untold,   30
Where Indus rolls his sluggish tide
  O'er glowing gems and sands of gold.

And Indian oceans waft the breeze
  Of renovated health to thee;
And odours of Arabia please   35
  Thy every sense from bower and tree.

And long as beats this kindred heart
  My love shall be as it hath been—
There shalt thou occupy thy part
  Though half the world lie us between!   40

MOUNT BENGER ON YARROW
June 17, 1828

The Minstrel Boy

By the Ettrick Shepherd

TREAD light this haunted grove of pleasure,
And list the fall of that dying measure;
O breathe not, stir not foot or hand—
There are visitants here from Fairy land!
For such a sweet and melting strain   5
Was never framed in this world of pain;
It had breathings of ecstasy and bliss—
Of a happier, holier sphere than this!

I see the vision—I see it now—
And the grey hairs creep upon my brow;   10
For I know full well, from a thrilling smart
And a joy that quivers through my heart,
That this most sweet and comely boy,
With his pipe and his looks of sunny joy,
Is either the prince of the land unseen,   15
The child of my loved Fairy Queen,
Or cherub sent from a region higher,
The son of Apollo the king of the lyre!

Painted by C.R.Leslie, R.A.

THE MINSTREL BOY.

Engraved by A.Duncan.

Hail lovely thing! Ah might it be
That I were again such a being as thee, 20
With my pipe and my plaid in the wild green wood,—
If thou art indeed of flesh and of blood!
But be thou a child of this world of strife,
Or a stranger come from the land of life,
Where the day of glory closes never, 25
And the harp and the song prevail for ever,
Still, vision fair, I long to be
A thing as holy and pure as thee.

Is it a dream of fairy trance,
This scene of grandeur and wild romance? 30
That chrystal pool with its sounding linn,
And the lovely vista far within,
The weeping birch and the poplar tall,
And the minstrel boy, the loveliest of all,
Thus singing his lay to the waterfall? 35
It is no vision of aught to be,
But a wild and splendid reality.
Then here let me linger, enwrapt, alone,
And think of the days that are past and gone—
Days of brightness, but fled as soon 40
As the bow from the cloud in the afternoon—
Gone like the purpled morning ray—
Gone like the blink of a winter day—
Gone like the strain of ravishing joy,
Late poured from the pipe of the minstrel boy, 45
That has left no trace in its airy flight,
Though the leaves were dancing with delight;
Gone like the swallow far over the main,
But never like her to return again!

Yes there was a time when memory twined, 50
(But time has left it a far behind),
When I, like thee, on a summer day
Would fling my bonnet and plaid away,
And toil at the leap, the race, or the stone,
With none to beat but myself alone. 55
And then would I raise my tiny lay
And lilt the songs of a former day:
Till I believed that over the fell

The fairies peeped from the heather bell;
That the lamb, so fraught with fond regard,   60
Had ceased to nibble the flowery sward;
That the plover came nigh with his corslet brown,
And the moorcock showed his scarlet crown;
Then I even beheld, with reverence due,
The goss-hawk droop his pinion blue,   65
And the tear in the eye of the good curlew:
These things I trowed in my ecstasy,
So they were the same as truth to me:
And I decided, with placid brow,
That at the leap, the race, or the throw,   70
Or tuneful lay of the greenwood glen,
I was the chief of the sons of men.

Well, time flew on; and this conceit,
This high resolve not to be beat,
So urged me on these sports to head,   75
Though rarely the first, I had no dread
With *all* the first my skill to try,
And little lose in the contest high.
—Without resolve that mocks controul,
A conscious energy of soul   80
That views no height to human skill,
Man never excelled and never will.
Forgive, dear boy, this barren theme,
But be this phrase thy apothegm—
Better in the first race contend,   85
Than all that follows to transcend.

But thou shalt rise, full well I know,
If health still beam on thy comely brow;
For thou hast a hand to lead thee on
That stands unequalled and alone,   90
While thy old monitor had none—
None save the song of the rural hind,
The bleating flocks, and the wailing wind,
The wildered glen with its gloomy pall,
The cliff, and the cairn, and the waterfall,   95
The towering clouds of ghastly form,
And the voice that spoke in the thunder storm!

Yes—there was another—a fervid flame,
Dear of remembrance, and dear of name,
With a thousand pains and pleasures blent,   100
But scarcely a thing of this element;
And thou shalt know it some time hence
To thy sweet and thy hard experience;
And thou shalt heave the burning sigh,
And be its slave as well as I.   105
Much do I owe to its sacred sway,
For he who sends thee this simple lay,
In his remote and green alcove
Was the pupil of NATURE and of LOVE.
With these and ART, shalt thou excel: 110
Dear Minstrel Boy! a while farewell.

MOUNT BENGER
June 14, 1828

A Scots Luve Sang

By the Ettrick Shepherd

I.

COULD this ill warld hae been contrived
    To stand without mischievous woman,
How peacefu' bodies wad hae lived,
    Released frae a' the ills sae common!
But since it is the waefu' case   5
    That man maun hae this teazing crony,
Why sic a sweet bewitching face?
    —O had they no been made sae bonny!

II.

I might hae wandered dale and wood,
    Brisk as the breeze that whistles o'er me,   10
As careless as the roe-deer's brood,
    As happy as the lambs before me;
I might hae screwed my tunefu' pegs,
    And carolled mountain strains so gaily,
Had we but wantit a' the Megs   15
    Wi' glossy e'en sae dark an' wily.

III.

I saw the danger, feared the dart,
   The smile, the air, an' a' sae taking,
Yet open laid my wareless heart,
   An' gat the wound that keeps me waking.   20
My harp waves on the willow green;
   O' wild witch-notes it has nae ony,
Sin' e'er I saw that pawky quean,
   Sae sweet, sae wicked, an' sae bonny!

The Fords of Callum

An Ower True Tale

By the Ettrick Shepherd

"Ye had better steek the door, Janet; I think there's a kind o' cauld sugh coming up the house the night."

"Gude forgie you for leeing, Wat; for the night is that muth an' breathless, I'm maist like to swairf, an' am hardly able to do a single turn. An' for you, ye are joost a' in ae thow, I see; an' hae muckle mair need that I suld clash a sowp cauld water on you than steek the door."

"It will be as weel to steek the door, Janet, my woman, an' let us take our chance o' swairfing. Ye ken the auld saying, 'at open doors the dogs come ben.' An' we little ken what may come in at that door the night."

Janet ran and shut the door, bolting it fast, and muttering to herself all the way, as she perceived a manifest alteration in her husband's looks and manner; for Wat Douglas was not one of your chicken-hearted timorous hinds, but as bold as a lion, fearing neither man nor beast; and as for bogles of all kinds, such as fairies, brownies, ghosts, wraiths, or water kelpies, Wat denied positively that any such creatures had existence. But he was very far wrong in so doing, as will appear in the sequel.

His wife was his cousin-german; they were married young, and had three comely daughters at service, one of whom, named Anne, was accounted particularly handsome. Janet was much of her husband's way of thinking with regard to these spiritual beings; but when she saw that he was alarmed at something, she became ten times more so.

"Now gude forgie us, Walter! tell us what's the matter wi' ye? Hae ye seen aught? Hae ye heard aught? Or hae ye grown unweel on the hill that has made ye a wee squeamish?"

"Bring me a drink o' water, Janet. It's only a bit dwam; it will soon gang aff (*drinks*). Hech whow! what a warld this is that we lieve in! Have ye been guilty of ony great sin lately, Janet?"

"No that I hae mind o' just now. But what a question that is to speir at your wife!"

"War ye ever guilty of ony great backsliding or transgression?"

"Aih! gudeness forbid, Walter! But what has set you upon sic questions the night?"

"Because I'm feared, Janet, that there's some heavy judgment gaun to happen to us very soon. I hae had a singular warning the night."

"Aih whow! Oh, Wattie, ye gar a' my heart groo within me! What kind o' warning have ye had?"

"I canna tell ye. It is out o' my power to tell ye. An' gin I could tell you, ye wadna believe me. Gang away to your bed, Janet, an' let us compose ourselves to rest in our Maker's name."

The lonely couple went to their bed, and commended themselves to the protection of heaven; but sleep was far from visiting their couch. Wat Douglas lay and groaned heavily, while his groans were audibly responded by his wife. At length he says to her, "When did ye hear from your daughter Annie, Janet?"

"No this lang while; no sin' Lockerbie tryste."

"Do ye think that Annie can hae been guilty of ony great sin in her days?"

"Aih! I hope our poor lassie has been better guidit. But she's a queer mysterious lassie, our Annie. There is something about her that I can never comprehend. I had some heavy, heavy dreams about her afore she was born. I think always there is something to happen to her."

"Ay, Janet, as sure as I am speaking to you, an' as sure as the starns are shining in heaven, there will something happen to her, an' that very soon.—Sae ye say ye haena seen nor heard o' her sin' Lockerbie tryste?"

"Na, no sin' syne."

"What wad ye think, Janet, gin I had seen her the night?"

"Gin ye saw her weel, I should be very happy."

"Oh! Janet, I hae gotten a warning the night that I canna comprehend. But we'll hear mair about it soon. Tell me just ae thing, an' tell me truly. Is Annie—? But hush! What's that I hear? Lord be wi' us, there it is again!"

At that instant, and before he pronounced these last words, a quick tap was heard at the window, and a sweet and well-known voice called from without in a melancholy key: "Mither, are ye waukin?"

"Yes, dear, I'm waukin," cried the agitated mother; "Gude forgie ye, what has brought you here at this time o' night? The like o' this I kend never! I think it be true what folks say—speak o' the deil an' he'll appear! I'll open the door this minent, Annie. Is there any body wi' ye?"

"Na, there's nae body wi' me; an' I wish there had been nane wi' me the night. Is Wat Douglas away to the Fords o' Callum?"

"Wat Douglas! Whaten a gate is that o' speakin about your father, Annie? Wat Douglas, as ye ca' him, is nane away to the Fords o' Callum, but lying snug in his bed here."

"Oh! lack-a-day! Then it is ower late now!" said the voice without; and as it said so, it seemed to pass away from the window on the breeze, so that the last words were scarcely audible. It was like the passing sound of a beetle or a bee pronouncing the melancholy words as it flew.

"Dinna gang near it, Janet! Dinna gang near it," cried Wat Douglas, shuddering, and shrouding himself deeper in the bed-clothes. "For the sake o' your soul, bide where you are, an' keep the wa's o' the house atween you an' it!"

"The man's wudd! Will I no gang an' open the door to my ain bairn? Ay, that will I, though a' the ghaists o' the folk o' Sodom and Gomorrah were letten loose!" And so saying, away flew Janet to the door with her clothes half on, while Wattie was calling all the while from under the clothes, "Ye dinna ken what ye're doing, Janet! Ye dinna ken what ye're doing!"

Janet opened the door, and went round and round the house calling her daughter's name; but there was none that answered or regarded. She once thought she heard a distant sound as of one wailing in the air, but it died away and she heard no more. She returned into her cot, breathless and dumb with astonishment; and after sitting a space, with crossed arms and her head hanging over them, she once more began speaking in a deep voice and half a whisper—"She's away! She's away! She's away! Can it hae been our daughter's wraith that spak to us through the window?"

"*Your* daughter say, Janet, for you hear I'm denied. But nevertheless, now when I think on it, it maun be a wraith, for it canna be aught else. I had sic an encounter wi't this night afore now, as mortal man o' flesh and blood never had wi' an unyirthly creature. But what passed atween us is a secret that maunna an' canna be revealed. But had I thought o't being a wraith I wadna hae been sae feared."

"What is a wraith, Wattie? for I thought you had denied a' thae things."

"Ay, but seeing's believing, Janet. An' as for a wraith, I tak it to be a guardian angel that comes to gie warning o' something that's to happen to its ward. Now a guardian angel can never be a bad thing, Janet."

"But think o' the warning, Wattie. Think o' the warning. What was it that the voice said about the Fords o' Callum?"

"That maun be considered, Janet. But the terrors o' this night had put that, an ilka thing else out o' my head. That maun be considered. The Fords o' Callum? Ay! That's the place where the spirit tried to take me to in spite of my teeth. Wha *is* Annie, Janet?"

"Gude forgie us! heard ony body ever sickan a rhame as that! She's her father's daughter to be sure.–But is this a night to begin wi' sickan queer questions, Walter? If ye gat wit that ony body in the hale country were perishing or in jeopardy, wad it be necessar to settle a' about their connections and parentage afore you set out to save them?"

"That's very true, Janet. She is a lassie that is weel worthy o' looking after, though I had never seen her face afore; an' a message frae heaven shoudna be neglekit."

"I'm no sae clear about the message being frae heaven, Wattie. But a message we certainly have had; an' I think it is incumbent on us to set out immediately, an' see what is going on at the Fords o' Callum."

"I think the same. It is but a step of a mile or twae, an' my conscience coudna be at ease without ganging there. An' yet it is daft like to be gaun away afore day-light to a particular spot to look for a body, an' that spot ten miles aff frae the place where the body is living."

"Na, na, it isna ten miles, Wat. It's na aboon nine miles and a half, if it be that."

It was not yet one o'clock, but it was a mid-summer night, still and beautiful, as well as the morning following; and when the couple reached the Fords o' Callum, the grey twilight began to shed its pale and eiry hues over that lonely upland: and ere they reached the Ford by two hundred paces, they perceived something like a human form lying on a small green sward on the other side of the river, or burn; for though called a river, or water, it is no bigger than an ordinary burn.

"What's yon lying yonder, Janet?"

"O the Lord in heaven kens what it is! My heart is beginning to fail me, Wattie. I canna gang ony farther. I think we shoudna gang ony nearer till we get somebody wi' us."

"It wad be a shame to stop here or turn again after coming sae far. Lean on me, and let us venture forward and see what it is. It is like a woman; but she's maybe sleeping."

"Na, na! yon's nae sleeping posture. She's lying athraw. I canna gang! I canna gang! dinna drag me; for though I hae stooden ower the bed o' death mony a time, yet it is a fearsome thing to look upon death in the open field. An' there's maybe blood, too. Think ye I can look upon a corpse swathed in blood, in a wild place like this? No, no, I hae nae power to gang a step farther!"

Janet Douglas would neither advance nor remain by herself; but hung upon her husband and wept. Wat called aloud to see if the form would awake and move, but he called in vain; and just as the two were returning to seek assistance, they perceived a gentleman coming toward them, which was a happy sight. This was Mr. George Brown of Callum, who was at that time a bridegroom, and had set out so early on horseback to go into Nithsdale by the Queensberry road. They told him their dilemma, and pointed out the form lying on the other side of Duff's Kinnel. Mr. Brown was as much appalled as they; but the three ventured across to the form, in breathless terror and awful suspense; and there, indeed, they found the body of Annie Douglas, lying a pale corpse, and her bosom still warm. She appeared to have been dead some hours. Mr. Brown, who was excellently mounted, gave up his journey, and galloped back straight to Moffat, where he procured a Dr. Johnstone then living in Moffat, said to have been a gentleman of great ability, and another young surgeon whose name I have forgot; and the three arrived at the spot in an inconceivably short time, the distance not being more than three miles. All endeavours to restore life proved vain and abortive; therefore their whole attention was next directed to ascertain the manner of her death. But there they were puzzled—nonplussed beyond the power of calculation. Her clothes were torn; but there was not the smallest mark of violence on any part of her body. She was dressed in all her best attire; and it was manifest that she had come there on horseback, with more in company than one, for there were many marks of horses' feet about the spot, as if they had been held or fastened there for a space.

Her death made a great noise in that district for a few months, and a hundred conjectures were framed concerning it; probably all wide of the truth. But there were some circumstances attending it that astounded every one. Mr. Brown of Callum's mind was so much confused at the time, and his pity so much excited by the untimely death of the beautiful young woman, that he never thought of one thing which occurred to him afterwards as having been very singular, namely, that the old couple should have been sitting in that remote place watching the corpse of their daughter at a distance before daylight. But the worst consequence of all was this:—During the time that Mr. Brown was seeking the surgeons, Janet was so ill that she fainted several times, and fell into hysterics, while her husband supported and assisted her with apparent command of his feelings, and perfect presence of mind. But before they reached home with the corpse, the case was altered. Janet was quite recovered and collected, while Wat looked so ill that it was fearful to see him. He immediately betook himself to bed, from which he never arose again, but died a fortnight afterwards, having rarely ever spoken from that morning forward.

Of course he could not attend Annie's funeral; and there was no circumstance more puzzling than one that occurred there. Among the mourners there was one gentleman quite unknown to every one who was present. Indeed, from the beginning, he took upon himself, as it were, the office of chief mourner, carrying the head almost the whole way to the churchyard, so that all the people supposed the elegant stranger some near relation of the deceased, sent for, from a distance, to take the father's part, and conduct the last obsequies. When they came to the grave, he took his station at the head of the corpse, which he lowered into the grave with great decency and decorum, appearing to be deeply affected. When the interment was over, he gave the sexton a guinea and walked away. He was afterwards seen riding towards Dumfries, with a page in full mourning riding at a distance behind him. How much were all the good people of Johnston astonished when they heard that neither father nor mother of the deceased, nor one present at the funeral knew any thing whatever of the gentleman; who he was; where he came from; or what brought him there. I have heard it reported, on what authority I do not know, that this stranger was subsequently traced to have been the late Duke of Q——. And as this unaccountable incident is well known to have happened when the late Mr. George Brown of Callum was a bridegroom, it settles the time to have been about sixty-six years ago.

MOUNT BENGER, ON YARROW
June 15, 1829

A Bard's Address to his Youngest Daughter

By the Ettrick Shepherd

COME to my arms, my dear wee pet!
My gleesome, gentle Harriet!
The sweetest babe art thou to me
That ever sat on parent's knee;
Thy every feature is so cheering,   5
And every motion so endearing.
Thou hast that eye was mine erewhile,
Thy mother's blithe and grateful smile,
And such a playful merry mien
That Care flies off whene'er thou'rt seen.   10

And if aright I read thy mind,
The child of nature thou'rt designed;
For, even while yet upon the breast,
Thou mimick'st child, and bird, and beast:
Canst cry like Maggy o'er her book,   15
And crow like cock, and caw like rook,
Boo like a bull, or blare like ram,
And bark like dog, and bleat like lamb:
And when afield in sunshine weather
Thou minglest all these sounds together,—   20
Then who can say, thou happy creature!
Thou'rt not the very child of nature!

Child of my age and dearest love!
As precious gift from God above,
I take thy pure and gentle frame,   25
And tiny mind of mounting flame;
And hope that through life's chequered glade,
That weary path that all must tread,
Some credit from thy name will flow
To the old bard who loved thee so.   30
At least thou shalt not want thy meed,
His blessing on thy beauteous head,
And prayers to Him whose sacred breath

Lightened the shades of life and death—
Who said with sweet benignity,   35
"Let little children come to me."

   'Tis very strange, my little dove!
That all I ever loved, or love,
In wondrous visions still I trace,
While gazing on thy guiltless face.   40
Thy very name brings to my mind
One, whose high birth and soul refined
Withheld her not from naming me,
Even in life's last extremity.
Sweet babe! thou art memorial dear   45
Of all I honour and revere!

   Come, look not sad: though sorrow now
Broods on thy father's thoughtful brow,
And on the reverie he would dwell—
Thy prattle soon will that expel.
—How darest thou frown, thou freakish fay!   50
And turn thy chubby face away,
And pout, as if thou took'st amiss
Thy partial parent's offered kiss?
Full well I know thy deep design;
'Tis to turn back thy face to mine,   55
With triple burst of joyous glee,
And fifty strains at mimicry!

   Crow on, sweet child! thy wild delight
Is moved by visions heavenly bright:
What wealth from nature may'st thou gain,   60
With promptings high to heart and brain!
But hope is all—though yet unproved,
Thou art a shepherd's best beloved:
And now above thy brow so fair
And flowing films of flaxen hair,   65
I lay my hand once more, and frame
A blessing, in the holy name
Of that supreme Divinity
Who breathed a living soul in thee.

The Musical Bijou

The Harp of Ossian

By the Ettrick Shepherd

Old Harp of the Highlands, how long hast thou slumber'd
  In cave of the correi, ungarnish'd, unstrung;
Thy minstrels no more with thy heroes are number'd,
  Or deeds of thy heroes no more dare be sung.
A seer late heard, from thy cavern ascending,   5
  A low sounding chime as of sorrow and dole;
Some spirit unseen, on the relic attending,
  Thus sung the last strain of the warrior's soul:

"My country, farewell! for the days are expir'd
  On which I could hallow the deeds of the free;   10
Thy heroes have all to new honours aspir'd,
  They fight, but they fight not for Scotia or me.
All lost is our sway, and the name of our nation
  Is lost in the name of our old mortal foe;
Then why should the lay of our last degradation   15
  Be forc'd from the old harp of Ossian to flow.

"My country, farewell! for the murmurs of sorrow
  Alone the dark mountains of Scotia become;
Her sons condescend from new models to borrow,
  And voices of strangers prevail in the hum.   20
Before the smooth face of our Saxon invaders
  Is quench'd the last ray in the eye of the free;
Then, oh! let me rest in the caves of my fathers,
  Forgetful of them as forgetful of me."

3

THE HARP OF OSSIAN.

Arranged by H. R. Bishop.

In moderate time, not too slow

Old Harp of the High-lands, how long thou hast slum-ber'd, In cave of the cor--rei un----gar--nished, un------strung; Thy

4

minstrels no more with thy he-roes are numberd, Or deeds of thy heroes no

more dare be sung: A seer late heard from thy cavern as--cending, A

low sounding chime, as of sorrow and dole; Some Spi--rit un---seen on the

relic at---tending, Thus sung the last strain of the war---rior's soul.

5

"My country fare-

...well! for the days are ex...pir'd, On which I could hallow   the deeds of the

free; My   heroes have   all   to new honours as....pir'd, They fight, but they

fight not for Scotia. or   me: All lost is our sway, and the name of our nation Is

6

lost in the name of our old mor__tal foe; Then why should the lay of our

last degra___dation Be forc'd from the old harp of Ossian to flow?"

"My country fare__well! for the

murmurs of sorrow A___lone the dark mountains of Sco_tia be__come; Her

7

sons con...de...scend from new models to borrow, And voices of strangers pre...

...vail in the hum: Be...fore the smooth face of our Saxon in...vaders Is

quench'd the last ray in the eye of the free; Then O let me rest in the

caves of thy fathers, For...getful of them as for...getful of me!"

My Emma, My Darling

By the Ettrick Shepherd

My Emma, my darling, from winter's domain
Let us fly to the glee of the city again,
Where a day never wakes but some joy it renews,
And a night never falls but that joy it pursues;
Where the dance is so light and the ball is so bright,   5
And life whirls onward one round of delight.
Would we feel that we live and have spirits refin'd,
We must mix with the world and enjoy human kind.

Mute nature is lovely in earth and in sky,
It cheers the lone heart and enlivens the eye;   10
But no where can beauty and dignity shine
So as in the human face fair and divine;
'Mongst these could I love thee, and that love enjoy;
But, ah! in the wilderness fond love would cloy.
To the homes of our kindred our spirits must cling,   15
And away from their bosoms at last take their wing.

100

MY EMMA, MY DARLING.

Arranged by H. R. Bishop.

101

day ne-ver wakes but some joy it renews, And a night never falls but that

joy it pursues: Where the dance is so light, and the ball is so bright, And

life whirls on-ward one round of delight; Would we feel that we live, and have

spirits re-fin'd, We must mix with the world, and en--joy human-kind.

103

these could I love thee, and that love en--joy; But ah! in the

wil--derness fond love would cloy; To the homes of our kin--dred our

spirits must cling, And a---way from their bosoms, at last take their

wing.

O Weel Befa' the Guileless Heart

By the Ettrick Shepherd

AIR—The Wauking o' the Fauld

1

O weel befa' the guileless heart
  In cottage bught or penn
And weel befa' the bonny thing
  That wons in yonder glen
The lovely flower I like sae weel   5
Wha's ay sae kind an' ay sae leel
An' pure as blooming asphodel
  Amang sae mony men
O weel befa' my bonny thing
  That wons in yonder glen   10

2

There's beauty in the violet's vest
  There's hinny in the haw
There's dew within the rose's breast
  The sweetest o' them a'
The sun may rise an' set again   15
An' lace wi' burning goud the main
The rainbow bend outower the plain
  Sae lovely to the ken
But there's naething like my bonny thing
  That wons in yonder glen   20

3

'Tis sweet to hear the music float
  Alang the gloaming lea
'Tis sweet to hear the blackbird's note
  Come pealing frae the tree
To see the lambkin's lightsome race   25
The speckled kid in wanton chace
The young deer cower in lonely place
  Deep in her flowery den
But O what's like the bonny face
  That smiles in yonder glen   30

Fairy Songs

By the Ettrick Shepherd

[Manuscript Source of 'The Song of Oberon']

Queen of the fairies—sings

Never, gentle spirits—never
   Yeild your cares of human kind
Can you leave the lonely river
From the moonlight valley sever
   All your guardian love resigned?   5
Thrown aside, and scorned the giver
   Never! gentle spirits—Never!

Chorus of fairies

Never till the dawn of day
   Dawn of truth that shine shall ever
Will we quit our polar way   10
Over greenwood glen and brae
   Over tree
   Over lea
Over fell and forest free
Over rock and over river   15
Over cairn and cloud to quiver
Never, gentle spirits, never!
Never! —Never!

Song second

By the Queen of the Fairies

1

Hie you away fairies hie you away
Lean to the breeze and ride in array   20
Over the land and the sea so fleet
Over the rain and the hail and the sleet
Be the springs of the dew your cool retreat
With the morning star far under your feet
And there we will sing our roundelay   25
Hie you away fairies hie you away

2

Keep the morning behind and the stars by your side
Be the moon-beam your path and her crescent your guide
For O her mild and her humid flame
Suits best with the fairies' airy frame   30
And meet me again to morrow at even
When the first star opens the window of heaven
And here such a palace of light shall be
As the world ne'er saw and never will see

3

For there shall the onyx and ruby be seen   35
And the amethyst blue and the emerald green
And our throne shall stand as the pine tree high
And its columns shall reach to the middle sky
Soft music shall flow of the spheres above
The songs of gladness and songs of love   40
And our feast shall be with glory and glee
Whatever the end of our days may be

The Song of Oberon

By the Ettrick Shepherd

[Published Extract from 'Fairy Songs']

HIE you away, fairies,—hie you away!
Lean to the breeze, and ride in array
Over the rain, and the hail, and the sleet,
By the springs of the dew—your cool retreat,
With the morning star far under your feet:—   5
And there we will sing our roundelay--
Hie you away, fairies,—hie you away.

Keep the morning behind, and the stars by your side,—
Be the moonbeam your path, and her crescent your guide:
For oh! her mild and humid flame,   10
Suit best with the fairie's airy frame;
And meet me again to-morrow at even,
When the first star opens the window of heaven!

And here such a palace of light shall be
As the world ne'er saw, and never will see. 15

For there shall the onyx, and the ruby be seen,
And the amethyst blue, and the emerald green;
And our throne shall stand as the pine tree high,—
And its columns shall reach to the middle sky:
Soft music shall flow of the spheres above, 20
The songs of gladness, and songs of love;
And our feast shall be with glory and glee,
Whatever the end of our days may be.

The Amulet

A Lay of the Martyrs

By the Ettrick Shepherd

"O where hae you been bonny Marley Reid
  For mony a lang night and day
I have missed ye sair at the Wanlock-head
  And the cave o' the Louther brae

Our friends are waning fast away   5
  Baith frae the cliff and the wood
They are tearing them frae us ilka day
  For there's naething will please but blood

And O bonny Marley I maun now
  Gie your heart muckle pain   10
For your bridegroom is a missing too
  And 'tis feared that he is ta'en

We have sought the caves o' the Enterkin
  And the dens o' the Ballybough
And a' the howes o' the Ganna linn   15
  And we wot not what to do"

"Dispel your fears good Marjory Laing
  And hope all for the best
For the servants of God will find a place
  Their weary heads to rest   20

There are better places that we ken o'
  And seemlier to be in
Than all the dens of the Ballybough
  Or howes o' the Ganna linn

But sit thee down good Marjory Laing   25
  And listen a while to me
For I have a tale to tell to you
  That will bring you to your knee

I went to seek my own dear James
  In the cave o' the Louther brae   30

For I had some things that of a' the world
    He best deserved to hae

I had a kebbuck in my lap
    And a fadge o' the flower sae sma'
And a sark I had made for his boardly back   35
    As white as the new dri'en snaw

I sought him over hill and dale
    Shouting by cave and tree
But only the dell with its eiry yell
    An answer returned to me   40

I sought him up and I sought him down
    And echos returned his name
Till the gloffs o' dread shot to my heart
    And dirled through a' my frame

I sat me down by the Enterkin   45
    And saw in a fearfu' line
The red dragoons come up the path
    Wi' prisoners eight or nine

And one of them was my dear dear James
    The flower of a' his kin   50
He was wounded behind and wounded before
    And the blood ran frae his chin

He was bound upon a weary hack
    Lashed both by hough and heel
And his hands were bound behind his back   55
    Wi' the thumbikins of steel

I kneeled before that popish band
    In the fervor of inward strife
And I spread to heaven my trembling hands
    And begged my husband's life   60

But all the troop laughed me to scorn
    Making my grief their game
And the captain said some words to me
    Which I cannot tell you for shame

And then he cursed our whiggish race   65
    With a proud and a scornful brow
And bade me look at my husband's face
    And say how I liked him now?

O I like him weel thou proud Captain
    Though the blood runs to his knee   70
And all the better for the grievous wrongs
    He has suffered this day frae thee

But can you feel within your heart
    That comely youth to slay
For the hope you have in heaven Captain   75
    Let him gang wi' me away

Then the captain swore a fearfu' oath
    With loathsome jest and mock
That he thought no more of a whigamore's life
    Than the life of a noisome brock   80

Then my poor James to the captain called
    And he beg'd baith hard and sair
To have one kiss of his bonny bride
    Ere we parted for evermair

I'll do that for you said the proud captain   85
    And save you the toil to day
And moreover I'll take her little store
    To support you by the way

He took my bountith from my lap
    And I saw with sorrow dumb   90
That he parted it all among his men
    And gave not my love one crumb

Now fare you well my very bonny bride
    Cried the captain with disdain
When I come back to the banks of Nith   95
    I shall kiss you sweetly then

Your heartiest thanks must sure be given
    For what I have done to day

I am taking him straight on the road to heaven
   And short will be the way   100

My love he gave me a parting look
   And blessed me ferventlye
And the tears they mixed wi' his purple blood
   And ran down to his knee"

"What's this I hear bonny Marley Reid   105
   How could these woes betide?
For blither you could not look this day
   Were your husband by your side

One of two things alone is left
   And dreadful one to me   110
For either your fair wits are reft
   Or else your husband's free"

"Allay your fears good Marjory Laing
   And hear me out the rest
You little ken what a bride will do   115
   For the youth she likes the best

I hied me hame to my father's ha'
   And through a' my friends I ran
And I gathered me up a purse o' goud
   To redeem my young goodman   120

For I kend the papish lowns would well
   My fair intent approve
For they'll do far mair for the good red goud
   Than they'll do for heaven above

And away I ran to Edinburgh town   125
   Of my shining treasure vain
To buy my James from the prison strang
   Or there with him remain

I sought through a' the city jails
   I sought baith lang and sair   130
But the guardsmen turned me frae their doors
   And swore that he was not there

I went away to the popish duke
   Who was my love's judge to be
And I proffered him a' my yellow store   135
   If he'd grant his life to me

He counted the red goud slowly o'er
   By twenties and by tens
And said I had taken the only means
   To attain my hopeful ends   140

And now said he your husband's safe
   You may take this pledge of me
And I'll tell you, fair one, where you'll go
   To gain this certaintye

Gang west the street and down the bow   145
   And through the market place
And there you will meet with a gentleman
   Of a tall and courteous grace

He is clad in a livery of the green
   With a plume aboon his bree   150
And armed with a halbert glittering sheen
   Your love he will let you see

O Marjory never flew blithsome bird
   So light out through the sky
As I flew up that stately street   155
   Weeping for very joy

O never flew lamb out o'er the lea
   When the sun gangs o'er the hill
Wi' lighter blither step than me
   Or skipped wi' sic good will   160

And ay I blessed the precious ore
   My husband's life that wan
And I even blessed the popish duke
   For a kind good-hearted man

The officer I soon found out   165
   For he could not be mistook

But in all my life I never beheld
   Sic a grim and gruesome look

I asked him for my dear dear James
   With throbs of wild delight   170
And begged him in his master's name
   To take me to his sight

He asked me for his true address
   With a voice at which I shook
For I saw that he was a popish knave   175
   By the terror of his look

I named the name with a buoyant voice
   That trembled with extacye
But the savage brayed a hideous laugh
   Then turned and grinned at me   180

He pointed up to the city wall
   One look benumbed my soul
For there I saw my husband's head
   Fixed high upon a pole

His yellow hair waved in the wind   185
   And far behind did flee
And his right hand hang beside his cheek
   A waesome sight to see

His chin hang down on open space
   Yet comely was his brow   190
And his een were open to the breeze
   There was nane to close them now

What think you of your true love now?
   The hideous porter said
Is not that a comely sight to see   195
   And sweet to a whiggish maid?

O haud your tongue ye popish slave
   For I downae answer you
He was dear dear to my heart before
   But never sae dear as now   200

I see a sight you cannot see
　　Which man can not efface
I see a ray of heavenly love
　　Beaming on that dear face

And weel I ken yon bonny brent brow   205
　　Will smile in the walks on high
And yon yellow hair all blood-stained now
　　Maun wave aboon the sky

But can you trow me Marjory dear
　　In the might of heavenly grace   210
There was never a sigh burst frae my heart
　　Nor a tear ran o'er my face

But I blessed my God who had thus seen meet
　　To take him from my side
To call him home to the courts above   215
　　And leave me a virgin bride"

"Alak alak bonny Marley Reid
　　That sic days we hae lived to see
For sickan a cruel and waefu' tale
　　Was never yet heard by me   220

And all this time I have trembling weened
　　That your dear wits were gone
For there is a joy in your countenance
　　Which I never saw beam thereon

Then let us kneel with humble hearts   225
　　To the God whom we revere
Who never yet laid that burden on
　　Which he gave not strength to bear"

A Tale of Pentland

By the Ettrick Shepherd

WOODROW mentions the following story, but in a manner so confused and indefinite, that it is impossible to comprehend either the connexion of the incidents with one another, or what inference he wishes to draw from them. The facts seem to have been these. Mr. John Haliday having been in hiding on the hills, after the battle of Pentland, became impatient to hear news concerning the suffering of his brethren who had been in arms, and in particular if there were any troops scouring the district in which he had found shelter. Accordingly, he left his hiding-place in the evening, and travelled towards the valley until about midnight; when, coming to the house of Gabriel Johnstone, and perceiving a light, he determined on entering, as he knew him to be a devout man, and one much concerned about the sufferings of the church of Scotland.

Mr. Haliday, however, approached the house with great caution, for he rather wondered why there should be a light there at midnight, while at the same time he neither heard psalms singing nor the accents of prayer. So, casting off his heavy shoes, for fear of making a noise, he stole softly up to the little window from whence the light beamed, and peeped in, where he saw, not Johnstone, but another man, whom he did not know, in the very act of cutting a soldier's throat, while Johnstone's daughter, a comely girl, about twenty years of age, was standing deliberately by, and holding the candle to him.

Haliday was seized with an inexpressible terror; for the floor was all blood, and the man was struggling in the agonies of death, and from his dress he appeared to have been a cavalier of some distinction. So completely was the covenanter overcome with horror, that he turned and fled from the house with all his might; resolved to have no participation in the crime, and deeply grieved that he should have witnessed such an act of depravity, as a private deliberate murder, perpetrated at such an hour, and in such a place, by any who professed to be adherents to the reformed religion of the Scottish church. So much had Haliday been confounded, that he even forgot to lift his shoes, but fled without them; and he had not run above half a bowshot before he came upon two men hasting to the house of Gabriel Johnstone. As soon as they perceived him running towards them they fled, and he pursued them, for when he saw them so ready to take alarm, he was sure they were some of the persecuted race and tried eagerly to overtake them, exerting his utmost speed, and calling on them to stop. All this only made them run the faster, and when they came to a feal-dike they separated, and ran different ways, and he soon thereafter lost sight of them both.

This house, where Johnstone lived, is said to have been in a lonely concealed dell, not far from West Linton, in what direction I do not know, but it was towards that village that Haliday fled, not knowing whither he went, till he came to the houses. Having no acquaintances here whom he durst venture to call up, and the morning having set in frosty, he began to conceive that it was absolutely necessary for him to return to the house of Gabriel Johnstone, and try to regain his shoes, as he little knew when or where it might be in his power to get another pair. Accordingly he hasted back by a nearer path, and coming to the place before it was day, found his shoes. At the same time he heard a fierce contention within the house, but as there seemed to be a watch he durst not approach it, but again made his escape.

Having brought some victuals along with him, he did not return to his hiding-place that day, which was in a wild height, south of Biggar, but remained in the moss of Craigengaur; and as soon as it grew dark descended again into the valley, determined to have some communication with his species, whatever it might cost. Again he perceived a light at a distance, where he thought no light should have been. But he went toward it, and as he approached, he heard the melody of psalm-singing issuing from the place, and floating far on the still breeze of the night. The covenanter's spirits were cheered, he had never heard any thing so sweet; no, not when enjoying the gospel strains in peace, and in their fullest fruition. It was to him the feast of the soul, and rang through his ears like a hymn of paradise. He flew as on hinds' feet to the spot, and found the reverend and devout Mr. Livingston, in the act of divine worship, in an old void barn on the lands of Slipperfield, with a great number of serious and pious people, who were all much affected both by his prayers and discourse.

After the worship was ended, Haliday made up to the minister, among many others, to congratulate him on the splendour of his discourse, and implore "a further supply of the same milk of redeeming grace, with which they found their souls nourished, cherished, and exalted." Indeed, it is quite consistent with human nature to suppose, that the whole of the circumstances under which this small community of Christians met, could not miss rendering their devotions impressive. They were a proscribed race, and were meet-ing at the penalty of their lives; their dome of worship a waste house in the wilderness, and the season, the dead hour of the night, had of themselves tints of sublimity which could not fail to make impres-sions on the souls of the worshippers. The good man complied with their request, and appointed another meeting at the same place, on a future night.

Haliday having been formerly well acquainted with the preacher, conveyed him on his way home, where they condoled with one another on the hardness of their lots; and Haliday told him of the scene he had witnessed at the house of Gabriel Johnstone. The heart of the good minister was wrung with grief, and he deplored the madness and malice of the people who had committed an act that would bring down tenfold vengeance on the heads of the whole persecuted race. At length it was resolved between them, that as soon as it was day, they would go and reconnoitre; and if they found the case of the aggravated nature they suspected, they would themselves be the first to expose it, and give the perpetrators up to justice.

Accordingly, the next morning they took another man into the secret, a William Rankin, one of Mr. Livingston's elders, and the three went away to Johnstone's house, to investigate the case of the cavalier's murder; but there was a guard of three armed men op-posed them, and neither promises, nor threatenings, nor all the minister's eloquence, could induce them to give way one inch. They said they could not conceive what they were seeking there, and as they suspected they came for no good purpose, they were deter-mined that they should not enter. It was in vain that Mr. Livingston informed them of his name and sacred calling, and his friendship for the owner of the house, and the cause which he had espoused; the men continued obstinate: and when he asked to speak a word to Gabriel Johnstone himself, they shook their heads, and said, "he would never see him again." The men then advised the intruders to take themselves off without any more delay, lest a worse thing should befal them; and as they continued to motion them away, with the most impatient gestures, the kind divine and his associates thought meet to retire, and leave the matter as it was: and thus was this mysterious affair hushed up in silence and darkness for that time, no tongue having been heard to mention it further than as above recited. The three armed men were all unknown to the others, but Haliday observed, that one of them was the very youth whom he saw cutting off the soldier's head with a knife.

The rage and cruelty of the popish party seemed to gather new virulence every day, influencing all the counsels of the king; and the persecution of the non-conformists was proportionably severe. One new act of council was issued after another, all tending to root the covenanters out of Scotland, but it had only the effect of making their tenets still dearer to them. The longed-for night of the meeting in the old hay-barn at length arrived, and it was attended by a still greater number than that on the preceding. A more motley group can hardly be conceived than appeared in the barn that night, and the lamps being weak and dim, rendered the appearance of the as- sembly still more striking. It was, however, observed, that about the middle of the service, a number of fellows came in with broad slouch bonnets, and watch coats or cloaks about them, who placed themselves in equal divisions at the two doors, and remained with- out uncovering their heads, two of them being busily engaged in taking notes. Before Mr. Livingston began the last prayer, however, he desired the men to uncover, which they did, and the service went on to the end, but no sooner had the minister pronounced the word *Amen*, than the group of late comers threw off their cloaks, and draw- ing out swords and pistols, their commander, one General Drummond, charged the whole congregation, in the king's name, to surrender.

A scene of the utmost confusion ensued; the lights being extin- guished, many of the young men burst through the roof of the old barn in every direction, and though many shots were fired at them in the dark, great numbers escaped; but Mr. Livingston, and other eleven, were retained prisoners and conveyed to Edinburgh, where they were examined before the council, and cast into prison; among the prisoners was Mr. Haliday, and the identical young man whom he had seen in the act of murdering the cavalier, and who turned out to be a Mr. John Lindsay, from Edinburgh, who had been at the battle of Pentland, and in hiding, afterwards.

Great was the lamentation for the loss of Mr. Livingston, who was so highly esteemed by his hearers: the short extracts from his sermons in the barn, that were produced against him on his trial, prove him to have been a man endowed with talents some- what above the greater part of his contemporaries. His text that night, it appears, had been taken from Genesis: "And God saw the wickedness of man that it was great in the earth, and that every imagination of the thoughts of his heart is only evil continually." One of the quoted passages runs thus:

"And while we have thus ample experience of the *effects* of sin, we have also abundance of examples set before us of sin itself, yea, in its most hideous aspect; for behold how it abounds among us all, but chiefly among the rulers and nobles of the land! Dare I mention to you those crimes of theirs which cause the sun of heaven to blush and hide his head as ashamed of the sight of their abominations? Dare I mention to you the extent of their blasphemies against that God who made them, and the Saviour who died to redeem them? Their cursing and swearing, Sabbath-breaking, chambering, and wantonness; and, above all, their trampling upon the blood of the covenant, and pouring out the blood of saints and martyrs like water on the face of the earth. Because of those the land mourneth, and by these, multitudes, which no man can number, are plunging their souls into irretrievable and eternal ruin. But some say, O these are honourable men! Amiable, upright, and good moral men—though no great professors of religion. But I say, my brethren, alack and well-a-day for their uprightness and honour! which, if ever they come to be tried by the test of the Divine law, and by the example of him who was holiness itself, will be found miserably short-coming. So true it is that the kings of the earth have combined to plot against the Lord and his anointed. Let us therefore join together in breaking their bands and casting their cords from us. As for myself, as a member of this poor persecuted Church of Scotland, and an unworthy minister of it, I hereby call upon you all, in the name of God, to set your faces, your hearts, and your hands against all such acts, which are or shall be passed, against the covenanted work of reformation in this kingdom; that we here declare ourselves free of the guilt of them, and pray that God may put this in record in heaven."

These words having been sworn to, and Mr. Livingston not denying them, a sharp debate arose in the council what punishment to award. The king's advocate urged the utility of sending him forthwith to the gallows; but some friends in the council got his sentence commuted to banishment; and he was accordingly banished the kingdom. Six more, against whom nothing could be proven, farther than their having been present at a conventicle, were sentenced to imprisonment for two months; among this number Haliday was one. The other five were condemned to be executed at the cross of Edinburgh, on the 14th of December following; and among this last unhappy number was Mr. John Lindsay.

Haliday now tried all the means he could devise to gain an interview with Lindsay, to have some explanation of the extraordinary scene he had witnessed in the cottage at midnight, for it had made a fearful impression upon his mind, and he never could get rid of it for a moment; having still in his mind's eye a beautiful country maiden standing with a pleased face, holding a candle, and Lindsay in the mean time at his horrid task. His endeavours, however, were all in vain, for they were in different prisons, and the jailor paid no attention to his requests. But there was a gentleman in the Privy Council, that year, whose name, I think, was Gilmour, to whose candour Haliday conceived, that both he and some of his associates owed their lives. To this gentleman, therefore, he applied by letter, requesting a private interview with him, as he had a singular instance of barbarity to communicate, which it would be well to inquire into while the possibility of doing so remained, for the access to it would soon be sealed for ever. The gentleman attended immediately, and Haliday revealed to him the circumstances previously mentioned, stating that the murderer now lay in the Tolbooth jail, under sentence of death.

Gilmour appeared much interested, as well as astonished at the narrative, and taking out a note-book, he looked over some dates, and then observed: "This date of yours, tallies exactly with one of my own, relating to an incident of the same sort, but the circumstances narrated are so different, that I must conceive, either that you are mistaken, or that you are trumping up this story to screen some other guilty person or persons."

Haliday disclaimed all such motives, and persevered in his attestations. Gilmour then took him along with him to the Tolbooth prison, where the two were admitted to a private interview with the prisoner, and there charged him with the crime of murder in such a place and on such a night; but he denied the whole with disdain. Haliday told him that it was in vain for him to deny it, for he beheld him in the very act of perpetrating the murder with his own eyes, while Gabriel Johnstone's daughter stood deliberately and held the candle to him.

"Hold your tongue, fellow!" said Lindsay, disdainfully, "for you know not what you are saying. What a cowardly dog you must be by your own account! If you saw me murdering a gentleman cavalier, why did you not rush in to his assistance?"

"I could not have saved the gentleman then," said Haliday, "and I thought it not meet to intermeddle in such a scene of blood."

"It was as well for you that you did not," said Lindsay.

"Then you acknowledge being in the cottage of the dell that night?" said Gilmour.

"And if I was, what is that to you? Or what is it now to me, or any person? I *was* there on the night specified; but I am ashamed of the part I there acted, and am now well requited for it! Yes, requited as I ought to be, so let it rest; for not one syllable of the transaction shall any one hear from me."

Thus they were obliged to leave the prisoner, and forthwith Gilmour led Haliday up a stair to a lodging in the Parliament Square, where they found a gentleman lying sick in bed, to whom Mr. Gilmour said, after inquiring after his health, "Brother Robert, I conceive that we two have found out the young man who saved your life at the cottage among the mountains."

"I would give the half that I possess that this were true," said the sick gentleman, "who or where is he?"

"If I am right in my conjecture," said the Privy Councillor, "he is lying in the Tolbooth jail, there under sentence of death, and has but a few days to live. But tell me, brother, could you know him, or have you any recollection of his appearance?"

"Alas! I have none!" said the other, mournfully, "for I was insensible, through the loss of blood, the whole time I was under his protection; and if I ever heard his name I have lost it: the whole of that period being a total blank in my memory. But he must be a hero of the first rank, and therefore, O my dear brother, save him whatever his crime may be."

"His life is justly forfeited to the laws of his country, brother," said Gilmour, "and he must die with the rest."

"He shall not die with the rest if I should die for him," cried the sick man, vehemently, "I will move heaven and earth before my brave deliverer shall die like a felon."

"Calm yourself, brother; and trust that part to me," said Gilmour, "I think my influence saved the life of this gentleman, as well as the lives of some others, and it was all on account of the feeling of respect I had for the party, one of whom, or, rather, I should say two of whom, acted such a noble and distinguished part toward you. But pray undeceive this gentleman by narrating the facts to him, in which he cannot miss to be interested." The sick man, whose name it seems, if I remember aright, was Captain Robert Gilmour, of the volunteers, then proceeded as follows:—

"There having been high rewards offered for the apprehension of some south-country gentlemen, whose correspondence with Mr. Welch, and some other of the fanatics, had been intercepted, I took advantage of information I obtained, regarding the place of their retreat, and set out, certain of apprehending two of them at least.

"Accordingly I went off one morning, about the beginning of November, with only five followers, well armed and mounted. We left

Gilmerton long before it was light, and, having a trusty guide, rode straight to their hiding-place, where we did not arrive till towards the evening, when we started them. They were seven in number, and were armed with swords and bludgeons: but, being apprized of our approach, they fled from us, and took shelter in a morass, into which it was impossible to follow them on horseback. But perceiving three men more, on another hill, I thought there was no time to lose; so giving one of my men our horses to hold, the rest of us advanced into the morass with drawn swords and loaded horse pistols. I called to them to surrender, but they stood upon their guard, determined on resistance; and just while we were involved to the knees in the mire of the morass, they broke in upon us, pell-mell, and for about two minutes the engagement was very sharp. There was an old man struck me a terrible blow with a bludgeon, and was just about to repeat it when I brought him down with a shot from my pistol. A young fellow then ran at me with his sword, and as I still stuck in the moss, I could not ward the blow, so that he got a fair stroke at my neck, meaning, without doubt, to cut off my head; and he would have done it had his sword been sharp. As it was, he cut it to the bone, and opened one of the jugular veins. I fell, but my men firing a volley in their faces, at that moment, they fled. It seems we did the same, without loss of time; for I must now take my narrative from the report of others, as I remember no more that passed. My men bore me on their arms to our horses, and then mounted and fled; trying all that they could to staunch the bleeding of my wound. But perceiving a party coming running down a hill, as with the intent of cutting off their retreat, and losing all hopes of saving my life, they carried me into a cottage in a wild lonely retreat, commended me to the care of the inmates, and, after telling them my name, and in what manner I had received my death wound, they thought proper to provide for their own safety, and so escaped.

"The only inmates of that lonely house, at least at that present time, were a lover and his mistress, both intercommuned whigs; and when my men left me on the floor, the blood, which they had hitherto restrained in part, burst out afresh and deluged the floor. The young man said it was best to put me out of my pain, but the girl wept and prayed him rather to render me some assistance. 'Oh Johnny, man, how can ye speak that gate?' cried she, 'suppose he be our mortal enemy, he is ay ane o' God's creatures, an' has a soul to be saved as well as either you or me; an' a soldier is obliged to do as he is bidden. Now Johnny, ye ken ye war learned to be a doctor o' physic, wad ye no rather try to stop the blooding and save the young officer's life, as either kill him, or let him blood to death on our floor, when the blame o' the murder might fa' on us?'

" 'Now, the blessing of heaven light on your head, my dear Sally!' said the lover, 'for you have spoken the very sentiments of my heart; and, since it is your desire, though we should both rue it, I here vow to you that I will not only endeavour to save his life, but I will defend it against our own party to the last drop of my blood.'

"He then began, and in spite of my feeble struggles, who knew not either what I was doing or suffering, sewed up the hideous gash in my throat and neck, tying every stitch by itself; and the house not being able to produce a pair of scissars, it seems that he cut off all the odds and ends of the stitching with a large sharp gully knife, and it was likely to have been during the operation that this gentleman chanced to look in at the window. He then bathed the wound for an hour with cloths dipped in cold water, dressed it with plaister of wood-betony, and put me to bed, expressing to his sweetheart the most vivid hopes of my recovery.

"These operations were scarcely finished, when the maid's two brothers came home from their hiding-place; and it seems they would have been there much sooner had not this gentleman given them chace in the contrary direction. They, seeing the floor all covered with blood, inquired the cause with wild trepidation of manner. Their sister was the first to inform them of what had happened; on which both the young men gripped to their weapons, and the eldest, Samuel, cried out with the vehemence of a maniac, 'Blessed be the righteous avenger of blood! Hoo! Is it then true that the Lord hath delivered our greatest enemy into our hands!' 'Hold, hold, dearest brother!' cried the maid, spreading out her arms before him, 'Would you kill a helpless young man, lying in a state of insensibility? What, although the Almighty hath put his life in your hand, will he not require the blood of you, shed in such a base and cowardly way?'

" 'Hold your peace, foolish girl,' cried he, in the same furious strain, 'I tell you if he had a thousand lives I would sacrifice them all this moment! Wo be to this old rusty and fizenless sword, that did not sever his head from his body, when I had a fair chance in the open field! Nevertheless he shall die; for you do not yet know that he hath, within these few hours, murdered our father, whose blood is yet warm around him on the bleak height.'

" 'Oh! merciful heaven! killed our father!" screamed the girl, and flinging herself down on the resting-chair, she fainted away. The two brothers regarded not, but with their bared weapons, made towards the closet, intent on my blood, and both vowing I should die if I had a thousand lives. The stranger interfered, and thrust himself into the closet door before them, swearing that, before they committed so cowardly a murder, they should first make their way through his body. A long scene of expostulation and bitter altercation then ensued, which it is needless to recapitulate; both parties refusing to yield. Samuel at the last got into an ungovernable rage, and raising his weapon, he said, furiously, 'How dare you, Sir, mar my righteous vengeance when my father's blood calls to me from the dreary heights? Or how dictate to me in my own house? Either stand aside this moment, or thy blood be upon thine own head!'

"'I'll dictate to the devil, if he will not hearken to reason,' said the young surgeon, 'therefore strike at your peril.'

"Samuel retreated one step to have full sway for his weapon, and the fury depicted on his countenance proved his determination. But in a moment, his gallant opponent closed with him, and holding up his wrist with his left hand, he with the right bestowed on him a blow with such energy, that he fell flat on the floor, among the soldier's blood. The youngest then ran on their antagonist with his sword, and wounded him, but the next moment he was lying beside his brother. He then disarmed them both, and still not thinking himself quite safe with them, he tied both their hands behind their backs, and had then time to pay attention to the young woman, who was inconsolable for the loss of her father, yet deprecated the idea of murdering the wounded man. As soon as her brothers came fairly to their senses, she and her lover began and expostulated with them, at great length, on the impropriety and unmanliness of the attempt, until they became all of one mind, and the two brothers agreed to join in the defence of the wounded gentleman, from all of their own party, until he was rescued by his friends, which they did. But it was the maid's simple eloquence that finally prevailed with the fierce covenanters, in whom a spirit of retaliation seemed inherent.

"'O my dear brothers,' said she, weeping, 'calm yourselves, and think like men and like Christians. There has been enough o' blood shed for ae day, and if ye wad cut him a' to inches it coudna restore our father to life again. Na, na, it coudna bring back the soul that has departed frae this weary scene o' sin, sorrow, and suffering; and if ye wad but mind the maxims o' our blessed Saviour ye wadna let revenge rankle in your hearts that gate. An' o'er an' aboon a', it appears to me that the young officer was only doing what he conceived to be his bounden duty, and at the moment was actually acting in defence of his own life. Since it is the will of the Almighty to lay these grievous sufferings on our covenanted church, why not suffer patiently, along with your brethren, in obedience to that will: for it is na like to be a private act of cruelty or revenge that is to prove favourable to our forlorn cause.'

"When my brothers came at last, with a number of my men, and took me away, the only thing I remember seeing in the house was the corpse of the old man whom I had shot, and the beautiful girl standing weeping over the body; and certainly my heart smote me in such a manner that I would not experience the same feeling again for the highest of this world's benefits. That comely young maiden, and her brave intrepid lover, it would be the utmost ingratitude in me, or in any of my family, ever to forget; for it is scarcely possible that a man can ever be again in the same circumstances as I was, having been preserved from death in the house of the man whom my hand had just deprived of life."

Just as he ended, the sick-nurse peeped in, which she had done several times before, and said, "Will your honour soon be disengaged d'ye think? for ye see because there's a lass wanting till speak till ye."

"A lass, nurse? what lass can have any business with me? what is she like?"

"Oo 'deed, Sir, the lass is weel enough, for that part o't, but she may be nae better than she should be for a' that; ye ken, I's no answer for that, for ye see because *like* is an ill mark: but she has been aften up, speering after ye, an' gude troth she's fairly in nettle-earnest now, for she winna gang awa till she see your honour."

The nurse being desired to show her in, a comely girl entered, with a timid step, and seemed ready to faint with trepidation. She had a mantle on, and a hood that covered much of her face. The Privy Councillor spoke to her, desiring her to come forward, and say her errand; on which she said that "she only wanted a preevat word wi' the captain, if he was that weel as to speak to ane." He looked over the bed, and desired her to say on, for that gentleman was his brother, from whom he kept no secrets. After a hard struggle with her diffidence, but, on the other hand, prompted by the urgency of the case, she at last got out, "I'm unco glad to see you sae weel comed round again, though I daresay ye'll maybe no ken wha I am. But it was me that nursed ye, an' took care o' ye, in our house, when your head was amaist cuttit off."

There was not another word required to draw forth the most ardent expressions of kindness from the two brothers; on which the poor girl took courage, and, after several showers of tears she said, with many bitter sobs, "There's a poor lad wha, in my humble opin-

Painted by David Wilkie, R. A.   Engraved by I. Mitchell

THE DORTY BAIRN

Published for the Proprietors of the Amulet.

Printed by H. Wilson

ion, saved your life; an' wha is just gaun to be hanged the day after the morn. I wad unco fain beg your honour's interest to get his life spared."

"Say not another word, my dear, good girl," said the Councillor, "for though I hardly know how I can intercede for a rebel who has taken up arms against the government, yet for your sake, and his, my best interest shall be exerted."

"Oh, ye maun just say, sir, that the poor whigs were driven to desperation, and that this young man was misled by others in the fervour and enthusiasm of youth. What else can ye say? but ye're good! oh, ye're very good! and on my knees I beg that ye winna lose ony time, for indeed there is nae time to lose!"

The Councillor lifted her kindly by both hands, and desired her to stay with his brother's nurse till his return, on which he went away to the president, and in half an hour returned with a respite for the convict, John Lindsay, for three days, which he gave to the girl, along with an order for her admittance to the prisoner. She thanked him with the tears in her eyes, but added, "Oh, sir, will he and I then be obliged to part for ever at the end of three days?"

"Keep up your heart, and encourage your lover," said he, "and meet me here again, on Thursday, at this same hour, for, till the council meet, nothing further than this can be obtained."

It may well be conceived how much the poor forlorn prisoner was astonished, when his own beloved Sally entered to him, with the reprieve in her hand, and how much his whole soul dilated when, on the Thursday following, she presented him with a free pardon. They were afterwards married; when the Gilmours took them under their protection. Lindsay became a highly qualified surgeon, and the descendants of this intrepid youth occupy respectable positions in Edinburgh to this present day.

[Three Sketches: A Tribute to David Wilkie]

The Dorty Wean

By the Ettrick Shepherd

I never see an interesting and original figure or a group but I uniformly think to myself "O if I had but Davie Wilkie here!" and no farther gone than yesterday I had a strong feeling of the same sort impressed on my mind on witnessing the following very simple scene.

As I was passing my shepherd's house in Benger-Hope I heard a great screaming on which I ran into the house thinking some of the children had fallen into the fire but seeing all right I only peeped over the hallan. And behold all the fray was no more than this that little Mary a very pretty child had taken the pet and got into a desperate rage because forsooth Andrew had got the piece of bread and butter which she had set her fancy on though I really thought to all appearance that the piece allotted to her was both the best and biggest. Jenny her mother was fleeching one while and flyting another and at length said to her in a coaxing manner "Fie fie Mary how can ye yammer on that gate when ye ken I hae nae better i' the house to g'ye. Gie ower greeting like a good bairn an' tak your bit piece or else the dog will tak it for see auld Yarrow has his nose just amaist at it."

"Aye let him tak it, he'll no be muckle upmade wi't."

"Aih! now ye little hempy skempy limmer! How can ye speak that gate to your mither? I am sure it is a very good piece an' far bigger nor Andrew's an' he's mumping away at his like a man an' a good bairn. Fie Yarrow come an' tak away Mary's piece."

"Ay let him tak it. It is mair like a bit piece for a dog or a cat than for a poor lassie wha hasna tastit oughts the day."

"But lakadaisey! Mary haud your tongue for there's the master comin' in an' gin he catch you that way he'll maybe mak a poet on you."

"Aye let him be doing. He may mak a poet on you too gin he likes."

"But he ca's ye ay sae bonny ye ken. Now if he should see you wi' sic a face as that what wad he think? Wow woman sic-a-like face as ye hae made that bonny face o' your's! I wish ye but saw it for aince I am sure you would never put it on again." Then taking the little family looking-glass down from its place on the wall she popped it in before the little crying urchin ere ever she was aware. The effect was instantaneous! It acted like a charm. It was nature itself! So true is the apothegm that all the sex old and young are the most affected by that which impairs their beauty. Little Mary took only one look of her distorted countenance and seemingly quite shocked at the figure she made instinctively lifted the corner of her pinafore and with repentant modesty held it up before her eyes to shield her features from the world's view and from her own.

The History of an Auld Naig

By the Same

I witnessed another scene in St. Boswell's fair very lately which amused me a good deal as a picture of the very lowest species of harmless yet overweening vulgarity and I would have given half a dozen of wine that my friend Mr Wilkie had seen it. I went into a tent with a friend to talk of some business and at the door of the tent there was standing a hard featured old horse who had the appearance of having seen better days, and he was whisking his tail, and looking about him with the greatest contempt. His owner the very prince and hero of vulgarity was sitting on a form, holding by the halter, and guzzling ale, and taking at least a quarter of a pound of bread at every bite. He was trying to sell the veteran steed to four others of the same class, who were manifestly intending to overreach him yet at the same time they could not help regarding him as a sort of natural curiosity. Such a group, taking in the horse and all, I never beheld! The following is a literal specimen of a part of their dialogue.

"Come now, maister, let us hear what ye're gaun to say about the naig? Are ye gaun to tak the thretty shillings for him or no?"

"Thretty shillings, mun! Thretty diels! Aw wudna tak your twapund-ten for him. As fack as death, aw wudna. He's a horse that, mun, that'll gang up hill an' down hill, through fire an' water, yird an' stane, an' never an ill word in his head. It's as fack as death, mun. He's a horse that'll never stand still, whatever he gangs to. Thretty *Shillings*! Aw wudna luk on the side o' the gate ye war on mun wi' your thretty shillings."

"The only thing I'm feared for" said one of the purchasers "is that we'll no get him hame for dogs' meat. Whar did ye pick him up, for I'm sure ye canna hae brought him far?"

"Aw think nae shame to tell where I got him, mun! Awm nane o' that sort! Ay nor what I gae for him neither. I coft him on the tap o' the street in the Gerse Merkat o' Edinbrough, frae auld Peter Dods, the coal-cawer, a gayan quirky carle. Aw thought the horse liftit his feet gayan' weel, for awm never at a loss to see what's what, and sae I says, 'Peter, what are auxing for the auld beast?' 'Thretty shillings', says he. 'Thretty puffs o tobacco reek mun!' says I. 'Ye munna speak that gate till me wha kens better. But come awa into Newbiggings, an' we'll hae a bottle o' yill. It'll no brik us baith.' As fack as death, aw said sae. 'It'll no brik us baith, Peter,' says I. Weel we get's the yill. 'An now, Peter,' says I. 'Awm nane o' the kind o' folks wha mak a great whitty-whattying an' arglebargaining about a thing, however big the soom. Awm just gaun to lay ye down five-an-twanty shillings for the naig, tak it or want it.'

"'Five-an-twanty puffs o' tobbacco reek!' quo the auld mockrife rascal. 'Ye maunna speak to me that gate, lad, wha kens better. But I'll tell ye what I'll do wi' ye; I'll just tak it.' An wi' that, nippit up my five-an-twanty shillings, an' pat it in his pouch, wi' a girn. 'An' now, lad' says he, 'The siller's mine an' the beast's your's, an' ye're very welcome to him.'

"Od, Sir, I thought I was fairly snappit, an' the vera countenance o' my face rose as I had been set in a lowe. 'If ye hae cheatit me wi' that beast, billy,' says I, 'I'll scorn to loup back or gang to the law w'ye, however great may be my loss. But I promise ye a good thresh-ing, an I'll keep my word too. Only tell me this. Is the beast no a good beast?'

"'Gin he be a good beast, ye'll be the better o' him' says he, an' off he gangs, laughin in his sleeve an' turnin the quid in his cheek.

"I was vera sair dung down. But what could I do? My siller was gane; sae I took my beast, an' pat him into the Meadow Park. I coudna sleep a wink that night wi' thinking about my bargain. 'I'm sair, sair taken in!' thinks I. 'For if the beast be useless there I hae to pay auld Gray aughteen pence a night for his gerse an' that mair nor I can gain through the day an' the best thing aw can do is to gie him again to auld Peter for naething. It's as fack as death.' Weel as soon as the daylight skairs the sky off I sets wi' a heavy heart to look after my beast, an' soon fand him feedin' closs to the hedge. Sae aw lays ma lugs i' ma neck to listen, an there is he ruggin an' rivin' an' craunchin away at nae allowance. 'There is some hope here yet,' thinks I 'for gin a beast dinna eat weel, it'll never work weel,' an' wi that I gies my apron a blatter at him an aw'll be the greatest leear ever was born if he didna spang up i' the air like a wild deer, till aw thought he was gaun to loup ower the chimla taps. As fack as death aw did. An' then he cockit up his head an' his tail till the twasome met thegither an he gae three skreeds o' snorks till a' the Hope-park-end yells again. 'There he goes that never saw the morn!' cries I 'There's mair mettle there by a hunder times than any body wad think! An' aw'll tell ye what it is, ma jolly auld rogue, aw'll no tak ony man's twa-pund-ten for ye, gin he war to lay it down this day!' As fack as death, aw said sae. An' that's the history o' the auld naig."

David Wilkie

By the same

I little wot what Mr Wilkie is doing now since I last saw him in Yarrow but I cannot help deeming it strange that he should ever delight in depicting scenes out of his native country for to me his genius is as completely Scottish as if I saw it walking our hills in the blue bonnet the grey plaid and the clouted shoes. There is not a trait of mind among our peasantry which he has not embodied and personified in tints never to be effaced. In particular there is a stupid effort at abstruse calculation at which he is inimitable and which even Mr Wm Murray has not yet outvied. This cast of thought is often given in a single touch and yet every muscle corresponds with that.

I remember of once in particular seeing a small piece of his I have forgot when or where but it was a number of years ago which was probably regarded by the artist as a trifle but if nature's first impressions are to be in aught believed it is a gem of the first water. I got only one slight look of it but I saw nature so beautifully depicted that in spite of all I could do the tears burst from my eyes and the impression made by it is as powerful at this moment as it was then. It is a scene from Allan Ramsay's Gentle Shepherd in which the lover is exerting all his power to play his sweetheart's favourite tune with proper effect while she is leaning on her cousin and asking her "If she has any guess what tune that is which the poor fellow is trying?" I never saw any thing equal to it! There is a cast of disdain in every muscle of Jenny's lovely rural form from the toe to the eyebrow which is indescribable. And the best of it all is that the looker at the picture percieves at once that it is an affected disdain, but neither the lover, nor Peggy, nor the colley discover aught of this but are all deploring her perversity by looks the most characteristic. The looks of dissapointed affection in the dog are exquisite. I have often wondered what became of that little picture, or how it was estimated, for there was never any thing of the kind made such an impression on me.

MOUNT-BENGER
August 6th, 1829

A Cameronian Ballad

By James Hogg

"O what is become o' your leel goodman,
  That now you are a' your lane?
If he has joined wi' the rebel gang,
  You will never see him again."

"O say nae 'the rebel gang,' ladye,   5
  It's a term nae heart can thole,
For they wha rebel against their God,
  It is justice to control.

When rank oppression rends the heart,
  An' rules wi' stroke o' death,   10
Wha wadna spend their dear heart's blood
  For the tenets o' their faith?

Then say nae 'the rebel gang,' ladye,
  For it gi'es me muckle pain;
My John went away with Earlston,   15
  And I'll never see either again."

"O wae is my heart for thee, Janet,
  O sair is my heart for thee!
These covenant men were ill advised,
  They are fools, you may credit me.   20

Where's a' their boastfu' preaching now,
  Against their king and law,
When mony a head in death lies low,
  An' mony mae maun fa'?"

"Ay, but death lasts no for aye, ladye,   25
  For the grave maun yield its prey;
And when we meet on the verge of heaven,
  We'll see wha are fools that day:

We'll see wha looks in their Saviour's face
  With holiest joy and pride,   30
Whether they who shed his servants' blood,
  Or those that for him died.

I wadna be the highest dame
   That ever this country knew,
And take my chance to share the doom   35
   Of that persecuting crew.

Then ca' us nae rebel gang, ladye,
   Nor take us fools to be,
For there is nae ane of a' that gang,
   Wad change his state wi' thee."   40

"O weel may you be, my poor Janet,
   May blessings on you combine!
The better you are in either state,
   The less shall I repine.

But wi' your fightings an' your faith,   45
   Your ravings an' your rage,
There you have lost a leel helpmate,
   In the blossom of his age.

An' what's to come o' ye, my poor Janet,
   Wi' these twa babies sweet?   50
Ye hae naebody now to work for them,
   Or bring you a meal o' meat;

It is that which makes my heart sae wae,
   An' gars me, while scarce aware,
Whiles say the things I wadna say,   55
   Of them that can err nae mair."

Poor Janet kissed her youngest babe,
   And the tears fell on his cheek,
And they fell upon his swaddling bands,
   For her heart was like to break.   60

"O little do I ken, my dear, dear babes,
   What misery's to be thine!
But for the cause we hae espoused,
   I will yield thy life and mine.

O had I a friend, as I hae nane,   65
   For nane dare own me now,

That I might send to Bothwell brigg,
   If the killers wad but allow,

To lift the corpse of my brave John,
   I ken where they will him find,   70
He wad meet his God's foes face to face,
   And he'll hae nae wound behind."

"But I went to Bothwell brigg, Janet,
   There was nane durst hinder me,
For I wantit to hear a' I could hear,   75
   An' to see what I could see;

And there I found your brave husband,
   As viewing the dead my lane,
He was lying in the very foremost rank,
   In the midst of a heap o' slain."   80

Then Janet held up her hands to heaven,
   An' she grat, an' she tore her hair,
"O sweet ladye, O dear ladye,
   Dinna tell me ony mair!

There is a hope will linger within,   85
   When earthly hope is vain,
But when ane kens the very worst,
   It turns the heart to stane!"

"O wae is my heart, John Carr, said I,
   That I this sight should see!   90
And when I said these waefu' words,
   He liftit his een to me.

'O art thou there, my kind ladye,
   The best o' this warld's breed,
And are you gangin' your liefu lane,   95
   Amang the hapless dead?'

I hae servants within my ca', John Carr,
   And a chariot in the dell,
An' if there is ony hope o' life,
   I will carry you hame mysel'.   100

'O lady, there is nae hope o' life—
   And what were life to me!
Wad ye save me frae the death of a man,
   To hang on a gallows tree?

I hae nae hame to fly to now,   105
   Nae country an' nae kin,
There is not a door in fair Scotland
   Durst open to let me in.

But I hae a loving wife at hame,
   An' twa babies dear to me;   110
They hae naebody now that dares favour them,
   An' of hunger they a' maun dee.

Oh, for the sake of thy Saviour dear,
   Whose mercy thou hopest to share,
Dear lady take the sackless things   115
   A wee beneath thy care!

A long fareweel, my kind ladye,
   O'er weel I ken thy worth;
Gae send me a drink o' the water o' Clyde,
   For my last drink on earth.' "   120

"O dinna tell ony mair, ladye,
   For my heart is cauld as clay;
There is a spear that pierces here,
   Frae every word ye say."

"He was nae feared to dee, Janet,   125
   For he gloried in his death,
And wished to be laid with those who had bled
   For the same enduring faith.

There were three wounds in his boardly breast,
   And his limb was broke in twain,   130
An' the sweat ran down wi' his red heart's blood,
   Wrung out by the deadly pain.

I rowed my apron round his head,
   For fear my men should tell,

And I hid him in my lord's castle,   135
    An' I nursed him there mysel'.

An' the best leeches in a' the land
    Have tended him as he lay,
And he never has lacked my helping hand,
    By night nor yet by day.   140

I durstna tell you before, Janet,
    For I feared his life was gane,
But now he's sae well, ye may visit him,
    An' ye's meet by yoursels alane."

Then Janet she fell at her lady's feet,   145
    And she claspit them ferventlye,
And she steepit them a' wi' the tears o' joy,
    Till the good lady wept to see.

"Oh, ye are an angel sent frae heaven,
    To lighten calamitye!   150
For in distress, a friend or foe
    Is a' the same to thee.

If good deeds count in heaven, ladye,
    Eternal bliss to share,
Ye hae done a deed will save your soul,   155
    Though ye should never do mair."

"Get up, get up, my kind Janet,
    But never trow tongue or pen,
That a' the warld are lost to good,
    Except the covenant men."   160

Wha wadna hae shared that lady's joy,
    When watching the wounded hind,
Rather than those of the feast and the dance,
    Which her kind heart resigned?

Wha wadna rather share that lady's fate,   165
    When the stars shall melt away,
Than that of the sternest anchorite,
    That can naething but graen an' pray?

A Hymn to the Redeemer

By the Ettrick Shepherd

O THOU adored in heaven and earth,
A being divine of human birth;
Son of the virgin, hear us, hear us;
Son of the living God, be near us:
Thou who art man in form and feature,   5
Yet God of glory, and God of nature;
Thou, who led'st the star of the east,
Yet hapless lay at a virgin's breast,
Slept in the manger, and cried on the knee,
Yet rulest o'er time and eternity;   10
Whose kind mediations never shall cease,
Thou mighty God, thou Prince of peace,
Pity thy creatures here kneeling in dust,
Pity the beings in thee that trust.

Thou, who fedst the hungry with bread,   15
And raised from the grave the mouldering dead,
Who walked on the waves of the rolling main,
Who cried to thy Father, and cried in vain;
Yet, wept for the woes and the sins of man,
And prayed for him when thy life-blood ran;   20
With thy last breath thou cried'st FORGIVE,
When dying by man that man might live;
O'er death and the grave thou hast victory won,
And now art throned by the stars and the sun,
For thy name's glory, hear us, hear us;   25
Son of the living God, be near us.

Oh, leave the abodes of glory and bliss,
The realms of heavenly happiness;
Come swifter than the meteor of even,
On the lightning's wing, in the chariot of heaven;   30
By the gates of light and the glowing sphere,
Oh, come on thy errand of mercy here.

But, Lord of glory, we know not thee,
    We know not what we say;
We cannot from thy presence be,   35
    Nor from thine eye away:

For, though on the right hand of our God,
Thou art here in this lowly drear abode.
Beyond the moon and the starry way,
Thou holdest thy Almighty sway,   40
Where spirits in floods of light are swimming,
And angels round the throne are hymning,
Where waters of life are ever streaming,
And crowns of glory are round thee beaming;
Yet present with all that call on thee   45
In this world of woe and adversity.

Then, O thou Son of the virgin, hear us,
God of love and of life be near us;
Our stains wash out, our sins forgive,
And before thee let our spirits live;   50
For thy dear faith be our bosoms steeled:
Oh, be our help, our stay, our shield;
Show thy dread power for mercy's sake,
For the souls of thy children are at stake.
Oh, save us! save us! blest Redeemer,   55
From the power of the scorner and blasphemer;
Oh, come as the floods of thy foes assemble,
That all may see, and fear, and tremble;
Bow down thy heavens, and rend them asunder,
And come in the cloud, in the flame, or the thunder, 60
That heaven and earth may see and know
How much they to a Virgin owe.

Morning Hymn

By the Ettrick Shepherd

Lauded be thy name for ever
Thou of life the guard and giver
Thou can'st guard thy creatures sleeping
Heal the heart long broke with weeping
Rule the ouphes and elves at will   5
That vex the air or haunt the hill
And all the fury subject keep
Of boiling cloud and chafed deep
I have seen and well I know it

Thou hast done and thou wilt do it   10
God of stilness and of motion
Of the rainbow and the ocean
Of the mountain rock and river
Blessed be thy name for ever
   I have proved thy wonderous might   15
Through the shadows of the night
Thou who slumber'st not nor sleepest
Blest are they thou kindly keepest
Spirits from the ocean under
Liquid flame and levelled thunder   20
Need not waken nor alarm them
No! they cannot cannot harm them
God of evening's yellow ray
God of yonder dawning day
That rises from the distant sea   25
Like breathings of eternity
Thine the flaming sphere of light
Thine the darkness of the night
Thine are all the stars of even
God of angels! God of heaven   30
God of life that fade shall never
Glory to thy name for ever

ALTRIVE-LAKE
the longest day, 1835

The Judgment of Idumea

Versified by the Ettrick Shepherd

COME near, ye nations! Around me gather
And list to the words of your God and your Father,
For my fury is forth on a city and nation,
That are doomed to the slaughter and dire desolation.
In Bozrah the Lord has his sacrifice fitted,   5
His altar the land where the sins were committed,
Let the dead and the living around him assemble,
And time and eternity hear and tremble.
   Oh, wail for Idumea, cast forth unforgiven!
My sword is bathed red in the vengeance of heaven;   10

And down on the mountains unnerved and supine,
They shall fall as the dead leaves descend from the vine,
Where heaps upon heaps shall their corpses remain,
And the mountains shall melt with the blood of the slain.
    'Tis the day of the Lord;—prepare thee! prepare thee!   15
And mark its approach that it may not ensnare thee;
Look well to the plain at its throes and its bending,
Lest it swallow you up in the gulf of its rending;
Attend to the sea when to blood it is turning;
Attend to the mountains when clothed in mourning;   20
Observe the pale moon when her radiance is clouded;
And look to the sun when his glory is shrouded;
To the stars when appearing in dimness involving,
In the breath of Jehovah annealed and dissolving;
Then to the blue heavens heaved hither and thither,   25
Then folded and rolled like a scroll up together;
Then, then, is approaching o'erwhelming and early,
The day of the Lord; prepare thee! prepare thee!
    It is past, it is over! The earth's in amazement;
The people stand silent in dreadful debasement   30
Before the dire wrath of the mighty Avenger
Of Israel, thus wreaked on the land of the stranger.
Idumea is fallen! No arm to deliver!
The contest of Zion is settled for ever.
    The beauty of Edom no age shall restore it,   35
The curse of the Lord is in it and o'er it,
The rivers and springs into pitch are turning
The dust is brimstone, the breeze is burning,
The city is shaken unto its foundations,
The land is a waste unto all generations.   40
    Her halls are of emptiness, grandeur's illusion;
And stretched out upon them the line of confusion;
In her palaces dark desolation is reigning,
And the briers and the nettle their foliage entwining;
The owl calls his court with a whoop and a knell,   45
And there shall the bittern and cormorant dwell,
The lamia shall lie in her chambers of state,
And open her bosom and cry for her mate;
The ostrich shall stand on her battlements proudly,
And the vultures assemble, discordant and loudly;   50
The satyrs shall dance with their howlings and yellings,
The spirits of darkness that haunt the low dwellings

Of mortals cut off in their greenness of sinning,
Ere grace had a spring or repentance beginning,
The toad and the adder shall come from the forest,   55
And dragons pant o'er it when thirst's at the sorest.
The gloom of oblivion shall over it centre,
Till time shall withdraw and eternity enter,
To all who despise their God and Forgiver,
A beacon of terror for ever and ever.   60

MOUNT BENGER
August 23, 1835

A Letter to the Ettrick Shepherd

SIR:—

A POOR widow from your sister kingdom humbly ventures to address you, in hopes that you will aid her with your advice and assistance in earning a little profit for the support of her orphan family, whose plaintive cries for bread every day wring her heart. Alas!
I once thought that heart was rendered callous for ever, and dead to
the thrilling ties of natural affection; for the hand of the Lord has
been laid heavily upon me, and I weened that my burden was greater
than female heart could bear. But, ever blessed be the Divine Goodness that, in my greatest extremity, sent resignation to my aid—humble and heavenly resignation to his holy will; and from that moment
my energies were restored, and my fondness for the remaining objects of my love redoubled.

What I desire of you, Sir, is, that as you appear to be deeply
interested in the periodical literature of both kingdoms, you will try
to procure me some remuneration for such little simple tales and
moral essays as I am able to write. Even the least acknowledgment
will be gratefully received; for what else can a poor widow do, who
was not bred to any manual employment? I have only once in my
life been paid for an article of my own writing; and never can I
forget the thrilling pleasure I experienced when I opened the franked
letter, and found the liberal enclosure. If there can be such things
conceived as *pangs* of delight, I may have been said to have experienced them that night. I did not only shed tears, but I wept outright,
and I hugged my two little girls, and kissed them, and said to them,
that they should not now want bread or clothes, though their mother
should toil night and day.

Alas! many a rebuff have I since that time experienced, with a coldly civil answer from the editor; and, when my hopes were high, and not a sixpence in my pocket, these returns were hard to bear. Among others, I sent you two pieces, one in prose, and one in verse, for Mr. Blackwood; but you never returned me any answer or acknowledgment whatever, which was rather ungracious: though I have heard a different account of you. And, it being from your friend Sir C. Sharpe's advice that I apply to you, I hope you will not neglect me altogether, as you did formerly.

My first must be a tale of juvenile delight, of love, of pain, and sorrow; for how can I tell any tale before that which lies nearest to my heart?

My father was a farmer, and once accounted wealthy, before the wealth of the British farmer began to melt from his grasp. We were bred at the village school, along with the vicar's family, and some others; but between our two families the greatest harmony subsisted. We drank tea together every Saturday and every Sunday, and joined in all the same rambles and amusements as if we had been one family. William Brand, the vicar's second son, and I, being of an age, our parents often spake to us jocularly of being married; at which I pretended to be highly offended, pouting and turning up my little nose with the greatest disdain, and answering with sauciness, to the amusement of all present; even pretty William laughed as heartily as any of them:–"I thank you, mamma; you are very kind and very officious; and, pardon me, if I think rather too ready at proposing certain wives and certain husbands for certain young people. Should *you* require another husband, you may chuse for youself; which, I assure you, I intend to do."

But, for all this coquetry, I liked well to have William by my side, from which he was seldom wanting. When we read together in the Bible, the language was far more sublime to my ear, and the histories more interesting, when read verse about with him. Nor was the Gospel of Jesus ever so sweet and affecting as when pronounced by his mellow voice. There was a cadence in it that often brought tears into my eyes; for William was a good boy, had a deep feeling of religion, and a strong sense of moral duty; so that all his actions and words became him, and sat on him with the most beautiful effect.

Whenever we went a flower-gathering, nutting, or bird-nesting, William and I went in fellowship, there being no girls in the two families of the same age with me; and, if there had, I don't think I would have gone with them, for William brought always the best things to me, which they would not have done. But girls should never go a bird-nesting with boys, for the latter will not desist from plundering; and it not only grieves the gentle spirit of the former that they cannot prevent it, but causes them often to regard their brethren and friends with a sort of abhorrence as monsters of inhumanity. I know that many a sore heart and bitter tear these doings cost me, for which I was only laughed to scorn by all but William Brand, whose heart shared in all my sympathies. There are very few good boys. They are a set of bullying, fighting, hard-headed, and still harder-hearted, reavers, which renders a real amiable and manly boy quite a treasure.

I remember being one day out on Beckwith Common, the boys in search of plover and lark nests, and the girls of heather bells and other flowers of the waste, when I unluckily perceived a very important bird fluttering round a bush of heath, and making a terrible uproar, chattering and chirping in the most vehement style. It was joined by another of the same species; and the two made such a work there, as if their lives depended on something which was in that bush leaving it. I durst not go to see what it was, for I was afraid it would be an adder, but kept where I was at a distance, and at length I saw a creature come out of the bush, something like a rat, with a short tail. The two birds tormented it terribly, so that it was obliged to sit down and watch them, often flying at them and trying to catch them. At length it came cowering straight toward me, small as it was, I liked its look very ill, and beginning to think I was too long there, I rose hastily and took to my heels.

But the battle now assumed a more serious aspect. The animal came to a heap of grey stones, where there was a hole, at which it wanted to enter. This the two birds set themselves to oppose with all their might. They placed themselves together in the mouth of the hole, fluttering, chattering, and screaming; and all the while they pelted so furiously at the creature's eyes and nose, that for the space of several minutes, they kept it at bay. And, when sundry times it got its head into the hole, the male bird, as a last resource, seized it by the tail with his bill, and nipped it with such energy that the creature was compelled to disengage itself from the hole and fly at its assailant. Never was there an entry more strenuously defended. The whole vigour of the two distressed parents was exerted without flinching; and had not the male bird suffered some injury (for I saw the creature bring feathers off him), I am persuaded the spoliator would have been ultimately beat off.

It however, at last, succeeded in its enterprize, entered the hole, and suddenly returned, bearing a fine full-grown nestling in its mouth, which was fluttering and crying most piteously. My philanthropy was aroused to the highest pitch by this incident, and all my fears of the voracious plunderer vanished. I could have seized it with my little delicate hands, and wrung its neck about. I pursued it with all my speed, screaming as if my own life had been at stake, while the two parent birds assisted me well, by harassing the little wretch, and impeding its flight. My two brothers, Edward and John, who were nearest to me, came running to my assistance; to whom, in breathless agony, I pointed out the aggressor. It was a grand business for them. They waylaid him, turned him, and pelted him with stones, till they soon compelled him to relinquish his prey, and then pursued him till he took earth. I asked them what he was, and they said he was *a capital weazel*. With a joyful heart I ran to the released captive, lifted it and placed it in my bosom, but it was in the throes of death, and died amid my caresses; and, when I thought of its hard and early fate, I shed some tears of genuine grief over it. My brothers laughed at me, and said, they wondered how I could grieve for the death of *an useless stone-chatter*.

Without the least hesitation, but as a natural consequence, I led them to the little crevice where the desperate battle took place; where, on raising a stone or two, we soon came to other four fine nestlings. Never did I think but that the boys would again cover them carefully up, bless them, and leave them to the kind parents who had fought so gallantly for them. There was no such humane project in their heads. They took one of them, and tossed it up in the air to a great height; it flew a space, and then, falling, tumbled over—a poor, helpless, inexperienced object, but, instead of pitying, they fell a pelting at it with stones. I screamed violently, and tried to hinder them; but they laughed still the more, and, taking aim time about, they continued throwing at it till they killed it. When I saw it fluttering and trying in vain to get away from them, and then falling over, gasping, and dying, I thought my heart would burst. I had never witnessed a deed of such enormity, and I remember I wondered that some visible judgment was not poured on the heads of these ruthless murderers, and destroyers of domestic happiness. Even the two bereaved parents, who had fought so bravely against their first invader, now sat at a melancholy distance, uttering now and then a hopeless chirp, as if astonished at a deed which had no motive but cruelty.

Yet it was a game of the highest zest for the boys. Away they ran for another to *get a fair batter at it*, as they said; but there I was beforehand with them; and throwing myself above the few grey stones that covered the remnant of the nestlings, I screamed, wept, and told them they should tear me in pieces before they should get another of the birds to murder out of mere wantonness. Finding they could not prevail without hurting me, they tried to reason me out of my resolution by insinuating many bad things against the general character of the stone-chat; but to none of these would I listen. They then set seriously to work to remove me by force; but I clung to the grey stones, and screamed without any intermission or mitigation of voice, till, at length, William Brand came running to my assistance in utter astonishment at what the boys were doing to their sister. "What is it? What is it?" cried he. "Off hands instantly, and tell me what is the matter."

"Oh, nothing at all," cried they; "but only that Alice is the greatest fool that ever was born." I showed him the two victims; told him how the parent birds had fought for the lives of their young, and the wanton cruelty of my brothers; and I shall never forget the glow on his countenance as he reprimanded and shamed them out of their ruthless intent. "I could not have believed that you would have hurt your sister's feelings by such an act of shameless barbarity," said he; "you say, 'What signifies the life of a stone chatter?' But it was her estimate that ought to have made it valuable in your eyes. And you should remember that these are all God's creatures; that a sparrow cannot fall to the ground without his knowledge; and for every act of wilful depravity you shall be answerable to him."

My brothers went away rather out of countenance, saying they did not want to hear any more of the minister's sermon. William and I watched the nestlings till their persecutors were out of sight; we then lifted them, and carried them carefully to a distance, where we watched them till we saw the dam come and feed them. This we did lest the boys or the weazel should find them again.

No, no! girls and boys should never go a bird-nesting together. They should go to the nut-wood together, for the boys are a sort of protection. I have seen them batter off an impertinent clown with stones, and make a boisterous bull-dog glad to take to his heels that he might escape with life. In both these instances, I felt that we girls would have been very helpless creatures. There is nothing that I know of so dangerous as the united attack of a set of resolute boys; there is no possibility either of eluding them or overpowering them; and the more danger to themselves, the more in proportion is such an assault endeared to them.

I shall relate another story of bird-nesting, which I never shall forget as an instance of maternal devotion and heroism without a parallel. I was constantly on the look out for birds' nests, though all that I wanted was the pleasure of knowing where they were, and visiting them every good day. But there was a small blue hawk which for years had wrought great devastation among my feathered songsters, and which I wished by all means to be revenged on. At length, after unwearied attention to the course he pursued through the air with his prey; and, following in that direction still farther and farther on, I discovered the nest. Joyfully did I hasten home with the information to my brothers. Edward and John both went with me. The tree was difficult to climb, and overhung a precipice. John ventured, and reached the nest; but the dam met him at a yard's distance, attacking his hands and face without mercy. He got so near as to perceive that there were young ones half feathered in the nest; but, with all his exertion, he could not get hold of one of them, and was obliged to return with his right hand and his nose terribly lacerated.

But John was incensed, and the young hawks a prize; he cut a strong sapling, took it in his teeth, and once more clomb the tree. The hawk had all this while been wheeling round and round in air, and with a laughing yell proclaiming her victory over poor John. Whenever she saw him begin again to ascend the tree, she alighted upon the nest, and, meeting him at the cleft below it, attacked him precisely in the same way as before. He had nothing but his hat to strike with the first time, but now the blows of the cudgel astounded her. She threw herself several times in his face with a maternal scream of despair; but, for all the blows that John aimed at her, she never thought of flying. Had the male been present, who was doubtless out on a foraging expedition, no boy could have reaved their nest without fire-arms. The last sight that I saw of her living, she was gasping and hanging her wings, and John's next blow felled her dead. She died on the side of the nest next to the intruder, and during the struggle never deserted her post one inch. She was a small bluish bird, with large black eyes. My brothers called her a merlin, which others disputed. The young were all kept and tamed, and turned out docile and the prettiest birds I ever saw. There was a majesty in their large black eyes, and the greater their danger the roll of those grew always the more proud and independent.

But these youthful reminiscences have drawn me from my tale. In this way, was William and I bred up together; by constant fellowship and reciprocal acts of kindness, endeared to one another; and, owing to the jokes and insinuations of our parents, I think, as far back as I remember, we both had a sort of vague feeling that our hearts were made for one another.

His elder brother having studied for the church, William was destined for a mercantile life; but the first year he went into a counting-house he was seized with a severe illness, and brought home to his father. It was then that I first felt how dear he was to my young heart. His own family were debarred from entering his apartment for fear of infection; but all their efforts could not keep me away. I sat by his bed the whole day, and let his nurse sleep. I held the wine and water to his parched lips, wept over him, and read portions of Scripture daily, and the service for a bed of sickness. Often would he take my hand, and press it to his burning brow, then to his lips, and feebly whisper, "Heaven bless you, dear Alice!" My heart was wrung almost beyond sufferance, for I thought him dying, and the purpose of my soul was not to tarry behind him. How gladly would I have suffered and died for him!—so sanguine are the feelings of the youthful bosom, before being ripened by the showers and suns of reason.

The mercantile world having been at this time completely paralyzed, poor William, after a slow recovery, could find no situation for the space of two years; and, though he tried all that he could to improve his mind, and fit himself for any situation, yet he was heartless and cast down, and even took care to shun my presence as much as possible. At length a sort of desperate situation was offered him in the island of Tobago, which he recklessly accepted, and then we two met every day to talk of our separation, and deplore our lot. We never talked of love, we were too young and too modest for that. But there was no occasion for it; for every look, every word, every action, bespoke how dear we were to one another. For me, when the day of his departure drew near, I wept day and night. My parents took alarm, for well they knew the cause; and my father, who was a true English farmer in kindness of heart and honest frankness of disposition, invited William by himself to take a family dinner with us before he set out on his destination.

We made great efforts to be cheerful that afternoon, but it would not do. My father took his ale heartily, but William almost none; and, at length, it so chancing that we three being left together, my father, after blowing his nose, began the following speech, "Why, Willie, lad, do you know that I don't much like this going away of your's to that plaguy tobacco place? It is a bad spot, and you will be a weary distance from us, should you be taken ill. You say, it is a fine island; that may be: but there's never any body comes home from it, man. I have never yet known a man who went to reside there come home again. I don't much like this, Willie. It's too like getting quit of a son. I think, for the little while a man has to live he might contrive to do so at home. I'll tell you what I have resolved, Willie, for I do not like to part with you; you have long been the same to me as one of my own; and, if you will stay at home, I will stock the farm of Renton for you, and put in the first year's crop for a beginning; and, as your father has a more numerous family than me, and not a great deal more to give them, I'll ask no security but your own honour."

I could stand this no longer, for my heart was bursting with gratitude for the disinterested generosity of my dear father. I sprang from my seat, clasped my arms around his neck, kissed him I know not how oft, and then laid my head on his bosom and wept.

"Alice! Alice!—behave yourself, girl. What means all this flummery? I cannot bear it." I looked up, and the tear was forcing itself slowly over his honest cheek, while William was at his other knee, pressing his hand between both his own. "Give over, children; give over, I tell you! Why will you cause an old man to play the child? Dang it, I was trying to gratify nobody but myself!"

I always loved my father with my whole heart and soul, for he ruled his family by sheer affection and kindness; but, oh, how I admired his manly generosity that night. There was no word said about me. No such hint as, "If you wed my Alice, I will do so and so." That was left to follow, or not to follow, as circumstances suited.

The result may be anticipated by any one; but these days of delirious joy it is painful to recapitulate. I cannot even remember them, for they passed over like a brilliant dream. The intense eagerness of William to succeed in this farming speculation, so generously conferred, ruined all. He began his improvements on the most brilliant and expensive scale; and the accommodation afforded by the banks at that period had no bounds. Before the soil could produce adequate returns, the banks were exterminated, their notes were of no avail, and the farmers found themselves involved in inextricable ruin. My husband, my poor William, was amongst the first that fell. Though he told me nothing, I saw, by his wan cheek, and the fond and rueful looks which he sometimes fixed on our children, that matters were far from being right. He failed, and brought in both our parents to heavy losses. Mine in particular; which, I am sure, broke my dear William's heart. After that, he never held up his head again. The thoughts of my father's affection, and the way in which he had involved him, was more than his gentle spirit could bear.

The privations, the miseries, that now hedged me in on every side, were indeed grievous, yet the Lord in his kindness afforded me strength to bear them. My beloved husband, than whom a more affectionate never lived, even before the prime of life, broken in heart and constitution, hasting to an untimely grave. Two helpless infants on my hand, and all of us dependent only on the bounty of those whom he had deeply injured. It was a heart-breaking condition to be placed in, but my poor old father, now brought to the verge of ruin, never remitted his attentions for a day; and, when my husband's effects were sold, and the proceeds parted among his creditors, my father returned me the whole of his reversion. His last meeting with William I never shall forget. He came to our lowly cottage to see him, and, with the tear in his sunken eye, tried to speak words of comfort and hope. Alas! it was too apparent they were both hasting to the same bourne! Both felt it; and, although seemingly unawares, their conversation turned again and again on the country beyond the grave. I never saw my father so much affected as when he blessed William, and took farewell of him. He was conscious it was for ever. I wept over both their death-beds on the same week, and they lie buried side by side in the little church-yard of the priory of St. John.

I have been obliged to curtail this little narrative of all its painful descriptions, in order to suit it to some of the juvenile periodicals; where, should it appear, I will in my next subscribe myself,
Your obliged,
ALICE BRAND.

To Miss M. A. C——e

By the Ettrick Shepherd

Maid of my worship thou shalt see
Though long I strove to pleasure thee
That now I've changed my timid tone
And sing to please myself alone
And thou wilt read when well I wot   5
I care not whether you do or not
    Yes I'll be querulous or boon
Flow with the tide change with the moon

For what am I or what art thou
Or what the cloud and radiant bow　　　　　10
Or what are waters winds and seas
But elemental energies?
The sea must flow the cloud descend
The thunder burst the rainbow bend
Not when they would but when they can　　15
Fit emblems of the soul of man!
Then let me frolic while I may
The sportive vagrant of a day
Yield to the impulse of the time
Be it a toy or theme sublime　　　　　　20
Wing the thin air or starry sheen
Sport with the child upon the green
Dive to the sea-maid's coral dome
Or fairy's visionary home
Sail on the whirlwind or the storm　　　　25
Or trifle with the maiden's form
Or raise up spirits of the hill
But only if, and when I will
　　Say may the meteor of the wild
Nature's unstaid erratic child　　　　　　30
That glimmers o'er the forest fen
Or twinkles in the darksome glen
Can that be bound? Can that be rein'd
By cold ungenial rules restrained?
No! leave it o'er its ample home　　　　　35
The boundless wilderness to roam
To gleam to tremble and to die
'Tis nature's error—so am I
Then leave to all his fancies wild
Nature's own rude untutored child　　　　40
And should he forfeit his fond claim
Pity his loss—but do not blame
　　Let those who list the garden choose
Where flowers are regular and profuse
Come thou to dell and lonely lea　　　　45
And cull the mountain gems with me
And sweeter blooms may be thine own
By nature's hand at random sown
And sweeter strains may touch thy heart
Than are producible by art　　　　　　　50

The nightingale may give delight
A while 'mid silence of the night
But the lark lost in the heavens blue
O her wild strain is ever new!

The Gem

A Highland Eclogue

By the Ettrick Shepherd

At the dawning of morn, on a sweet summer-day,
Young Mary of Moy went out to pray,—
To pray, as her guileless heart befitted,
For the pardon of sins that were never committed;
A grateful homage to render Heaven   5
For all its gifts and favours given,—
For a heart that dreaded the paths of sin;
For a soul of life and light within;
And a form, withal, so passing fair
That the rays of love seem'd centering there.   10

Mary felt that her eye was beaming bright,
For her bosom glow'd with a pure delight:
As over the green-wood sward she bounded,
A halo of sweets her form surrounded;
For the breezes that kiss'd her cheek grew rare,   15
Her breathing perfumed the morning air;
And scarce did her foot, as she onward flew,
From the fringe of the daisy wring out the dew.

She went to her bower, by the water-side,
Which the woodbine and wild-rose canopied: 20
And she kneeled beneath its fragrant bough,
And waved her locks back from her brow;
But just as she lifted her eye so meek,
A hand from behind her touch'd her cheek:
She turn'd her around with a visage pale,   25
And there stood Allan of Borlan-dale!

ALLAN
Sweet Mary of Moy, is it so with thee?
Have I caught thee on thy bended knee,
Beginning thy rath orisons here,
In the bower to the breathings of love so dear?   30
Oh tell me, Mary, what this can mean!
Hast thou such a great transgressor been?
Is the loveliest model of mortal kind

A thing of an erring, tainted mind,
That thus she must kneel and heave the sigh,   35
With the tear-drop dimming her azure eye?
To whom wert thou going thy vows to pay?
Or for what, or for whom, wert thou going to pray?

MARY

I was going to pray in the name divine
Of Him that died for me and for mine;   40
I was going to pray for them and me,
And haply, Allan, for thine and thee.
And now I have answer'd as well as I may
Your questions thus put in so strange a way:
But I deem it behaviour most unmeet,   45
Thus to follow a maid to her lone retreat,
To hear her her heart of its sins unload,
And all the secrets 'twixt her and her God.
For shame, that my kindred should hear such a tale
Of the gallant young Allan of Borlan-dale!   50

ALLAN

Sweet Mary of Moy, I must be plain:
I have told you once and tell you again,
Though in love I am deeper than woman can be,
You must either part with your faith or me.

MARY

What! part with my faith? You may as well demand   55
That I should part with my own right hand!
Than part with that faith I would sooner incline
To part with my heart from its mortal shrine.

ALLAN

Ah! Mary! dear Mary! how can you thus frown,
And propose to part with what's not your own?   60
For that heart now is mine; and you must, my sweet
    dove,
Renounce that same faith on the altar of Love.

Then Mary's sweet voice took its sharpest key,
And rose somewhat higher than maiden's should be;
But ere the vehement sentence was said,   65

A gentle hand on her lips was laid,
And a voice to her that was ever dear,
Thus whisper'd softly in her ear:—

LADY OF MOY

Hush, Mary! dear Mary! what madness is this?
These dreams of the morning, my darling, dismiss: 70
Awake from this torpor of slumber so deep;
You are raving and clamouring through your sleep:
Up, up, and array you in scarlet and blue;
For Allan of Dale is come here to woo.

MARY

Tell Allan of Dale straight home to hie,   75
And court Helen Kay, or his darling of Sky:
This positive message deliver from me,
For I list not his heretic face to see.

LADY

My Mary! dear Mary! what am I to deem?
Arouse you, my love; you are still in your dream: 80
Your lover's views of things divine
May differ in some degree from thine;
But I think he is one who will not pother
Betwixt the one faith and the other.

MARY

That is worse and worse; for my lover must be   85
Attach'd to my faith as well as to me:
We must kneel at one beloved shrine,
And the mode of his worship must be mine.
For why should a wedded pair devout,
By different paths seek heaven out?   90
Or in that dwelling happy be,
Who of the road could never agree?
O mother! this day, without all fail,
I had given my hand to young Borlan-dale;
But I've had such a hint from the throne on high,   95
Or some good angel hovering nigh,
That tongue of mortal should never prevail
On me to be bride to this Allan of Dale,

Unless he sign over a bond, for me
In the path of religion his guide to be.   100

Young Allan to all his companions was known
As a sceptic of bold and most dissolute tone,
Who jeer'd at the cross, at the altar, and priest,
And made our most holy communions his jest;
Yet Mary of this had of knowledge no gleam,   105
Till warn'd of her danger that morn in her dream.
He loved his Mary for lands and for gold,
For beauty of feature and beauty of mould,
As well as a cold-hearted sceptic could love
Who held no belief in the blessings above;   110
And whene'er of his faith or his soul she spoke,
He answer'd her always with jeer and with joke.

The frowns of the maiden, and sighs of the lover,
With poutings and nay-says, were all gotten over;
And nothing remain'd but the schedule-deed gerent,   115
The bonds and the forms of the final agreement,—
A thing called a contract, that long-galling fetter!
Which parents love dearly, and lawyers love better.
In this was set down, at the maiden's inditement,
One part, to devotion a powerful incitement,   120
That her lover should forfeit, without diminution,
Her fortune redoubled, (a sore retribution!)
If ever his words or his actions should jostle
With the creed she revered, of the holy apostle.
The terms were severe, but resource there was none;   125
So he sign'd, seal'd, and swore, and the bridal went on.

Well was it for Mary! for scarce were got over
The honey-moon joys, ere her profligate lover
Began his old jibes, when in frolicksome mood,
At all that the Christian holds sacred and good;   130
But still, lest the terms might be proven in law,
The bond and the forfeiture kept him in awe;
Which caused him to ponder and often think of it,—
This thing that he jeer'd at, and where lay the profit?
Till at last, though by men it will scarce be believed,   135
A year had not pass'd, ere he daily perceived
The truths of the Gospel rise bright and more bright,

Like the dawning of day o'er the darkness of night,
Or the sun of eternity rising to save
From the thraldom of death, and the gloom of the
    grave.   140

Then Mary's fond heart was with gratitude moved
To her God, for the peace of the man that she loved;
And her mild face would glow with the radiance of
    beauty,
As he urged her along on her Christian duty;
For, of the two, his soul throughout   145
Grew the most sincere and the most devout.

Then their life pass'd on like an autumn day,
That rises with red portentous ray,
Threatening its pathway to deform
With the wasting flood and the rolling storm;   150
But, long ere the arch of the day is won,
A halo of promise is round the sun,
And the settled sky, though all serene,
Is ray'd with the dark and the bright between;
With the ruddy glow and the streamer wan,   155
Like the evil and good in the life of man;
And, at last, when it sinks on the cradle of day,
More holy and mild is its sapphire ray.
O why should blind mortals e'er turn into mirth
The strange intercourse betwixt heaven and earth,   160
Or deem that their Maker cannot impart,
By a thousand ways, to the human heart,
In shadows portentous of what is to be,
His warnings, His will, and His final decree?

This tale is a fact—I pledge for't in token,   165
The troth of a poet, which may not be broken;
And, had it not been for this dream of the morn,
This vision of prayer, intrusion, and scorn,
Which Heaven at the last hour thus deign'd to deliver,
The peace of the twain had been ruin'd for ever.   170

MOUNT BENGER
July 6, 1829

The Remembrance

A Boy's Song

By the Ettrick Shepherd

Where the pools are bright and deep,
Where the grey trout lies asleep,
Up the river and o'er the lea,
That's the way for Billy and me.

Where the blackbird sings the latest, 5
Where the hawthorn blooms the sweetest,
Where the nestlings chirp and flee,
That's the way for Billy and me.

Where the mowers mow the cleanest,
Where the hay lies thick and greenest, 10
There to trace the homeward bee,
That's the way for Billy and me.

Where the hazel bank is steepest,
Where the shadow falls the deepest,
Where the clustering nuts fall free, 15
That's the way for Billy and me.

Why the boys should drive away
Little sweet maidens from the play,
Or love to banter and fight so well,
That's the thing I never could tell. 20

But this I know I love to play,
Through the meadow, among the hay;
Up the water and o'er the lea,
That's the way for Billy and me.

The Two Valleys
A Fairy Tale

By the Ettrick Shepherd

I wish to ask all the pretty maidens of England, Scotland, and Ireland, if they ever heard of the sweet and retired valley of Luran? If they have not it will be a great pleasure to them; for such a pattern of virtue, beauty, and happiness is not to be found in our country nor in any other.

It must be understood that this name Luran is a Celtic term, and signifies the valley of beautiful women. And never was there in Britain a valley that so well deserved the name as the peaceful and happy valley of Glen-Luran. There the young men are brave, sprightly, and courteous, having been all bred up in the pure and simple tenets of the true religion; and the girls are mild and gentle, and all as comely as angels; for where there is no sin there can be no real sorrow of heart, and a happy and heavenly frame of soul makes always a beautiful and benign countenance.

Right over against this place, and at a very short distance, there lies another little retired valley called Dual, which is likewise a Celtic term, and signifies the valley of vice; and never was there a greater contrast in nature than has existed for ages between these two valleys, although so near to each other. And each of them too contains a village, a school, and a place of worship.

Now I would not have any of my dear young friends take up a prejudice against any system of religion, merely because it is not their religion. On the contrary, I would have them believe that it is most consistent with Christian love and charity to pay a certain respect and deference to every sort of religion, out of regard to the feelings of our fellow creatures who know no better. But it so happened, and I cannot help it, that the community that inhabited the valley of Dual were of a different religion, or at least professed different tenets of the same faith, and had done so from generation to generation without a single instance of a convert having been made from the one to the other.

All that I know is that the people of Glen-Dual were very poor, very ignorant, and generally vicious. They could not read their Bibles, and of course were ignorant of all the great things which God had done for his ancient people Israel. They could not read their New Testaments, and therefore were ignorant of all the great things which the Son of God had done for us. They knew nothing of his mild and sinless character, or of the heavenly example he left us; and alas! what is all other earthly knowledge to the knowledge of these!

Now, what do you think was the consequence of this long-continued system of ignorance and superstition? It was just this,—that there was not a cleanly, comfortable cottage, a handsome and courteous young man, nor a lovely and amiable maiden in the whole valley: no; there never was one. They were a gloomy and morose race, who quarrelled and fought with their neighbours and with one another, kidnapped their neighbours' sheep, stole their deer, shot their game, and poached their river; and many of them were so openly and desperately wicked that the evil genii of the glen got the power over them, and carried them no one knew to what place, but few entertained hopes that it was to a good one.

But every young man and maiden in Glen-Luran could read their bibles, their psalms, and their books of prayer, and so well were they acquainted with all these that they could turn to any mentioned part. And how lovely a thing was it to see that amiable and comely race in their sequestered valley, all kneeling to the same God and Redeemer, with the most heartfelt devotion; all singing the same psalm or hymn, or bowing to the same strain of prayer or thanksgiving. They were like a community of beings of a sinless and happy world; for they all loved one another like brothers and sisters, and the guardian spirits of the glen got a commission from above to watch over them for good, and preserve them from the wicked elves that possessed Glen-Dual, and hated them, and tried every means to do them a mischief.

Well, it so happened, on a particular holiday, that all the little maidens of Glen-Luran went to pull berries in the wood of Dual, which abounded with blackberries that were peculiarly delicious and healthful. As they went along the bridge of Luran, they met with a beautiful little lady, dressed in green satin, with a wreath of roses and flowers on her head. Every one of the group curtsied to the lovely little stranger—for they were all as civil and well bred as they were virtuous—on which she smiled sweetly on them, and asked where all the flowers of Glen-Luran were going on such a day? "But I need not ask," added she; "for I see by your baskets you are going to gather blaeberries in the wood of Dual." And they said, "We are going there, and if you will go with us you shall have a part of our nice provisions and the choice of all our baskets, once they are full."

"I thank you for your courtesy, my generous and kind young friends," said she, "and in return I will give you some advice. Go not to the wood of Dual to day, but return home to your parents and friends; for there is danger, and methinks the very name of the place should deter good girls from going to it. For do you not know that in the primitive language of the country it is called the place of vice or wickedness?" And they smiled and said, "What is in a name? Our parents and school-mistress have given us leave to go for this day, and why should we return because the place has an unpropitious name?"

Then the little creature shook her sunny locks till the odour flew from the flowers over her brow, and filled the breeze with the perfume of paradise. And she said "True, there is not much in a name. But as the name of the place is, so is its nature; for there is more wickedness perpetrated in that wood every season than any of you virtuous children of Luran can conceive. And moreover you must have heard that it is haunted by evil and malignant spirits, which is true though you may not believe it, but without better protection than your own you will believe it before your return. At all events you know how many wicked and malevolent boys there are in that valley. Are you not afraid that they may fall on and maltreat you?"

And the lively and frolicsome group smiled at her fears, and asked who she was that took such an interest in them? And she said, "My name is May-lily, of Rainbow-hill, and since you will not return at my behest I must even go with you and make the most of you."

So away they all went to the wood, and began to pull berries with great joy, happiness and glee being the constant attendants of innocent amusement. But their hilarity was a little damped at the sight of a very ruffian-looking boy, who took a scrutinizing look at them and vanished. They tried to banish any lurking fears owing to this encounter, by saying to one another that the poor fellow took them for fairies and was frightened. But May-lily bade them keep together; for she dreaded he was gone to raise his wicked associates to fall on them; and accordingly it was not above half an hour before they saw a band of young ruffians who had got between them and their homes, and were coming straight towards them, so eager to attack them that they were running all the way.

Then May-lily said, "Do not run away and scream and scatter yourselves over the wood, like thoughtless foolish girls; for then they will catch you separately, and then what will your cries or strength avail against such as these? Keep all in a body beside me;

look them steadily in the face, and show no tokens of alarm; for there is something in the looks of innocence and purity that can appal even the wild beasts of the desert, and strike the most dissolute and abandoned with a temporary awe."

The maids did as they were commanded, standing in a close row, with their faces straight to their assailants, which so confounded the ruffians that when they came within a certain distance they seemed to have no power to advance farther, but stood still and gazed. Twice they retired for a space and whispered, and then again faced about, but still had not power to lay a hand on any of the damsels, although their looks became more and more ferocious every instant.

May-lily, who stood at the head, perceiving this, asked them mildly what they wanted? or if they had any commands for her and her playmates? One fierce-looking fellow, with a bare head and matted locks, who seemed to be a sort of commander-in-chief among them, then said that he and his associates were come to beat them soundly and take their fine clothes from them, for presuming to come and pull all their fine berries. "The berries are as much ours as yours," said May-lily; "for our fathers' possessions bound more than the half of this wood."

"Aye, you are proud and saucy madams," said he; "but we will teach you that all the world is not yours, for as high as you carry your heads."

"You are good for frightening cowards," said May-lily; "but I warn you off, and tell you that if you dare but to touch us with one of your fingers, it will be the dearest bought benefit you ever received." And at these words of the tiny elf the whole fraternity actually retreated, laughing and mocking as they went.

However, May-lily told her protegees that she was well aware they were as yet far from being out of danger; for, now that the blackguards were by themselves, they would to a certainty spirit up one another to some desperate deed.

"But here is a peeled wand to each of you," said she, "pure and white as your own souls; and, if they do attack us, ply these well, and I shall answer for the result."

Accordingly on listening they heard that the young ruffians were once more returning to the charge, vowing vengeance on the proud and saucy lasses of Luran. On coming close up to the girls, the great burly leader of the boys, finding his courage again beginning to give way, rushed forward and made a desperate effort to seize little May-lily of Rainbow-hill by the locks; but the lovely fay with a smiling countenance, and without flinching, struck her antagonist carelessly across the eyes with her white wand, and that moment the fellow fell back, over and down the hill, heels-over-head, roaring out like a bull. His associates were astonished, and flew to the charge, but every one of the maidens followed the example of their queen, and struck her assailant across the eyes with her wand, and the effect in all cases was the same. Down the brae headlong the lubberly boys went, stumbling, and floundering, and shouting out *murder!* and the little girls after them screaming with laughter, and flogging the rascals as if they had been highland bullocks or so many wild colts.

For the truth turned out to be that these strokes with the fairy wands had struck all the boys with a temporary blindness, so that when any of them got on their feet, and tried to run at their assailants, they were sure to run in a contrary direction, dashing in among thorns and brambles, which redoubled the sport, and the little good and lovely maidens had nothing to do but to laugh and lay on. Never did virtue obtain so complete a victory over vice; for after these wicked boys got mostly clear of the wood and into the road that led up the side of the river, still, not being able to see, some of them ran into pools of the river over their heads, others into quagmires and ditches, so terrified were they with the strokes of the fairy wands. By this time many of the little maids had fallen down quite powerless with laughter, but others at the instigation of May-lily, and by her example, pursued them all the way to their dirty village, belabouring the wickedest of them to great purpose.

Then the news rang through the whole country how the little lovely maidens of Luran had beat the great ragamuffin boys of Dual in a set skirmish, and pursued them home, pelting them all the way. The boys could not deny it, and then they were so much laughed at that they could not hold up their heads, and they now thirsted for ample revenge, a passion which all wicked boys and girls are apt to indulge in, but which every one who reveres the injunctions of his Saviour will carefully shun. Even the parents of these boys, who were no better than themselves, stirred them up to it, and, in the first place, told them to send a challenge to the boys of Glen-Luran, to meet them at the boundary, and they would fight them man to man. But these returned for answer that they would disdain to fight with a set of poltroons who had suffered themselves to be beaten by their little sisters, and to be pursued and thrashed by them like so many bullocks. This answer put the boys of Dual into such a rage that they were almost beside themselves, and from that time forth they watched every opportunity to do any of the young people of

Luran a mischief, until matters came to that pass that such insolence could no longer be borne, while the peaceful inhabitants of Glen-Luran knew not in what way to obviate it.

Just when things were at the worst, it chanced that all the little maids of Glen-Luran were assembled on the village green. It was St. Cyprian's day, and they were all dressed in their best apparel, with fillets of roses and various other flowers around their heads: and sure a lovelier sight was not to be seen in the walks of nature.

As they were taking counsel how to spend the day, behold, little May-lily of Rainbow-hill came among them! They were all so over-joyed to see her, that they shouted and danced around her in rings, and it was long ere any order could be restored among them, so loud and joyous was their merriment. She asked them how they meant to spend that holiday, and they all with one voice declared that they would spend it as she liked. She then said that, as the nuts were at the ripest, she thought they should go once more to the wood of Dual and fill their baskets. Then they all went rejoicing and brought their baskets and went with her.

Just as they entered Glen-Dual, the village dominie came riding by them upon an ass, viewing them with great curiosity, on which May-lily said to him, "Sir, will you be so kind as to order your boys not to molest us to day, as we are only going to pull our baskets full of nuts and go peaceably home again, and evil be to those who evil design." The dominie answered neither good nor bad, but galloped away home on his donkey, thrashing it all the way.

The girls, however, soon filled their baskets with fine nuts, and by the time this was done they perceived the boys of Glen-Dual coming, half running all the way to attack them. The villains were so intent on ample revenge that they had all stripped off their rag-ged coats, and had staves in their hands. May-lily had manifestly expected this; for, when she saw them, a smile of joy beamed on her face. Then she led her maids to an open space in the wood where there was a fairy ring, around which she danced three times back-ward, singing these lines:

> "Whoever comes first within this ring,
> Be he a lord or be he a king,
> He shall be changed in spirit and frame
> Into the thing that I first shall name."

She then arranged her maids behind this circle, so that the ruffians were obliged to come through it to the attack. They rushed into it, however, with oaths and cursing, and their eyes gleaming with passion; but the moment they entered it they fell flat on their faces, and lay motionless. "What is the matter now, brave boys?" said May-lily, "are you going to fall on your knees instead of maltreating us? Up to the combat, and let us see what mettle is in you to fulfil your threats." She then went among them, and gave every one of them three gentle strokes with her wand, muttering some mystic words, and behold the whole rabble rout stood up as many goodly jack-asses as there had been boys, and they were all shaking their long ears and braying most piteously; yet the girls could not help remarking that their braying resembled in some degree the crying of a herd of lubberly boys.

Then every one of the maidens mounted her donkey, and with May-lily at their head rode away home, each with her basket of nuts hanging at her donkey's neck. Never was there a more ridiculous cavalcade seen than these wicked boys when changed into asses, and forced to carry those they detested. They seemed not rightly to comprehend what had befallen them, but there they cantered away, kept quite in subjection by the white wands, and always laying back one long ear, and the other forward, with faces of the most stupid perplexity.

As for the girls, they never had such fun in their lives; for they rode races, lost bonnets, and scattered nuts, but all these added only to their merriment, and as they rode up the street of the village all the people came to the doors and windows, shouting and clapping their hands at seeing their little school maidens so well mounted. The boys hurraed, the dogs barked, and the bells rang, till at the common stable beside the church the maids alighted, and into that place they each put their donkeys.

May-lily then desired her associates to go home with their nuts, and bring their papas and the village pastor to look at their fine beasts. But it happened that in the common stable that day there were a number of wild highland ponies confined, and such a din arose between these and the asses as never was heard in the vale of Luran before. May-lily remained behind to guard the door, but when the parson and the men came in a body she was gone, and only a hideous noise was heard within. When the minister opened the door there were no asses there, but the whole of the ruffian boys of Glen-Dual stripped of their coats, and the wild ponies yerking at them with their heels in every corner. When they saw the minister and the fathers of the girls, they cried out to them for mercy, kneeling and beseeching them, and promising never again to offer wrong to an inhabitant of Glen-Luran.

The good pastor and the serious part of his flock took pity on the boys, released them, and gave to every one of them a new coat, that they might not leave their happy village naked and disgusted. Then the little maidens gathered round, and presented each boy with a sweet cake and a book: it was the book of all books, the book of life; and, from that day to this, there has not only been peace between the two valleys, but there is not a young man of Dual who will not risk his life any day for a maid of Glen-Luran.

There is no way in which I like so well to address my dear young friends as in a whimsical moral tale. I wish to impress upon their tender and flexile minds this delightful assurance, that around the truly virtuous there will always be a shield of defence, whether seen or unseen; for there is an arm of power around them which the strength of the wicked can never remove.

The Covenanter's Scaffold Song

By the Ettrick Shepherd

Sing with me! sing with me!
Weeping brethren, sing with me!
For now an open heaven I see,
And a crown of glory laid for me.
How my soul this earth despises! 5
How my heart and spirit rises!
Bounding from the flesh I sever!
World of sin, adieu for ever!

Sing with me! sing with me!
Friends in Jesus, sing with me! 10
All my sufferings, all my woe,
All my griefs I here forego.
Farewell terror, sighing, grieving,
Praying, hearing, and believing,
Earthly trust and all its wrongings, 15
Earthly love and all its longings!

Sing with me! sing with me!
Blessed spirits, sing with me!
To the Lamb our song shall be,
Through a glad eternity!   20
Farewell earthly morn and even,
Sun and moon and stars of heaven;
Heavenly portals ope before me,
Welcome, Christ, in all thy glory!

The May Flower

Song

By the late James Hogg, the Ettrick Shepherd.*

DEAR is the blush o' the rosy red rowan,
Sweet is the breath o' the young clover lea;
Pure is the breast o' the bonny ewe-gowan,
For Oh! my young May, they are emblems o' thee.
Then when the bee to his moor-bink is winging,   5
And the woods are alive wi' the coo o' the dove;
And the gloamin' afar its mantle is flinging,
Come to my shieling, Oh! come to me, love.

If vice for one moment my true heart be leading,
To injure thy beauty, my guide and my stay,   10
Cast thy mild modest glance in purity pleading,
And my error will vanish like darkness 'fore day.
Then when the bee to his moor-bink is winging,
And the woods are alive wi' the coo o' the dove,
And the gloamin' afar its mantle is flinging,   15
Come to my shieling, Oh! come to me, love.

* Never before published.

Juvenile Annuals

*Ackermann's Juvenile
Forget Me Not*

A Child's Prayer

By the Ettrick Shepherd

O God I am a little child
  Who fain to thee would pray
But am so mazed in folly's wild
  I know not what to say

O teach my light and erring tongue   5
  To render thanks to thee
And mould my simple heart while young
  To deep humility

For thou hast made me what I am
  With brightest hopes before   10
And put a living soul within
  To live for evermore

That thou art kind, and great, and good,
  I joyfully believe;
But O thy boundless love to man   15
  My soul cannot concieve!

That thou should'st send thine only son
  From regions of the sky
And for this sinful race of mine
  A dreadful death to die   20

I cannot frame! But teach me Lord
  With grateful heart to bow
And be that reverenced and adored
  Which none concievest but thou

Dramas of Infancy

By the Ettrick Shepherd

[Manuscript Version]

No 1

What is Sin?

Jessie–Shall we then not go to the nut wood to day sister, for as fine as the day is, and the flowers all blooming, and the birds all singing, and the nuts so brown and so ripe? Pray now, do let us go Elen.

Elen Indeed we shan't go to day Jessie. So content yourself; for Mamma forbade us to go and it would be a great sin in us to disobey our good Mamma.

Jessie Well that is so teasing! I could sit down and cry till night I am so angry! I never heard such a business as with that sin! Always sin sin with you and Mamma. Pray Elen can you tell me this What *is* sin?

Elen What is sin? That is a single question. "Sin is any want of conformity unto or transgression of the law of God."

Jessie I think it be a double question. At least, it is so to me, for I do not understand a word of it. But tell me what sin is in your own words, and I'll warrant you I understand it.

Elen Well then you know my dear little sister that when ever we break any of God's commands then we sin. Big men sin when they drink, and swear, and fight, and steal–

Jessie Oh horrible! Such monsters as they are! I like big men very ill sister Elen.

Elen But you ought not to do that Jessie. For that is very wrong and a sin of itself. There are many good men who fear and love the Lord who made us, with all their hearts.

Jessie Oh! I think the big vulgar men are very bad creatures! They fight and kill one another like wild beasts, and they kill poor women too. They are all bad ugly disgusting creatures except the pretty gentlemen.

Elen Alas my dear little sister how far you are wrong! For the gentlemen are generally the worst and the most dissolute of mankind, and God chooses the greater part of his elect from among the poor and the indigent.

Jessie Oh I cannot think so, it is so contrary to nature. I have always concieved that the rich and genteel people were the good people, because my Maker I saw was best to them, and gave them good houses, and good meat, and fine things. And then I was sure the poor shabby people were all the bad people, for I saw that God did not like them but gave them bad houses, and bad clothes, and dirty children, and nothing to eat but tobacco. The pretty gentlemen for my taste I assure you Elen. But tell me this. Do the ladies sin any?

Elen I suppose they do though I cannot tell you in what way. But my good book says that we were all born to sin, and can do nothing of ourselves but sin.

Jessie Then it is not a very good book sister let me tell you that. For I know full well that I never sinned any nor ever intend it. Do you think that you or I would kill or steal or swear? Or that Mamma would? Or any of the pretty Misses Brown? Or any elegant young lady whatever. No no! I will not believe that any young lady has the heart or the face to commit sin and if any women do sin it must be the ugly old wives and old maids that play at cards and scold one another and never look at little pretty misses like me. Some of them are very like sin itself.

Elen Hold your peace my dear little sister for you are too young and too wild and too petulant to talk about these matters, and I am afraid we may both be guilty of sin in thus trying to find out what it is.

Jessie I am afraid of no such thing I assure you! I am resolved to keep free of sin and have nothing to do with it. It is a bad vulgar thing.

Elen I am forced to laugh at you my dear Jessie while at the same time you see the tears standing in my eyes for you. You think you are quite above committing sin but in that you are grieviously mistaken for you are a great sinner and there is not a day on which you do not commit sin. Now tell me truly. Do you never break the Sabbath?

Jessie O never! unless sometimes when I get out of Mamma's sight.

Elen Ah Jessie Jessie! And do you not sometimes tell lies?

Jessie N–n–no.

Elen Speak truly now?

Jessie If ever I *do* tell any lies they are very little ones, and not worth minding. They are only such as saying NO when I should say YES or YES when I should say NO.

Elen But then you perhaps do not intend that?

Jessie Yes. I do.

Elen What then are your motives for doing so Jessie?

Jessie Just because I think it would have better if it had been the way that I say it is. And so I say it; and then it don't make Mamma angry with me.

Elen These are two very great and crying sins that you have confessed yourself guilty of. And if you do not guard against them they will still grow on you, and may ruin both your soul and body in the end.

Jessie I am very sorry for them sister, and will take care never to do any of them again.

Elen I think you may always note and remember this Jessie; that when ever you do that which your God forbids or that your Mamma forbids you are doing wrong and committing a great sin. And I must tell you that you are very cross with Mamma and vex her kind heart every day, which is a bad fault in you and one that our father in heaven will not overlook. We have lost our father and who has our good Mamma to love her and be kind to her if we are not so? If you would but think how she nursed you on her breast brought you up in her bosom cradled you on her knee and fondled and watched over you night and day when you could do nothing for yourself you would surely never wring the heart of that tender mother with your perversity and unkindness.

Jessie O dear sister do not break my heart and I promise never to do it again. I thought I had been a very good little miss and I find that I am a very naughty bad one. But I am always the better of talking with you and I will therefore try to make you my example.

Dramas of Infancy

By the Ettrick Shepherd

[Manuscript Version]

No 2
What is Death?

George Who is this fellow Death that kills so many people brother Tom?

Tom I don't know who he is. I never saw him, but I have seen his picture. He is a fellow without either skin or flesh on his bones;

a mere skeleton. A very ugly fellow indeed, with a long scythe over his shoulder with which he cuts down and kills all the men and women and children of the whole world when ever he can get at them.

George He must be a giant; and a very bad wicked fellow too. I do not understand him. Did not God make all the men women and children in the world brother?

Tom Yes—God made them all.

George Then what has Death ado to kill them? If George were God him would fight him.

Tom I have often thought that if I were a big strong man I would like to fight him and thrash him and smash him dead; for you know he killed our dear good sister, George, our kind little Laura.

George So he did. And you are to let me help you to kill him Tom for I like him very bad. Did God make Death too brother?

Tom I don't know. I do not think God would make him; for I think he would not make so many strong men, and lovely women, and good pretty children, and then make an ugly monster of a rascal to kill them all again. I rather think he is a ghost.

George Hold your peace and don't say so brother else you will make me frightened for him, and that is what I cannot bear to think of: for if I live I intend to meet him face to face, and dare him, and smite him down with a sharp sword, or a very long spear on the end of a pole. But if he be a ghost how can I do that?

Tom I suspect he is the ghost of some wicked cruel king, or perhaps that of Cain the first shedder of human blood. But I really don't know who or what he is. However yonder comes cousin Mary to take us home to school we will ask her. Can you tell us cousin who death is, or who made him? For George and I want to fight him for killing our poor sister.

Mary You are brave little boys, of manly and generous natures; but you speak you know not what. And you must learn to speak of death with more awe and reverence.

Both Who is he Mary? Who is he?

Mary He is the soveriegn of the Grave, and sends forth his invisible emissaries in thousands over the whole face of the earth to cut off mankind in every stage of their life. Yet no man needs to be afraid of Death, for there is one who is his master, and he can only take such as God hath appointed him.

George Did God make him at first cousin Mary?

Mary No my dear boy. Men brought death upon themselves. God made man at first pure and upright; but man brought sin into the world, and Death came with it; and so Death still passes upon all men for all have sinned.

Tom Who is it then that has mastered him?

Mary It is Jesus Christ the son of the living God; he who came from heaven and redeemed us with his own blood. These our bodies that grow up here like flowers to perish and decay are all subject to death, and the grave. But Jesus Christ by the sacrifice of himself conquered both, and we shall all rise again in the vigour of youth and beauty, go to a better and more glorious country, and continue to improve in knowledge righteousness and holiness to all the ages of Eternity.

George Will we improve in strength too cousin Mary?

Mary Yes both in strength and beauty.

George Then poor little George likes no body so well as Jesus Christ. He always loved him, but he felt that he loved his father and mother better. But they have not died for him and now George loves his saviour better than all the world.

Mary May the blessing of heaven rest upon my two little good cousins. And now come away home with me to school.

What is Sin?

By the Ettrick Shepherd

[Published Version]

Jessie. Shall we, then, not go to the nut-wood to-day, sister, though the day is so fine, and the flowers all blooming, and the birds all singing, and the nuts so brown and so ripe? Pray, now, do let us go, Ellen.

Ellen. Indeed, we sha'n't go to day, Jessie; so content yourself; for mama forbade us to go, and it would be a great sin in us to disobey our good mama.

Jessie. Well, that is so teasing! I could sit down and cry till night, I am so angry. I never heard such a fuss as with that sin. Always sin, sin, sin, with you and mama. Pray, Ellen, can you tell me one thing,--what is sin?

Ellen. What is sin? That is a single question. "Sin is want of conformity to, or transgression of, the law of God."

Jessie. I think it is a double question; at least, it is so to me; for I do not understand a word of it. But tell me what sin is, in your own words, and I'll warrant you I understand it.

Ellen. Well, then, you know, my dear little sister, that whenever we break any of God's commands, then we sin. Big men sin, when they swear, and fight, and steal.

Jessie. O horrible! such monsters as they are! I hate big men very much, sister Ellen.

Ellen. But you ought not to do so, Jessie; for that is very wrong, and a sin of itself. There are many good men, who fear and love God, who made us, with all their hearts.

Jessie. Oh, I think the big vulgar men are very bad people. They fight and kill one another like wild beasts; and they kill poor women, too. They are all ugly disgusting creatures, except the pretty gentlemen.

Ellen. Alas! my dear little sister, how mistaken you are! Some of those whom you call gentlemen are among the most wicked of mankind.

Jessie. I cannot think so either. I have always supposed that the rich and genteel people were the good people, because I observed that God had been kindest to them, and given them good houses, and good living, and fine clothes. And then I made sure that the poor, shabby people, were the bad people, because God did not seem to like them, but gave them mean houses, and mean clothes, and dirty children, and nothing to eat but tobacco. The pretty gentlemen for my taste, I assure you, Ellen. But tell me, do the ladies ever sin?

Ellen. I suppose they do, though I cannot tell you in what way. But my good book says that we were all born to sin, and can do nothing of ourselves but sin.

Jessie. Then it is not a very good book, sister,--let me tell you that; for I know full well that I never sinned, nor ever intend it. Do you think that you or I would kill, or steal, or swear; or that mama would, or any of the pretty Misses Brown, or any elegant young lady whatever? No, no; I will not believe that any elegant young lady has the heart or the face to commit sin; and if any women do sin, it must be the ugly old wives and old maids, who play at cards and scold one another.

Ellen. Hold your tongue, my dear little sister, for you are too young and too wild to talk about these matters; and I am afraid we may both be guilty of sin, in thus trying to find out what it is.

Jessie. I am afraid of no such thing, I assure you. I am resolved to keep clear from sin, and to have nothing to do with it. 'Tis a bad, vulgar thing.

Ellen. I am forced to laugh at you, my dear Jessie, while at the same time you see the tears standing in my eyes for you. You think yourself quite above committing sin; but in that you are grievously mistaken; for you are a great sinner, and there is not a day on which you do not commit sin. Now, tell me truly, do you not sometimes tell lies?

Jessie. N–n–no.

Ellen. Speak the truth, now.

Jessie. Well, if I ever do tell lies, they are very little ones, and not worth minding. They are only such as saying No, when I should say Yes; or Yes, when I should say No.

Ellen. But then, perhaps, you do not intend that.

Jessie. Yes, I do.

Ellen. And what are your motives for doing so, Jessie?

Jessie. Just because I think it would have been better if it had been the way I say it is; and so I say it, and then it don't make mama angry with me.

Ellen. But this is a very great sin that you have confessed yourself guilty of, Jessie; and if you do not guard against it, it will grow on you, and nobody can tell all the bad consequences to which it may lead.

Jessie. I am very sorry for it, sister, and will take care not to do it again.

Ellen. Always remember this, Jessie,–that when you are doing any thing that God has forbidden, or that your mama forbids, you are doing wrong, and committing a great sin. And I must tell you, too, that you are very cross with mama, and vex her kind heart every day, which is a bad fault in you, and one that our Father in heaven will not overlook. We have lost our earthly father, and whom has our good mama to love her and be kind to her, if we are not so? If you would but think how she nursed you on her breast, brought you up on her bosom, cradled you on her knee, and fondled and watched over you night and day, when you could do nothing for yourself, you would surely never wring the heart of that tender mother with your perversity and unkindness.

Jessie. O, dear sister, do not break my heart, and I promise never to do it again. I thought I had been a very good little girl, and I find that I am a very naughty one. But I am always the better for talking with you, and I will try to make you my example.

The Poachers

By the Ettrick Shepherd

BENJAMIN LITTLE, or little Benjy, as he was more generally called for a long period, was the son of a poor man of all work, who lived on the property of Sprinkell, on the Scots side of the Border. His name was Jacob. He could dress a hedge, work in a garden, mend a wheelbarrow, gird a cog, or put a gravel-walk in order. But, having no set post under his master, the baronet, he had no set wages; and for all these little odd jobs to which he was constantly putting his hand, he got literally nothing. He had one qualification, however, not yet mentioned, which was, that he could shoot a hare or black cock at any time without particular orders from the baronet. This was the cause of great trouble to him, for first one nobleman's game-keeper found him in a transgression, then another. It is the leading principle of these men's tenets to have no mercy. They stripped Jacob of every thing. They sold his split new household furniture by public auction, at his own cottage door, for ready money. Alas! it brought not one-third of its value. The eight-day clock fetched only seventeen shillings and sixpence. They sold the new blankets off the bed. They sold the bed itself; and, worst of all, they sold the double-barrelled gun for forty shillings.

This ruinous business was the death of Jacob's wife, a young creature, who had lately become the mother of a pretty boy. Whether her health was broken by reason of the loss of her bed-clothes, and her heart by the loss of her husband's effects, or by the loss of his good name, which was far worse, and which, till then, she had deemed unimpeachable,—which of these two it was, or whether it was the effect of both combined, that killed her, I do not know; but a few days afterwards, a woman named Mabel Irving called by chance on going by, and found her and her babe lying on a shakedown, in the cold corner of the empty cottage, without any covering, save a plaid and an old window-cloth. She was weeping over her unchristened boy, and calling him Benoni, the son of her sorrow, blessing him with every blessing, in the name of the Lord, praying that he might be kept from the errors that had brought ruin on his hapless father, and taught to revere and keep the laws of his country, and all the while baptising him with a dying mother's tears.

The woman Irving having apprised some of the wives of the baronet's people, one of them went up to Jacob's cottage in the morning, and found poor Helen dead. She was lying pale, stretched on her lowly bed of rushes, covered with the old window-cloth, and Jacob was busy, feeding his infant boy with a soup made from a hare which he had snared for the purpose, having no other earthly thing to give him; and the little urchin seemed to be enjoying it mightily. The feelings of the country people were excited: they exclaimed against the cruelty of gamekeepers, and denounced the judgment of God on their heads; but the men defended themselves by saying that they were only doing their duty, and that if he had ceased meddling with the game intrusted to their charge, they should never have meddled with him. Jacob christened his little boy by the name of Benjamin, sent him to nurse, and continued his old practices.

His old practices, did I say? Alas! he now became ten times worse than ever! He had nothing more that the law could seize, save his person, and of that he was reckless. He contrived to buy an old gun with only one barrel, but it was a thumper. He could bring down game almost at any distance with her, and the depredations which he now made in the preserves were prodigious; and as he was grown rather a desperate character, men were not rash in meddling with him. He made a deal of money of the game, all of which he transmitted to London, so that he paid punctually for little Benjy's maintenance, but never put any furniture into his house, for fear of another seizure.

As soon as the little fellow could run about, his father brought him home to his empty dwelling, feeding him on fish and game, and taking him out poaching with him by night, to drive the hares and the game to him. When blamed for thus initiating the pretty boy so early into crime, the father said he could not help it, for he could not leave the dear little fellow sleeping by himself; and, besides, there was nothing he liked better than a bout at the hares, pheasants, and black cocks.

For the space of five or six years did the father and son and little Cocket, their dog, carry on this work of lawless depredation, and wanted for nothing; but it was a depredation so notorious as no longer to be borne: so one night as little Benjy was driving a plantation, he heard loud words and a scuffle at a distance, in the direction where he knew his father to be; and with the natural dread of an evil-doer, he hid himself in a tree. There he sat till all was again silent, and till he heard his father call his name in an under-voice; he then came down, and the two went home to their lowly couch, without any game, and as usual lay down together in the dark with little Cocket upon their feet.

Benjy was awaked at an early hour by the fierce and desperate baying of Cocket; and when the boy raised his head, he perceived that three ill-looking fellows had entered the house, and that the fury of the little pointer was keeping them at bay. Benjy only said "Whisht, Cocket!" and the little fellow cowered down on his master's feet and ceased barking, but kept uttering an ill-suppressed growl indicative of the most heartfelt dissatisfaction. One of the men then inquired of Benjy if his father was there? He answered that he was! "Father, here are some men wanting you," added he; but his father made no reply.

"Oh! this is all fudge, Mr. Jacob," said they;—"a mere sham sleep, out of some evil design. Have you fire-arms beside you, rascal?" "Ay," said Benjy, with great simplicity. The three men then made a bolt forward to seize Jacob; but little Cocket fairly fought and beat off all the three, tearing them without mercy or mitigation of his resentment. Little Benjy now, from an internal movement of terror, tried with all his force to rise, but found himself locked to the spot; and it was not till after the most violent exertions that he disengaged himself, and when he did he was covered with one sheet of blood. When he saw this the poor fellow uttered a loud cry of horror. His father was lifeless. He had died with his child clasped to his bosom; for, with all his faults, want of affection was none of them. The constables who had come to seize Jacob now retreated in dismay with the woful tidings, leaving poor little Benjy with the bloody corpse of his father. A distressed boy was he that morning: nay, he was in such a state of distraction as is scarcely to be expressed. Both his parents had now finished their lives with him in their bosoms, and both their deaths had been caused by the same crime; for poor Jacob had died of the wounds he received in the affray with the keepers the night before; and though there can be no doubt that he felt the hand of death upon him, he never mentioned the circumstance to the boy, as if unwilling to witness his distress.

Benjy now, for the first time in his life, abhorred the crime of poaching from his very soul, and resolved never more to indulge in that which had cost both his dear parents their earthly existence. Of his mother he remembered nothing, but his father had often mentioned her to him as the sweetest and most loving creature on earth, whose death was caused by those most detestable of all earthly creatures, the gamekeepers. His father he loved with a more than ordinary affection. In him and Cocket all the fond feelings of his heart were centered. He knew of no other friends, and he cared for no other; and now that he had lost the principal, his undivided affection was set on the one that remained.

Now little Cocket himself was the greatest poacher in Scotland; not a hare, rabbit, or any game bird, could lurk within a hundred yards of his master's route, that he would not find and point as steadily as the needle to the pole. His mode was to squat close down on his belly, turn his little nose towards the game, and lie there in an agony of solicitude till his master came up. And with this little dog and a tremendous gun, called Johnnie Cope, as his sole portion, was left this poor boy, who had taken up the resolution never to poach more as long as he lived.

On the day of Jacob's funeral, poor Benjy laid his father's head in the grave, with many bitter tears and sobs that were like to rend his young heart in twain; and when the interment was over, one man thought Benjy would be going to such a place to stay, another to such another place, and the consequence was that Benjy got the offer of going to no place whatever; and not knowing where to go, he naturally, as by instinct, took the only road he had ever been accustomed to go, away to the lonely shieling at the back of the plantations. Alas! what a habitation for the poor fellow now to retire to! an empty shieling, and a lowly couch stained with the blood of his dear father! But what could he do? So he jogged slowly along, weeping as he went, and eagerly cherishing the virtuous resolution *never* to poach more, *no, never, never*, as long as he lived and breathed in the world!

As he went up by the Winter Cleuch Foot, Cocket made a dead point on the opposite brae. "I may ay gang an' see what it is," said Benjy to himself: "the creature will be nae the waur o' me looking at it; and unless I spring it, Cocket will be there till the morn." So away went Benjy across the glen to see what it was that little Cocket was pointing at so steadily. He was determined not to poach any more, but he had a stone of about half a pound weight in either hand just to throw at the creature for fun when it rose. With his arm stretched backward at its full length, ready to throw with great force, Benjy ran in on the game—turned—ran this way, and that way:—no—there was no game there, at least none that Benjy could see. Cocket still kept the point, and that so eagerly that his eyes were set in his head like the eyes of a dead creature. "Seize him, Cocket!" cried Benjy. No sooner said than done: the word was hardly out of the boy's mouth ere the dog had hold of a great fat rabbit that had ensconced himself beneath the long grass out of Benjy's sight, and every other creature's sight; but to elude the scent of Cocket was out of his power.

How Benjy did laugh as the rabbit screamed and Cocket shook him by the throat! and when he had done worrying it, Benjy picked up his rabbit, and stroking Cocket's crown, said "he was a little, fine, clever fellow."

Now it is a curious fact that, as long as Jacob carried the gun, no cajoling, no pressing, could make Cocket break point and run in. For why? he well knew his master would bring the bird, or whatever it was, down, when once it was properly sprung; but when he saw his poor young master coming armed only with a stone in either hand, he took the first hint to make sure of the rabbit himself, and he contrived to play a hare the same trick before he and Benjy reached home.

There was no man in Scotland could skin and dress a hare or rabbit more cleverly than Benjy; and what a capital supper Cocket and he made of one of their prizes that night! He then carried out the bloody hay, took plenty of the sweetest-scented meadow hay he could find into another corner of the shieling, and without any thing, either above or below him, save hay, he took little Cocket in his bosom and slept soundly till the morrow, when the sun was high up in the east.

After a hearty breakfast, he began with a heavy heart to look at auld Johnnie Cope. "It was a pity to let his father's gude auld gun gang a' ower wi' roost; he had cleaned and oiled her oft–he wad do it again–no that he meant to mak ony use o' her–that was out o' the question, for the poaching had been the death o' baith his father an' mither; but it was as purpose like to hae a clean thing as a dirty thing standing in a body's house." Thus did Benjy apostrophise himself; and, cleaning the gun well, he set her out of his hand with a satisfied look, quite ready for action.

He next went to his father's hidden treasure of springes, gins, nets, and snares for every sort of game, and surveying them all with great interest, he put a few in his pocket; and then, purposing a walk to put off the wearisome day, he took a long look at Johnnie Cope, such a look as a dog takes of a morsel which he is compelled against his will to quit. "It coudna do muckle ill to tak her wi' ane in case ane might fa' in wi' a fox, or a hawk, or a glede. The country wad be weel quat o' a wheen o' them. But then Johnnie Cope made sic a noise through the country, an' it didna do for ane to be making a *verra* grit noise the day after ane's father's burial." Johnnie Cope was actually left at home that day; and away went Benjy and Cocket to take their forenoon's walk.

Where do you suppose Benjy and Cocket would take their walk that day? Of course along the highway or some bare moor where there was no temptation, you will say. Such were undoubtedly the most proper places for a youth to walk who was resolved *never* to poach more. But Benjy's walk lay through the richest cover of the country, for he had some of his father's old snares to lift, and some other cogent reasons for taking that direction. He returned literally laden with game, for, besides other shifts, Cocket seemed to apprehend that on himself depended his master's subsistence. Scarcely any thing could escape him;—rabbits never did, and of these there was an overflowing superabundance. But he likewise frequently caught hares and black cocks, by creeping on his belly close along the ground till within a leap of his prey, when he very seldom missed them. Benjy was thus naturally established as a poacher by circumstances which he could not avert, and against which his better judgment and feeling remonstrated.

During the day above mentioned he made a very affecting discovery. When he went out to walk, he put on his poaching jacket with wide tails and large pockets, in one of which he felt something terribly heavy thumping against his thigh: he took it out and looked at it: it was something rolled up in a clout, and the clout was glued together with blood. The boy wondered; but, sitting down, he opened it, and there was a whole hoard of guineas, more than he could count. The poor little fellow was deeply affected, for he easily conceived that they had been placed there by the bloody hand of a dying father, the only gift that he had to bequeath to his son, whom he seems to have loved above measure. Although doubtless this was a treasure earned by the sale of game, I have always regarded it as one of the most affecting incidents I ever heard.

Day passed on after day, and week after week, and nobody seemed to regard or care for poor Benjy. He was abandoned to a lonely and lawless life; and when it was discovered that he still occupied his late father's shieling, no sympathy was evinced for the young outlaw. In proof of this I need only relate a conversation that took place in the house of James Ferguson, one of Sir John's tenants.

"Can ony o' you tell me, sirs, what is become o' the poor fatherless an' motherless callant Benjamin Little? I am feared that creature will either dee for hunger or learn to steal."

"As for him dying for hunger, there is nae fear o' that as long as there is game in Annandale or the woods o' Cannobie. Aih! but he is a hardened desperate wretch, and just living in the desolate cottage where his father died sae lately, an' picking up every thing o' game kind. I saw him at the guard o' the London coach wi' a box yesterday. He's gaun to the gallows as fast as he can, an' it is little matter how soon."

"O, fie, fie, Jamie, how can ye say sae! It is a hard case to abandon a human being awthegither, without at least giving him a chance o' doing better, for as yet the poor fellow has had none. Think you he has ony sense o' religion?"

"His father Jacob had a deep *sense* o' religion, but I doubt the practice was laid aside; for how can a man who is living in the daily breach of the laws of his country engage in the ordinances of religion? He is sensible that it is a mockery of both God and man, and he cannot do it. He has not the face. And as to the reclaiming o' this little rascal, that is a thing impossible, for I doubt if he kens ony mair about religion than just this—that there is a God who created man, hares, partricks, an' moorcocks, an' that his own right to these is as good as the greatest man's in the kingdom. These are Benjy's leading tenets, and he will pursue them till they bring him to his end. There's naebody feels for him, for naebody expects ony good o' him."

When Ferguson had gone thus far, the other speaker (who was an old man, named Adam Little) went straight to Sir John, and laid the boy's case before him: the baronet instantly ordered the poor boy to be brought down to the hall and seen to, and sent to school. This was done, and Benjy left the empty house with Johnnie Cope over his shoulder, loaded, and Cocket gambolling about him. Under the guardianship of these only remaining friends, he found that he could scarcely be in bad circumstances. His gold he had hidden in the middle of a stone dike, under an elm tree, which he well knew, and in which he had often hidden game, so that Benjy felt himself rather "an independent callant."

But, alas! in a few days it was announced to him by the steward and gamekeeper that he must part with Cocket, who was a condemned criminal, having been caught in the preserve destroying game without mercy. This was a rending up of the last affections of Benjy's heart. He burst out a-crying, and said, he would rather part with his life than poor Cocket; he was his own, the sole friend he had on earth; and nothing but death should part them.

The gamekeeper said that then death should soon part them—the sooner the better for both; and taking out a cord, he prepared to hang up the little animal before his master's eyes. Benjy darted off like an arrow, and Cocket before him. They were pursued, and would soon have been overtaken, but Benjy had a protector for Cocket in view; and, presenting Johnnie Cope, who was loaded with swan-shot, he cocked, and then said to his assailants, "Now touch outher me or my dog gin ye daur for the blood o' ye! I shall

lay your heads where ye never shall lift them again. My dog is a
treasure left me by my poor father, an' ye hae nae mair right to take
him frae me than I hae to come an' take Sir John's house an' garden
frae him."

The man, perceiving the little veteran's determination in his looks,
wisely kept back, and Benjy made good his retreat, keeping a sharp
eye on his enemies, and his finger still at the trigger, for fear of an
attack in rear.

Adam Little witnessed this scene, and could not help admiring
the boy's strong affection for the little animal, as well as his un-
daunted resolution, and began to expostulate with the men, observ-
ing, that in his opinion they were heinously wrong and the boy was
right. They answered that the separating him from that dog was the
only thing that could save the poor little fellow from perdition; and
for his own sake they were resolved to dispatch the dog privately,
which they ought to have done at first. Old Little's heart could not
approve this, and, instantly following Benjy to the shieling, he told
him what he had heard, and that it was vain now to think of finding
an asylum on Sir John's property on any other conditions than giving up his favourite.

Benjy said he would "see them a' hanged afore he did ony sic
thing; an' they had better let alone than meddle wi' him an' his dog.
He wad keep possession o' his father's bit house till the neist term,
in spite o' them."

Adam said that would be all fair, if he could remain there without
breaking the law, which he thought very dubious; and, that he might
not perish on the same rock with his hapless parents, he had resolved to take him to his sister and brother-in-law at Kirtonholm,
who had no son of their own, lived beside the school, and to whom
such a boy would be of great value. There he might keep little Cocket
as long as he lived, and the more rabbits and hares he worried the
better, for there were none in that place to find fault.

Benjy burst out into tears of gratitude; and from that moment old
Little resolved to assist him with his whole protection and influence,
for he saw that his heart was in the right place, and that he had a
desire to be good and virtuous, if Providence would open a path for
him to virtue and goodness. That night the two set out on their
journey to the house of Mr. Beattie, of Kirtonholm.

This single incident in Benjy's life, his resolute defence of his little
dog, changed all his circumstances, and opened to him new sources
of pleasure, emulation, and ambition. He lived with Mr. Beattie seven
years, attending the school with his three daughters, and at the end

of that period went to the college. Many wondered how he got so easily and readily through his classes, but the hoard in the bloody clout under the elm-tree helped well with that. From this store Benjy took a portion every year, and no more than what he actually needed; and many a tear it cost him when he thought of the affectionate heart that had bestowed it with that heart's last earthly throbs.

But I must hasten to the end of my simple tale. As soon as Benjy had passed his *trials*, as we say, Sir John interested himself earnestly in his fortunes, and soon procured him a living. He married his benefactor's second daughter, and there is not at this present time a more respectable presbyterian clergyman that I know of. True, on the 12th of August he is the first and the deadliest shot on the moors, and the latest perhaps that traverses the bare winter fields, and beats up the bushes and hedgerows. This is accounted an aberration by some, but, at all events, it is a manly, healthy, and invigorating exercise; and to an active frame often absolutely necessary, to enable him to follow his sedentary and mental labours with energy and effect. To traverse the blooming heath swathed in the breeze of the wilderness; to look far abroad on all the goings on of nature; to bring down the black cock among his native brackens, and the moorcock on his dark and heathery waste; to mark the unerring sagacity of a favourite dog; the flights of the fowls, which, after a certain round, return always to their native spot as a place of rendezvous; to drink of the silver fountain, and rest on the flowery sward, in some lone retired fairy nook—if these are crimes, or even errors, may He whose bounty has granted us the delightful privilege forgive all who indulge in it, and among others the old Shepherd of Ettrick and the Minister of Shootinglees!

Play up my Love
A Song

By the Ettrick Shepherd

[Published as 'The Shepherd Boy's Song']

Play up my love my darling Sue
   That strain was rather mair than common
The lambies darena chump nor chew
   For listening to my bonny woman
And see how Bawtie's brockit crown   5
   Is gee'd up to the cope o' heaven
He thinks the fairies are come down
   Our wilder'd correi to enliven

Play up my love—That pipe I vow
   Is mellower than I e'er could trow it   10
It never play'd sae sweet till now
   Wi' the sweet breath that passes through it
Strike A and B then half the C
   And then a minim soft an' evenly
But O tis a' the same to me!   15
   If there's a tone the music's heavenly

Music has power to still the waves
   To break the cloud and bend the willow
To wake the dead out o' their graves
   An' bang frae 'neath the stormy billow   20
To make the fays of glen and grove
   Skip wildly o'er their velvet flooring
But when it pours frae lips we love
   O 'tis sae sweet 'tis past enduring

H. Warren, pinx.t

Pub.d by R.Ackermann, London.

H. Robin sculp.t

THE SHEPHERD'S BOY.

Gift-Books

The Casket

The Admonition

AULD GEORDIE sat beside a board
Wi' routh o' hamely meltith stored,
Threw off his hat, composed his face,
An' just was thinkin' o'er the grace,—
When a wee say, that chanced to pass   5
Atween his wife and only lass,
At aince pu'd Geordie's mind away,
To something lang he wished to say.—
He turned, an' wi' a fervent air,
That weel bespak a parent's care,   10
Soft, yet severe, tho' kind, yet keen,
And thus addressed his darling Jean.—
His auld wife by his elbow staid,
Assentin' weel to a' he said.—
"Ah, lassie! thou art a' we hae,   15
For Heaven has left us now nae mae!
Thy ilka faut we grieve to see,
For a' our care on earth's for thee.—
If thou but ken'd by night an' day
How for thy weal we wish an' pray,   20
How sair o'er thee our bosoms yearn,
Jean, thou wad be a mindfu' bairn!
I've lately seen, and grieved to see,
Your frequent rambles o'er the lea;
When gloamin' draws her darknin' screen   25
Around the holms and woodlands green;
When birds are singing in the grove,
An' ilka note's a tale of love!—
What gars ye daunder out your lane,
In wrapper braw, an' tippet clean,   30
Your hair caimbed up fu' dink to see,
And gouden curls aboon your bree?—
Ah, Jean, beware, my bonnie bairn!
The love o' virtue's hard to learn;
The pleasant way oft leads to death;   35
The adder lurks in flowery path;
I ken ye gae—an' grieve to ken—
To meet young Jamie o' the glen;
But gang nae mair:—I ken fu' weel

Your virtue fair, your bosom leal;   40
But, oh my child! by night and day
Keep out o' sin and danger's way!
Your health is high, your blossom fair,
Your spirits dance as light as air;
Yet, trust me, Jean, ye're lightly poising   45
Atween the winning an' the losing;
On youthfu' passion's firm controul
Depends your fair, immortal soul!
Oh think! if sic a thing should be,
As that these walks by greenwood tree,   50
These nightly daunderings by the river,
Should gar us lose our bairn for ever!
Be good, my love!—Ye canna' be
For aye aneath a parent's ee;
But mind, there's ANE, will aye be near ye,   55
Will ever see, will ever hear ye,
An' if ye're gude, he'll be your friend,
And mak' ye happy in the end."—
Young Jeanie's heart was saft an' kind,
A tender thought shot through her mind;   60
It came unsought, an' came again,—
'Twas about Jamie o' the glen!
But she was gude as she was fair,
An' i' the gloamin' walk'd nae mair.

A Father's
New Year's Gift

My Dearest Children,

As a small token of assurance that you are never from my remembrance, and likewise as a hint that I wish you to remember me, I send you this little New Year's Present, in hopes that I shall hear you recite them all beautifully and impressively on your knees before your Maker on my return. Receive also with it the most fervent blessing of your affectionate Father,

James Hogg.

London, January 1st, 1832.

Prayer for the Sabbath Morning

O MY God and my Father, behold in mercy and compassion a poor offending and helpless creature here kneeling at the footstool of thy grace. I acknowledge thee as my Creator, my Redeemer, and my most bountiful benefactor; and once more I desire to dedicate and devote myself to thee and to thy service. Do with me, or keep from me, what thou wilt; but take never away thy loving-kindness through Christ Jesus. I thank thee, O Lord, for thy goodness to me through the last week; and for the return of this Sabbath morning, and the comforts thereof. Be with me through this thy holy day, to assist me in every piece and part of duty. Give me a new heart to serve thee in newness of life, and teach me to chasten all the irregularities of my temper by the sweet influences of the Christian religion. Bless all who are near and dear to me in this world of sin and sorrow, whether related to me by the ties of nature or of grace: be their God and their guide; and hear their prayers on my behalf, for I am unworthy of thy notice.

Our Father, which art in Heaven; hallowed be thy name. Thy kingdom come. Thy will be done in earth, as it is in Heaven. Give us this day our daily bread: and forgive us our trespasses, as we forgive them that trespass against us. And lead us not into temptation; but deliver us from evil: for thine is the kingdom, the power, and the glory, for ever and ever. *Amen.*

Prayer for the Sabbath Evening

ALMIGHTY Father, Lord of Heaven and Earth; how shall I, a child, approach thy Divine presence, or take thy holy name into sinful lips. I know thee to be the great God who inhabitest the praises of Eternity, and dwellest in that light that is inaccessible and full of glory, into which no mortal eye can penetrate. But I know also that thou lovest thy creatures, and that thou sentest thy Son from Heaven to redeem them from death, and to die that we might not die eternally. Therefore, O Lord, beneath the cross of my Redeemer, beneath his bleeding love for mankind, do I lay my guilty and polluted self. Own me, O Lord Jesus, and I shall never be ashamed. Defend me, and I shall never be afraid. Take me under the shadow of the wings of thy imputed righteousness, and my soul shall magnify the Lord, and my spirit rejoice in God my Saviour. Pardon all the sins which I have committed against thee through this thy holy day, whether of omission or commission. May they all be blotted out of the book of thy remembrance; and take me under thy protection through the dark and silent watches of the night. May I lie down in thy fear, and awake in thy favour, that my mouth may be filled with thy praises. May my friends be friends to Christ, and my relations related to him by the ties of the covenant of grace. I thank thee for this day, and for the mercies thereof both special and common; and I thank thee for the health and happiness which I enjoy. But, above all, I thank thee for Jesus Christ thy unspeakable gift. And I pray for all those who love him, and trust in thee through his mercy. Bless them all, O Lord, with thy best blessing; and bless me, even me also, O my Father, and the praise shall be thine in Christ Jesus for ever. *Amen.*

Hymn for Sabbath Morning

I LOVE, O Lord, this holy day
    In mercy sent to me,
A day the youthful heart to sway
    With thankfulness to thee.

On it this world at first was made   5
    By thy creative might;
The ample heavens above it spread,
    The day form'd and the night.

This day the earth arose from night
    With spirit unendued;   10
A second time to glorious light
    It rose, by grace renew'd.

In shadow'd and in doubtful faith
    Of life we groped the way;
But Jesus burst the bonds of death,   15
    And darkness fled away.

O blessed day! sent from above
    Despondence to controul;
The beacon of Redeeming love,
    The rainbow of the soul.   20

For the return of this thy day,
   O Lord, I bless thy name;
Lead me unto thy house to pray
   With heart in praying frame:

And never may this blessed day   25
   Dawn o'er the eastern sea,
On which I do not kneel and pray
   With grateful heart to thee.

Father of Life, do thou approve,
   And my Redeemer dear;   30
And Spirit of grace, bow down in love
   A simple child to hear.

Hymn for the Sabbath Evening

WHEN, O my Saviour! when shall I
   Behold thee all serene,
Blest in perpetual Sabbath day
   Without a veil between?

Assist me while I wander here   5
   Amid this world of cares;
Incline my heart to pray with love,
   And then accept my prayers.

Thy Spirit, O my Father, give,
   My erring steps to tend;   10
And light my path to ceaseless joys
   In Sabbath without end.

Morning Prayer for Week Days

I ADORE thee, O Lord, as my Creator, Preserver, and bountiful
Benefactor: thou hast watched over me with a father's care, and made
the outgoings of the evening and morning to rejoice over me. O
make me a new creature created in Christ Jesus unto good works.
May his precious blood blot out all my sins, his perfect righteousness make me accepted of thee, and his blessed Spirit lead me and

guide me in the way of truth. I thank thee for preserving me through the last night and this morning: watch over me through this day. Keep me in thy fear continually. Guide me by thy Spirit while I live, and afterwards receive me into thy glory. Bless all whom I ought to remember at a throne of Grace: may they be united to Christ by a true and living faith. Increase the limits of the Redeemer's kingdom, and enable me to love him more and serve him better than I have hitherto done. O keep me from the evils of my own heart, the evils of the world, and the temptations of the devil; and bring me to Heaven at last for Christ's sake. *Amen.*

Evening Prayer for Week Days

ACCEPT of my thanks, O Lord, for thy preservation of me through this day. Pardon any sins of which I have been guilty in any part of it; and take me under thy protection through another night. Thou watchest over thy people by night and by day, so that nothing can harm those who are followers of that which is good. Bless all those who are near and dear to me. May my relations be related to Christ, my friends be the friends of the Redeemer, my benefactors partake of thy spiritual bounty, and my enemies partake of thy pardoning mercy. Sympathise, O Lord, with the poor and distressed; supply their wants, and sanctify their troubles: and enable me to improve the health which thou givest me, so that when I die, I may have the testimony of my conscience that I have lived with thee; for all that I ask is for Jesus Christ's sake. *Amen.*

Hymn for the Close of the Week

BEFORE thy footstool, God of Truth,
    A humble child bows down,
To thank thee for the joys of youth,
    And errors all to own.

I know thou art the fountain-head   5
    Whence all my blessings flow;
But all thy glory and thy good
    I dare not seek to know.

Whether thy way is on the wind,
    The pathway of the storm,   10

Or on the waste of waters wide,
    Which rolling waves deform;

I only know, by flood or wild,
    Thou see'st me night and day,
And grievest o'er the wayward child   15
    That goes from thee astray.

Through all this week thy kindly sway
    Hast round me been for good;
At task or play—by night or day—
    In wilderness or wood.   20

And when I lay me down to sleep
    Thy guardian shield be spread;
And angel of thy presence keep
    A watch around my bed.

O teach me to adore thy name   25
    For all thy love to me;
Thy guardian goodness to proclaim,
    Thy truth and verity.

And through the darkness of the night
    Watch o'er my thoughts that stray;   30
And lift mine eyes upon the light
    Of a new Sabbath day.

And in a holy frame employ
    Thy day, due praise to give
To Him who wept that I might joy,   35
    And died that I might live;

Who rose again, and went above
    That sinful ones like me
Might glory in redeeming love
    To all eternity.   40

For all thy blessings shower'd around
    My kindred and my race,
I bless thee, Lord; but, most of all,
    For riches of thy grace.

For peace of mind, and health of frame,   45
    And joys—a mighty store,
Accept my thanks; and to thy name
    Be glory evermore.

Hymn for General Use

O GOD of yonder starry frame,
    How should a thing like me
Dare to pronounce thy holy name,
    Or bow to thee the knee!

I know not of my spirit's birth,   5
    How dust and soul combine,
Nor being of one thing on earth;
    And how can I know thine!

I only know that I was made
    Thy purpose to fulfil,   10
And that I gladly would be good
    And do thy holy will.

For this my being rational,
    For this my dwelling-place,
I bless the Lord; but, most of all,   15
    For Gospel of thy grace.

Direct my soul to search and know
    What Jesus did for me,
And teach my little heart to glow
    With thankfulness to thee.   20

And when this weary life is done,
    And dust to dust declines,
Then may I dwell beyond the sun,
    Where thy own glory shines.

Take my dear parents[1] to thy care,   25
    My little kinsfolk too;
And listen to their humble prayer
    When they before thee bow:

[1] Instead of "*dear parents*"—"*relations*," if the child has no parents.

And when they pray for sinful me
   With fervour that exceeds,   30
Do thou return the blessing free
   And double on their heads.

Hymn on the Omnipresence of the Deity

DWELLER in heaven, and ruler below,
Fain would I know thee, yet tremble to know.
How can a mortal deem—how may it be,
That being can not be but present with thee?
Is it true that thou saw'st me ere I saw the morn?   5
Is it true that thou knew'st me before I was born?
That nature must live in the light of thine eye?
This knowledge for me is too great and too high!

That fly I to noonday or fly I to night,
To shroud me in darkness or bathe me in light,   10
The light and the darkness to thee are the same,
And still in thy presence of wonder I am?
Should I with the dove to the desert repair,
Or dwell with the eagle in clough of the air,
In the desert afar, on the mountain's wild brink,   15
From the eye of Omniscience still must I shrink:

Or mount I on wings of the morning away,
To caves of the ocean unseen by the day,
And hide in those uttermost parts of the sea,
Even there to be living and moving in thee;   20
Nay, scale I the cloud in the heavens to dwell,
Or make I my bed in the shadows of hell,
Can science expound, or humanity frame,
That still thou art present, and all are the same?

Yes, present for ever!—Almighty!—Alone!   25
Great Spirit of nature, unbounded, unknown!
What mind can embody thy presence divine?
I know not my own being, how can I thine?
Then humbly and low in the dust let me bend,
And adore what through life I can ne'er comprehend.   30
The mountains may melt, and the elements flee,
Yet a universe still be rejoicing in thee.

The Young Lady's Sabbath Companion

Manuscript Fragment

The history of woman since the creation of the world is very like the history of an individual of the sex. They are all liable to the same passions and the same errors though not in the same degrees. Now as I look upon carelessness about religion amounting almost to an unbelief in it as the leading vice of the young of the age I regard it my duty to contribute towards the preservation of the sublime truths of Christianity fully convinced of the pernicious effects of the least shade of infidelity on the virtue and happiness of those for whom I am inditing these simple lessons. it leads to levity as certainly as the sparks fly upward.

It is the great error of this age to believe too little. Indeed not to believe implicitly in any thing unless it be extravagantly rediculous such as the gift of tongues. I entreat therefore my young readers to make up their minds to despise every redicule that the profane can throw on the religion of Jesus and never to let such eradicate from their belief one item of the truth of that divine institution and if my simple and humble efforts can but establish one wavering soul how well I should consider my time bestowed If you deserve either happiness in this world or the world

A Parting Gift

To Mrs James Cochrane

[Manuscript version]

O Mary dear Mary let gratitude move
Your soul for the peace of the man that you love
That your life may pass on like an Autumn day
That rises with red and portentous ray
But long ere the arch of the day is won   5
A halo of promise is round the sun
And the settled sky though all serene
Is rayed with the dark and the bright between
With the ruddy glow and the streamer wan
Like the evil and good in the life of man   10
And at last when it sinks in the cradle of day
More holy and mild is its sapphire ray
                                        James Hogg

Waterloo-place
March 20th 1832

To Mary

[Published version]

O MARY, dear Mary! let gratitude move
Your soul for the peace of the man that you love!
That your life may pass on like an autumn day,
That rises with red and portentous ray;
But long ere the arch of the day is won,   5
A halo of promise is round the sun!
And the settled sky, though all serene,
Is rayed with the dark and the bright between;
With the ruddy glow and the streamer wan,
Like the evil and good in the life of man;   10
And at last, when it sinks in the cradle of day,
More holy and mild is its sapphire ray!
                                        HOGG

A Listing of Hogg Texts in Annuals and Gift-Books

Janette Currie

I

Part One lists all known contributions by Hogg that were published in annuals and gift-books, arranged in the order in which these texts are discussed in the present edition's Introductory and Textual Notes. The page numbers given below relate to the original annual or gift-book.

Literary Souvenir

for 1825
    'Invocation to the Queen of the Fairies', pp. 122–26.
for 1826
    'Love's Jubilee', pp. 121–27.
    'The Border Chronicler', pp. 257–79.
for 1827
    Stanzas for Music', p. 232.

The Bijou

for 1828
    'An Aged Widow's Own Words', pp. 26–27.
    'Ane Waefu' Scots Pastoral', pp. 108–11.
for 1829
    'Woman', pp. 93–96.
    'Superstition and Grace', pp. 129–34.

Forget Me Not

for 1828
    'The Sky Lark', p. 27.
    'The Descent of Love', pp. 217–20.
for 1829
    'St. Mary of the Lows', pp. 25–29.
    'Eastern Apologues', pp. 309–23.
for 1830
    'Seeking the Houdy', pp. 399–413.
for 1831
    'A Sea Story', pp. 19–31.
for 1832
    'Maggy o' Buccleuch', pp. 182–83.
    'The Battle of the Boyne. A Dramatic Sketch', pp. 299–304.

The Remembrance

for 1831
> 'A Boy's Song', pp. 74–75.
> 'The Two Valleys', pp. 121–32.
> 'The Covenanter's Scaffold Song', p. 255.

Ackermann's Juvenile Forget Me Not

for 1830
> 'A Child's Prayer', pp. 176–77.
> 'What is Sin?', pp. 223–27.
for 1831
> 'The Poachers', pp. 99–116.
> 'A Hymn for Sabbath Morning', pp. 172–73.
for 1832
> 'The Shepherd Boy's Song', pp. 157–58.

The Juvenile Forget Me Not

for 1830
> 'A Child's Prayer', pp. 114–15.
for 1831
> 'A Child's Hymn for the Close of the Week', pp. 78–80.

The Casket

(1829)
> 'The Admonition', pp. 150–52.

A Father's New Year's Gift

(1832)
> Letter of Dedication.
> 'Prayer for the Sabbath Morning', p. 3.
> 'Prayer for the Sabbath Evening', pp. 4–5.
> 'Hymn for Sabbath Morning', pp. 6–7.
> 'Hymn for the Sabbath Evening', p. 8.
> 'Morning Prayer for Week Days', p. 9.
> 'Evening Prayer for Week Days', p. 10.
> 'Hymn for the Close of the Week', pp. 11–12.
> 'Hymn for General Use', pp. 13–14.
> 'Hymn on the Omnipresence of the Deity', pp. 15–16.

II

Part Two lists items that were contributed by Hogg to a specific annual or gift-book, but in the event were not published there.

Forget Me Not

'A Love Ballad': see Introductory and Textual Notes, p. 301.

The Anniversary

'Katie Cheyne': see Introductory and Textual Notes, pp. 307–09.

The Musical Bijou

'O Weel Befa' the Guileless Heart': see Introductory and Textual Notes, pp. 319–21.

'Fairy Songs': see Introductory and Textual Notes, p. 321.

The Amulet

'The Dorty Wean': see Introductory and Textual Notes, pp. 325–30.

'The History of an Auld Naig': see Introductory and Textual Notes, pp. 325–30.

'David Wilkie': see Introductory and Textual Notes, pp. 325–30.

'To Miss M. A. C.——e.': see Introductory and Textual Notes, pp. 335–36.

Ackermann's Juvenile Forget Me Not

'What is Death?': see Introductory and Textual Notes, pp. 344–45.

The Young Lady's Sabbath Companion

See Introductory and Textual Notes, pp. 357–58.

III

Part Three lists items by (or relating to) Hogg which appeared in an annual or a gift-book, but which do not seem to have been directly contributed to the publication in question by Hogg himself. Part III is divided into two sub-sections. Items in each sub-section are listed in chronological order

III A
Items Not Previously Published

The May Flower for 1846, ed. by Robert Hamilton (Boston: Saxton and Kelt). 'Song. By the late James Hogg, the Ettrick Shepherd', p. 147: see Introductory and Textual Notes, pp. 340–41.

A Parting Gift (Edinburgh: Nelson, 1846). 'To Mary', pp. 248–49: see Introductory and Textual Notes, pp. 358–61.

III B
Items Reprinted from Earlier Publications

The Poetical Scrap Book, by W. Clapperton (Edinburgh: John Fairburn [and nine others]; London: T. Tegg, 1824). 'The Battle of Busaco', pp. 19–21. [From Hogg's *The Spy* for 9 February 1811: see S / SC Edition, ed. by Gillian Hughes, pp. 253–54.]

The Pledge of Friendship (London: W. Marshall, 1827). 'A Night Piece. By James Hogg, the Ettrick Shepherd. Written in Autumn 1811', pp. 231–32. [Reprinted from *The Poetical Register*, 8 (1810–11), 90–91.]

The Casquet of Literary Gems, 2 vols, ed. by Alex. Whitelaw (Glasgow: Blackie, Fullarton, 1829). 'The Sky Lark', II, 241; 'An Aged Widow's Own Words', II, 297–98. [From the *Forget Me Not* for 1828 and the *Bijou* for 1828 respectively.]

Cameo (London: William Pickering, 1831). 'Woman', p. 146. [Reprinted from the *Bijou* for 1829.]

The Poetical Album; or, Register of Modern Fugitive Poetry, ed. by Alaric A. Watts (London: Hurst, Chance, 1830). 'Invocation to the Queen of the Fairies', pp. 174–77; 'Love's Jubilee', pp. 323–27; 'Stanzas for Music', p. 373. [From the *Literary Souvenir* for 1825, for 1826, and for 1827.]

The Bouquet: A Collection of Tales, Essays, and Poems, Original and Select (London: S. Robinson, 1832). 'Katie Cheyne', pp. 39–57. [From *Sharpe's London Magazine*, 2 (1829), 56–63: see also Part Two of this Listing, under *The Anniversary*.]

Englische Bibliothek (Karlsruhe: G. Braun, 1834). 'Die Heumahd und Alexander in Schottland', pp. 301–10. [This is a translation of 'Scottish Haymakers' from the *Forget Me Not* for 1834.]

The Gift: A Poetical Remembrance, Selected from the Works of Native and Foreign Authors (Concord, NH: Currier and Hall, and Asa M'Farland, 1835.) 'A Boy's Song', pp. 222–23. [From the *Remembrance* for 1831.]

Youth's Keepsake: A Christmas and New Year's Gift for Young People (Boston: Otis, Broaders, 1835). 'What is Sin?', p. 146. [From *Ackermann's Juvenile Forget Me Not* for 1830.]

A Port Folio for Youth, by Robert Ramble (Philadelphia: J. Crissy, 1835). 'The Shepherd's Dog', pp. 229–31. [Extracted from *The Shepherd's Calendar*, 2 vols (Edinburgh: William Blackwood; London: T. Cadell, 1829), II, 293–326 (pp. 298–302).]

The Cabinet of Literary Gems, ed. by Bernard Bowring (London: Renshaw, 1836). 'A Tale of Pentland', pp. 131–48. [From the *Amulet* for 1830.]

A Mother's Present to her Daughter, (London: Charles Tilt, 1836). 'The Sabbath', pp. 42–43. [This is 'A Child's Hymn for the Close of the Week', from the *Juvenile Forget Me Not* for 1831.]

The Book of Gems: The Modern Poets and Artists of Great Britain, ed. by S. C. Hall, 3 vols (London: Saunders & Otley, 1836–38: vol. 3 published by Whittaker). 'The Stranded Ship', 'The Wee Housie', 'The Broken Heart', 'Mary Gray', 'The Skylark', and 'An Arabian Song', III, 129–33. [Extracted from Hogg's *Poetical Works*, 4 vols (Edinburgh: Constable, 1822), III, 289–93, and from *Songs by the Ettrick Shepherd* (Edinburgh: Blackwood; London: Cadell, 1831), pp. 307–09, 271–73, 296–97, 15–16, 35–36.]

The Poetic Wreath: Consisting of Passages from the Works of English Poets from Chaucer to Wordsworth (Philadelphia: Lea & Blanchard, 1839). 'The Gude Greye Katt' and 'Kilmeny', pp. 81, 184. [Passages extracted from Hogg's *Poetical Works*, 4 vols (Edinburgh: Constable; London: Hurst, Robinson, 1822), III, 193–220 (pp. 207–08) and I, 176–93 (p. 178).]

Youth's Keepsake: A Christmas and New Year's Gift for Young People (Boston: Otis, Broaders, 1840). [In the following year this annual was reissued with the same contents, under the title *The New Year's Gift and Juvenile Souvenir*.] 'The Shepherd Boy's Song', p. 191. [From *Ackermann's Juvenile Forget Me Not* for 1832.]

The Remembrancer; or, Fragments for Leisure Hours, compiled by the Association for the Improvement of Juvenile Books (Philadelphia: T. Ellwood Chapman, Marshall, Williams & Butler, 1841). 'Hymn of Praise', pp. 71–72. [This is 'Morning Hymn' from the *Amulet* for 1836.]

The New Year's Gift and Juvenile Souvenir (Boston: Otis, Broaders, 1841). [See also *Youth's Keepsake*, 1840, above.] 'The Shepherd Boy's Song', p. 191. [From *Ackermann's Juvenile Forget Me Not* for 1832.]

The Forget Me Not for 1844, ed. by Frederic Shoberl (London: Ackermann, [1843]). 'Original Letter of Lord Byron's to the Ettrick Shepherd', pp. 353–54. [Communicated by 'Delta'.]

A Parting Gift (Edinburgh: Nelson, 1846). 'An Arabian Song', p. 247. [see Introductory and Textual Notes, pp. 357–60.]

The Ladies' Casket, and Friendship's Gift for 1849 (New York: Rev. E. T. Winter, [1848]). 'The Skylark', p. 95. [From the *Forget Me Not* for 1828.]

The Hyacinth; or, Affection's Gift: A Christmas, New Year, and Birth-Day Present for 1850 (Philadelphia: Henry F. Anners, 1850). 'A Child's Prayer', pp. 91–92. [From *Ackermann's Juvenile Forget Me Not* for 1830.]

The Gift of Friendship: A Token of Remembrance for 1851 (Philadelphia: Henry Anners, [1850]). 'The Two Valleys', pp. 178–96. [From the *Remembrance* for 1831.]

Friendship's Offering: A Christmas, New Year, and Birthday Present for 1854 (Philadelphia: E. H. Butler, [1853]). 'Maggy o' Buccleuch', p. 220. [From the *Forget Me Not* for 1832.]

The Hyacinth; or, Affection's Gift for 1855 (Philadelphia: Henry Anners, [1854]). 'The Bard of Ettrick and his Daughter', pp. 112–14. [This is 'A Bard's Address to his Youngest Daughter' from *Friendship's Offering* for 1830.]

Ornaments of Memory; or, Beauties of History, Romance and Poetry with Eighteen Engravings (New York: D. Appleton, 1856). 'An Aged Widow's Own Words', p. 158. [From the *Bijou* for 1828.]

Harp of Judah; or, Gems of Sacred Poetry Original and Selected (London: Nelson, 1868). 'A Hebrew Melody', pp. 18–20; 'Adoration', pp. 108–09. [These items appear together in *The Poetical Works of the Ettrick Shepherd*, 5 vols (Glasgow: Blackie, 1838–40), v, 10–13, where 'A Hebrew Melody' appears as 'On Carmel's Brow' (pp. 11–13) and 'Adoration' appears as 'Dweller in Heaven' (pp. 10–11): see also the present edition's Introductory and Textual Notes, pp. 356–57 (note on 'Hymn on the Omnipresence of the Deity').]

The Drawing-Room Annual: A Present for All Seasons (Philadelphia: Lindsay & Blakiston, [n.d., *c.* 1842–55?]). 'An Arabian Song', p. 59. [From *Songs by the Ettrick Shepherd* (Edinburgh: Blackwood; London: Cadell, 1831), pp. 35–36.]

The Bouquet; or, Spirit of the English Poetry, 3rd ed. (Philadelphia: Henry Anners, [n.d.]). 'A Hymn to the Redeemer', pp. 178–81. [From the *Amulet* for 1835.]

Gift of Affection: A Souvenir (New York: Leavitt and Allen, [n.d.]). 'The Broken Heart', p. 121. [From *Songs by the Ettrick Shepherd* (Edinburgh: Blackwood; London: Cadell, 1831), pp. 271–72.]

IV
Item Wrongly Attributed to Hogg

The Scottish Annual, ed. by William Weir (Glasgow: John Reid; Edinburgh: Oliver and Boyd; London: Whittaker, 1836). 'A Psychological Curiosity. James Hogg', pp. 25–33. [In fact written by Robert Macnish: see *The Modern Pythagorean: A Series of Tales Essays and Sketches by the late Robert Macnish with the Author's Life by his friend D. M. Moir*, 2 vols (Edinburgh: Blackwood; London: Cadell, 1838), I, 351–52.]

Introductory and Textual Notes

Gillian Hughes

One important aim of the Stirling / South Carolina (S/SC) Edition is to reveal the true status of James Hogg as a major writer, a status which has been obscured in the past by editions that presented a bland, bowdlerised, and lifeless version of Hogg's writings to the public. The social production of a literary work by author, publisher, and printer is normally a benign process, but it was not invariably so in Hogg's case, because his low social and financial status made him particularly vulnerable in the literary market-place. As a result Hogg's work was sometimes mangled and bowdlerised in the publication process, and a core task of the S/SC Edition is to make his texts available to readers in their unmangled and unbowdlerised form. This policy is followed in the present volume, as in other parts of the S/SC Edition. However, Hogg's contemporaries read his published work rather than the work he prepared for publication, and his published work inevitably formed the basis of his reputation and literary influence, as well as providing a context within which the work he prepared for publication must now be understood. This is particularly true of Hogg's contributions to annuals, given the interest and importance of annuals as a publishing phenomenon. Even when weakened by bowdlerisation, then, the published versions of Hogg's texts have their own particular kind of interest and importance, and for this reason the present edition sets out to give its readers access to the published versions as well as to Hogg's originals, when they differ from one another. In cases where the differences are few, this is done by listing the significant differences in the textual notes. Where the differences are many they are summarised in the textual notes, and both versions of the text are printed. This should be convenient to readers, because many of the original annuals are now rare volumes and difficult to locate.

The S/SC *Contributions to Annuals and Gift-Books* contains all the known texts created or revised by Hogg for publication in an annual or a gift-book. It also contains those Hogg items which, in the event, were first published in an annual or a gift-book, although not composed for publication there. However, it does not include the numerous items that were simply reprinted in annuals or gift-books from previous Hogg publications. Such items often appeared without Hogg's knowledge: indeed, many of them appeared long after his death. The known ones are, however, included in Section III of this volume's 'Listing of Hogg Texts in Annuals and Gift-Books' (pp. 275–81).

Hogg's role as a collaborator in the production of annuals could be positive and consensual: he wrote text to partner a specific engraving, and lyrics to be fused with music by a fashionable composer into song. Hogg's contributions to the annuals concerned would not be fully comprehensible in these cases without the engravings or printed music, and these have accordingly been included in the present volume.

Eight of Hogg's contributions to the annuals were included in *A Queer Book*, a collection of twenty-six of his longer poems published in 1832. These eight poems duly take their place in Peter Garside's S/SC edition of *A Queer Book* (1995). For the convenience of readers, they are also included here: a degree of duplication within the S/SC Edition was thought to be preferable to the exclusion from the present volume of a significant part of Hogg's work for the annuals. For each of these eight poems Peter Garside chose as his copy-text either the printing in the annuals, or a pre-annuals manuscript, and it has therefore seemed appropriate to reprint seven of them here (with his permission) from the S/SC *Queer Book*. However, as is explained below at pp. 315–16, we have based our text of 'A Bard's Address to his Youngest Daughter' on the version printed in *Friendship's Offering*, rather than on the private family manuscript version presented by Peter Garside.

Hogg contributed to one annual, Anna Maria Hall's *The Juvenile Forget Me Not*, for which there is no section of text printed in the present volume. This is because Hogg subsequently incorporated both items published in this annual into his own gift-book, *A Father's New Year's Gift*. They are included in that section of the present volume, therefore, as part of a larger Hogg work. To omit all discussion of *The Juvenile Forget Me Not* would, however, give an incomplete picture of Hogg's contributions to annuals, so a brief note about it is included in the Introductory and Textual Notes to Juvenile Annuals.

The present text is arranged in sections by annual, and within sections items are arranged in chronological order. The abbreviations employed in the Introductory and Textual Notes are common to the Explanatory Notes and are listed at the start of those.

Literary Souvenir
Four published contributions

Although the *Literary Souvenir* was not the first of the English annuals to appear, its editor, Alaric A. Watts (1797–1864), claimed that it was the first in conception—see the 'Preface' to the *Literary Souvenir* for 1825, pp. iii–vii (p. iii). It also contains the earliest of Hogg's annual contributions, 'Invocation to the Queen of the Fairies', which appeared in the volume for 1825. Altogether Hogg made four contributions to this annual, three in prose and one poem. The *Literary Souvenir* continued to be published up to 1835, but no Hogg items occur after the volume for 1827.

It is not clear from Hogg's surviving correspondence with Watts how he became a contributor to the *Literary Souvenir*, or precisely why his communications ceased. Poor communication between Watts in London and Hogg in Altrive may have been a problem: Watts seems to have been unlucky in selecting D. M. Moir as his Edinburgh intermediary in sending letters and parcels on to Hogg. These clearly took a long time to get to Altrive, and Hogg additionally mistrusted Moir because of his role as publisher's reader for William Blackwood and for *Blackwood's Edinburgh Magazine*. On one occasion he grumbled to Blackwood, 'I care nothing about More. [...] Do you remember of showing me a letter of his once advising you to have nothing to do with a M. S. publication of mine for that I was incapable of producing any work that would go down with the public. Mr A A Watts has written to me thrice respecting a parcel he sent to me to the care of Mr More but I despised the fellow so much I would not even enquire what became of it' (see Hogg to Blackwood, 28 March [1829], in NLS, MS 4021, fols 277–78).

Hogg himself attributed his ceasing to continue to contribute to the *Literary Souvenir* partly to annoyance at Watts's failure to return his unused literary manuscripts, warning Allan Cunningham on 31 December 1828, 'If one M. S. of mine is lost I write no more for that editor which Mr A A Watts and several others can tell you' (Beinecke Rare Book & Manuscript Library, Yale University, James Hogg Collection, GEN MSS 61, Box 1, Folder 7). However, Watts's letter to Hogg of 18 July 1827 (in NLS, MS 2245, fols 104–05) seems to indicate that, having recently straitened himself financially by buying out a former partner, he was proposing to cut payments to at least some of the contributors to the 1828 volume: Hogg would be paid partly with 'puffs' in newspapers such as the *Standard* and *St James Chronicle* and only partly in cash. This would be unacceptable, for Hogg (who was losing money on his nine-year lease of Mount Benger farm in Yarrow) was dependent upon the income generated by his pen. Hogg was also plainly offended to receive advice on how to write effective poetry from Watts, for in his letter to Cunningham of 19 January 1830 (Trinity College Library, Cambridge: Cullum N.8.2) he instructs him:

> Don't give any thing of mine to Mr Alaric A Watts he is the greatest fool and puppy ever I had ought to do with. Pray is the poor affected fellow supposed among his contemporaries to be a rational being? I should like particularly to know as he has favoured me with a great many most sage and sapient remarks how to write poetry and the advices are so serious that I really think them well meant but I cannot tell whether to follow them or not till I know for certain that the man is not daft.

Whatever the reason for Hogg's withdrawal as a contributor, Watts seems to have regretted it, writing 'I am sorry that the Literary Souvenir is almost the only annual of this year without a contribution from your pen. [...] if you would write me a little prose sketch of a legendary character I should be most happy to offer you liberal pecuniary recompense', adding 'Please to accept a copy of my new volume in its most attractive form and if I have not offended you pray let me hear from you soon' (Watts to Hogg, 5 November 1827, in NLS, MS 2245, fol. 106). Watts was one of Hogg's targets among the annuals editors in his poem 'The Miser's Grave' in the issue of *Blackwood's Edinburgh Magazine* for June 1831 (see Introduction, p. xxi), and seems to have retaliated in 'The Conversazione' in the *Literary Souvenir* for 1832 (pp. 222–51): accusing Allan Cunningham and Hogg of mutual puffing, he declared that

> [...] every Magazine's a stye,
> With Ettrick Jamie's eulogy;

And Hogg the fulsome praise returns,
And, eulogising Robert Burns,
Informs his friends—he's surely funning 'em—
That 'Rab' was nought to Allan Cunningham! (p. 224)

Invocation to the Queen of the Fairies (pp. 3–6)

This was the first of Hogg's contributions to the *Literary Souvenir* and appeared in the volume for 1825 (pp. 122–26), published in early November 1824 for sale as a Christmas and New Year gift-book. Another version appeared in December 1824 as the opening lines of 'Book Sixth' of Hogg's epic poem *Queen Hynde* (published jointly by Longman in London and Blackwood in Edinburgh), and it is not entirely clear which of these versions was the first to be written. The available evidence regarding the date of composition of the two poems is incomplete, and somewhat confusing.

A manuscript version headed 'Invocation to the Queen of the Fairies' (NLS, MS 1002, fol. 103) is roughly equivalent to lines 1–59 of the *Literary Souvenir* text. The slip of paper on which the poem is written has been pasted onto Hogg's letter to Watts of 2 February 1825, a conjunction which misleadingly associates the manuscript poem with the letter. There are verbal differences between the text of this manuscript and the equivalent passage of the *Literary Souvenir* text, which also contains two lines not present in the manuscript, so that it is clear that the manuscript was not copy for the *Literary Souvenir*. The letter's mention of 'Invocation to the Queen of the Fairies' as having already appeared in Watts's newly-published annual confirms this conclusion. The poem may represent a presentation holograph created by Hogg from the *Literary Souvenir* text itself, minor verbal differences and the accidental omission of two lines being the result of eye-slip and a general carelessness in transcription on Hogg's part. It is unclear how far back the joint provenance of the two separate items extends, except that the National Library of Scotland acquired them together. A pencil note on the blank page of Hogg's letter states, 'The poem was received in the National Library pasted in thus'. At some point the poem clearly fell into the hands of the owner of a Hogg letter that mentioned that poem, and he or she thought it was appropriate to join the two separate items together. Speculation that this former owner may have been Watts himself and that the holograph poem may have been given to him by Hogg is tempting, but there is no evidence that it was ever in Watts's possession. This particular manuscript provides no clear evidence as to whether 'Invocation to the Queen of the Fairies' or the equivalent lines in *The Queen's Wake* were written first.

Hogg appears to have finished or almost finished the composition of *Queen Hynde* by 10 July 1824, and to have mostly revised the proofs of it by 13 November 1824—see *Queen Hynde*, ed. by Suzanne Gilbert and Douglas S. Mack (S/SC, 1998), pp. 221 and 227. 'Invocation to the Queen of the Fairies' is dated '*Altrive Lake, Oct.* 6, 1824' in the *Literary Souvenir*, which would seem to suggest that the poem in the annual was revised from lines in *Queen Hynde*. However, this is an improbable date of composition for a poem included in a volume published in London early in the following month—the *Literary Souvenir* for 1825 was advertised as 'In a few days will be published' in the *Literary Gazette* for 30 October 1824 (p. 704), and reviewed in the issue for 13 November 1824 (pp. 721–23). That the lines form a self-contained unit at the start of Book Sixth of *Queen Hynde* might suggest that the *Literary Souvenir* version is the earlier of the two, but on the other hand the closing reference to Hogg's poem as 'the last' seems more relevant to Hogg's long-abandoned *Queen Hynde* than to a contribution to the newly-emerging annuals. Hogg's own letter to Watts of 2 February 1825 (NLS, MS 1002, fols 102–03) in fact declares that the annuals version was written first: 'The Queen of the Fairies was so decidedly in my best stile that I could not help popping her into the last book of Queen Hynde, and I regretted that my work appeared so soon after yours [...]'. The two versions must in fact have been created very close together, given the narrow time scale involved. Nevertheless there are many differences between the two (lines are rearranged and rewritten, words and phrases changed), and even though the overall purpose of these changes is unclear it is plain that Hogg created two versions of these lines, one to take its place in his epic poem, and one as a contribution in his popular visionary 'Kilmeny' style to the *Literary Souvenir*. Although Hogg's manuscript for the relevant section of *Queen Hynde* has survived, the manuscript he sent to Watts for 'Invocation to the Queen of the Fairies' does not appear to have done so, and this version was never subsequently reprinted. The poem is printed here from the *Literary Souvenir* without emendation.

Love's Jubilee (pp. 6–10)

Peter Garside provides the following introductory and textual notes to 'Love's Jubilee' in his edition of *A Queer Book* (S/SC, 1995), pp. 248–49:

> First published in *The Literary Souvenir* for 1826 (pp. 121–27), 'Love's Jubilee' is the earliest among those *Queer Book* poems which were derived from the new annuals. Hogg submitted it to the editor Alaric A. Watts on 2 February 1825, shortly after having received a complimentary copy of the 1825 number: 'I [...] have written rather a happy poem for the next Souvenir which I send with a promise that it shall not appear in any other work for a year at least after its appearance in your work. I have no copy, not a scrap, you have the first and last and therefore if you do not publish take care and do not lose it' (NLS, MS 1002, fol. 102).
>
> Both the date of Hogg's letter and the end inscription of the published version suggest that the poem was actually completed at Candlemas [2 February], one of the Scottish quarter-days and the Feast of the Purification of the Virgin Mary. The candles burned then have an origin in the Roman festival for Februa, the mother of Mars; and in Scotland the day before Candlemas was dedicated to St Bride, the successor to a Celtic goddess of the same name—the Day of Bride being the old Celtic festival of spring. The poem's dialogue between supernatural Spirits, with their respective male and female charges, is also reminis-

cent of traditional representations of Mars and Venus; while tone and imagery both evoke, without ever exactly paralleling, Shakespeare's *A Midsummer Night's Dream*. In a letter of 16 February 1826, Alan Cunningham praised the piece as being in his friend's 'happiest' manner: 'it is pure and graceful, warm yet delicate and we have nought in the language to compare to it save Kilmeny. In other portions of verse you have been equalled and sometimes surpassed, but in scenes which are neither on earth nor wholly removed from it—where fairies speak and spiritual creatures act, you are unrivalled' (NLS, MS 2245, fol. 90). In its *Queer Book* context, 'Love's Jubilee' links with several other items (e.g. 'Ringan and May') which explore the relationship between physical and spiritual love.

Textual Notes on 'Love's Jubilee'
No manuscript of the poem apparently survives, and it is not improbable that the only copy was destroyed in London after printing. The present edition follows the text in the *Literary Souvenir*, in preference to the more formal version in the 1832 *Queer Book*, except for the two following emendations where the *Queer Book* punctuation is preferred:
(l. 107) spell] spell, (*Literary Souvenir*)
(l. 108) be, by] be by (*Literary Souvenir*)

The Border Chronicler (pp. 10–22)
Hogg seems to have sent 'The Border Chronicler' to Watts with his letter of 17 April 1825 (Manuscripts Division of the Department of Rare Books and Special Collections of the Princeton University Library, Alaric A. Watts Correspondence Collection, Box CO 619, Folder 12: extract below published with the permission of the Princeton University Library), and this corresponds to the date at the end of the story as published in the *Literary Souvenir* for 1826, pp. 257–79. In his letter to Watts Hogg stated:

> In looking over my papers I alighted on a tale of mine copied by my amanuensis several years ago for the Winter Evening tales, but left out on account of being imperfect. I have now gone over it and made large additions in order to give it some more point and interest, and as it is I send it you for your next *Souvenir*.

The tale in fact originates in an anonymous contribution 'To the Editor of the Sale-Room', in no. 10 of John Ballantyne's weekly paper *The Sale Room* for 8 March 1817, pp. 72–76. For further details see Gillian Hughes, 'James Hogg's Contributions to *The Sale Room*', *The Bibliotheck*, 23 (1998), 64–68. This essay corresponds roughly to the 'Charlie Dinmont' section of 'The Border Chronicler' up to the point where the narrator introduces himself to Charlie after his conversation with the radical at the auction room. The narrative device of a city editor retailing the Border legends he has heard from the mouth of a countryman is reminiscent of the contrasting figures of the Spy and John Miller in Hogg's earlier essay-periodical *The Spy*: while it is useful here to mediate Hogg's legends to an English readership, it would be redundant in

Hogg's 1820 collection of *Winter Evening Tales* where the title itself acts as a framing device, informing Hogg's reader of the kind of stories he or she is to encounter. Charlie's final tale, 'The White Lady of Glen-Tress' also looks back to an earlier collection of Hogg's fiction, being a retelling and expansion of one of Barnaby's legends in 'The Wool-Gatherer' from *The Brownie of Bodsbeck and Other Tales*, 2 vols (Edinburgh: Blackwood; London: Murray, 1818), II, 142–43. At the end of 'The Border Chronicler' Hogg's narrator promises to relate more of Charlie Dinmont's stories in the following volume of the *Literary Souvenir* (p. 22), and Watts seemed to have welcomed this intimation of a sequel, writing to Hogg on 18 July 1827 (in NLS, MS 2245, fols 104–05), 'I mentioned in my former letter my great wish to have [...] some little short prose legend similar to those with which you favoured me for my volume in 1826'. This request for a continuation is perhaps surprising in view of Charlie Dinmont's allusions to prostitution in Edinburgh (pp. 15–16): Watts's early annual clearly permitted an author more freedom than later ones such as Thomas Pringle's *Friendship's Offering*. No more of the series appeared, however.

Hogg clearly rewrote and extended his earlier paper specifically for sending to Watts, though his manuscript does not survive. 'The Border Chronicler' has never been reprinted after its appearance in the *Literary Souvenir*. In his letter of 17 April 1825 Hogg explained that he would need to see the proofs 'as my broad Scots is not easily made out by an Englishman and any mistake in that offends me particularly': nevertheless a number of English misunderstandings appear to have gone through to the printed text, among them the mistaken possessive of 'Galashiel's grey', and there are also omissions and inconsistencies in the use of speech marks. The present editors in printing 'The Border Chronicler' from the *Literary Souvenir* for 1826 have silently completed and regularised these according to the following conventions: double speech marks are used to enclose speech, and single speech marks for speech within speech, the double opening speech marks being repeated at the start of each new paragraph within a speech. In addition to this, the following emendations have been made:

p. 10, l. 9 Galashiels grey] Galashiel's grey (*Literary Souvenir*) [the town is called Galashiels]

p. 12, l. 18 into Edinbroch] nto Edinbroch (*Literary Souvenir*)

p. 12, l. 25 ane a farm] ane a' farm (*Literary Souvenir*)

p. 12, l. 32 caution] cation (*Literary Souvenir*)

p. 13, l. 2 the kirn!"] the kirm!" (*Literary Souvenir*)

p. 13, l. 36 New Town o' Edinbroch] new town o' Edinbroch (*Literary Souvenir*) [a specific area is intended]

p. 14, l. 42 " 'Now Charlie] "now Charlie (*Literary Souvenir*)

p. 15, l. 17 a degree of prejudice] a degree of prejudices (*Literary Souvenir*)

p. 16, l. 34 'What can] "what can (*Literary Souvenir*)

p. 16, l. 40 'Past *twall*] "past *twall* (*Literary Souvenir*)

p. 17, l. 2 adding, "Eh!] adding, "eh! (*Literary Souvenir*)

p. 17, l. 21 world this wad be] world, this wad be (*Literary Souvenir*)

p. 18, l. 14 the troop.] the troop." (*Literary Souvenir*)

p. 18, l. 17 'Whae the deil] "whae the deil (*Literary Souvenir*)

p. 18, l. 34 said Little. 'But] said Little. [N.P.] "But (*Literary Souvenir*) [Little is still the speaker]

p. 20, l. 1 for a broose.] for a broose." (*Literary Souvenir*)

p. 20, l. 2 ane; 'Come on!] ane; "come on! (*Literary Souvenir*)

p. 20, l. 23 said,–'You] said,–"you (*Literary Souvenir*)

Stanzas for Music (p. 23)

This poem was published in the *Literary Souvenir* for 1827, p. 232. It had originally been the song of the insane Sally Niven, as she nurses an imaginary baby among the devastation of the aftermath of Culloden in Hogg's earlier Romance *The Three Perils of Woman*, 3 vols (London: Longman, 1823), III, 350–51. Although this is the only Hogg item to appear in the *Literary Souvenir* for 1827, Watts's letter to Hogg of 18 July 1827 (in NLS, MS 2245, fols 104–05) about the volume seems to indicate that 'Stanzas for Music' was one of a number of pieces submitted by Hogg in 1826: 'You will have seen that I only printed the song you sent me last year Unless however I am favoured with something I like better I shall use one of these articles this year'. Although the revised version is printed as a poem in the *Literary Souvenir* the title given suggests that Hogg still envisaged it as a song. It was not reprinted subsequently within Hogg's lifetime.

In revising Sally Niven's song for the *Literary Souvenir* Hogg has strengthened the mother's anxiety that the child has not been baptised. The original context of the genocidal aftermath of the Jacobite defeat at Culloden was a sufficient explanation of this in the original context, but in the new context may imply that the singer is a solitary parent, an unmarried mother: Sally's 'O, sweet little cherub' becomes 'My sweet little cherub', and the child which was formerly 'unshriven' is now 'unblest and unshrieven'. Hogg's plain-speaking appears to reflect the relative liberality of this early annual. Sally Niven's song can be read in *The Three Perils of Woman*, ed. by David Groves, Antony Hasler, and Douglas S. Mack (S/SC, 1995), p. 399: this is a version of Hogg's lines distinct from the revised 'Stanzas for Music'. No manuscript appears to have survived for the later version of his lines, which are reprinted here from the *Literary Souvenir* without emendation.

The Bijou
Four published contributions

The Bijou; or, Annual of Literature and the Arts was published in London by William Pickering and edited by William Fraser: three volumes appeared, for 1828, 1829, and 1830 respectively. How Hogg became a contributor has not been ascertained, though *The Bijou* may be the work Thomas Pringle refers to in his letter to Hogg of 19 May 1827 (in NLS, MS 2245, fols 100–01), which opens, 'I wrote you a hasty note some time ago to solicit your literary aid for the projected work of Mr. Fraser'. (Pringle's earlier letter does not appear to have survived.) Hogg contributed two poems to each of the volumes of *The Bijou* for 1828 and 1829.

An Aged Widow's Own Words (p. 27)

'An Aged Widow's Own Words' was published in *The Bijou* for 1828, pp. 26–27. It is undated, and the manuscript does not appear to have survived, nor does it seem to be referred to in Hogg's surviving correspondence. Hogg's daughter, Mrs Garden (p. 154) writes that it expresses the feelings of Hogg's aged mother-in-law on the death of her husband. A death notice for Peter Phillips appeared as follows in the *Dumfries and Galloway Courier* of 29 May:

> At Altrive Lake, on Yarrow, on the 16th curt. Mr Peter Phillips, aged 79. He was upwards of 40 years tenant of Longbridge Muir, and other lands in this country, and was highly respected for every moral and religious virtue. His numerous relations in Dumfries-shire and Gallo-way will please accept this notification of his death.

A set of anonymous verses representing an early version of 'An Aged Widow's Own Words' appeared in the same paper a week later on 5 June 1827, and were clearly written by Hogg in the immediate aftermath of his father-in-law's death. The differences between this version and the one published in *The Bijou* are substantial, and imply that Hogg subsequently revised and rewrote his poem before sending it to London for inclusion in *The Bijou* for 1828: for example 'that weary space' of line 7 became 'that happy time' and 'Nor languish nor despond;' in line 22 was changed to 'Nor fret nor yet despond'. Although the poem was included subsequently in *The Casquet of Literary Gems*, ed. by Alexander Whitelaw, 2 vols (Glasgow, 1829), II, 297–98 it was flagged as 'from the *Bijou*' and there is no indication of authorial re-engagement with this later printing. The poem is printed here from *The Bijou* for 1828 without emendation.

Ane Waefu' Scots Pastoral (pp. 28–30)

'Ane Waefu' Scots Pastoral' was published in *The Bijou* for 1828, pp. 108–11. It is dated 'Mount Benger, April 24th, 1827', and Hogg states in a footnote that it was composed 'on the evening of the 23rd April, 1827, about the time the great storm of snow was at the height'. It forms a natural companion-piece to 'An Aged Widow's Own Words' as a personal poem about the author's life, in which he expresses the feelings and shares the sorrows of those who surround him in his country home. It seems likely that both poems were sent to London together for publication in *The Bijou* during the late spring or summer of 1827. Hogg's manuscript for 'Ane Waefu' Scots Pastoral' does not appear to have survived, nor was the poem reprinted during his lifetime. It is printed here from *The Bijou* for 1828 with the following emendation:

l. 44 cauldrife stane,] cauldrife stane; (*Bijou*)

Woman (pp. 30–32)

The precise textual history of 'Woman' is in some respects a mysterious one, the poem in *The Bijou* for 1829 (pp. 93–96) seeming to bear a relationship to

Hogg's long poem 'Love's Legacy' rather like the one his 'Invocation to the Queen of the Fairies' bears to *Queen Hynde* (see above).

A fair-copy manuscript end-dated 'Mount Benger | April 6th 1827' and entitled 'Hogg on Women!!!' (NLS, MS 1809, fols 86–87) appears to have been prepared by Hogg as a contribution to *Blackwood's Edinburgh Magazine*, and returned to him by William Blackwood on 25 May 1827, for Blackwood's letter of that date (NLS, MS 30,310, pp. 128A–30) discusses various contributions submitted by Hogg and says 'I now enclose you the Verses on Women'. Hogg's poem in *The Bijou* is almost identical to this (allowing for the normal addition and adjustment of punctuation during the printing process) apart from the omission of eight lines of satire after line 26 and surrounding adjustments to take account of it. Hogg probably recast this poem for *The Bijou*, excising the satirical passage that would have been inappropriate in the context of an annual, though there is the alternative possibility that the editor of *The Bijou* himself made this obvious and necessary change. The relevant passage in 'Hogg on Women!!!' reads as follows in MS 1809:

> But as well woman may compare
> A David Haggart with a Blair
> A Hunt with a Southey or I wot
> A lord of Buchan with a Scott
> A Jeffery with a tailor spruce
> Strutting with ellwand and with goose
> A Peter Rob'son with a clown
> Or Doctor Brown with Dr Browne
> As man take one degraded mind
> For model of dear womankind
>   Nay let us rise in our compare
> To beauties of the earth and air

David Haggart was a murderer executed in 1821, while Hugh Blair, a clergyman and academic, was author of *Lectures on Rhetoric and Belles Lettres* (1783). Two radicals (Leigh Hunt and David Erskine, 11th Earl of Buchan) contrast with the more conservative figures of Robert Southey and Walter Scott, while Francis Jeffrey was editor of *The Edinburgh Review*. Patrick Robertson (1794–1855) was an advocate and (from 1843) a judge. A friend of John Wilson ('Christopher North'), Robertson 'was commonly called by the endearing Scottish diminutive Peter, and was renowned for his convivial and social qualities' (see the article on him by G. F. R. Barker, revised by H. J. Spencer, in the *Oxford DNB*). David Groves has suggested that 'Doctor Brown' may be the Edinburgh minister John Brown (1776–1832), and that 'Dr Browne' is probably James Browne (1793–1841), who in 1832 fiercely criticised Hogg's 'Memoir of the Author's Life': see Hogg, 'Love's Legacy', ed. by David Groves, *Altrive Chapbooks*, 5 (1988), 1–53 (p. 52).

The substance of 'Hogg on Women!!!' from line 7 onwards also appears in a slightly longer version in the conclusion to Canto Second of Hogg's long poem 'Love's Legacy' (the fair-copy manuscript of which survives in the Alexander Turnbull Library, Wellington, New Zealand, James Hogg Papers (Item 74). MS-Papers-0042-07). 'Woman' in *The Bijou* is clearly more closely related to 'Hogg on Women!!!' than to the equivalent passage in 'Love's Legacy' and almost certainly derives from it: in addition to the fact that the two shorter poems begin with seven lines not in the 'Love's Legacy' passage, 'Woman' generally follows the reading of 'Hogg on Women!!!' where that differs from the reading of 'Love's Legacy.'

It is unclear, however, whether 'Hogg on Women!!!' or 'Love's Legacy' was written first. In his letter to Blackwood of 12 February 1828 (NLS, MS 4021, fols 275–76) Hogg describes 'Love's Legacy' as then complete ('I have likewise a poem about the length of The Pleasures of Memory. Entitled LOVE'S LEGACY or A FAREWELL GIFT but after my grievious dissapointment with Queen Hynde neither dare I offer it to the public'). While giving the impression that the poem has been lying on his hands unpublished he provides no indication as to whether the actual date of composition was before or after 6 April 1827, the date given for 'Hogg on Women!!!'. It is thus unclear whether 'Hogg on Women!!!' was written first and subsequently incorporated into 'Love's Legacy', or whether a passage from the pre-existing 'Love's Legacy' was extracted and shaped into a shorter poem.

However, it does seem probable that 'Woman' was sent to London for inclusion in *The Bijou* after 27 May 1827, while its appearance in *The Bijou* for 1829 indicates that the editor must have received it by the early autumn of 1828 at the latest (the volume being published in time for sale as a gift for Christmas 1828).

Hogg recycled portions of his tribute to the fair sex several times after 'Woman' was published in *The Bijou* for 1829, incorporating lines into other works such as the fifty-six line poem included in his prose article 'A Letter about Men and Women' dated 'MOUNT-BENGER, *July* 13, 1829' and published in *Blackwood's Edinburgh Magazine*, 26 (August 1829), 245–50 (pp. 246–47), and a presentation holograph manuscript entitled 'Woman' and dated 'Altrive Lake | May 5th 1833' (NLS, MS 581, fol. 15). A second presentation holograph from Hogg's 1832 London visit, dated 'Waterloo Place | March 1st 1832' and corresponding roughly to lines 69–88 of the present text survives in the Fales Library & Special Collections, New York University (Fales MS 89: 21).

Eventually he was also able to publish his long poem 'Love's Legacy', though not all in one place. The manuscript's Canto Third was retitled 'Mora Campbell' and published in *Blackwood's Edinburgh Magazine*, 35 (June 1834), 947–54, while Canto First and Canto Second were turned into three cantos of a revised 'Love's Legacy' and published later the same year in *Fraser's Magazine*, 10 (October, November, and December 1834), 403–08, 556–60, and 639–44. Lines included in 'Woman' recur in sections of the final three pages of 'Love's Legacy. Canto Third' in the December 1834 issue of *Fraser's Magazine*.

Clearly Hogg's 'Woman' from *The Bijou* for 1829, pp. 93–96 is the version of his lines appropriate to *Contributions to Annuals and Gift-Books*, and this is the one reprinted in the present volume. The earlier 'Hogg on Women!!!', however, has allowed the editors to understand that two rather odd-looking words in *The Bijou* text almost certainly stem from the editor's or printer's misreading of Hogg's hand, where 'delirious' was misinterpreted as 'oblivious' (line 4) and 'reverses' as 'revenges' (line 31). The following emendations have been made:

l. 4 delirious] oblivious (*Bijou* [as NLS manuscript])
l. 31 their reverses–] their revenges (*Bijou* [as NLS manuscript])

Superstition and Grace (pp. 33–36)

This poem has its roots in 'The Harper's Song', which forms part of the first canto of Hogg's *Mador of the Moor* (1816), and which was reprinted (as 'The Gyre Caryl') in the second volume of Hogg's *Poetical Works (1822)*. Hogg subsequently re-cast the poem (as 'Superstition and Grace') for publication in *The Bijou* for 1829, and 'Superstition and Grace' was then included in *A Queer Book* (1832). Peter Garside provides the following introductory and textual notes in the S/SC *Queer Book* (pp. 263–64):

> This poem first appeared in *The Bijou* for 1829 (pp. 129–34), an eclectic literary annual, edited by William Fraser, whose first issue in the previous year had included items by J. G. Lockhart, Coleridge, Southey, and Hogg himself. While no correspondence with Fraser has apparently survived, there is little reason to doubt that 'Superstition and Grace' was submitted in May 1828 as its end subscription suggests. [...] In subject matter and much of its wording the present poem derives directly from 'The Gyre Caryl', written in Hogg's 'ancient stile', which appeared in the *Poetical Works (1822)*, II, 167–78. The latter's positioning in *Poetical Works* also indicates that it was once conceived as part of a larger project to be titled *Midsummer Night Dreams*. For further information on this scheme, which occupied Hogg in about 1814, see *Selected Poems and Songs*, ed. by Groves, pp. 211–12.

> *Textual Notes on 'Superstition and Grace'*
> No manuscript of the poem first published in the *Bijou* has been found, nor of 'The Gyre Caryl' on which it is so closely based. Collation of the printed texts, however, shows how Hogg thinned out much of his original 'ancient stile', transposed certain passages, and also removed some of the more arcane chants in the earlier poem. Another interesting difference, reflecting perhaps the organs of publication in view, is the substition of 'Ladies' for 'lordyngs' as a form of address to the reader. The extent to which the *Bijou* editor was aware of being offered a recycled poem is unclear. Even as late as the 1838–40 *Poetical Works of the Ettrick Shepherd*, published by Blackie and Son, the two poems were presented as if autonomous works (vol. II, pp. 93–98, 141–45).

> The present text is based on the *Bijou* of 1829, as the version of the poem nearest to Hogg's original manuscript. However, the printer in London appears to have had some difficulty in reading Hogg's hand, especially when confronted with Scots terms. The *Queer Book* worked hard to correct errors of this nature, but some of its solutions appear to

be based on guesswork, and more than once 'The Gyre Caryl' of the 1822 *Poetical Works* proves to be a better guide. The following emendations seek to correct misreadings and faulty punctuation by the *Bijou* printer.

(1. 16) fauldit] faulelit (*Bijou*) [*Poetical Works* 1822 fauldit; *Queer Book* 1832 faul't]

(1. 21) grew] grew, (*Bijou*)

(1. 37) fell] fell, (*Bijou*)

(1. 38) bell,] bell. (*Bijou*)

(1. 42) sang] sung (*Bijou*) [*Poetical Works* 1822 and *Queer Book* 1832 sang]

(1. 51) feres] fires (*Bijou*) [*Poetical Works* 1822 and *Queer Book* 1832 feres]

(1. 55 rase] rage (*Bijou*) [*Poetical Works* 1822 and *Queer Book* 1832 rase]

(1. 57) list–for the choral band] list for the choral band, (*Bijou*)

(1. 67) Lammer-muir] lammer-muir (*Bijou*)

(1. 71) heaven] Heaven (*Bijou*)

(1. 73) quake,] quake (*Bijou*)

(1. 77) viol and ayril] viol ayril (*Bijou*) [*Poetical Works* 1822 vele and ayril; *Queer Book* 1832 viol, and ayril]

(1. 83) Ring! ring!] King! king! (*Bijou*) [*Poetical Works* 1822 Ryng! ryng!; *Queer Book* 1832 Ring! Ring!]

(1. 98) adieu;] adieu (*Bijou*)

(1. 102) Spirits' King] spirits' king (*Bijou*)

(1. 115) asklent] artlent (*Bijou*) [*Poetical Works* 1822 and *Queer Book* 1832 asklent]

(1. 124) pain] pain, (*Bijou*)

Forget Me Not

Ten published contributions: one additional
unpublished contribution is included in the present volume

Forget Me Not was the earliest and one of the most successful English annuals, volumes appearing from 1823 right up to 1847. Its publisher Rudolph Ackermann (1764–1834) was an established London fine-art publisher and technical innovator of German extraction, and therefore well-placed to realise the potential of combining new engraving processes with the German pocket-book. In Frederic Shoberl (1775–1853) he had an editor with whom he had collaborated harmoniously ever since 1809. The close relations between the publisher and the editor of *Forget Me Not* are perhaps reflected in the fact that Hogg corresponded with either member of the partnership. Ackermann and Shoberl appealed on a number of occasions to Hogg's interest in the visual arts, sending him advance copies of engravings and requesting him to write letterpress to accompany these. 'Scottish Haymakers', for example, was written in this way and is itself an exuberant meditation on the subject of painting and the arts in general. Shoberl subsequently sent Hogg a copy of 'Mabel Gray', painted by Cattermole and engraved by Davenport, later published in

Forget Me Not for 1835, although in this instance Hogg replied on 21 April 1834 (NLS, MS 10998, fols 176–77), 'But remember I do not promise to illustrate it for the best of all reasons. I do not understand it nor do I know whether the hero is an officer or a common trooper'. Another attraction of this annual may have been its beautiful and accurate typography–there are fewer apparent errors in reproducing Hogg's work in *Forget Me Not* than in almost any other annual.

Ten Hogg items were published in this annual, more than in any other, and the present volume also includes another poem written specifically for it though never actually published within its pages.

Hogg's work was first published in the volume of *Forget Me Not* for 1828, almost certainly in response to a request made by Ackermann in the spring of 1827, for Hogg's letter to him of 1 April 1827 (NLS, MS 8887, fols 36–37) is plainly the reply to such an invitation: 'I recieved your letter accompanying your elegant present of the FORGET ME NOT for this year. I have written the romantic stories &c accompanying this solely for your work and request of you to show them to Mr Shoberl without loss of time, and if they do not suit your publication to return them to me to the care of any of the Edin^r booksellers to whom you chance to be sending parcels'. While Hogg did not contribute to every subsequent volume of *Forget Me Not* for the rest of his life, his work does appear in most of them. On 4 June 1831 (Historical Society of Pennsylvania: Frank M. Etting [family] Collection, Collection 193, European Authors) he wrote to Shoberl, '[...] you are likely to be the only editor this year who has aught from my pen which I hope will be no dishonour to you. It is not because they paid me ill for they paid me well but on none can I depend for unpublished pieces but yourself and such as are not returned are all lost to me'. He even seems to have felt that an apology was due when the 1833 volume was published without a Hogg contribution, writing to Shoberl on 2 March 1833 (in NLS, MS 1809, fol. 85), 'I was sorry I was obliged to break my word to you last year but it was the same with all other editors. My literary engagements are getting beyond my power to execute for always as I grow older and less qualified the demand on me is growing the greater'. Hogg's last contribution to *Forget Me Not* appeared in the volume for 1836, published shortly before his death on 21 November 1835.

The Skylark (p. 39)

'The Skylark' appeared in *Forget Me Not* for 1828, p. 27, after previous publication united to music as a song. Hogg's first manuscript forms part of a letter to Dr John Clarke Whitfeld of 8 April [1816] (see *Letters 1*), and appeared as song no. 5 in that composer's *Twelve Vocal Pieces*, published soon afterwards. Hogg then published it set to an old air as 'The Lark' in his own *A Border Garland: Containing Nine New Songs* around 1819 (pp. 14–15), and again in the revised and extended *The Border Garland: Containing Twelve New Songs* around 1828 (pp. 13–15). A subsequent musical version, 'Bird of the Wilderness: A Favourite Scotch Song' with music by 'J. Clifton', published by the London firm of Collard & Collard around 1835 and sold at one shilling and sixpence may or may not have been authorised by Hogg himself. Although the poem was included in *The Casquet of Literary Gems*, ed. by Alexander Whitelaw, 2 vols (Glasgow, 1829), II, 241, it was flagged as 'from the *Forget Me Not*' and there is no evidence of authorial engagement with this printing.

Hogg appears to have published 'The Skylark' for the first time as independent verse in the *Forget Me Not* itself. Although there is a second undated manuscript of these verses in the National Library of Scotland (MS, 10279, fol. 82), Hogg's fair-copy manuscript for this particular printing, complete with the customary header and dated 'Altrive Lake | April 2^d 1827', survives in the Huntington Library, San Marino, California, MS HM 12409. It is part of a paper folded to make a four-page booklet also containing a similarly dated manuscript of 'The Descent of Love'. This poem also appeared in *Forget Me Not* for 1828, suggesting that both pieces were among the manuscripts accompanying Hogg's letter to Ackermann of 1 April 1827, referred to above. An examination of this four-page manuscript shows that Hogg's work was altered before being typeset: there are various changes in Shoberl's hand, and he has then written the instruction 'Proof' on the top left-hand corner of the first page of 'The Descent of Love'. In the case of 'The Sky Lark' line 18, 'Musical cherubim hie thee away!' has been altered to 'Musical cherub hie, hie thee away!', presumably because Shoberl knew that 'cherubim' was the plural of 'cherub' and somewhat pedantically corrected Hogg's grammar, doubling the following word to preserve the rhythm of the line. He also deleted Hogg's end-date to the poem. These editorial changes then went through to the text printed in *Forget Me Not*, which also disturbs a gradual accelaration of the poem signalled in the punctuation of Hogg's manuscript. While the close of the fourth stanza repeats the close of the first verbally, Hogg's increased use of exclamation marks in the repetition signals the poem's climax. The printer, however, has added exclamation marks to the ends of lines 4 and 5 to create a mechanical parallel with lines 22 and 23, and has also modernised Hogg's spelling of 'desart' to 'desert'.

It is unclear whether or not Hogg saw proofs for his contributions to *Forget Me Not* for 1828: his letter to Ackermann of 1 April 1827 (NLS, MS 8887, fols 36–37) had included a postscript, 'In the event of the articles proving acceptable I believe it will be necessary that I see the proofs', but there is no surviving indication that they were in fact sent. Another manuscript in NLS, MS 4805, fol. 30 relates to *Songs (1831)*, (pp. 15–16). When 'The Sky Lark' was revised for this, line 18 was changed again to 'Musical cherub, soar, singing, away!', perhaps indicating some unease on Hogg's part with Shoberl's 'hie, hie thee away!'

A subsequent presentation holograph, dated 'Altrive-Lake Septr 7th 1832' (NLS, Acc. 8879) is addressed to 'W. Forbes Mackenzie Esq | Stobo Castle'.

'The Sky Lark' is printed in *Contributions to Annuals and Gift-Books* from Hogg's fair-copy manuscript for *Forget Me Not* in the Huntington Library. Since the substantial differences between this and the published version are significant rather than numerous and have been summarised above, the published version is not printed here. The following emendation has been made to Hogg's fair-copy manuscript:

l. 14 O'er moor] Oe'r moor (MS) [to agree with the word in lines 13 and 15]

The Descent of Love (pp. 40–44)

In one respect the textual history of 'The Descent of Love' parallels that of 'Woman' as published in *The Bijou* (see note above, pp. 291–93), in that it is also related to a section of Hogg's manuscript poem of 'Love's Legacy' (Alexander Turnbull Library, Wellington, New Zealand, James Hogg Papers (Item 74). MS-Papers-0042-07). Although the concluding section of Canto First of 'Love's Legacy', from 'Ah youthful love! thy votarist' onwards, corresponds roughly to 'The Descent of Love' there are substantial verbal differences between the two, with lines transposed and some lines appearing in the relevant section of the longer poem but not in the *Forget Me Not* version.

Hogg's fair-copy manuscript for 'The Descent of Love', with the usual header and dated 'Altrive Lake by Selkirk | April 2^d 1827' survives in the Huntington Library, San Marino, California, MS HM 12409. It is part of a four-page booklet which includes 'The Skylark', also published in the 1828 *Forget Me Not*, and both poems were almost certainly among the items sent to Ackermann by Hogg for *Forget Me Not* with his letter of 1 April 1827, referred to above. But as the date of composition of 'Love's Legacy' is not known (see note to 'Woman' above), it is not possible to establish whether it or 'The Descent of Love' was written first. The lines from the longer poem equivalent to 'The Descent of Love' like those equivalent to 'Woman' were also revised with the rest of 'Love's Legacy' for subsequent republication and appeared as the concluding lines of 'Love's Legacy. Canto First' in *Fraser's Magazine*, 10 (October 1834), 403–08.

A presentation holograph manuscript of the poem's opening lines dated 'Altrive Lake | May 11th 1831' survives in the Thomas Cooper Library, University of South Carolina (Spec PR4791.D4 1831). This appears to be the one Mrs Garden describes Hogg attempting for 'the album of a young lady residing in Alloa' (p. 68), when his inspiration ran dry and after composing a few lines he was forced to close with a note, 'I have sticket this poem'. As a complete and self-contained poem, however, 'The Descent of Love' was first published in *Forget Me Not* for 1828, pp. 217–20, and was not reprinted in Hogg's lifetime.

A number of significant changes were made to Hogg's fair-copy manuscript by Shoberl before 'The Descent of Love' was typeset for *Forget Me Not*, the instruction 'proof' also appearing in his hand on the top left-hand corner of the first page of the manuscript, just above Hogg's title. As with the change from 'cherubim' to 'cherub' in 'The Skylark' there is a touch of pedantry about some of these alterations: Hogg's reference to the rivers Euphrates and Tigris joining in 'Arabian lands' for example was changed to the more geographically-accurate 'Assyrian lands'. Others seem designed to eliminate Hogg's more unusual and obscure vocabulary, words such as 'adventine' and 'compend' being deleted, presumably in the interests of the wider and more domestic readership of the annuals compared to that, say, of the standard monthly magazines. Hogg's end-dating was also deleted at this stage.

Another layer of revision clearly took place after the intial typesetting had been completed. Hogg's 'angels know not youthful love;' in line 12 and 'In a new world' in line 59 (unchanged by Shoberl in the manuscript) read 'angels feel not youthful love;' and 'In a blest world' respectively in *Forget Me Not*. Changes to the couplet forming lines 13–14 demonstrate the process of revision most clearly: Hogg had originally written 'Their's is a flame without compend, | An holy ardor without end:', which Shoberl changed on the manuscript to 'Their's is a flame without decrease | A holy fire that neer can cease', while the printed text has 'Theirs is a flame we cannot know, | A holy ardour free from wo;'. In a postscript to his letter to Ackermann of 1 April 1827 accompanying 'The Descent of Love' (NLS, MS 8887, fols 36–37) Hogg had stated 'In the event of the articles proving acceptable I believe it will be necessary that I see the proofs' but there is no surviving indication that proofs were actually sent. While it is quite possible that Shoberl himself incorporated fresh revisions at the proof stage, the insistence on the word 'ardour' may be that of Hogg himself, suggesting that the printed text as well as the fair-copy manuscript reflects authorial involvement. Accordingly, the editors have included the printed version of 'The Descent of Love' as well as a text from Hogg's fair-copy manuscript in *Contributions to Annuals and Gift-Books*. The following emendations have been made to Hogg's fair-copy manuscript:

l. 45 heavenly art] heavinly art (MS)
l. 46 and divine.] and divine (MS)

St. Mary of the Lows (pp. 44–47)

Peter Garside provides the following introductory and textual notes to this poem in his edition of *A Queer Book* (S/SC, 1995), pp. 255–56:

'St. Mary of the Lows' first appeared in the *Forget Me Not* for 1829 (pp. 25–29). This was the oldest of the London annuals, having been established in 1823, and the numbers from 1827 were edited by Frederic Shoberl. Hogg first sent material on 1 April 1827, having received a complimentary copy from its publisher, Ackermann: 'I have written the romantic stories &c accompanying this solely for your work and request of you to show them to Mr Shoberl without loss of time' (NLS, MS 8887, fols 36–37). Though no evidence about the present contribution has apparently survived, most probably it was written and submitted at a later point during the early months of 1828. Hogg's combination of two current reflective modes, the churchyard meditation and romantic expression of grief over a lost love, was well directed at Shoberl's popular and relatively eclectic literary miscellany.

St Mary's Churchyard is located on a hill side on the northern bank of St Mary's Loch, in the Yarrow Valley, and affords spectacular views over the loch, which at its southern point connects with the smaller Loch of the Lowes. The church burial ground, which served local farming communities, was still in use in Hogg's day. An earlier note by Hogg to his ballad 'Mess John' (1807) suggests that remnants of the original Chapel or Church also survived: 'The ruins of St Mary's Chapel are still visible, in a wild scene on the banks of the lake of that name [...] The chapel is, in some ancient records, called *The Maiden Kirk*, and, in others, *The Kirk of Saint Mary of the Lowes*' (*The Mountain Bard*, (Edinburgh, 1807), p. 86). By projecting a feudal origin, the poem effectively offers a historical panorama of Ettrick Forest: from its early days as a royal hunting-ground, through border conflict and civil strife, to a new domestic calm marked by the advent of sheep-farming. The graveyard (somewhat fancifully) is depicted as mingling pre-Reformation warriors and Presbyterian martyrs, while elements of both the Catholic and Protestant creeds are traceable in Hogg's closing reflections on the premature death of an unnamed woman.

Textual Notes on 'St. Mary of the Lows'
No manuscript of this poem has been discovered, and it is not unlikely that the copy sent to London was destroyed after printing. Nonetheless there is reason to believe that the text in the *Forget Me Not* represents a reasonably fair version. When first sending contributions on 1 April 1827, Hogg had made a point of asking for proofs; and he still enjoyed good relations with Shoberl ('the only editor this year who has aught from my pen') as late as 4 June 1831.

The *Queer Book* of 1832 introduced a number of minor changes in accidentals, its main verbal alteration being the substitution of 'Border' for 'forest' at line 41 (arguably diminishing the focus on Ettrick Forest at this point). More remarkably, it left out the final stanza of the original poem altogether, ending with the penultimate stanza at the foot of a page (p. 256). Although it is tempting to conclude space was a factor– procedure would have demanded a whole page for the remaining verse– the failure of the normally punctilious printer to provide a concluding mark is more indicative of a production error.

The present edition reprints the text from the *Forget Me Not* for 1829, without alteration.

Eastern Apologues (pp. 48–56)

'Eastern Apologues' appeared in *Forget Me Not* for 1829, pp. 309–23. Hogg seems to have composed it around the 1827–28 Christmas and New Year holidays, for he wrote to William Blackwood on 5 January 1828 (NLS, MS 4021, fols 271–72) 'I have written several Eastern Appologues but am thinking of sending them to Ackerman as I am rather encumbering you with articles'. The date is significant in view of Hogg's self-portrait as the old lame bard Ismael, happy despite many personal misfortunes because of his possession of 'the gift of song [...] an emanation from the Deity' (p. 49), but shown to be indiscreet and lacking in worldly wisdom compared with his interlocutor Sadac. Hogg himself was temporarily crippled at the time 'Eastern Apologues' was written, as his previous letter to William Blackwood of 21 December [1827] (NLS, MS 4007, fols 48–49) reveals. Announcing the birth of his third daughter Harriet on 18 December 1827 Hogg declares, 'I have not been fortunate otherwise for last week I got a stroke from a horse in the dark by which I am rendered quite lame and confined to my room and ran a great risk of being rendered lame for life'. By 5 January, when 'Eastern Apologues' had been written, Hogg had still not fully recovered from this accident, reporting to Blackwood 'I am walking about again but have not been able as yet to fish any'. In 'Eastern Apologues' Hogg confronted the threat of 'being rendered lame for life', and compensated himself for his enforced physical inactivity by the exercise of his pen. Its moralising and religious but non-denominational tone was well suited to the annuals, combining the attractions of Aesop's fables, and works on the topic of the search for happiness such as Johnson's *Rasselas* (1759) or Prior's *Solomon* (1718). It is also clearly a forerunner of New Age twentieth-century classics such as Kahlil Gibran's *The Prophet* (1923). Although a presentation holograph of a few lines from 'Eastern Apologues' dated 7 December 1828 has survived (NLS, MS 3218, fol. 38) Hogg's manuscript for *Forget Me Not* has not apparently done so, and 'Eastern Apologues' was not reprinted in his lifetime. It is given here from *Forget Me Not* for 1829 without emendation.

Seeking the Houdy (pp. 56–64)

Nothing is known of the circumstances surrounding the publication of 'Seeking the Houdy' in *Forget Me Not* for 1830, pp. 399–413. Hogg's manuscript does not appear to have survived, the printed version is undated, nor are there any references to it before publication in his surviving correspondence. Hogg may have sent it to Ackermann during 1829 for its appearance in the next volume of his annual, or it may have been sent for a previous volume and held back until the issue for 1830. A reprinting in the anthology *The Outlaw's Bride and Other Tales*, ed. by Leitch Ritchie, 2 vols (Philadelphia: E. L. Carey, 1833), II, 67–78 appears to have been made from *Forget Me Not*. Otherwise it was not reprinted in Hogg's lifetime, and is given here from *Forget Me Not* for 1830 without emendation.

A Sea Story (pp. 64–71)

'A Sea Story' was first published in *Forget Me Not* for 1831, pp. 19–31, and never reprinted in Hogg's lifetime. Following after Coleridge's eerie creation of a haunted ship in 'The Rime of the Ancient Mariner' Hogg brilliantly recreates in print the fireside tale-telling of his youth for the domestic readership of the annuals, pointing the moral that deeds of wickedness done in the dark are sure to come to light. The circumstances of its composition are unknown. Hogg's letter to Blackwood of 10 November 1830 (NLS, MS 4027, fol. 200) refers to a payment due from Ackermann in October 1830, either for this tale or for Hogg's contributions to *Ackermann's Juvenile Forget Me Not* for 1831: 'Mr R Ackerman wrote to me last month to draw upon him for £15= at ten days sight. Pray can you do that for me and send it?' There is no surviving manuscript for the tale. 'A Sea Story' is given in the present volume from *Forget Me Not* for 1831 without emendation.

A Love Ballad (pp. 71–73)

Although this poem was never actually published in *Forget Me Not* the manuscript forms part of Hogg's letter to Shoberl of 4 June 1831 (Historical Society of Pennsylvania: Frank M. Etting [family] Collection, Collection 193, EuropeanAuthors), transmitting items intended for *Forget Me Not* and *Ackermann's Juvenile Forget Me Not* for 1832: 'I got your letter only with our carrier this day and have dashed you off three verses for the picture besides a ballad which I would wish to be in the old FORGET ME NOT as you are likely to be the only editor this year who has aught from my pen [...]'. 'A Love Ballad' is a charming, light-hearted account of courtship in Hogg's best Scottish pastoral mode, and seems far better suited to *Forget Me Not* than 'The Battle of the Boyne. A Dramatic Sketch' which did appear in the volume for 1832. Ackermann and Shoberl may perhaps have hesitated over the lines 'Yet never till the break of morn | Did she propose to leave me mair' despite the assurance in the following stanza that Jane is 'virtuous'.

Another version of Hogg's rejected ballad was published shortly after the appearance of *Forget Me Not* for 1832, right at the start of his London visit: 'A Scottish Ballad. By the Ettrick Shepherd' appeared in the *Athenæum* of 7 January 1832 (p. 8). The manuscript of 'A Scottish Ballad' in NLS, MS 10279, fols 74–75 would appear to be Hogg's fair-copy manuscript for this version since the differences between manuscript and print are either punctuational or the result of an English compositor misreading Hogg's hand (a note 'To Correspondents' on p. 38 of the following week's paper points out a number of printing errors as 'mostly corrected in a second edition').

However, there can be no doubt that the version sent to Shoberl is the one Hogg intended to contribute to this annual. The editors of the present volume follow Hogg's own expressed wish in reprinting this from his manuscript among his contributions to *Forget Me Not*. The following emendation has been made:

l. 43 lad. Befa'] lad Befa' (MS) [end of sentence]

Maggy o' Buccleuch (pp. 73–74)

Hogg's literary song 'Maggy o' Buccleuch' was printed in *Forget Me Not* for 1832, pp. 182–83, and probably not reprinted by Hogg himself. Although it is not fully realised for singing (as several of his contributions to *The Musical Bijou* were) Hogg does name a suitable tune, thus providing the clue for a competent amateur or professional musician to turn it into an accompanied or unaccompanied song for performance. Hogg thus presents himself to the reader of *Forget Me Not* as a Scottish song-writer, the successor to Robert Burns, and there is perhaps a distant echo of Burns's well-known 'A red red Rose' with its melting rocks, drying sea, and ten-thousand-mile journey in Hogg's geographical range from the 'cauldrife north' to 'far ayont the burning line'.

Unsurprisingly, his words were subsequently set to music by a composer named E. J. Nielson and published (as 'sung by Mr Wilson, at the Theatre Royal') by W. H. Aldridge of 204 Regent Street price two shillings (see British Library H.1654.mm.5). Whether Hogg received a payment for this popular theatrical number, or even knew of its publication, is a matter for speculation. However, this fully-realised performance song clearly belongs with others of the kind and is distinct from the literary song Hogg himself contributed to *Forget Me Not* for 1832.

Hogg's manuscript has not apparently survived, his literary song is not dated in *Forget Me Not*, nor is there any direct reference to it in his surviving correspondence. 'Maggy o' Buccleuch' is reprinted here without change from *Forget Me Not* for 1832.

The Battle of the Boyne (pp. 74–77)

Although 'The Battle of the Boyne. A Dramatic Sketch' was first published in *Forget Me Not* for 1832, pp. 299–304, it seems to have been composed originally for *Blackwood's Edinburgh Magazine* since Blackwood mentions 'The Battle of the Boyne' among a number of manuscripts returned to Hogg with his letter of 26 February 1831 (NLS, MS 30,312, pp. 154–56), stating 'All these are good in their kind, but not so good as what would be expected from you'. The subject-matter of the sketch with its implicit championing of the Protestant over the Catholic cause in Ireland does indeed seem more relevant to a Tory magazine than to the more ecumenical annuals. Presumably the sketch was forwarded to Ackermann in London not long after its return to Hogg at Altrive. Hogg's letter to Blackwood of 24 October 1831 (NLS, MS 4029, fols 264–65) refers to a letter sent to him by Ackermann of 15 October acknowledging a debt of £10, but it is unclear whether this refers to payment for contributions to *Forget Me Not* or to *Ackermann's Juvenile Forget Me Not* for 1832. Hogg's manuscript does not appear to have survived, and this dramatic sketch was not reprinted with his authority in his lifetime, though included in a showcase article entitled 'The Spirit of the Annuals' in *Royal Lady's Magazine*, 2 (1831), 322–24. It is given in the present volume from *Forget me Not* for 1832, without change.

Scottish Haymakers (pp. 78–84)

'Scottish Haymakers' was published in *Forget Me Not* for 1834, pp. 327–35, and composed specifically for that issue, to accompany an engraving of a picture of the same title painted by William Kidd and engraved by James Mitchell. The annual's editor Frederic Shoberl must have sent Hogg an early copy in the spring of 1833, for Hogg's letter of 2 March 1833 (NLS, MS 1809, fol. 85) is a detailed response to the engraving:

> I will furnish you with something for the Haymakers if God spare me life and health. [...] But I write this line principally to tell you that the hay-rake in the picture is wrong the semi-circular bow being sufficient the other two supporters I never saw in Scotland. All the rest is in fair keeping perhaps the hay on the cart is rather too roughsome and touzy.

These initial remarks on the distortion of a familiar agricultural scene by the artist contain the elements of the story Hogg subsequently wrote to accompany this engraving. Hogg's Ettrick Shepherd persona is emphasised both in his recollections of personal labour in the hayfield and in his anecdotes of the celebrated men he became acquainted with during his career as a writer, while Alexander Nasmyth's remarks on artistic selection and Alexandre's deceptive ventriloquism both comment on the nature of art and the ways in which it both represents and distorts reality.

Hogg's manuscript for 'Scottish Haymakers' has not apparently survived, and the story does not seem to have been reprinted with Hogg's authority during his lifetime although a German version, 'Die Heumahd und Alexander in Schottland' appeared in the *Englische Bibliothek* (Karlsruhe: G. Braun, 1834), pp. 301–10. The present volume prints the tale from *Forget Me Not* for 1834, accompanied by the illustration which is a vital part of its meaning. The following emendation has been made:

p. 84, l. 23 Alexandre] Alexander (*Forget Me Not*) [the error undoes Hogg's careful distinction earlier between the ventriloquist and Nasmyth]

The Lord of Balloch (pp. 84–87)

Hogg's poem was originally published as 'A Ballad from the Gaelic' in the *Edinburgh Literary Journal* of 10 July 1830, p. 30 before its appearance as 'The Lord of Balloch' in *Forget Me Not* for 1836, pp. 352–57. No details about the process of composition are known, and neither of Hogg's manuscripts appear to have survived, but a comparison of the two printed versions reveals that Hogg substantially revised his poem before submitting it to *Forget Me Not*. Besides a number of minor local adjustments Hogg also carefully adapted his ballad to the family readership of the annuals, adding moral lines to emphasise the wickedness of the murder and deleting the macabre description of the hanged and decaying bodies of the twenty clan perpetrators. In effect, therefore, there are two distinct versions of this poem of which the second, printed in *Forget Me Not* for 1836, is appropriate to the present volume and is printed without change.

The Anniversary

*Two published contributions: one additional unpublished
contribution is included in the present volume*

Only one volume of this annual appeared, for 1829. It was published by John Sharpe of London, edited by Allan Cunningham (1784–1842), and cost one guinea, the general price of an annual being twelve shillings. The higher price implied an intended rivalry with *The Keepsake*, which tried to import an aristocratic distinction to the annual and also secured the prestige of having Sir Walter Scott among its contributors. Cunningham showed his awareness of this in a letter to Ritchie of 20 October 1828 (quoted from David Hogg, *Life of Allan Cunningham* (Dumfries: J. Anderson, 1875), p. 288), commenting that 'the "Keepsake" purchased authors and bribed lords at a prodigious expense'. He tried to make his own annual of the highest literary quality rather than social prestige, and although *The Keepsake* had Scott, *The Anniversary* was also a fashionably Scottish production, numbering not only Hogg but also Wilson, Lockhart, and Pringle among its contributors. In his letters to Hogg of 12 and 23 December 1828 (NLS, MS 2245, fols 132–33 and 136–37 respectively), he reported proudly, 'My Book—*Our* Book—for Scotchmen have made it, will succeed very well', adding that 'the name of the Anniversary stands higher than any other Annual for its Poetry'. In a letter to an unnamed correspondent of 27 November 1828 (The Brotherton Collection, Leeds University Library: BC Miscellaneous Letters, PRI (Pringle album)) Hogg discusses *The Anniversary* among other annuals, stating, 'I find that Cunningham with a little application has a chance of all our Scottish literary might and *We* are the most powerful party to be on one side'.

To this single volume Hogg contributed 'The Cameronian Preacher's Tale' in prose and 'The Carle of Invertime' in verse, while his dramatic dialogue 'Katie Cheyne' was accepted for the projected second volume for 1830.

In contributing to *The Anniversary* Hogg was responding to a direct appeal from an old and valued friend. The editor, Allan Cunningham, was like Hogg a peasant-poet and the two had formed a close and mutually-supportive friendship in Dumfriesshire in about 1806, when Hogg was a shepherd and Cunningham a stone-mason—see 'Memoir', pp. 69–71, and also Cunningham's letter to Hogg of 6 March 1828 in NLS, MS 2245, fols 114–15. Cunningham's tone in writing to Hogg on 6 March 1828 to ask for his assistance was naturally both confident and affectionate:

> To you I naturally turned my thoughts when I undertook my task and I wish for one or more of those happy little pieces of poetry which you make out so readily by the side of your beloved Yarrow. [...] I can afford to pay at the rate of something like a pound per page and five or eight pages from your pen in your happy manner will be of much service to me. See a vision for me or dream a dream—converse with a spirit or do what you please. (NLS, MS 2245, fols 114–15)

The warmth of Hogg's response to this appeal is demonstrated in the quality of his contributions. In his letter to Hogg of 26 May 1828 Cunningham declared 'I hardly think you ever wrote aught better than some of what you sent me', and in that of 12 December (after publication) he stated 'No praise of mine can add to the warm and handsome things which are spoken here of your two communications—they please every body; and I am proud to think that a country man and a brother Peasant has seen so much distinction in giving his help to me' (NLS, MS 2245, fols 120–21 and 132–33). Cunningham also began to negotiate an arrangement whereby Hogg would be paid a premium to confine his contributions in future years to *The Anniversary* and to *Friendship's Offering*, edited by his friend and fellow-Scotsman Thomas Pringle— see his letters to Hogg of 23 December 1828 and 7 January 1829, in NLS, MS 2245, fols 136–37 and Garden, pp. 221–23.

His jubilation, however, was clearly not shared by *The Anniversary*'s publisher, John Sharpe, who finally decided against publishing a second volume of *The Anniversary* for the following year, 1830.

The Carle of Invertime (pp. 91–96)

Peter Garside provides the following introductory and textual notes to this poem in his edition of *A Queer Book* (S/SC, 1995), pp. 242–43:

This poem first appeared in the 1829 number of *The Anniversary* (pp. 100–07), the short-lived annual edited by Hogg's friend and fellow-poet Allan Cunningham, who had written to Hogg on 6 March 1828 soliciting a contribution: 'I can afford to pay at the rate of something like a pound per page and five or eight pages from your pen in your happy manner will be of much service to me. See a vision for me or dream a dream—converse with a spirit or do what you please. I have little room for my work is a varied one and the pages will hold some 30 or 34 lines each' (NLS, MS 2245, fol. 114). From the evidence of the poem in *The Anniversary* Hogg obliged on several counts. 'The Carle' is cast in the visionary, 'Kilmeny' style Cunningham must have been hoping for; and the idea that Hogg is here operating as a poet of the first rank is reinforced by its attribution to 'the author of The Queen's Wake'. Furthermore, in length the poem seems tailor-made to suit Cunningham's requirements—its 204 lines taking up less than eight of *The Anniversary*'s pages. Cunningham expressed his pleasure in a letter to Hogg on 26 May 1828: 'Your poem is excellent' (NLS, MS 2245, fol. 120).

   Hogg's subject-matter also meshed neatly with the topic of 'Time' which Cunningham's Preface announced as a running theme in the collection. In imaginative scope 'The Carle' is reminiscent of larger 'philosophical' poems by Hogg, notably *The Pilgrims of the Sun* (1815). Its Christian allegory, the leading of the 'old gray wife' by Hope towards Eternity, is also similar in some respects to Christiana's pilgrimage with Mercy in Part II of Bunyan's *Pilgrim's Progress*.

Textual Notes on 'The Carle of Invertime'
No manuscript of this poem, as published in *The Anniversary*, survives. However, a fragment of another version is held in the National Library of Scotland (MS 9634, fols 3–4). This consists of two leaves, paginated by Hogg 5, [6], 7, 8, and covers an area approximating line 110 to the end of the poem. The clean script and presence of an end inscription ('Mount-Benger | March 29th 1828') both indicate that it was intended as a final draft. Collation against the *Anniversary* text reveals large areas of rewriting, and a more obtrusive religious dimension in the NLS version (which ends with the chorus 'Halleluiah'). One explanation is that Hogg rewrote the poem to order; another, that Cunningham made his own changes owing to pressure of space. The *Queer Book* of 1832, in following the *Anniversary* text, made a number of formal changes, including the creation of fresh lines to show double rhymes at lines 67, 69, 77,

79, 109, 111, 145, 147–a characteristic also evident in the NLS fragment.

The present edition of 'The Carle of Invertime' is reprinted from the
Anniversary of 1829. A 'new' verse paragraph is created at line 195, through
indentation and spacing, matching the *Queer Book* of 1832 and the NLS
MS fragment. Additionally, the following emendations have been made:

(l. 152) the sole] thy sole (*Anniversary*) ['the' as in MS 9634 and *Queer
Book* 1832]

(l. 196) Time] time (*Anniversary*) [MS 9634 Time]

(l. 202) Eternity back to Time] eternity back to time (*Anniversary*) [MS
9634 and *Queer Book* 1832 Eternity back to Time]

The Cameronian Preacher's Tale (pp. 96–108)

'The Cameronian Preacher's Tale' was first published in *The Anniversary* for
1829, pp. 170–95. Hogg probably wrote it in 1828, as part of a series about
the Covenanters, as he indicates in his letter to William Blackwood of 3 June
1829 (NLS, MS 4024, fols 292–93):

> The tale and ballad of the Covenanters are part of a series which I
> wrote last year for publication by themselves but I sent Allan
> Cunningham one Mr Hall another and this is a third so that the series
> is fairly broken up.

It is possible that this series was inspired by Cunningham's own series of
'Recollections of Mark Macrabin, the Cameronian' in *Blackwood's Edinburgh
Magazine* between 1819 and 1821, the first number of which was praised by
Hogg as 'so like him and so graphic' in his letter to Blackwood of 30 Novem-
ber 1819 (quoted from *Letters I*). At any rate it seems tailored for Cunningham
himself, in being set in his part of Dumfriesshire with a narrator whom
Cunningham had known in his youth.

An incomplete and entirely different telling of the same story occurs in
Hogg's manuscript 'The Two Drovers' at the Beinecke Rare Book & Manuscript Library, Yale University, James Hogg Collection, GEN MSS 61, Box 1,
Folder 27). This manuscript, consisting of five sheets of paper folded into
Hogg's customary four-page booklets, was paginated [1]–20 by Hogg, and
the sheets are watermarked with a crowned shield and a date of 1823. In this
version the piper (only a minor character in 'The Cameronian Preacher's
Tale') is much more prominent—the tale begins with his discussion of the
murder of Johnston and breaks off with his trial for attempting to rob the
widowed Mrs Johnston of the treasure restored to her by the Cameronian
minister, in this case not Farley but Macmillan.

Hogg's manuscript of 'The Cameronian Preacher's Tale' does not apparently survive but there are indications that the original tale was shortened by
Cunningham for its appearance in *The Anniversary*: in his letter to Hogg of 26
May 1828 (NLS MS 2245, fols 120–21), acknowledging receipt of Hogg's
pieces he says 'Your Poem is excellent–your tales capital–but too long for my

space—but this I can manage without injuring them in any little abridgement which I make'. This seems to have been done purely to shorten the tale, for Cunningham seems otherwise to have been extremely pleased with it, calling it 'a noble Tale' in his letter of 9 October 1828 (NLS, MS 2245, fols 128–29), though admitting that he was not able to pay so well for prose as for verse contributions (£17 for 22 pages of prose, rather than the pound a page for verse).

'The Cameronian Preacher's Tale' was not reprinted in Hogg's lifetime, and the text included in *Tales and Sketches by the Ettrick Shepherd*, 6 vols (Glasgow: Blackie & Son, 1836–37), II, 339–54 appears to have been set from the text in *The Anniversary*, with a few minor and mostly punctuational differences.

The tale is reprinted here from *The Anniversary*. A line space has been introduced before the final paragraph of the tale, the only one not narrated by Farley. The following emendations have also been made:

p. 105, l. 25 piper," said the widow, "ye're] piper, said the widow, ye're (*Anniversary*)

p. 106, ll. 7–8 "'Clavers and his Highlandmen',] "Clavers and his Highlandmen, (*Anniversary*) [this is the title of a song]

p. 106, l. 37 'Clavers'] Clavers (*Anniversary*) [this is the shortened title of a song]

p. 107, l. 10 piper, "he's] piper, he's (*Anniversary*)

Katie Cheyne (pp. 108–19)

An early version of the story known as 'Katie Cheyne' appears to have been written by Hogg for *Blackwood's Edinburgh Magazine* as one of a series of 'Dramas of Simple Life'. Hogg's manuscript of the story under the title 'A Pastoral Love Scene, or Dramas of Simple Life Drama First' survives in the Mitchell Library, Glasgow (MS 308865). An edited version, along with the story of its rejection by William Blackwood in 1826, has been published by Janette Currie in her 'Two Early Versions of Tales from Annuals', *Studies in Hogg and his World*, 11 (2000), 87–121. This story differs markedly from the later 'Katie Cheyne'— at its end, for example, Duncan is shot in a graveyard by his rival in Katie's affections.

Hogg clearly rewrote his tale before sending it to Allan Cunningham for inclusion in *The Anniversary* for 1829. The manuscript pieces sent to Cunningham as potential contributions included at least two other prose tales besides 'The Cameronian Preacher's Tale': in his letter of 26 May 1828, acknowledging their receipt (NLS, MS 2245, fols 120–21), Cunningham mentions returning 'the one on the Polar discoveries', while in his subsequent letter of 9 October (NLS, MS 2245, fols 128–29) he states that he had intended to print two of Hogg's tales, 'but other important communications came in and for the sake of variety I was obliged to omit for this year one of yours'. On 23 December, soliciting Hogg's contributions for the proposed second volume for 1830, Cunningham refers to this as a 'pleasant story' to match the serious one he hoped to receive from Hogg (NLS, MS 2245, fols

136–37). Hogg responded doubtfully on 31 December: 'I am not sure about the drama in your hands My reccollections of it are not very favourable. I would not wish any thing of mine to appear in your work now that was not rather superior to my other pieces' (James Hogg Collection, Beinecke Rare Book & Manuscript Library, Yale University, GEN MSS 61, Box 1, Folder 7). Writing just over a week later on 7 January 1829 Cunningham rebuked Hogg for this remark: 'The domestic "Prose Tale", my good friend, is a capital one, and the characters *original*, and you must not allow your memory to influence you against it' (Garden, pp. 221–23). Clearly the piece was firmly scheduled to appear in *The Anniversary* for 1830 despite the author's temporary misgivings as to its quality, misgivings perhaps instilled by Blackwood's earlier rejection of the first of his 'Dramas of Simple Life'.

Unfortunately Cunningham was obliged to announce on 15 July 1829 that his publisher John Sharpe had declined to publish the projected second volume of *The Anniversary*: he had, however, placed those of Hogg's manuscripts intended for the volume in the publisher's hands as 'he intreats to insert them in a New Magazine which he has planned with Dr Maginn and Th^r Hook for Editors' (NLS, MS 2245, fols 152–53).

Sharpe's London Magazine was not a successful venture, only three issues appearing, for July, August, and September 1829. The first issue in particular clearly shows signs of its annual origins, as it includes several engravings and even a piece entitled 'The Splendid Annual' (pp. 1–14), which refers directly to *The Anniversary*. Hogg's 'Katie Cheyne' appears in the second issue, for August 1829, pp. 56–63, and is clearly the second tale Cunningham had not room for in *The Anniversary* for 1829, but intended to appear in the following issue for 1830.

'Katie Cheyne' is therefore included in the present volume, as it was sent by Hogg and accepted by Cunningham for inclusion in *The Anniversary*. Hitherto the tale has only been known in the version which appeared in *Tales and Sketches by the Ettrick Shepherd*, 6 vols (Glasgow: Blackie & Son, 1836–37), III, 171–82. That makes a number of verbal changes to the text of the tale in *Sharpe's London Magazine* for which no overall reason is discernable: sometimes English words are substituted for Scots ones, and sometimes vice versa, for example. Also, the beginning of the fourth scene (where Katie's own letter gives her reaction to Duncan's breach of promise of marriage) is cut from the 1836–37 version, perhaps for reasons of space or perhaps because Blackie and Son's corrector of the press thought that a jilted girl should not be flirting with another man at a dance: without this scene, though, there is no explanation of Katie's sudden wedding to Jock at the end of the tale.

Hogg's tale, after appearing in an annual-derived magazine, returned to an annuals context in 1832, being reprinted in *The Bouquet* for 1832 (pp. 39–57). This volume consisted mainly of reprinted pieces, its preface acknowledging an obligation to various magazines, among them 'the unfortunate (because no longer existing) one of Sharpe', and a textual comparison demonstrates that the story in *The Bouquet* was indeed reprinted from *Sharpe's London Magazine*. It seems likely that this was an unauthorised reprinting, but it is of interest in that Hogg's tale was accompanied in *The Bouquet* by an engraving by J. Shury of a painting by William Kidd (reproduced on p. 109 here). It is not known whether 'Katie Cheyne' was the inspiration for Kidd's picture, or whether Hogg's story of rural courtship simply happened to tie in well with Kidd's painting of such a scene.

The present volume reprints 'Katie Cheyne' from *Sharpe's London Magazine* with the following changes:

p. 108, l. 27 yere very heart] ye're very heart (*Sharpe's*)
p. 108, l. 33 "It's bleating] "Its bleating (*Sharpe's*)
p. 111, l. 14 it's nae matter] its nae matter (*Sharpe's*)
p. 112, l. 8 leaped o'er the linn] leaped o'er the line (*Sharpe's*)
p. 113, l. 24 hap step and loup] hapstep and loup (*Sharpe's*)
p. 115, l. 1 says she, 'If] says she, 'if (*Sharpe's*)
p. 116, l. 1 grow daft, break] grow daft break (*Sharpe's*)
p. 116, l. 18 cozie plaidie."] cozie plaidie. (*Sharpe's*) [Duncan's speech ends with his song]
p. 117, l. 20 cousin,' says I, 'has] cousin, says I, has (*Sharpe's*)
p. 118, ll. 13–14 'Dear Duncan,'] "Dear Duncan," (*Sharpe's*) [Katie's letter is read aloud within Duncan's soliloquy]
p. 118, l. 17 she, 'Dear Duncan,] she, "Dear Duncan, (*Sharpe's*) [Katie's letter is read aloud within Duncan's soliloquy]
p. 118, l. 26 ye'se] yese (*Sharpe's*)
p. 118, l. 34 sic a touzle.'] sic a touzle." (*Sharpe's*) [not the end of Duncan's soliloquy but only of Katie's letter within it]
p. 118, l. 35 laughing too."] laughing too. (*Sharpe's*) [end of Duncan's soliloquy]

Friendship's Offering
Seven published contributions

Although *Friendship's Offering* began publication as early as 1824 and continued in modified form up to 1844 Hogg contributed only to the issues for 1829 and 1830. The beginning of his connection with this annual was related to a change of ownership, when the firm of Smith, Elder and Co. replaced Lupton Relfe as publisher and Hogg's old friend Thomas Pringle replaced Thomas K. Hervey as editor. Smith, Elder and Co. seem to have acquired this annual so late in 1827 as to make its production in time for Christmas rather a rushed affair, as the 'Preface' to the volume for 1828 (pp. v–viii) relates: 'The Proprietors have, indeed, had many disadvantages to contend with, from the very short space of time allotted to its preparation; whilst the Editor had to succeed, at an advanced period of the year, to the duties which had previously been performed by a gentleman of acknowledged taste and ability' (p. v). Alexander Elder seems to have acted as the centre of an expatriate group of literary Scotsmen in London, as Hogg demonstrates in his letter to him of 14 January 1833 (Beinecke Rare Book & Manuscript Library, Yale University,

James Hogg Collection, GEN MSS 61, Box 1, Folder 8) in sending compliments to 'kind-hearted, honest, pragmatical Pringle and all our other Scottish literati that congregate about you'. There is no indication, however, that Hogg was intimate with Elder before his 1832 visit to London. Thomas Pringle, on the other hand, was an old friend, the author of the 'Epistle to Mr. R— S—' in Hogg's *The Poetic Mirror* (London: Longman; Edinburgh: John Ballantyne, 1816), pp. 27–51 and the man whom Hogg had suggested to William Blackwood as a suitable editor for his newly-projected magazine in 1817 (see 'Memoir', pp. 43–44). Pringle had recently returned from South Africa to London, and having accepted the editorship of *Friendship's Offering* wrote a number of letters to Hogg appealing for his assistance as a contributor. His letter to Hogg of 22 May 1828 (NLS, MS 2245, fols 118–19) is clearly a final appeal, saying 'if your other avocations do not admit of your sending me even a scrap of poetry I w^d never think of importuning you on that score. Only write to tell me so', adding a characteristic sentence of Scottish solidarity: 'Cunningham & I though editors of rival Annuals have agreed to write for each other in scorn of the paltry jealousy which actuates some of our compeers'. Hogg must have replied immediately with some of his literary manuscripts, for Pringle wrote again less than a week later on 28 May 1828 (NLS, MS 2245, fols 122–23) to acknowledge their receipt and give more specific details of terms of payment and the kind of material he wished to include in his annual. *Friendship's Offering* was to pay a liberal 12 guineas a sheet, comparing very favourably with the 10 guineas a sheet paid to Hogg by *Blackwood's Edinburgh Magazine* (see Blackwood's letter to John Grieve of 13 February 1833, in NLS, MS 30,313, pp. 80–83), especially in view of the difference between the letterpress contained in a sheet of an annual and in the sixteen-page double-columned magazine sheet. The real difficulty in Hogg's contributing to this annual lay in Pringle's excessively cautious approach to what was then termed 'delicacy', a careful avoidance of all explicit sexual allusion and / or theological unorthodoxy. Pringle, though admiring a 'strange wild ballad' Hogg had sent him for its 'wild originality' rejected it in terms that irresistibly recall Dickens's Mr Podsnap, because of his rule 'to admit not a single expression which would call up a blush in the cheek of the most delicate female if reading aloud to a mixt company' (NLS, MS 2245, fol. 123). The difference of outlook plainly recurred, Pringle telling Hogg on 1 June 1831 (in Garden, pp. 224–27) that his publisher and literary friend 'did not think your prose tale quite suitable for the book, it seems—its humour, they say, was *too broad*'. Pringle was still anxious, however, that Hogg should contribute to his annual, urging him to write a short poem for it on the death of their mutual friend James Gray, and even alluding in a good-humoured way to Hogg's 'quizzing me with other annualists in *Blackwood* this month [...]', a reference to Hogg's poem 'The Miser's Grave' in *Blackwood's Edinburgh Magazine*, 29 (June 1831), 915–18. Hogg presumably tired of Pringle's particularity, and discontinued his contributions.

Hogg's earlier willingness to serve his old friend is demonstrated in the seven items, all but one in verse, that he contributed to *Friendship's Offering* for

1829 and 1830, and in the care with which most of these were suited to Pringle's specific requirements.

Auld Joe Nicholson's Bonny Nannie (pp. 123–24)

'Auld Joe Nicholson's Bonny Nannie' was first published in *Friendship's Offering* for 1829, pp. 263–64, and though undated was presumably one of a number of shorter pieces sent to Pringle to replace the 'strange wild ballad' rejected by Pringle in his letter of 28 May 1828 (see above). It certainly fulfils Pringle's criterion of total inoffensiveness, being a metrically-lively celebration of the charms of a pretty and innocent young country girl.

Hogg's song was reprinted in 'Noctes Ambrosianae. No. XL' in the December 1828 issue of *Blackwood's Edinburgh Magazine* (vol. 24, p. 688) where North notes admiringly, 'You have sent that song to our friend Pringle's Friendship's Offering—haven't you, James' and the Shepherd responds, 'I hae—and anither as gude or better–', a neatly-placed advertisement for *Friendship's Offering* as well as for song-writer James Hogg. It was subsequently included by Hogg in his *Songs (1831)*, pp. 268–70 with some minor alterations, mostly of spelling and punctuation.

As with 'Maggy o' Buccleuch' (see note above) Hogg's words were subsequently set to music. There is an undated copy of 'Niddity Noddity Nannie, A Ballad in the Scottish Style' with words by the Ettrick Shepherd and music by 'J. Blewit' in the British Library (H.1650.gg.(16)). Promoted as 'Sung by Mr Wilson with Great Applause at the Theatre Royal Covent Garden' it was published by Mori & Lavenn of 28 New Bond Street priced at two shillings. It has not been possible to determine whether or not Hogg knew of this theatrical number, or whether he received anything for its publication.

'Auld Joe Nicholson's Bonny Nannie' is reprinted in the present volume from *Friendship's Offering* without change.

Ballad (pp. 124–25)

Hogg's 'Ballad' was first published in *Friendship's Offering* for 1829, pp. 415–16, and although undated is perhaps one of a group of poems sent to Pringle to replace the 'strange wild ballad' rejected in Pringle's letter of 28 May 1828 (see above). In requesting a poem for 'The Minstrel Boy' (see below) Pringle had shown that verse reflecting Hogg's own life-experiences would be welcome, and 'Ballad' is also a poem of this type. He subsequently described it as 'written in detestation of the behaviour of a gentleman (can I call him so?) to a dearly-beloved young relative of my own, and whom, at the time I wrote this, I never expected to recover from the shock her kind and affectionate heart had received' (*Songs (1831)*, p. 271). The broken-hearted girl in question was Mary Gray, the niece of Hogg's wife and daughter to his old Edinburgh friend James Gray. When Gray and his second wife went to India early in 1826 his daughters Mary and Janet had not accompanied him because both were engaged to be married: instead they were left at Mount Benger in the care of their aunt, Margaret Hogg. However, neither of these engagements came to anything, and Mary was apparently broken-hearted at being jilted—see Mary Gray Garden, *Margaret Phillips (Wife of The Ettrick Shepherd)* (Privately printed for family circulation, 1898), pp. 13–14.

'Ballad' was subsequently revised and reprinted as 'The Broken Heart' in *Songs (1831)*, pp. 271–73, Hogg's manuscript for this version surviving in NLS, MS 4805, fol. 84. The revised version tones down the girl's initial despair, and also removes the specific location of Yarrow in the final stanza, so that there are in fact two versions, the one appropriate to the present volume being that in *Friendship's Offering* for 1829. It is printed here without change.

Verses to a Beloved Young Friend (pp. 125–26)

'Verses to a Beloved Young Friend', like 'Ballad', was first published in *Friendship's Offering* for 1829, pp. 417–18, and is also concerned with Margaret Hogg's niece, Mary Gray. After the engagements of Mary and Janet Gray had been broken it seems to have been decided that they should go out to India to rejoin their father, after an interval of visits among their other Scottish relations. When Hogg wrote to Blackwood on 15 July 1828 (NLS, MS 4021, fol. 281) the girls were clearly in Edinburgh, for he wrote, 'I am moreover uncertain that every day I may not be summoned to town to take leave of my young friends and perhaps be obliged to accompany them to London'. A subsequent letter of 27 August [1828] sent from Altrive to Margaret Hogg in Edinburgh reveals that the two girls were still in Edinburgh and that Hogg no longer intended to see them embark for India: the 'Verses to a Beloved Young Friend' are almost certainly the 'few verses' written for Mary Gray as his farewell gift to her:

> My great desire was to see my two dear girls on shipboard and see how they were accommodated and under whose care but now harvest having come on and not one of my summer bargains sold it is out of my power to get to Liverpool but perhaps it may yet be in my power to see them before leaving Scotland I inclose for Mary the few verses I promised her and am sorry I have not had the opportunity of inserting it in her Album and to Jannet I send an inscription to be bound in with a copy of The Queen's Wake for which I enclose her an order on Mr Blackwood. Would to God it had been in my power to have bestowed something more valuable on two that I love so truly and with all my heart but a simple memorial of my affection is all I have to bestow. (Norah Parr, *James Hogg at Home: Being the Domestic Life and Letters of the Ettrick Shepherd* (Dollar: Douglas S. Mack, 1980), pp. 57–58)

Hogg's poem commemorates Mary's departure from his house at Mount Benger, the 'last look' being his last sight of her as well as her last sight of his Yarrow home, both of course prefiguring the ultimate parting of death. Hogg's poem in *Friendship's Offering* is dated '*Mount Benger on Yarrow,* | *June* 17, 1828' whereas Hogg's letter accompanying the verses sent to Mary Gray was written on 27 August. It may be that the date of the published poem is a part of its meaning rather than the true date of composition, the date when Mary

Gray actually said farewell to Hogg and to Mount Benger. At any rate there are clearly two versions of these verses, a private one for family circulation and one for publication in an annual. In *Songs (1831)*, p. 273 Hogg cites a different version of lines 21–24 of this poem and follows this with four lines that do not occur in it at all, presumably quoted from the private version for Mary Gray's album. As these are not part of the public version of 'Verses to a Beloved Young Friend' it would not be appropriate to integrate them into the present text. However, they are given below for the reader's interest:

> Woe to the guileful tongue that bred
>   This disappointment and this pain!
> Cold-hearted villain! on his head
>   A minstrel's malison remain!
> Guilt from his brow let ne'er depart,
>   Nor shame until his dying day;
> For he has broke the kindest heart
>   That ever bow'd to nature's sway!

'Verses to a Beloved Young Friend' is printed in the present volume from *Friendship's Offering* without change.

The Minstrel Boy (pp. 126–31)
When Pringle rejected Hogg's 'strange wild ballad' in his letter of 28 May 1828 (see above) he suggested an alternative contribution in its place, requesting that Hogg should write for one of the engravings ordered for *Friendship's Offering* for 1829:

> You w^d doubly oblige me if you could give me a few lines or stanzas under the title of "The Minstrel Boy"–for the illustration of one of our plates. It is a boy of perhaps 7 or 8 years of age with a shepherds pipe in his hand & a highland bonnet & plaid lying beside him–lying in the midst of a scene of wild magnificence–woods, hills and waterfalls. In short the idea seems to be taken from Beattie's Edwin–only the boy is rather young even for my idea of Edwin's earliest minstrelsy. But if the subject pleases you never mind age.–but give me some of the glorious romance of your own boyhood when the spirit of poetry & romance first began to pour over you the visions of fairyland which afterwards found expression in the immortal "Kilmeny", & others of your loftiest Lays.

The child in this picture of 'The Minstrel Boy', engraved by A. Duncan from a painting by C. R. Leslie, is a rather genteel version of the comparatively untended and ragged boy Hogg describes in his 'Memoir', pp. 12–13, but he did his best to fulfil Pringle's directions in this poem dated '*Mount-Benger, June 14, 1828*'. Hogg describes the pictured child in visionary Kilmeny-like terms, as a possible 'child of my loved Fairy Queen', emphasising his beauty and unproved potential as a contrast to the poet's own knowledge and experience and to his own childhood strivings after excellence. The poem thus set the characteristic tone of Hogg's contributions to *Friendship's Offering* in being a sentimental account of his own life-experiences.

Hogg's manuscript of 'The Minstrel Boy' has not apparently survived and it was not reprinted in his lifetime. The poem is given here from *Friendship's Offering* for 1829, with the following change:

l. 109 Was the pupil] Was it the pupil (*Friendship's Offering*)

A Scots Luve Sang (pp. 131–32)

'A Scots Luve Sang' was published in *Friendship's Offering* for 1830, pp. 185–86. Its first appearance had been as early as 8 December 1810 as 'Scotch Song' in no. 15 of *The Spy*, an admiring tribute to the then Margaret Phillips, whom Hogg met at about this time although he did not marry her until almost ten years later–see *The Spy*, ed. by Gillian Hughes (S/SC, 2000), pp. 163, 595. Subsequently Hogg sent it to the Scottish song-collector George Thomson in his letter of 25 October 1815 (see *Letters 1*) to be set to music, and it was published in the fifth volume of Thomson's folio edition of *A Select Collection of Original Scottish Airs* (1818), no. 204. Hogg, however, appears to have carefully revised and altered his verses for each of their subsequent appearances, the most noticeable differences being in the second stanza, so that each forms a distinct version. 'A Scots Luve Sang' in *Friendship's Offering* for 1830 is thus a third version of the lines, and a fourth printing subsequently formed part of *Songs (1831)*, pp. 196–97 (though this appears to be a reprinting of the words from Thomson's musical setting of 1818). Part of Hogg's manuscript for this version survives in NLS, MS 4805, fol. 76. There are no indications in Hogg's surviving correspondence of when he sent 'A Scots Luve Sang' to London for *Friendship's Offering*, and his manuscript for this version does not appear to have survived. An undated manuscript 'Sang' in the Pierpont Morgan Library, New York (MA 2406 R–V Autogr. Misc. Eng.) consists of only the first and third stanzas of the poem, signed by Hogg at the end, and was probably produced as an autograph. The following change has been made to the present text, reprinted from *Friendship's Offering* for 1830:

l. 6 teazing crony] teazing wony (*Friendship's Offering*)

The Fords of Callum (pp. 132–37)

'The Fords of Callum. An Ower True Tale' was published in *Friendship's Offering* for 1830, pp. 187–96, Hogg's only prose contribution to this annual. It is dated '*Mount Benger on Yarrow, | June 15, 1829*' and was presumably sent to London not long afterwards: it may or may not be the tale referred to in an undated letter from Hogg to Pringle (Fales Library & Special Collections, New York University, Fales MS 89: 20), 'I have dashed you off a ghost story but in spite of my teeth it has run on to too great a length'.

Although this is a splendidly eerie supernatural tale with characteristically humorous touches it seems less specifically tailored to Pringle's taste than Hogg's other contributions to *Friendship's Offering*–Pringle might well have objected, for example, to the clear implication that Annie Douglas is not the child of her mother's husband but the offspring of an illicit long-past love-affair.

Hogg's manuscript has not apparently survived, and the tale was not reprinted during his lifetime. However, the earlier editions of Hogg's prose tales produced after his death by the firm of Blackie and Son of Glasgow were apparently printed partly at least from copy provided by Hogg in his final years in preparation for an edition of his collected prose tales. Hogg's revisions are alluded to in the prefatory 'Advertisement' to the six-volume *Tales and Sketches by the Ettrick Shepherd* published in 1836–37, which nevertheless reveals a nervousness about sexual and religious reference that undoubtedly led to a degree of bowdlerisation. 'The Fords of Callum' does not appear in this 1836–37 edition, but does appear in a later undated reprint which seems to consist of the same sheets as the 1836–37 edition with the exception of the second volume, where 'The Bush Aboon Traquair' has been replaced by several of Hogg's tales, including 'The Fords of Callum', occupying pages 332–38. The possibility that this substituted copy may have been revised by Hogg, however, seems to be remote when the two versions are compared. The later version appears to have been set from a copy of the text in *Friendship's Offering*, with two important cuts near the beginning. These cuts eliminate Wat and Janet Douglas's scepticism about spiritual beings and Hogg's assertion that they were wrong in this and may have been made from a desire to avoid the implication that Hogg was superstitious, but it is also possible that the tale was truncated so that it did not overrun the space originally allocated to 'The Bush Aboon Traquair' (pp. 275–338) in the 1836–37 edition.

The present text is taken from *Friendship's Offering* for 1830, with the following changes:

p. 135, l. 5 "Ay, but] Ay, but (*Friendship's Offering*)
p. 136, l. 6 venture forward] venture foreward (*Friendship's Offering*) [a 'foreward'
    is the front rank of an army]
p. 136, l. 37 She was] Shewas (*Friendship's Offering*)

A Bard's Address to his Youngest Daughter (pp. 138–39)

'A Bard's Address to his Youngest Daughter', like several of Hogg's other poems for *Friendship's Offering*, relates to his own life-experiences, in this case his relationship with his third daughter, Harriet Sidney Hogg, born on 18 December 1827 (Yarrow OPR). As in the case of 'Verses to a Beloved Young Friend' there appear to have been two versions of this poem, one written for the person addressed and primarily for a family readership and another intended for publication. Peter Garside has outlined the publication history of 'A Bard's Address to his Youngest Daughter' in his edition of *A Queer Book* (S/ SC, 1995), pp. 252–53. It was first published in *Friendship's Offering* for 1830, pp. 312–14, and subsequently in *A Queer Book* published by William Blackwood in 1832, pp. 239–42: a surviving manuscript of the poem appears to be that of a private version for family reading, rather than the one on which the version in *Friendship's Offering* was based, and it is this version of 'A Bard's

Address to his Youngest Daughter' that has been published in Garside's volume within the Stirling / South Carolina Edition (pp. 144–46 with textual and explanatory notes on pp. 251–53).

Hogg's published version of the poem, however, is also of considerable interest and the present volume therefore includes it, complementing the private version given in the Stirling / South Carolina Edition volume of *A Queer Book*. Hogg's manuscript for this version does not appear to have survived, and a comparison of the versions published in *Friendship's Offering* and *A Queer Book* (Edinburgh, 1832), pp. 239–42 reveals that the two printings made in Hogg's lifetime are substantially the same, with the exception of a ten-line section beginning 'And now, sweet child, one boon I crave' given in *A Queer Book* but not in the earlier version of *Friendship's Offering*. As Hogg's manuscript for *Friendship's Offering* does not appear to have survived, it is impossible to tell whether or not it included this passage: Peter Garside has noted (p. 252) that in *Friendship's Offering* 'the poem ends exactly at the foot of page 314' concluding that there is a possibility that 'cuts were made to make space in the periodical itself' (p. 252), but has also suggested the alternative possibility that in preparing his text for *A Queer Book* of 1832 Hogg was almost certainly working from his memory of the private version which was current in his family (p. 253). It is therefore impossible to say which of the two printed versions most closely resembles the missing manuscript sent to Pringle for inclusion in *Friendship's Offering*.

The editors of the present volume have therefore decided to use as their copy-text the version that was actually read by the purchasers of *Friendship's Offering*, supplementing this here with the additional lines published in *A Queer Book* of 1832, which come between lines 22 and 23 of the present text:

> And now, sweet child, one boon I crave,–
> And pout not, for that boon I'll have,–
> One kiss I ask for grandam's sake,
> Who never saw thy tiny make;
> And one for her who left us late,
> Laid low, but not forgotten yet;
> And thy sweet mother, too, the nearest
> To thee and me, the kindest, dearest,–
> Thou sacred, blest memorial,
> When I kiss thee, I kiss them all!

'A Bard's Address to his Youngest Daughter' is reprinted in the present volume from *Friendship's Offering* for 1830 without change.

The Musical Bijou

*Three published contributions: one additional unpublished
contribution and one additional part-published contribution
are included in the present volume*

The success of the early annuals led to the development of sub-species, as the editor of *The Musical Bijou* noted in the preface to his first volume produced for 1829:

> Among the numerous and elegant Annuals presented to the notice of the public, none have as yet been produced of a character blending the sister Arts of Poetry and Music; with such an impulse the Editor submits to public attention the first volume of The Musical Bijou, trusting that the names contained in the list of contributors will at least secure for it the same degree of patronage that has attended its literary brethren.

Hogg, as a well-known Scottish song-writer and editor of *Jacobite Relics* (1819–21), was a desirable contributor to this miscellany of prose tales, poems, and printed music for singing. His connection seems to have been rather with the annual's publishers, Goulding & D'Almaine of 20 Soho Square, London, than with its editor, F. H. Burney. This firm were the publishers of Hogg's song-collection *Select and Rare Scotish Melodies* produced at about this time and containing thirteen songs with words by Hogg and music by the fashionable composer Henry Rowley Bishop (1786–1855). The collection was a stylish printing of songs for drawing-room performance, priced at twelve shillings and dedicated to the Ladies Ann, Margaret, and Harriet Scott of Buccleuch 'By their devoted Bard, | The Ettrick Shepherd'. Hogg seems to have been proud of it, writing to Allan Cunningham on 17 October 1828, 'There is a musical work of mine publishing in London just now which looks like as it would do me some credit. The music is most beautifully set and arranged by Bishop' (Beinecke Rare Book & Manuscript Library, Yale University, James Hogg Collection, GEN MSS 61, Box 1, Folder 7). Although Bishop is widely criticised now for his maladroit adaptations of music by Mozart, Rossini, and Beethoven, his contemporaries viewed him as a leading composer, especially for his songs, which were produced at the London theatres of Covent Garden and Drury Lane and at Vauxhall Gardens, each of these establishments employing him as musical director at different times. (Even today Bishop's 'Home Sweet Home' is still well-known.) From his letter to Goulding & D'Almaine of 17 March 1829 (Beinecke Rare Book & Manuscript Library, Yale University, James Hogg Collection, GEN MSS 61, Box 1, Folder 11) Hogg subsequently tried to persuade them to publish a selection of his Cameronian songs, indicating his contentment with *Select and Rare Scotish Melodies*. It seems likely that Hogg had sent the firm a number of songs, some of which were combined into *Select and Rare Scotish Melodies* and others chosen to appear in the new musical annual, for Hogg wrote to complain that 'there is also one of my best songs a wanting out of the *select melodies* as well as your other work'.

The financial terms upon which Hogg contributed to *The Musical Bijou* for 1829 are unknown, but his work was handsomely featured within its pages, his two songs being set to music by Bishop as a prominent composer and the words being also printed separately on another page. This makes it somewhat surprising that only one song of his appeared (without music) in *The*

Musical Bijou for 1830, and none thereafter, although the annual continued to be produced in modified form until at least 1838.

The Harp of Ossian (pp. 143–48)

This song first appeared in *The Musical Bijou* for 1829, pp. 2–7, the words by Hogg being given first on a single page and then slightly adapted and set to music by Henry Rowley Bishop, and it was subsequently revised and re-printed without the music in *Songs (1831)*, pp. 75–76. (Hogg's manuscript for this version is in NLS, MS 4805, fols 42–43.) It was probably one of a group of songs sent to Goulding & D'Almaine, of which some were included in *Select and Rare Scotish Melodies* (see above). The title of the song evokes the ancient Scottish bard Ossian, and it accordingly expresses Hogg's regret over the loss of a distinctively Scottish national identity. This is unusual, for Hogg generally proposes a continuity of feeling between the ancient Scottish Highlander and the modern inhabitant of North Britain—see for example his earliest song 'Donald Macdonald', where the Jacobite who fought for 'Charlie' is now the stalwart supporter of 'Geordie' against Napoleon. Hogg's subsequent comments suggest that this expression of his regret for a lost national independence was received unfavourably by some of his contemporaries:

> I have been sorely blamed by some friends for a sentiment expressed
> in this song; but I have always felt it painfully that the name of SCOT-
> LAND, the superior nation in every thing but wealth, should be lost,
> not in Britain, for that is proper, but in England. In all dispatches we
> are denominated *the English*, forsooth! We know ourselves, however,
> that we are not English, nor ever intend to be. (*Songs (1831)*, p. 75)

'The Harp of Ossian' is given in the present volume from the version printed in *The Musical Bijou* for 1829, as the one most appropriate to a collection of Hogg's contributions to the annuals. (Hogg's manuscript for this version does not appear to have survived, and the later version belongs to *Songs (1831)*.) *The Musical Bijou* for 1829 in effect contains two slightly different versions of Hogg's words, an independent set of verses written by Hogg and Hogg's verses as adapted to music by Bishop: while it is possible that the differences between the two could be the result of hasty transcription by Bishop or the musical engraver it seems more likely that they represent deliberate changes intended to guide the performance of the singer. Hogg seems to have accepted such minor adjustments quite happily, describing 'The Harp of Ossian' as 'finely set by H. R. Bishop, in one of the Musical Bijous' (*Songs (1831)*, p. 75). The present volume therefore gives an edited text of Hogg's words from p. 2 of the *Musical Bijou* for 1829, followed by a facsimile of those words as adapted by Bishop to music from pages 3–7. The following emendation has been made to Hogg's independent verses:

l. 2 cave of the correi] cave of the Correi (*The Musical Bijou*) [correi is a
     landscape feature, not a proper name]

In addition the rather confusing speech marks of the printing in *The Musical*

Bijou, which occur at the start of every line in the second and third stanza, have been regularised so that they occur only at the start of the speech, the start of the third stanza, and at the end of the speech.

My Emma, My Darling (pp. 149–53)

The textual history of this song parallels that of 'The Harp of Ossian' exactly: it seems probable that it formed one of a group of songs sent to Goulding & D'Almaine from which a selection was made for both *Select and Rare Scottish Melodies* and the firm's new musical annual. It was set to music by the fashionable composer Henry Rowley Bishop and published in *The Musical Bijou* for 1829 (pp. 93, 100–03), being subsequently revised and printed without the music in *Songs (1831)* (pp. 85–86).

'My Emma, My Darling' clearly shows Hogg tailoring his work to the drawing-rooms of London. Members of fashionable society would spend the autumn on their country estates and then proceed to London for the winter season, a movement which Emma is urged to make likewise from 'winter's domain' in the country to 'the glee of the city' with its balls and other amusements. Hogg himself also sometimes spent the autumn in country sports at Altrive, and then had a winter trip to Edinburgh visiting friends and publishers and enjoying the social life of the Scottish capital.

'My Emma, My Darling' is given in the present volume from *The Musical Bijou* for 1829. Hogg's manuscript for this version does not appear to have survived, but the manuscript for the version in *Songs (1831)* is at NLS, MS 4805, fol. 46. Hogg's words as set to music by Bishop differ in punctuation and capitalisation from his words printed independently within *The Musical Bijou,* perhaps as a result of Bishop's wish to guide a singer in performance. The present volume therefore gives an edited text of Hogg's words from p. 93 of *The Musical Bijou* for 1829 (in fact without change), followed by a facsimile of those words as adapted by Bishop to music from pages 100 to 103.

O Weel Befa' the Guileless Heart (p. 154)

In a note in his *Songs (1831)* (pp. 117–18), Hogg stated that this song had been composed on a visit to John Wilson at his house of Elleray near Windermere in the Lake District, a visit which also produced 'Superstition', a poem he first published in his *Pilgrims of the Sun* in 1815. Hogg's visit to Elleray in September 1814 thus gives a rough date of composition for the piece.

It was originally published as the conclusion to Act Two of Hogg's incomplete fairy-drama 'The Haunted Glen', in his *Dramatic Tales,* 2 vols (London: Longman; Edinburgh: John Ballantyne, 1817), II, 189–271 (pp. 269–70), and when 'The Haunted Glen' was reprinted in his four-volume *Poetical Works (1822),* II, 179–228 (pp. 227–28) it was virtually unaltered, minor differences in punctuation and orthography probably being accounted for by the change of house-style that came with a change of publisher.

Songs from the Shepherd were always in demand for inclusion in the 'Noctes Ambrosianae' of *Blackwood's Edinburgh Magazine,* and in an undated letter to William Blackwood of [June 1826] Hogg included a note for the fictitious

'Christopher North', stating 'Last night we were at Ambrose's you asked me for one or two pastoral love songs. I send you them An edition of the one was once published I know not where or when but not at all I believe as it is here' (NLS, MS 4017, fol. 141). 'O weel befa' the maiden gay,' duly appeared (together with 'Bonny Mary') in *Blackwood's Edinburgh Magazine*, 20 (July 1826), 108, and Blackwood from his letter to Hogg of 24 June 1826 (NLS, MS 30,309, pp. 229–30) was well pleased with both songs: 'They enliven the Noctes, and I hope you will send me some more very soon. I have credited your acc^t with two Guineas for them'. Hogg's song from 'The Haunted Glen' had been substantially rewritten to appear in *Blackwood's*—there are many verbal changes, the introduction of a new stanza and the removal of stanza two to the end of the song. Hogg's magazine song therefore represents a distinct version which belongs with his other contributions to *Blackwood's Edinburgh Magazine*.

On 24 August 1829 Hogg wrote to the firm of Goulding & D'Almaine (Lilly Library, Indiana University, Bloomington, IN, English Literature MSS), including in his letter the text of three songs in what he termed 'my own wild stile' intended as contributions to *The Musical Bijou* for 1830. In preparing the first of these, 'O weel befa' the guileless heart', he plainly returned to 'The Haunted Glen' rather than making use of the version published in *Blackwood's* for July 1826 since it corresponds to the three verses of the 1817 version. Hogg clearly revised that, however, to suit it to an annuals context, making a number of substantive changes of which the most significant is probably a completely new line 5. He also added an instruction for the composer H. R. Bishop, who had set his contributions to the previous year's volume of *The Musical Bijou*: 'The above song was written to a very old air the original of The Wauking o' the Fauld. If Mr Bishop would therefore approximate the air to that it would please me best'. Clearly Hogg had created a distinct version of 'O Weel Befa' the Guileless Heart' which he intended to be set to music and published in this musical annual.

Goulding & D'Almaine did not use the song Hogg sent them in his letter of 24 August 1829 for *The Musical Bijou* for 1830, but a very similar song was published in another London musical publication shortly afterwards, in the *Monthly Musical and Literary Magazine* for February 1830 (p. 30) where it was simply entitled 'Song. By the Ettrick Shepherd'. The differences between Hogg's manuscript and the magazine version can probably be attributed to a wish to make the song more accessible to an English readership. For instance, each of the three printed stanzas has for its final line 'That smiles in yonder glen', whereas only the third stanza in the manuscript version concludes with this line, the others ending 'That wons in yonder glen'. It seems likely that *wons*, meaning 'lives' or 'dwells', was incomprehensible to the magazine's English editor or compositor, who also failed to understand the second line of the song in Hogg's manuscript, 'In cottage, bught, or pen' and instead printed 'In cottage bright, or pen'. From this it seems unlikely that Hogg saw proofs of the song in the *Monthly Musical and Literary Magazine*, and at least possible that the transfer of Hogg's manuscript was effected in London unbeknown to him. For further information about this short-lived periodical see Gillian Hughes, 'Hogg and the *Monthly Musical and Literary Magazine*', *Studies in Hogg and his World*, 15 (2004), 120–25.

Hogg's song subsequently appeared in *Songs (1831)* (pp. 117–20), the manuscript for which survives in NLS, MS 4805, fols 52–53. This appears to be a further revision of the version published in *Blackwood's Edinburgh Magazine* for July 1826. A second appearance in *Blackwood's Edinburgh Magazine*, 29 (1831), 546–47 was clearly designed to advertise the publication of Hogg's 1831 song collection.

'O Weel Befa' the Guileless Heart' has a common origin to 'O Weel Befa' the Maiden Gay' in that both derive from 'The Haunted Glen', but it was developed quite independently. It is printed here from Hogg's letter to Goulding & D'Almaine of 24 August 1829 as one of his contributions to *The Musical Bijou* for 1830. The tune to which it was written ('The Wauking o' the Fauld') is named after the title, so that, although Mr Bishop can no longer 'approximate the air to that', a modern reader may bear it in mind. The following emendations have also been made:

l. 1 weel befa'] weel befa (MS) [as at lines 3 and 9]
l. 23 'Tis] Tis (MS) [as at line 21]

Fairy Songs (pp. 155–57)

This contribution to *The Musical Bijou* for 1830 also originated in lines from Hogg's fairy drama 'The Haunted Glen', published in *Dramatic Tales*, 2 vols (Edinburgh, 1817), II, 189–271 (pp. 238–39 and 267–68). Both passages are addressed to the fairies by Lu, a being part mortal and part fairy, who must choose between becoming King of the fairies or the lover of the country maiden Lula. The relevant lines were then reprinted almost verbatim with the rest of Hogg's fairy-drama in his *Poetical Works (1822)*, II, 217–18 and 225–27.

In shaping these two sections of his fairy drama for *The Musical Bijou* Hogg abandoned their previous dramatic context, uniting the two passages and adopting a more conventional scenario of a group of fairies headed by their Queen, probably already sensing the Victorian fairy obsession that led to Gilbert and Sullivan's *Iolanthe* among other musical and theatrical productions. Directions such as '*Queen of the fairies–sings*' and '*Chorus of fairies*' imply that Hogg expected his words to be set to music (probably by Bishop) for drawing-room or concert performance by a female soloist and accompanying chorus. For the first song Hogg's manuscript follows 'The Haunted Glen' almost exactly except for being much more lightly punctuated, but the second was extensively revised: some lines are cut, fresh lines are introduced, and the overall form and rhythmn of a three-verse song is constructed from what was formerly a passage of verse narrative.

Only the second of these fairy songs was published in *The Musical Bijou* for 1830 with the title of 'The Song of Oberon' (p. 7), and no musical setting was provided. The change of title was presumably made by the annual's editor with the object of associating Hogg's fairy verse with Shakespeare's *A Midsummer Night's Dream*, though interestingly it makes the speaker male again, as in the original version included in 'The Haunted Glen'.

The present editors recognise the importance of Hogg's conception of two linked songs and have chosen to print them together from his fair-copy manuscript as he intended, though of course without the musical setting he expected to be created for them. 'The Song of Oberon' published in the rare annual, *The Musical Bijou* for 1830, is of some interest too, though, so it is also printed in the present volume. 'Fairy Songs' is printed from Hogg's manuscript without change.

The Amulet
Seven published contributions: two additional unpublished contributions are included in the present volume

The subtitle of *The Amulet: A Christian and Literary Remembrancer* clearly indicates that it was intended for a more serious and a more evangelically-inclined readership than most of the annuals. Although the first issue was published for 1826 Hogg's involvement seems to have arisen when the annual changed publisher with the issue for 1829 from Baynes and Sons to Westley & Davis, who employed Samuel Carter Hall as editor. Hall's application to Hogg for his assistance was well-received from Hogg's reply of 15 March [1829]: 'I certainly wish well to the Amulet from the sweet and heavenly spirit manifested throughout and there is no species of composition I am fond of than such as have a religious tendency' (Fales Library & Special Collections, New York University, Fales MS 89: 20). The only problem was that he had agreed to write exclusively for the 1830 issues of *The Anniversary* (edited by Cunningham) and *Friendship's Offering* (edited by Pringle) for a sum of £35—see Cunningham's letter to Hogg of 23 December 1828, NLS, MS 2245, fols 136–37. However, Hogg felt that as Hall's annual 'embraces a different sphere of literature my contributions to it could hardly be detrimental to either of their's' and Hall therefore obtained permission from Cunningham and Pringle for Hogg to write for *The Amulet* too—see his letter to Hogg of 8 April [1829] (NLS, MS 2245, fols 144–45), in which he expressed his hope of receiving 'a prose tale and a poem from you at your earliest convenience'. Hall had also sent Hogg a copy of *The Amulet* for 1829 so that he would have an idea of the general tone of the work: in his letter to Hall of 17 April 1829 (NLS, MS 1002, fols 104–05) Hogg accordingly promised to 'send off immediately two articles in prose and two in verse', adding:

> I have some charges to give you which I lay strictly on all editors. "Be sure to preserve such M. S. S. as do not suit your miscellany and return them" for I write all off hand and have no duplicates And for the same reason "Take every liberty of pruning adding or diminishing" to suit the fastidious taste of the day for I am like Gallio I care for none of those things. You are sure to have something rather original from me but all of them will be no the worse of going over [...].

Peter Garside in his article 'Vision and Revision: Hogg's MS Poems in the Turnbull Library' in *Studies in Hogg and his World*, 5 (1994), 82–95, has demonstrated that Hogg shaped his work through a series of drafts, commonly keeping an earlier draft manuscript when he sent his fair copy one to an editor or publisher. One possible reason for Hogg's insistence on the return of his manuscripts here and elsewhere is that he wished to keep track of the publication of his work and of the payments made to him on that account. An unscrupulous editor might retain a manuscript for subsequent unauthorised and unpaid publication, and Hall himself appears to have behaved in this way to Coleridge over his 'Fragments of a Journey Over the Brocken' (see Introduction, p. xxxix note 40). Hogg contributed seven items, two in prose and five in verse, to *The Amulet* and the present volume also includes two further items sent specifically to Hall for this particular annual though not actually published there.

A Lay of the Martyrs (pp. 161–67)
Peter Garside provides the following introductory and textual notes to this poem in his edition of *A Queer Book* (S/SC, 1995), pp. 239–40:

> Originally published in *The Amulet* for 1830, pp. 145–54, this was the first poem featured in the *Queer Book* to have an origin in the annuals rather than in *Blackwood's Edinburgh Magazine*. On 8 April 1829 S. C. Hall, the *Amulet*'s editor, had invited 'a prose tale and a poem from you at your earliest convenience' (NLS, MS 2245, fol. 144). Hogg not only acted expeditiously, but also heeded Hall's tacit warning about the need for respectability in a religious publication. Two poems were offered, an early version of 'Elen of Reigh' and 'A Lay of the Martyrs'. Hall's letter of 25 June 1829 indicates that proofs of the latter had already been seen by Hogg: 'I have to apologise for so long delaying my reply to your most welcome communications–"a tale of Pentland" & "a tale of the Martyrs" I have printed in the Amulet, and duly received the corrected proofs from you' (NLS, MS 2245, fol. 148).
>
> From childhood Hogg had heard stories about the persecution of the Covenanters in later 17th-century Scotland, and his first published novel, *The Brownie of Bodsbeck* (1818), drew heavily on family traditions in Ettrick. As a shepherd and farmer in the Nithsdale region *c.* 1805–09, he would also have come into contact with tales about atrocities committed by the Royalist forces in SW Scotland. Locations mentioned early in the 'Lay' connect its events with the wild mountainous country of Upper Nithsdale, to the east of Sanquhar (itself a centre of Covenanting resistance). Another probable source is Robert Wodrow's *The History of the Sufferings of the Church of Scotland* (1721–22), which Hogg knew intimately. More particularly, the incidents in the poem could stem from Wodrow's account of the Enterkin Pass Rescue, in July 1684, an ambush which led to the release of a number of Covenanting prisoners and ultimately to the execution of three participants in the Edinburgh Grassmarket the

following December. The harrassing of the country about Enterkin after the incident is described in some detail by Wodrow, and it seems likely that the poem's events in part reflect this situation.

The ballad was well suited for *The Amulet*, whose devout female readership would have identified with the Covenanters' plight, especially as seen from the vantage point of its two women speakers.

Textual Notes on 'A Lay of the Martyrs'
The present text is based on Item 63 in MS Papers 42 in the Turnbull Library, Wellington, New Zealand. With a full header at the beginning, it bears all the marks of a final manuscript copy by Hogg. The poem is written in double columns on both sides of a single sheet (*c.* 42cm x 26cm; watermark G WILMOT | 1827), in a similar pen stroke, and virtually without alteration. At the top another hand has written in pencil the legend 'Amulet', and the presence of printer's ink marks also points to this having been the copy used for setting in London. An earlier MS version also survives in the Turnbull collection. Item 40 consists of a 4-page booklet (leaf size 23cm x 18cm), bearing an 1825 watermark, and its packed pages are characteristic of Hogg's early drafts. Collation shows quite a few local changes between items 40 and 63, perhaps the result of the poem having been laid aside for a while previous to its writing up for *The Amulet*.

If Hogg did receive and return proofs, he can only have given them cursory attention. Deteriorations in *The Amulet* printed version include: the transference from Marley (as found in both Turnbull drafts) to Morley Reid; the interpretation of 'goodman' as 'good man'—most obtrusive among several anglicisations; and the disruption of Hogg's upper case 'C' when the Royalist 'captain' is being directly addressed. *The Amulet* also supplied standard punctuation, a process furthered by the *Queer Book* of 1832, which introduced a more complex system of speech marks.

The present text reproduces Hogg's final (unpunctuated) manuscript version, as found in Turnbull Item 63, with only the following alterations: the provision of speech marks at lines 113 and 228; the insertion of two commas in line 143; and the raising of 'god' to 'God' at line 226. 'Edinburgh' is also preferred to 'Edenburgh' at line 125, where the manuscript is ambiguous.

A Tale of Pentland (pp. 168–81)

This was originally published in *The Amulet* for 1830, pp. 219–41, and appears to have been sent to Hall in the spring of 1829 in response to his invitation to Hogg to contribute to his annual. Writing to Hogg on 25 June [1829] (NLS, MS 2245, fols 148–49) Hall apologised 'for so long delaying my reply to your most welcome communications—"a tale of Pentland" & "a tale of the Martyrs" I have printed in the Amulet, and duly received the corrected proofs from you—the remainder I return you herewith [...]'. 'A Tale of Pentland' seems to have originally been part of a collection of poetry and prose by

Hogg about the Scottish Covenanters, as he subsequently explained to William
Blackwood in his letter of 3 June 1829 (NLS, MS 4024, fols 292–93):

> The tale and ballad of the Covenanters are part of a series which I
> wrote last year for publication by themselves but I sent Allan
> Cunningham one Mr Hall another and this is a third so that the series
> is fairly broken up.

Hogg's tales about the sufferings of the Covenanters in the cause of their
religion were well-suited to the devout readership of *The Amulet*. This particular story seems to be an adaptation of a similar episode in the title-story of
The Brownie of Bodsbeck and Other Tales, 2 vols (Edinburgh: Blackwood; London:
Murray, 1818), II, 43–44 where Walter Laidlaw, returning to his own house
by night after his imprisonment looks through a window and sees his daughter Katherine sitting with her hands around the throat of a corpse, surrounded
by her band of seemingly unearthly associates: though she appears to be
involved in a murder she has in fact been nursing and comforting a dying
Covenanter.

Hogg's manuscript does not appear to have survived, and 'A Tale of
Pentland' was probably not reprinted by Hogg in his lifetime, although it did
appear in *The Cabinet of Literary Gems* (London: Renshaw, 1836), pp. 131–48. It
was included in *Tales and Sketches by the Ettrick Shepherd*, 6 vols (Glasgow: Blackie
& Son, 1836–37), I, 317–32, an edition which claimed to have the benefit of
Hogg's revisions during the final years of his life (see the prefatory 'Advertisement') while also revealing a nervousness about sexual and religious reference that undoubtedly led to a degree of bowdlerisation. A comparison of this
story in *Tales and Sketches* with the text in *The Amulet* shows that the one was set
from the other, with minor changes, mostly of punctuation and capitalisation.
The present text is taken from *The Amulet* for 1830 with the following emendations:

p. 173, l. 31 to him.] to him (*Amulet*)
p. 177, l. 34 for ae day] for a'e day (*Amulet*)
p. 178, l. 16 and said, "Will] and said, "will (*Amulet*)

[Three Sketches: A Tribute to David Wilkie] (pp. 181–85)

Writing to Hogg on 25 June [1829] (NLS, MS 2245, fols 148–49) to thank
him for his contributions to *The Amulet* for 1830, S. C. Hall asked him to write
the letter-press to accompany an engraving prepared for the same issue of his
annual:

> I enclose a print from a picture by Mr Wilkie–it is entitled "the
> Dorty Bairn"–and I believe he painted from some lines by his uncle (I
> believe)–It represents a little girl who has quarrelled with her bread &
> butter–her mother is saying "look at your pretty face" and showing
> her a looking glass. Can you be good enough to write for me, a few
> lines to accompany this plate–I should far prefer them in the dialect of
> your country. If so, it will be well that I have them soon–

Wilkie had painted *The Dorty Bairn* around 1818, and it had been engraved for *The Amulet* by James Mitchell by the permission of its owner Sir Willoughby Gordon: it appeared facing page 101 of the issue for 1830 and is reproduced in the present volume.

Hogg had a general interest in Scottish painting (see 'Hogg, Art and the Annuals' in the present volume, pp. xlii–liv) and a particular interest in the work of David Wilkie (1785–1841). While Wilkie was passing part of a holiday with Scott in 1817 he had been introduced to Hogg, who had noted his youthful appearance and complimented, 'Thank God for it. I did not know that you were so young a man!'–see J. G. Lockhart, *Memoirs of the Life of Sir Walter Scott, Bart.*, 7 vols (Edinburgh: Cadell; London: Murray and Whittaker, 1837–38), IV, 98. Hogg responded by sending three sketches in which he both attempted to fulfil Hall's request and at the same time to give a wider personal tribute to an artist he particularly admired. Hogg's manuscript, which survives in the Beinecke Rare Book & Manuscript Library, Yale University (James Hogg Collection, GEN MSS 61, Box 1, Folder 21), consists of two sheets of paper, the first of which bears the watermark 'G WILMOT | 1827' and the second an address to 'S. C. Hall Esqr | Westly & Davis | Booksellers and publisher | London' with a postmark date of 7 August 1829.

Hogg's first sketch, 'The Dorty Wean', is a comical little scene in Scots as requested, set on Hogg's own farm of Mount Benger and so also providing the personal, autobiographical touch so much appreciated by editors and readers of annuals. 'The History of an Auld Naig' which follows gives a Scottish genre scene in prose of a kind that Wilkie would have embodied in paint, with an oblique reference to his well-known early picture of *Pitlessie Fair*. The third sketch demonstrated the affinity of Wilkie's Scottish painting with Scottish literature, through analysis of a specific picture based on a scene from Allan Ramsay's pastoral comedy *The Gentle Shepherd*. Although Hogg would be aware that reproductions of the last two Wilkie pictures would not be included in *The Amulet* they are included here to help the reader to see what Hogg had in mind when he was writing his tribute to Wilkie. Further information on these paintings by Wilkie is given in the Explanatory Notes.

Hogg's response to the engraving of *The Dorty Bairn* is wide-ranging and intelligent, greatly superior to the pedestrian verses by Rev. William Wilkie that actually accompanied the picture in *The Amulet* for 1830, pp. 101–02. Unfortunately Hogg's letterpress must simply have arrived too late to be used for *The Amulet* for 1830: Hall's letter of 25 June (quoted above) makes it clear that the annual was then in an advanced state of preparation and he urges that if Hogg intends to write a few lines to the engraving 'it will be well that I have them soon'. The cover to Hogg's manuscript is postmarked 7 August 1829, some six weeks later, while the vagueness of the address given clearly caused some delay in the delivery of the letter since an endorsement reads 'Not known by Mr Westly & Co | Strand | J Haws'. It seems likely that Hall had decided before he finally received Hogg's manuscript that he was not going to receive this contribution from Hogg, and had consequently reverted to the lines that he had mentioned in his letter to Hogg of 25 June as

David Wilkie, *Pitlessie Fair*

David Wilkie, *A Scene from 'The Gentle Shepherd'*

© The National Gallery of Scotland

the original inspiration of Wilkie's painting. As the annuals were sold as Christmas and New Year's gifts it was essential that publication should not be delayed, nor would it be feasible to omit from the volume a print that was both laboriously and expensively produced. *The Amulet* for 1830 seems to have been published by mid-October, for a review in the *Literary Gazette* of 17 October 1829 (pp. 675–76) opens by stating that the volume 'has reached us too late for a detailed review' in that issue. Hogg's three sketches, however, were written specifically for *The Amulet* in response to a direct request from its editor and are therefore included in the present volume.

Although these sketches were never published in Hogg's lifetime an abridged and altered version of the second of them was published after his death as 'The History of an Auld Naig' in *Chambers's Edinburgh Journal* for 10 August 1839, p. 232, with the following note by the paper's editor:

> Amongst a few papers contributed some years ago to a London *annual* by the Ettrick Shepherd, and which (no opportunity having occurred for using them) have been transferred to us, is one under the above title.

Perhaps Hogg's widow hoped to earn something by placing one of his unused works in a popular periodical publication. Hogg's manuscript bears definite signs of its use for *Chambers's Edinburgh Journal*. The manuscript has been cut at one time and then reassembled using strips of printer's waste (including one on the second sheet which seems to be from an advertisement for *Chambers's*), and various changes have been made to 'The History of an Auld Naig' in darker ink and in a hand which does not appear to be Hogg's. This hand has crossed through the words 'By the Same' in the sub-heading, for instance, and substituted 'A hitherto unpublished Sketch | by the late Ettrick Shepherd', besides making various additions and deletions to suit 'The History of an Auld Naig' to separate publication. Other deletions have been made to this sketch in pencil and punctuation added. These changes have been ignored in the version of 'The History of an Auld Naig' in the present volume, which presents Hogg's intended contribution to *The Amulet*. The present volume reprints all three sketches from Hogg's fair-copy manuscript in the Beinecke Library. Speech marks have been silently regularised according to the following convention: double speech marks enclose a speech, single speech marks enclose a speech within a speech, and the double opening speech marks are repeated at the start of each new paragraph within a speech while speeches should end with a full stop as well as closing speech marks. Full stops have also been added where a following upper-case letter indicates the end of a sentence. The following changes have also been made:

p. 183, l. 7 days, and] days. and (MS)
p. 183, l. 31 Gerse Merkat] gerse merkat (MS) [a place name]
p. 183, l. 37 Newbiggings] newbiggings (MS) [a place name]
p. 184, l. 7 tell ye] tell y (MS)
p. 184, l. 20 Meadow Park] meadow park (MS) [a place name]

p. 185, l. 19 Allan Ramsay's Gentle Shepherd] Allan Ramsay's gentle shepherd MS [the name of a play or its hero]

A Cameronian Ballad (pp. 186–90)

Peter Garside provides the following introductory and textual notes to this
poem in his edition of *A Queer Book* (S/SC, 1995), pp. 241–42:

This ballad featured in *The Amulet* for 1831 (pp. 173–80), and, as with 'A
Lay of the Martyrs' in the previous number, its focus on two female
speakers was well calculated to appeal to *The Amulet*'s readership. A
more complex situation is nevertheless found in the juxtaposition of the
religious / class antagonism shown by the Cameronian Janet with the
more pragmatic and humane values of her aristocratical lady. The
Cameronians, so named after their leader Richard Cameron (*d.* 1680),
steadfastly refused to accept secular authority in religious matters, and
this, together with their denial of good works as a means of salvation, is
reflected in Janet's readiness to accept her husband's death at the battle
of Bothwell Bridge in 1679 as a martyrdom. Her patroness, in contrast,
observes both spiritual and material priorities ('The better you are in
either state, | The less shall I repine'), and intervenes to rescue John
Carr from the field of slaughter. While Hogg characteristically allows
both attitudes to stand, a softening is sensed in Janet's later responses,
while the poem as a whole expresses a wider conviction that compassion is what matters, not the cause, and that good is possible on both
sides. In this respect, Hogg manages to satisfy the expectations of a
contemporary religious readership without losing hold of his own values.

Textual Notes on 'A Cameronian Ballad'
In addition to *The Amulet* for 1831, 'A Cameronian Ballad' appeared in
another contemporary journal, *The Annual Register, or A View of the History,
Politics, and Literature, of the year 1830* (London, 1831), pp. 529–32. A
superficial reading of dates might suggest that the *Annual Register* contains the earlier version. But whereas the *Register* was offering a *retrospec-
tive* view of public events, and must have been published after 1830, the
Amulet (as a keepsake for the following year) would have been ready for
sale well in time for Christmas 1830. Collation between the two texts
suggests that the *Annual Register* version was almost certainly taken from
the *Amulet*. Scots terms are anglicised on at least 30 occasions ('wha' to
'who', 'sae' to 'so' etc.); more tellingly still, 'your leel goodman' in line 1
becomes 'your leel, good man', and later 'the water o' Clyde' (i.e. the
river) is changed to 'the waters o' Clyde'. The *Annual Register* also regularised stanza structure by placing the whole poem in eight-line stanzas,
unlike the *Amulet* which includes six quatrains among its octets. The
Queer Book of 1832–which used *The Amulet* for its copy-text–then divided
the whole poem into quatrains. The title also became 'Bothwell Brigg',
and a number of routine adjustments were made (e.g. the raising of

'ladye' to 'Ladye'). A few substantive changes (such as the substitution of 'Earlston' for 'Earylton') appear to correct misreadings of the original manuscript.

The present text is based on *The Amulet* for 1831, the earliest version known to have survived. It nevertheless follows the *Queer Book* of 1832 in placing the poem in quatrains, largely on the grounds that no fully consistent pattern can be discerned in the *Amulet*'s mixture of octets and quatrains (it is not impossible that Hogg's crowding of stanzas in the manuscript was the original source of confusion). The following emendations have also been made:

(l. 10) rules] rubs (*Amulet*) [*Queer Book* 1832 rules]

(l. 15) Earlston] Earylton (*Amulet*)

(l. 60) break.] break; (*Amulet*)

(l. 64) thy life and mine] my life and thine (*Amulet*) [This emendation follows the wording found in the *Annual Register* (1831), which, though not authorial, offers the best solution to the awkwardness of the *Amulet* text at this point.]

(l. 95) liefu] liefe (*Amulet*) [*Queer Book* 1832 leifou]

(l. 115) sackless] sachless (*Amulet*)

(l. 127) bled] bled, (*Amulet*)

(l. 137) land] land, (*Amulet*)

(l. 139) hand, [...] night] hand [...] night, (*Amulet*)

(l. 144) yoursels] yoursel's (*Amulet*)

(l. 158) trow] traw (*Amulet*)

A Hymn to the Redeemer (pp. 191–92)

Hogg's next contribution to *The Amulet*, 'A Hymn to the Redeemer', did not appear until the volume for 1835 (pp. 118–20), no Hogg items being published in the volumes for 1832, 1833, or 1834. This is somewhat surprising, especially in view of Hogg's letter to Hall of 6 March 1830 (Beinecke Rare Book & Manuscript Library, Yale University, James Hogg Collection, GEN MSS 61, Box 1, Folder 10), with which he inclosed 'The Female Covenanters' (which may have been the poem published in the volume for 1831 as 'A Cameronian Ballad', see above), and also two other items entitled 'A Hymn' and 'The Judgment of Idumea'. Hogg additionally stated that he had 'ordered Mr Cunningham to furnish you with one or two that are in his hand' and promised 'you may have more if you want them'.

After selecting 'A Cameronian Ballad' for the volume for 1831 Hall may simply have retained Hogg's other manuscripts intending to use one or more of them in the 1832 volume and then have neglected to do so. 'A Hymn to the Redeemer' in *The Amulet* for 1835 is undated and may possibly be 'A Hymn', mentioned by Hogg in his letter of 6 March 1830. 'The Judgment of Idumea' also mentioned in this letter was certainly published in the issue for 1836, though this may have been from a freshly-prepared manuscript (see below). On the other hand it seems improbable that Hall would have retained Hogg's manuscripts for several years in view of Hogg's earlier insistence that his manuscripts should either be used or returned to him: if Hall felt that Hogg's articles were not up to standard he could have returned them and demanded others, and if he had insufficient space to include them in the 1831 volume it is difficult to see why he did not print one or more in the volume for 1832.

Hogg's maintenance of friendly relations with Hall argues against the idea that Hall retained his unused manuscripts for several years and then published them without his immediate consent: he visited at Hall's house in London during the early months of 1832 (see Garden, pp. 246, 263–64), describing the Halls in a later undated letter as 'a couple whom I love and admire' (Beinecke Rare Book & Manuscript Library, Yale University, James Hogg Collection, GEN MSS 61, Box 1, Folder 10). He also continued to send Hall and his wife fresh manuscripts (see the textual note on 'Morning Hymn' below). It should also be remembered that Hogg was a regular rather than an occasional contributor to *The Amulet*, and Hall would have known that there was a very high risk that any wrongful appropriation of Hogg's work would have been drawn to his attention immediately after publication. Furthermore the appearance of Hogg items in the subsequent volume for 1836 seems to indicate that Hogg was satisfied with Hall's treatment of him as a contributor.

It may be that by the close of 1831 Hogg had simply got into a muddle about which of his literary manuscripts were in London and when and to whom they had been submitted. His letter to an unnamed correspondent of 27 November 1828 (The Brotherton Collection, Leeds University Library: Miscellaneous Letters PRI (Pringle album)) suggests that he had certainly been in a state of confusion previously about his contributions to the annuals:

> But so perfectly am I confounded by the number of annuals that if take me book sworn at this moment I do not know which is your's and which I have wrote for and which not!

If Hogg's later contributions to *The Amulet* appeared there without his immediate consent then he would not have been given an opportunity to inspect proofs.

'Hymn to the Redeemer' had originally appeared within 'The Poet's Tale' in *The Three Perils of Man*, 3 vols (London: Longman, 1822), III, 48–49, sung by three Christian maidens about to be martyred by heathen Norsemen. Hogg had clearly revised it extensively before submitting it to Hall for *The Amulet*, however, introducing a number of completely new lines and removing the earlier contextual references to idolatry and sacrifice. He also transposed the surrounding 'The Poet's Tale' into verse, and this was published as 'The Three Sisters' in *Fraser's Magazine*, 11 (1835), 666–79. Whether the two poems were extracted from *The Three Perils of Man* at much the same time is unknown.

Hogg's manuscript of 'Hymn to the Redeemer' has not apparently survived, and the poem was not subsequently reprinted during Hogg's lifetime. The poem is printed in the present volume from *The Amulet* for 1835 without change.

Morning Hymn (pp. 192–93)

'Morning Hymn' was published in *The Amulet* for 1836, pp. 42–43, and Hogg's fair-copy manuscript with the usual header and dated like the printed text 'Altrive Lake the longest day 1835' survives in the Beinecke Rare Book & Manuscript Library, Yale University (James Hogg Collection, GEN MSS 61, Box 1, Folder 26). The manuscript consists of a single sheet of paper, bearing signs of having been folded into a letter, and with the direction 'Mrs. S. C. Hall' on the verso. Probably, therefore, the poem was originally intended as a contribution to Anna Maria Hall's *The Juvenile Forget Me Not*, and enclosed in a letter to her husband. Since Hogg's contributions to Mrs Hall's annual were intended as personal gifts (see the introductory and textual note to *The Juvenile Forget Me Not*, pp. 346–47) it seems possible that Hogg may not have received a payment for it when it was transferred to *The Amulet*.

An earlier version of 'Morning Hymn' had previously appeared as 'The Palmer's Morning Hymn' in the fourth canto of Hogg's narrative poem *Mador of the Moor* (Edinburgh: Blackwood; London: Murray, 1816), pp. 108–10. A copy, entitled 'Blessed be thy name for ever' (NLS, MS 842, fols 18–20) is not in Hogg's hand but forms part of the music book, dated 1827, of Alicia Anne Spottiswoode of Spottiswoode. Hogg subsequently revised these lines from *Mador of the Moor* slightly in preparing copy for *The Amulet*. In transforming the manuscript into a printed text Hall or his printers misread Hogg's 'ouphes' on line 5 as 'auphes', and also introduced a much heavier style of punctuation which occasionally overrides Hogg's own punctuation marks. Line 22 of Hogg's manuscript for example reads 'No! they cannot cannot harm them' whereas the printed text has 'No; they cannot, cannot harm them', while on line 2 Hogg's 'the guard and giver' is capitalised to 'the Guard and Giver,'. Hall's adoption of the more conventional spelling 'wondrous' for Hogg's 'wonderous' on line 15 arguably distorts the poem's rhythm slightly. These kind of changes had a subtle, cumulative effect on the poem, rendering the text printed in *The Amulet* inferior to that of Hogg's fair-copy manuscript. The editors felt that in this case an analysis of the overall change would be a more effective way of indicating the different feel of the manuscript and printed versions than printing them successively, and have printed 'Morning Hymn' from Hogg's manuscript without change.

The Judgment of Idumea (pp. 193–95)

'The Judgment of Idumea' was published in *The Amulet* for 1836, pp. 79–81 and end-dated in accordance with Hogg's usual practice 'Mount Benger, August 23, 1835'. This date agrees with the claim made at the start of a transcription of the poem in another hand (in NLS, MS 2245, fols 268–69) that it was 'written by the Ettrick Shepherd a short while before his death'. This transcription, headed 'The Fall of Idumea' contains the poem published in *The Amulet* with the exception of its first eight lines and is dated 'Stobohope 2 February 1846': Stobohope was the home of Hogg's elder brother William, and the transcription is therefore likely to have been made by William Hogg or a member of his immediate family. An earlier date for 'The Judgment of

Idumea' is given, though, in Hogg's letter to Samuel Carter Hall of 6 March 1830 (Beinecke Rare Book & Manuscript Library, Yale University, James Hogg Collection, GEN MSS 61, Box 1, Folder 10) which mentions it as one of the contributions then sent for *The Amulet*. Unfortunately no fair-copy manuscript prepared by Hogg for *The Amulet* appears to have survived, the only extant version of the poem in Hogg's hand being a rough draft in the Alexander Turnbull Library, Wellington, New Zealand (James Hogg Papers (Item 39. iii). f MS-Papers-0042-04).

It is possible that Hogg may have sent Hall two different versions of this poem, an earlier one in 1830 and a later one in 1835, the evidence of the transcription by a family member seeming to render it unlikely that the text of 'The Judgment of Idumea' in *The Amulet* was printed from a manuscript sent in 1830 and retained by Hall until 1835 when it was given a suitably revised date to make it seem fresher to the annual's readers. The presence of Hogg's 'Morning Hymn' in the same volume from a manuscript dated to 21 June 1835 would also seem to imply that Hogg had sent Hall and his wife items for 1836 during the preceding summer. No other version of 'The Judgment of Idumea' was published during Hogg's lifetime. The present volume prints the poem from *The Amulet* for 1836, with the following emendation:

l. 45 court] count (*Amulet*) [as MS draft]

A Letter to the Ettrick Shepherd (pp. 195–203)

'A Letter to the Ettrick Shepherd' was published in *The Amulet* for 1836, pp. 212–25. However, it does not seem to have been written originally for Hall's annual but for *The Juvenile Forget Me Not* edited by his wife. Hall seems to have solicited contributions for his wife's annual at the same time as for his own, and Hogg agreed to write for both. His verses 'A Child's Prayer', for example, were printed in *The Juvenile Forget Me Not* for 1830, pp. 114–15, and following their appearance Hogg wrote to Hall on 6 March 1830 (Beinecke Rare Book & Manuscript Library, Yale University, James Hogg Collection, GEN MSS 61, Box 1, Folder 10) enclosing contributions for their next annuals including for 'Mrs Hall "A Child's Hymn for the close of the Week" And "The Death of W. Watson" a tale of considerable length, both of which I send her as a present of course and she is welcome to more if she need them'. 'The Death of W. Watson' seems to have been a ghost story, and in rejecting it Mrs Hall requested Hogg in her letter of 2 April 1830 (James Hogg Collection, Special Collections, University of Otago Library: in a copy of the *Juvenile Forget Me Not* for 1831) to send her instead 'a simple tale, telling about your own pure and immortal Scottish children—without love—or ghosts—or fairies'. Hogg's subsequent letter of 22 May 1830 (Historical Society of Pennsylvania: Ferdinard Julius Dreer Collection, Collection 175, English Poets) in sending this substitute declares 'as I think shame to put my name to such mere common place things as you seem to want I have sent you a letter from an English Widow'. 'A Letter to the Ettrick Shepherd', which is signed Alice Brand, fits this description exactly: it opens 'A poor widow from your sister kingdom ventures to address you' and concludes with the writer's intention to try to insert it in 'some of the juvenile periodicals'. Mrs Hall did not however insert it in her annual, and it presumably remained with the Halls until its insertion in *The Amulet* for 1836.

Hogg's letter to S. C. Hall of 6 March 1830 (quoted above) implies that he regarded his contributions to Mrs Hall's *The Juvenile Forget Me Not* as personal gifts rather than as work to be paid for (for further details see the notes to *The Juvenile Forget Me Not*, pp. 346–47 below), and it may be that no payment was made for 'A Letter to the Ettrick Shepherd' even when it was transferred to *The Amulet*. Hogg's fair-copy manuscript does not appear to have survived, and it was not reprinted in his lifetime. The present volume reprints the tale from *The Amulet* for 1836 with the following emendations:

p. 198, ll. 36–37 their first invader] their first invaders (*Amulet*) [the weasel was a solitary invader]

p. 202, l. 32 exterminated] extirminated (*Amulet*)

To Miss M. A. C——e (pp. 203–05)

The final item in Hogg's contributions to *The Amulet* forms part of an undated letter to S. C. Hall (Beinecke Rare Book & Manuscript Library, Yale University, James Hogg Collection, GEN MSS 61, Box 1, Folder 10), clearly written towards the end of Hogg's life, since the paper on which it is written bears the watermark 'J WHATMAN | TURKEY MILL | 1835'. In this letter he declares: 'I send you and Mrs Hall a small poem each merely to see my name in the list of a couple whom I love and admire'. The young lady to whom the poem is addressed is probably the adolescent daughter of Hogg's London publisher James Cochrane, Mary Anne Cochrane. Hogg had been intimate in Cochrane's family during his London visit and had been quite openly and innocently captivated by Mary Anne. In his letter to his son James of 18 January 1832 (Hogg Letters Project Papers, University of Stirling) Hogg describes her as 'the age of Jessie', his own eldest daughter who was born on 23 April 1823. She is probably, therefore, the Mary Anne Cochrane christened at St Martin Ludgate, London on 2 September 1822, the daughter of James and Mary Cochrane (*International Genealogical Index*), and would be nine years old when Hogg first became acquainted with her in January 1832. In his letter to James Cochrane of 4 November 1832 (Beinecke Rare Book & Manuscript Library, Yale University, James Hogg Collection, GEN MSS 61, Box 1, Folder 6) Hogg sends his love to his publisher's family remarking 'I love them all as dearly as they were my own but Mary Anne I find still clings closest to my heart which I think arises merely from my fondness for the *women folks* for they were all alike obliging to me dear little fellows', adding 'I would like very much to have Marianne here and one of mine to come to London with her year about. Mine would be so much benefited by her conversation and she by the pure mountain air of Yarrow. She is a dear girl and I have ordered Mr M,Crowne to bless her in my name but not to kiss her I cannot afford him that privilege'. The subsequent correspondence between Hogg and Cochrane mentions Mary Anne from time to time, although she did not come to live at Altrive and Hogg presumably never saw her again. She was clearly not forgotten, though, Margaret Hogg writing to Cochrane on 30 January 1836, after her husband's death, 'I have heard much of Miss Cochrane she will now be a fine girl'—see R. B. Adam, *Works Letters and Manuscripts of James Hogg 'The Ettrick Shepherd'* (Buffalo: privately printed, 1930), p. 25.

Hogg's fair-copy manuscript, headed 'To Miss M. A. C——e | By the Ettrick Shepherd', is in fact a reworking of lines from Book I of his earlier epic poem *Queen Hynde* (London: Longman; Edinburgh: Blackwood, 1824), pp. 53–56. Apart from differences in punctuation and capitalisation, regarded at the time as matters falling within the purview of the printer, these lines have been adapted for publication in *The Amulet* in two main ways: firstly the poem is now addressed to the 'Maid of my worship' rather than the 'Maid of Dunedin' (who in *Queen Hynde* personifies the female poetry-reading public), and six lines from the earlier poem (which would have occurred between lines 38 and 39 of the present text) have been omitted. The earlier version of Hogg's lines may be read in *Queen Hynde*, ed. by Suzanne Gilbert and Douglas S. Mack (S/ SC, 1998), pp. 30–31. 'To Miss M. A. C——e' shows Hogg once again refashioning earlier material to an annuals context, and in accordance with his expressed wish it is included among his contributions to *The Amulet* in the present volume, without change.

The Gem
One published contribution
A Highland Eclogue (pp. 209–13)

Peter Garside provides the following introductory and textual notes to this poem in his edition of *A Queer Book* (S/SC, 1995), pp. 257–58:

> This poem was first published in *The Gem* for 1830 (pp. 194–200), a literary annual edited by Thomas Hood, whose first number a year earlier had included items by Scott, Keats, and John Clare. Hood had originally written to Hogg on 22 April 1828 asking for contributions: 'It is my *earnest* wish to see you numbered with the Contributors who grace my list' (NLS, MS 2245, fol. 116).
>
> The particular history of the poem, which has some of the characteristics of a rough sketch, is unknown. A number of details point to an imaginative overlap with the tragic Highland events of the last volume of *The Three Perils of Woman* (1823). In the present case, however, divisions are healed through two positive factors: human good sense, which insists on the setting of preconditions before marriage; and the benign influence of religion, seen from the broadest vantage point.

Textual Notes on 'A Highland Eclogue'

Though no manuscript has been found, the relatively free punctuation in *The Gem*, together with the survival there of several idiosyncratic spellings, suggests a fairly uncomplicated transcription of the poem on its first printing. For the *Queer Book* of 1832, the title was changed to 'Allan of Dale', introducing a hint of the Allan-a-dale of the Robin Hood ballads (as well as of Scott's recent *Ivanhoe* (1820)) which is arguably inappropriate to the poem as a whole. The *Queer Book* also endeavoured to standardise grammar and orthography (e.g. 'knelt' for 'kneeled' (l. 21) and 'indictment' for 'inditement' (l. 119)), in the process taking the poem further away from Hogg's original text.

The present text is reprinted, without alteration, from *The Gem* for 1830.

The Remembrance
Three published contributions

When the London publishers Jennings and Chaplin published their new annual, *The Remembrance* for 1831, they had secured the services of Thomas Roscoe (1791–1871), the fifth son of Hogg's old Liverpool correspondent, the poet William Roscoe, as editor. The first volume of his *Landscape Annual* for 1830, subtitled 'The Tourist in Switzerland and Italy', had been published in 1829, and he was also the editor of a childrens' annual entitled *Juvenile Keepsake*, two issues of which were published by the firm of Hurst, Chance & Co. for 1829 and 1830 respectively. From surviving correspondence Roscoe seems to have first applied to Hogg to contribute to this juvenile annual, although the date of his application cannot be precisely established because unfortunately neither he nor Hogg dated their correspondence in full. Roscoe's otherwise business-like application to Hogg states:

> Mr T. Roscoe does himself the honour of applying to Mr Hogg, whose highly pleasing and popular productions are so universally admired,— to ascertain if it may be agreeable to Mr H. to contribute some little poetical effusions to a little annual of which M^r R is the Editor and part proprietor
>
> It is called the J. Keepsake, and Mr R. will feel proud of attaching Mr H.'s name to the HEAD list of his contributors, if an early answer could be received—Copies of the work & remuneration will be sent on publication of the work (NLS, MS 2245, fols 321–22)

Hogg's response, dated merely 'Octr 15th', accedes to this request: 'You shall have one or two contributions of mine cheerfully But if no number of the work is yet published I would be the better of a prospectus or some directions from you regarding the nature of it lest I should do as I have often done send pieces the very reverse of what was wanted' (National Archives of Scotland, GD205/47/17/78 (1)). At some point Hogg must have followed up this letter with three contributions for *Juvenile Keepsake*, as a Roscoe letter to him of 'March 15' acknowledges the receipt of 'three little pieces from your hand for the purpose of inserting in the "Juvenile Keepsake"', which he had approved of 'with some slight alterations which you are considerate enough to leave open to me' (NLS, MS 2245, fol. 323). However, no Hogg contributions appeared in either of the two volumes of *Juvenile Keepsake* for 1829 and 1830. Roscoe may well have held Hogg's pieces over, with his permission, for insertion in his new annual, *The Remembrance*: certainly at least two of Hogg's three contributions to *The Remembrance* seem to be targeted at a juvenile audience even though *The Remembrance* was not a juvenile annual. Hogg clearly authorised the appearance of his work in *The Remembrance*, however, for he received a copy of the work during a visit to Edinburgh in December 1830, writing to his wife on 9 December, 'Mr Brooks' poem is not in Roscoe's Remembrance for [which] I am very vexed. It has been too late in going There are four of my things in it' (Alexander Turnbull Library, Wellington, New Zealand, James Hogg Papers (Item 110). MS-Papers-0042-12). Following Hogg's statement here the present editors have minutely examined the contents of the volume, but were forced to conclude that, Hogg to the contrary, there are only three Hogg items in *The Remembrance* for 1831, 'A Boy's Song', 'The Two Valleys: A Fairy Tale', and 'The Covenanter's Scaffold Song'.

   The Remembrance appears to have been intended for a general family audience with Royalist affinities, the work being dedicated to Queen Adelaide as 'a combined display of national taste and genius, as well in literature and art' (pp. iii–iv). A proportion of topographical articles (including descriptions of the Roman forum, the Coliseum, and Warwick and Windsor castles) suggests that Roscoe may have re-used material collected for the *Landscape Annual* as well as material originally intended for *Juvenile Keepsake*. Although a most attractive annual, *The Remembrance* for 1831 was not followed by other volumes in the succeeding years: the original volume was merely opportunistically reprinted 'with additions' in 1837 for the accession of Queen Victoria.

A Boy's Song (p. 217)

This was first published in *The Remembrance* for 1831, pp. 74–75 and not reprinted in Hogg's lifetime, even though it seems to have rapidly become one of his best-known poems during the nineteenth century.

   Hogg's fair-copy manuscript does not appear to have survived, although there is a rough draft in Stirling University Library (MS 25, Box 1 (1a)). This version of 'A Boy's Song' contains a stanza missing from the published version, and an earlier version of the penultimate stanza, Hogg's second thoughts being inserted above the line without the deletion of the previous words.

   Hogg's manuscript forms part of a single sheet of paper, covered on both sides by Hogg's writing in double columns and mostly comprising fair copies of items sent to *Ackermann's Juvenile Forget Me Not* for 1830, 'A Child's Prayer', 'What is Sin?' and its unpublished companion-piece 'What is Death?'. Presumably the sheet was returned to Hogg by Shoberl or Ackermann because the third item was not used for *Ackermann's Juvenile Forget Me Not*, the other two items being each carefully scored with a large pencil cross to indicate that they had been used. The draft of 'A Boy's Song' occupies about two-thirds of the final column: it seems probable that Hogg, being short of paper one day, utilised a vacant space at the end of this old manuscript for drafting a new composition. Hogg's rough draft of 'A Boy's Song' thus provides the only clue as to the date of composition: it was probably written after the summer or early autumn of 1829 when his unused contributions to *Ackermann's Juvenile*

Forget Me Not for 1830 are likely to have been returned to him.

'A Boy's Song' is given in the present volume from *The Remembrance* for 1831 without change. For the reader's interest the somewhat ineffective stanza from the rough draft (occurring after the third stanza) which does not appear in the printed version is given here:

> Where the poplar grows the smallest
> Where the old pine waves the tallest
> Pies and rooks know who are we
> That's the way for Billy and me

'Pies' here means *magpies* (from Scots *pyot*).

The Two Valleys: A Fairy Tale (pp. 218–25)

The history of 'The Two Valleys: A Fairy Tale' is not entirely clear, although its style and tone suggest that it was probably intended for publication in one of the juvenile annuals, perhaps Roscoe's own *Juvenile Keepsake* (see above). On the other hand Hogg's letter to Blackwood of 6 August 1829 (NLS, MS 4024, fol. 296) mentions 'two little tales for a juvenile Annual of Ackerman's' that he had just finished writing, describing one as 'quite in my own fairy stile', a description which is suggestive but not sufficiently detailed for a firm identification with this particular story to be made.

'The Two Valleys: A Fairy Tale' was published in *The Remembrance* for 1831, pp. 121–32, and Hogg's fair-copy manuscript for this does not appear to have survived. An incomplete fair-copy manuscript headed 'The Two Vallies By the Ettrick Shepherd' (in NLS, MS 1704, fols 65–66) is not the copy-text for the tale published in *The Remembrance*, but an alternative and undated version, differing in many individual details and in its more explicit references to Catholicism. This version has been edited by Janette Currie in her 'Two Early Versions of Tales from Annuals', *Studies in Hogg and his World*, 11 (2000), 87–121, where a fuller account of this manuscript is given.

The present volume reprints 'The Two Valleys: A Fairy Tale' from *The Remembrance* without change.

The Covenanter's Scaffold Song (pp. 225–26)

'The Covenanter's Scaffold Song' was first published in Roscoe's *The Remembrance* for 1831, p. 255, and not reprinted in Hogg's lifetime. The date of composition is unknown. A manuscript version of this short poem seems to have been located in Ettrick kirk until the 1970s, though it has since gone missing: it is not clear whether it was the fair copy used by the printer of *The Remembrance* or merely a rough draft.

Hogg seems to have written an entire collection of songs about Covenanters and sent them to Goulding & D'Almaine, the London music publishers of his collection of *Select and Rare Scotish Melodies* (*c*. 1829). Writing to the firm on 17 March 1829 (Beinecke Rare Book & Manuscript Library, Yale University, James Hogg Collection, GEN MSS 61, Box 1, Folder 11) he demanded the return of these songs:

340 INTRODUCTORY AND TEXTUAL NOTES

> As I have recieved no answer or notification of any sort anent my
> Cameronian poetry I of course draw the conclusion that the songs are
> not of that cast you wish to encourage. I therefore intreat you to
> return them without farther delay as I have some pressing demands
> for things of the same nature and no duplicates.

Hogg's work about the Scottish Covenanters clearly appealed to pre-Victorian evangelical piety, and several items of this kind were placed with annuals
such as S. C. Hall's *The Amulet; A Christian and Literary Remembrancer*. The 'pressing demands for things of the same nature' of Hogg's letter to Goulding &
D'Almaine may well refer to his work for annuals, and it is tempting to specu-
late that 'The Covenanter's Scaffold Song' may have originally been part of
Hogg's intended musical publication of Cameronian songs.

'The Covenanter's Scaffold Song' is given in the present volume from *The
Remembrance* for 1831, without change.

The May Flower
One poem published
Song (p. 229)

'Song. By the late James Hogg, the Ettrick Shepherd' appears on p. 147 of *The
May Flower* for 1846, an annual edited by Robert Hamilton and published in
Boston by Saxton & Kelt. In general, American annuals are a rather later
publishing phenomenon than their British equivalents, and Hogg items included in them turn out to be reprintings (presumably made without his
knowledge or permission) of items from British annuals or other British publications by James Hogg. These reprintings are of some interest because important and influential American writers, such as Edgar Allan Poe, contributed to American annuals and encountered Hogg's work there. For this reason known reprintings of Hogg items in American annuals are included in the
present volume's 'Listing of Hogg Texts in Annuals and Gift-Books'. 'Song',
however, is a special case in that Hamilton's claim in a footnote that these
verses were 'Never before published' appears to be accurate, so far as the
present editors have been able to discover. Hamilton edited the Saxton & Kelt
annual *The May Flower* for only that one year, the editor's names on the titlepages of the 1847 and 1848 volumes being given as 'Mrs E. Oakes Smith'.
Hamilton's Preface to *The May Flower* for 1846 reveals that the volume was a
mixture of original and reprinted pieces, arguing that pieces 'selected from the
most popular periodicals and other sources, little known to the American
public' would 'prove more acceptable than a boasted array of entirely original
articles, of only mediocre composition'.

James Hogg died on 21 November 1835, about ten years before the publication of *The May Flower* for 1846, so that the poem could not have been
contributed by him to this annual nor is it clear indeed that it was written for
an annual of any description whatever. It seems likely that a Hogg manuscript, either a fair-copy or a rough draft, came into Hamilton's possession

and that he then decided to include these verses by a well-known and well-regarded poet among his volume's attractions. Janette Currie points out that Hamilton (of whom almost nothing is known) also edited a New York magazine entitled *Ladies Companion*. Hogg's poem 'The Rose of Plora' was published in the May 1841 number of the *Ladies Companion*, 15 (1841), 42, and the editor explained in a note that this had reached him via an unnamed correspondent who had visited Hogg at Altrive in the summer of 1830. This person had requested a holograph poem from Hogg as a souvenir, and been politely refused:

> To this he seemed averse, alleging as an excuse, '*that it was not at a' times that his muse would jingle*'. A young lady who was present, perceiving my disappointment, as a kind of palliative, told me that I was welcome to a copy of an *original poem* which the shepherd had contributed to her album. As a curiosity, I transcribed it, and which the poet kindly authenticated with his autograph.

The passage illustrates Hamilton's general interest in Hogg's work, though there is no evidence that 'Song' in *The May Flower* was also collected in Scotland in the summer of 1830. Although the editors of the present volume recognise that 'Song' is not, strictly speaking, part of Hogg's work for the annuals they have decided to reprint it in the present volume, as the most logical place for it within the S/SC Edition. It is therefore reprinted from *The May Flower* for 1846. *The May Flower*'s footnote declaring that this 'Song' had not been previously published is reproduced in this second printing.

Juvenile Annuals

Ackermann's Juvenile Forget Me Not

*Five published contributions: one additional unpublished
contribution is included in the present volume*

Ackermann's Juvenile Forget Me Not seems to have been a much more congenial outlet for Hogg's work than the similarly-titled children's annual edited by Mrs Hall (see below), for besides two sets of religious verses this annual in the three years of its existence also printed an infant dialogue, a story about a boy-poacher, and a poem describing pastoral music-making by James Hogg. The present volume also contains a second infant dialogue from Hogg's fair-copy manuscript.

Like its parent *Forget Me Not* this children's annual was produced by the fine-art publisher Rudolph Ackermann and edited by Frederic Shoberl, and although the 'Preface' (pp. iii–iv) to the volume for 1830 reassured parents that the volume contained 'nothing but what is conducive to moral improvement, combined with pleasing instruction and innocent amusement' the primary description of the work was of 'an elegant miscellany, adapted to their age and capacity'. The engravings were also designed to be 'of a higher order than those with which it has hitherto been usual to illustrate books destined exclusively for the juvenile reader'. Ackermann and Shoberl argued that 'we are convinced that the formation of the taste [...] commences at a much earlier period, in the mind of inquisitive and observant infancy, than even the professed instructor is always aware of'. In effect, their aim was to educate their future fine-art customers.

In projecting a juvenile annual Ackermann naturally enough applied to Hogg for material as he was a regular contributor to the *Forget Me Not*. In his letter to S. C. Hall of 17 April 1829 (NLS, MS 1002, fols 104–05) Hogg recounts that 'At Mr Ackerman's pressing request I sent off some time ago to the charge I think of Constable & Co two articles in prose and two in verse for a Juvenile Annual of his', and writing to Blackwood on 6 August 1829 (NLS, MS 4024, fol. 296) Hogg mentioned that he had just finished writing 'two little tales for a juvenile Annual of Ackerman's', presumably in addition to the material sent earlier in the year.

A Child's Prayer (p. 233)

'A Child's Prayer' was published in *Ackermann's Juvenile Forget Me Not* for 1830, pp. 176–77. Hogg's fair-copy manuscript survives in the University of Stirling Library (MS 25, Box 1 (1A)), on a sheet which also contains the manuscript of another item published in the volume, 'What is Sin?'. This manuscript is undated but has the usual header 'By the Ettrick Shepherd' and is neatly written throughout. The printed version introduces a heavier system of punctuation, and also corrects Hogg's spelling of words such as 'concieve'. There are also several differences in wording between these two versions of the little prayer, as follows:

l. 11 living soul (MS) | reasoning soul (*AJFMN*)
l. 16 My soul (MS) | My mind (*AJFMN*)
l. 19 And for this sinful race (MS) | For this whole sinful race (*AJFMN*)
l. 21 I cannot frame! (MS) | I cannot grasp (*AJFMN*)

While it is hard to determine whether these changes were made by the printer or editor of *Ackermann's Juvenile Forget Me Not* or Hogg himself (if he was ever sent an author's proof), the fact that they tend to weaken the sense of mystery in religion and shift the emphasis from the soul to the mind suggests that they were not made by Hogg. The original reading of 'living soul' at line 11, for example, irresistibly recalls his sense of wonder in 'A Bard's Address to his Youngest Daughter' that God has 'breathed a living soul' into the little girl. The differences between manuscript and published version of 'A Child's Prayer' are significant but not numerous, and the editors have therefore decided that an analysis of these makes them clearer than a successive printing of the two versions in the present volume would do. 'A Child's Prayer' is therefore printed from Hogg's manuscript without change.

Dramas of Infancy No. 1. What is Sin? (pp. 234–36, 238–40)

'What is Sin?' was published in *Ackermann's Juvenile Forget Me Not* for 1830, pp. 223–27, a conversation in which a little girl and her elder sister attempt to understand and come to terms with one of the central mysteries of human existence. Instructive conversations appeared elsewhere in the juvenile annuals, like Miss Isabel Hill's 'Impulse and Amiability' in *The Juvenile Forget Me Not* for 1831, pp. 84–100, for instance, where Jane's tutor Mr Tyndale tells a story to distinguish between the two qualities and she responds, 'Thank you, dear Sir. Now I understand what amiability *should* be, and shall in future be careful not to obey mere impulse' (p. 100). Hogg's 'Drama of Infancy' differs from such a tale in exploring a major human problem rather than a fine moral distinction and in the prominence he gives to the children's own ideas and insights into the matter.

Hogg's fair-copy manuscript survives in Stirling University Library (MS 25, Box 1 (1A)), on the same sheet as 'A Child's Prayer' which was also published in the 1830 volume of this juvenile annual. Hogg's manuscript is neatly written and lightly punctuated, with the speakers carefully distinguished from one another and it has the usual header of 'By the Ettrick Shepherd' after the title. It is clear from this manuscript that 'What is Sin?' was the first of a two-part series entitled 'Dramas of Infancy', the second following immediately afterwards and entitled 'What is Death'.

'What is Sin?' occupies exactly five pages in *Ackermann's Juvenile Forget Me Not* and may have been shortened slightly by the editor to fit that space, a consideration which may also have determined the jettisoning of 'What is Death'. The differences between Hogg's fair-copy manuscript and the printed version, however, are extensive and coherent and suggest another motivation. Hogg had been carefully and comprehensively instructed in the Calvinist beliefs of the Church of Scotland, a theological grounding which underpins a slight piece like 'What is Sin?' just as it underpins *The Private Memoirs and Confessions of a Justified Sinner*. To some extent this upbringing was suited to the pre-Victorian evangelical piety of religious annuals such as *The Amulet* or those which aimed at the moral and religious instruction of children, but it could also seem too intellectually rigorous, too forthright, and not ecumenical enough for that particular market. The answer given by Hogg to 'What is Sin?', for example, is the reply to Question 14 of *The Shorter Catechism* word for word, which the printed version modernises by substituting 'to' for 'unto'. Hogg's original discusses Sabbath-breaking as a sin, which is entirely omitted by the printed version presumably out of deference to the less stringent practices of other churches, and his reference to God's choice of the elect from among the poor and indigent was also deleted. Elen's stern reference to sin as that which 'may ruin both your soul and body in the end' is transformed into the comparatively anodyne 'nobody can tell all the bad consequences to which it may lead'. Other changes seem designed to remove Hogg's more colloquial expressions: Jessie says 'though the day is so fine' rather than 'for as fine as the day is' (p. 234), and the reference to the old women looking as ugly as sin is omitted. Altogether the printed version is much more bland than Hogg's original. 'Dramas of Infancy No. 1. What is Sin?' from Hogg's manuscript is a much more interesting dialogue, but the printed version may also be seen as worthy of attention, particularly as it shows the kind of generalised and rather prim religious instruction that was deemed suitable for middle-class children of the period. The present volume therefore prints 'Dramas of Infancy No. 1. What is Sin?' from Hogg's fair-copy manuscript, following it up with the second number of the 'Dramas of Infancy', after which 'What is Sin?' is printed from *Ackermann's Juvenile Forget Me Not*. Hogg's fair-copy manuscript of 'What is Sin?' is printed with the silent addition of full stops or question marks at the end of sentences. The following emendations have also been made:

p. 235, ll. 17–18 and if any women do sin] and any women do sin (MS)
p. 235, l. 22 too petulant] to petulant (MS)
p. 235, ll. 29–30 you are grieviously mistaken] you err grieviously mistaken (MS) [an imperfectly implemented choice between two expressions]

Dramas of Infancy No. 2. What is Death? (pp. 236–38)

This dialogue between two boys about one of the great mysteries of human existence was clearly written by Hogg as a companion-piece to the similar conversation of two girls in 'Dramas of Infancy No. 1. What is Sin?', and follows on from it in Hogg's fair-copy manuscript in the University of Stirling Library (MS 25, Box 1 (1A)), although it was not published in *Ackermann's Juvenile Forget Me Not* for 1830, or indeed anywhere else in Hogg's lifetime. The story elaborates on an exchange between the twelve-year old Flora and her six-year old brother Sandy in Hogg's 'Cousin Mattie' of 1820—see *Winter Evening Tales*, ed. by Ian Duncan (S/SC, 2002), pp. 433–41. As the children approach their home Flora comments on its quietness, saying 'It's like death' and Sandy responds by asking her what death *is* like:

> "You will may be see that ower soon. It is death that kills a' living things, Sandy."
> "Aye; aih aye! Sandy saw a wee buldie, it could neilel pick, nol flee, nol dab. It was vely ill done o' death! Sistel Flola, didna God make a' living things?"
> "Yes; be assured he did."
> "Then, what has death ado to kill them? if Sandy wele God, him wad fight him."
> "Whisht, whisht, my dear; ye dinna ken what you're sayin. Ye maunna speak about these things." (pp. 436–37)

Consciously or unconsciously this little exchange seems to have provided the basis for 'What is Death?' ten years later.

Shoberl may have rejected 'What is Death?' because space in the annual was limited, or he may simply have felt that the dialogues were too much alike to be printed together in a volume which needed to provide as much variety of articles and contributors as possible. While to modern tastes the topic of death may seem unsuitable for young children, nineteenth-century evangelical readers did not share such scruples—on the contrary, life was particularly uncertain for children and preparation for death as essential to them as to older people.

Hogg clearly intended 'What is Death?' to be read with 'What is Sin?' when he gave it the same series title of 'Dramas of Infancy' and included it on the same sheet for Ackermann. It is accordingly printed here from Hogg's fair-copy manuscript with the silent addition of full stops or question marks at the end of sentences. The following emendations have also been made:

p. 237, ll. 9–10 If George were God] If Gorge were God (MS) [not a representation of a child's imperfect articulation since he calls himself 'George' correctly at p. 220, ll. 28 and 30]

p. 237, l. 13 our dear good sister, George,] our dear good sister George, (MS)

The Poachers (pp. 241–49)

'The Poachers' was published in *Ackermann's Juvenile Forget Me Not* for 1831, pp. 99–116, and was not reprinted during Hogg's lifetime, nor does his manuscript appear to have survived. Just as Hogg's 'Dramas of Infancy' show children struggling to comprehend the big issues of life, so this tale presents a moral problem to the reader in the figure of the boy Benjy. Benjy, as the orphaned child of a poacher, does wrong in pursuing his father's trade, but Hogg shows clearly that being outside the sympathies of the society which surrounds him he finds it almost impossible to live within the law even though he possesses good qualities such as loyalty and generosity. As Adam Little remarks, 'It is a hard case to abandon a human being awthegither, without at least giving him a chance o' doing better' (p. 247): when Adam helps him to a settled home and a decent education he ceases to be a social nuisance and eventually becomes a Church of Scotland minister. The tale forms an interesting commentary on Scott's presentation of the similarly disreputable Benjie in his novel *Redgauntlet* (1824), dismissed by Darsie Latimer as 'the blackguard vermin'—see *Redgauntlet*, ed. by G. A. M. Wood and David Hewitt, EEWN 17 (Edinburgh: Edinburgh University Press, 1997), p. 51.

'The Poachers' is reprinted in the present volume from *Ackermann's Juvenile Forget Me Not* with the following emendations:

p. 245, l. 24 as purpose like] ae purpose like   (*AJFMN*)
p. 246, l. 42 how soon."] how soon. (*AJFMN*)
p. 247, l. 2 at least] at best (*AJFMN*)
p. 248, l. 21 he would "see them a'] he would see them a' (*AJFMN*) [the paragraph modulates from indirect to direct speech, and at some point opening speech marks are required to match the closing ones]

Hymn for Sabbath Morning (see pp. 261–62)

Hogg's 'Hymn for Sabbath Morning' was first published in *Ackermann's Juvenile Forget Me Not* for 1831, pp. 172–73, and subsequently in his own gift-book *A Father's New Year's Gift* (1832), pp. 6–7. These two printings have different layouts on the page in that the first is continuous verse and the second divided into four-line stanzas, while the punctuation and capitalisation (matters normally deemed to be the printer's province) also vary slightly. This does not appear to warrant two appearances of 'Hymn for Sabbath Morning' in the present volume, and so it is not printed here but under the heading of *A Father's New Year's Gift*, pp. 261–62 as part of a collection created by Hogg himself.

Play up my Love (pp. 250–51)

These verses were published under the title of 'The Shepherd Boy's Song' in *Ackermann's Juvenile Forget Me Not* for 1832, pp. 157–58, and were obviously produced at the editor's request to accompany an engraving by H. Rolle from a painting by H. Warren of that title. Hogg's letter to Shoberl of 4 June 1831 (Historical Society of Pennsylvania: Frank M. Etting [family] Collection, Collection 193, European Authors) includes his fair-copy manuscript of these verses, explaining:

> I had completely forgot the picture which was the more natural as I did not promise unless you gave me the name of the artist and the story. I got your letter with our carrier this day and have dashed you off three verses for the picture

Hogg entitled his verses 'Play up my Love | A Song', which Shoberl must then have altered to agree with the title of the accompanying engraving. He or the printer also changed 'my bonny woman' of line 4 to 'my little woman', besides conventionalising spelling ('O' becomes 'Oh!', for instance) and adding a more explicit and heavier style of punctuation to the poem. While Hogg would have expected the printer of the work to complete the punctuation indicated in his fair-copy manuscript, the punctuation of the published text also over-rides and misrepresents the punctuation he did provide. The exclamation mark of 'Play up, my love!' in line 9, for example, eliminates the pause created by Hogg's dash at this point, and oddly enough given the editor's dislike of the Scots word 'bonny' there is an attempt to make Hogg's verses seem more colloquial and Scottish by changing 'and' to 'an'' (lines 5 and 18), and 'of' to 'o'' (line 21). The editors have decided to print 'Play up my Love' from Hogg's fair-copy manuscript, providing this analysis of the differences between it and the (only slightly different) published poem for the reader who does not have easy access to that version. No emendations have been made.

Note on a Juvenile Annual
Unrepresented in the Present Volume

The Juvenile Forget Me Not

Two published contributions

As the success of the annuals escalated, several specifically designed for children were published—an account of *The Christmas Box*, the first of these, is given in the Introduction to the present volume (p. xvi). A popular adult annual might well be linked to a children's annual, and the editor of *The Juvenile Forget Me Not*, Anna Maria Hall, was the wife of S. C. Hall, the editor of *The Amulet*. She was also a professional writer (her emphasis on Irish national culture paralleling Hogg's interest in a distinctively Scottish one), and had published her *Sketches of Irish Character* in 1829 as well as writing for various periodicals. Hogg's letter to Allan Cunningham of 19 January 1830 (Trinity College, Cambridge: Cullum N.8.2) implies that he had read and enjoyed her work so much that he wished his contributions to *The Juvenile Forget Me Not* to be considered as personal gifts to an admired colleague:

> That lady is a particular favourite of mine. Her simplicity, her humour and her pathos are all delightful and her careless easy manner most of all. Give my kindest love to her and say that whatever she accepts of mine she must take as a gift of homage even though it should amount to a third of the volume. To her husband I make no such concessions but when I come to London I shall see them both.

In view of this extravagant proffer it seems at first sight rather surprising that only two Hogg contributions in fact appeared in *The Juvenile Forget Me Not*.

When S. C. Hall had applied to Hogg for contributions to *The Amulet* he included a request for work for his wife's annual at the same time. Initially Hogg seems to have confused this children's annual with Ackermann's production of the same name, but Hall wrote to him on 24 April [1829] (NLS, MS 2245, fols 146–47) clearing up the matter:

> I beg that the tales &c. may be sent direct per mail, to me at Messrs Westley & Davies, Stationers Court London—pray let those intended for my wife be sent also,—as her book and that about to be published by Mr Ackermann are totally distinct—she will write you herself after she has received them,—and express how much she feels gratified at being enabled to rank you among her contributors.—You did not say whether I sent you one of the "Juvenile Forget Me Not" [...].

Hall's subsequent letter to Hogg of 25 June, however, reveals that Mrs Hall had by that date written to Hogg about the tales he had sent her for *The Juvenile Forget Me Not* and he then returned them, although he also stated, 'My wife means to insert in her little volume, your beautiful verses—the Childs Prayer—and desires me to present her best respects & remembbcs to you' (NLS, MS 2245, fols 148–49). The rejected tales may possibly have been those described by Mrs Hall in her subsequent letter to Hogg of 2 April 1830 (quoted below) as a tale of seduction and 'a wanderer from fairyland'.

A Child's Prayer (see pp. 265–66, 'Hymn for General Use')
From S. C. Hall's letter to Hogg of 25 June 1829 (quoted above) 'A Child's Prayer' was sent to Mrs Hall during the spring or early summer of that year, and it was first published in *The Juvenile Forget Me Not* for 1830, pp. 114–15. It was then reprinted as 'Hymn for General Use' in Hogg's own gift-book, *A Father's New Year's Gift* (London: Cochrane, 1832), pp. 13–14. The relationship between these two printings (as well as a holograph presentation manuscript under the title of 'A Young Girl's Prayer') is discussed in the introductory and textual note to 'Hymn for General Use' below, together with the reasons for the decision of the present editors not to print both versions in this volume.

A Child's Hymn for the Close of the Week (see pp. 263–65)

'A Child's Hymn for the Close of the Week' was sent to the care of S. C. Hall with Hogg's letter of 6 March 1830 (already quoted), and was printed in *The Juvenile Forget Me Not* for 1831, pp. 78–80. 'A Child's Hymn for the Close of the Week' was subsequently reprinted in Hogg's own gift-book *A Father's New Year's Gift* (London: Cochrane, 1832), pp. 11–12. The differences between the two printings are discussed under the heading 'Hymn for the Close of the Week' below, together with the reasons for the decision of the present editors not to print both versions in this volume.

Hogg's traditional religious upbringing and the pre-Victorian evangelicism of the Halls united in placing great emphasis on the religious training and education of the young, and his hymns and prayers for children were there-fore extremely welcome to Mrs Hall–'your Hymns for children are exquisite' she told him in a letter of [2 March 1832] (NLS, MS 2245, fols 203–04). But her attitude to children was otherwise much more repressive than that of James Hogg. The 'Preface' to *The Juvenile Forget Me Not* for 1831 (pp. iii–iv) reminded its readers that 'mere amusement is not much better than idleness, and that even "a merry Christmas and a happy New Year" [...]—may bring information to their cheerful fire-sides, and that knowledge and Pleasure may go hand in hand to visit them'. Hogg by contrast was a man who could de-scribe his own children to Mrs Hannah Lamont in a letter of 23 June 1834 as 'noisy romping healthy brats but good learners' (NLS, Acc. 9430, no. 107). While Hogg's prayers and hymns for children were appreciated his fiction was not, and the following letter from Mrs Hall to Hogg of 2 April 1830 (see this volume's Introduction, pp. xxiii–xxiv) reveals that the fiction he sent her in 1830 was rejected just as the tales he had sent her during the previous year had been:

> "The Prayer" for my "Juvenile" is all that I can wish, and the tale you intended for me also, is interesting and powerfully written–but surely my dear Sir, you would not wish my young readers to credit super-natural appearances?–I could not take it upon my conscience to send the little darlings tremblingly to bed after perusing the very perfection of Ghost Stories from your pen. I find it most singularly perplexing–that the first tale you sent me was one of Seduction–Your Second (a thing by the way of extraordinary spirit and beauty)–was a wanderer from fairy land. [...] Your last is a Ghost Story!–which kept even me awake half the night–it is a downright destruction of peace for you to write them so well–pray pray, write me a simple tale something about your own pure and innocent Scottish children–without love–or ghosts– or fairies (James Hogg Collection, Special Collections, University of Otago Library: in a copy of the *Juvenile Forget Me Not* for 1831)

Clearly Mrs Hall appreciated Hogg's tales from a literary point of view even though she did not approve of children reading them. Hogg's response of 22 May 1830 (Historical Society of Pennsylvania: Ferdinand Julius Dreer Collec-tion, Collection 175, English Poets), though gallant towards Mrs Hall personally, was uncompromising in its rejection of her attitude towards children's reading-matter:

> I sent you a very good tale and one of those with which I delight to harrow up the little souls of my own family I say it is a *very good* tale and *exactly* fit for children and no body else; and your letter to me occassioned me writing one of the best poems ever dropped from my pen in ridicule of your's and the modern system of education [...] As I think shame to put my name to such mere common place things as you seem to want I have sent you a letter from an English Widow

This was probably 'A Letter to the Ettrick Shepherd' subsequently published in *The Amulet* (see pp. 334–35 above): although it was tailored specifically to the moral instructional tone of *The Juvenile Forget Me Not* in repudiating cruelty to animals, it nevertheless also contains a love-story which may be the reason for Mrs Hall's rejection of this too.

For all his generosity towards Mrs Hall personally Hogg must have found her constant rejection of his fiction tiresome: his letter of 22 May 1830, quoted above, declares that 'of all creatures ever I met with you are the most capricious and the worst to please'. Nothing by Hogg was published in *The Juvenile Forget Me Not* after the issue for 1831.

Gift-Books
The Casket
One poem published

Although the title may give the impression that *The Casket* is a similar volume to the annuals of the late 1820s and early 1830s it is a much more old-fashioned and dignified-looking octavo gift-book, published not by a fine-art publisher but by John Murray of Albemarle Street. The title-page has a motto from Moliere's *The Miser* which continues the idea expressed in the title that the book is a casket of poetic treasures.

A paragraph about the forthcoming publication in the 'Literary Novelties' column of the *Literary Gazette* of 28 February 1829 (p. 150) reported that it was 'to be published by subscription, for the relief of a family that has seen better days', and names the Ettrick Shepherd among the contributors, who included 'almost every name of note in our poetical sphere'. The editor of this poetry anthology (named as a Mrs Blencowe in a review of the volume in the *Literary Gazette* of 13 June 1829, pp. 385–86) also implies in the prefatory Advertisement that it was compiled for charitable purposes, from 'the earnest wish of benefiting a friend', and her gratitude to John Murray for 'the liberality of the terms on which he has engaged to publish' the volume reinforces the idea. The family to be benefited is not named, while nothing more than her name is known of the editor.

A fourteen-page list of subscribers is headed with the names of six members of the royal family, and includes many aristocrats and churchmen, including the Archbishop of Canterbury. This list occupies the place normally as-signed to the contents pages, and the titles of the poems included in the volume with the names of their equally illustrious authors are given instead in an Index at the back of the book. The volume included poems by Samuel Rogers, Thomas Moore, William Wordsworth, L. E. L., Mrs Hemans, Bernard Barton, Lord Byron, Theodore Hook, T. H. Bayly, Joanna Baillie, Edward Lytton Bulwer, and George Crabbe.

The Casket was advertised in the *Literary Gazette* of 2 May 1829 (p. 295) as to be published on 1 May 1829 by John Murray by subscription, but no price to subscribers is mentioned. It seems likely that publication was delayed by a few weeks, since a review did not appear in the paper until 13 June and the *Literary Gazette* was often the earliest periodical to notice a work once it became available.

The title-page termed *The Casket* 'A Miscellany, Consisting of Unpublished Poems', and the Editor explains accordingly, 'The poetry contained in this volume consists of pieces written expressly for "The Casket," and of others which have never before been published' (p. vi). Scrupulously, she goes on to note in the 'Advertisement' that the lines by Samuel Rogers 'were extracted from a poem, which, though unpublished at the time, has since been given to the public', and a similar footnote to the Index adds that 'Since the Casket was sent to the Press, the Editor has heard that the three Charades marked with an asterisk have been printed' (p. 451).

The Admonition (pp. 255–56)

Hogg's poem 'The Admonition' was published on pp. 150–52 of *The Casket*, but his surviving correspondence provides no information about his connec-tion with either the publication or its editor. John Murray had published a number of Hogg's poems during the 1810s in partnership with William Blackwood and had been among Hogg's correspondents until the early 1820s, while a link between the two men still existed through J. G. Lockhart, an Edinburgh friend of Hogg's who had moved to London and was now editor of Murray's prestigious *Quarterly Review*. It is possible that Murray, as publisher of *The Casket*, might have solicited a contribution from the well-known Ettrick Shepherd either directly or through Lockhart.

An early version of 'The Admonition' had been published in no. 44 of Hogg's own essay-periodical *The Spy*, on 29 June 1811 (see *The Spy*, pp. 443–45), and was reprinted by Archibald Constable with minor revisions in Hogg's *Poetical Works (1822)*, IV, 270–73. The revised version of the poem in *The Casket* tends to follow *The Spy* rather than *Poetical Works (1822)* when the two earlier texts differ: presumably Hogg, having been asked for a poem for *The Casket*, decided to revise something from *The Spy* (a work little remembered by the public in 1829), forgetting that 'The Admonition' had been included in *Poetical Works (1822)*. The version of the poem in *The Casket* is tailored to meet the requirements of a genteel, English poetry miscellany. The suggestion that Jeanie is about to lie to her father about the purpose of her nightly wander-ings ('Ye needna lie—ye gang, I ken, | To meet young Jamie i' the glen' in *The*

Spy) is softened in lines 37–38 to 'I ken ye gae–an' grieve to ken– | To meet young Jamie o' the glen'. A homely Scots 'Be good, my bairn!' in *The Spy* is anglicised to 'Be good, my love!', and the lines 'But that's no' a'–by night an' day | Keep out o' sin an' danger's way.' become 'But, oh my child! by night and day, | Keep out o' sin and danger's way!' (lines 41–42). Furthermore, the four lines from 'O! think if sic a thing should be,' to 'Should gar us lose our bairn for ever.', which in *The Spy* precede six lines beginning 'Your health is high', follow the equivalent passage in the version printed in *The Casket*, a change which is more likely to have been the work of the author than of an editor or compositor. There are also several changes in words and in word-order that also suggest the revising author at work: 'weal' (line 20) replaces 'good' in *The Spy*, for instance, and Hogg's 'ilka note's a tale of love' (line 28) avoids the repetition of 'note' in *The Spy*'s 'ilka note's a note of love'.

On balance it appears more likely that Hogg supplied a revised version of one of his previously-published poems as a new one than that the editor of *The Casket* (who seems to have been nervously scrupulous to acknowledge when contributions to her volume had in fact appeared in print elsewhere) had printed a previously-published poem without the author's permission. It is improbable, however, that Hogg saw proofs of his poem, which contains evidence of misunderstanding by an English editor or compositor. 'The Admonition' is therefore reprinted in the present volume from *The Casket* with the following emendations which seek to correct these errors:

l. 10 bespak] bespak' (*The Casket*) [emendation matches *The Spy*]
l. 31 fu' dink] fu'dink' (*The Casket*) [*The Spy* has: sae dink]
l. 45 poising] posing (*The Casket*) [emendation matches *The Spy*]
l. 52 Should gar us] Should gae us (*The Casket*) [emendation matches *The Spy*]

A Father's New Year's Gift

Of all Hogg's work for juvenile annuals his prayers and hymns for children were probably the most acceptable, his own traditional presbyterian upbringing coinciding with the new pre-Victorian evangelicalism in placing great emphasis on the religious education and instruction of the young. Hogg warned parents, for example, of the seriousness of this responsibility in his *Lay Sermons* (1834), urging 'You are breeding up flowers of immortality, and what will be your reckoning at the last day if you do not train them up in the way that they should go!'–see *A Series of Lay Sermons on Good Principles and Good Breeding*, ed. by Gillian Hughes with Douglas S. Mack (S/SC, 1997), p. 75. During his London visit in 1832 Hogg published a little sixteen-page devotional manual of prayers and hymns for the use of children, partly intended as a keepsake for his own young family in the distant Yarrow valley, as the title and dedicatory letter reveal.

The date of composition of the work remains unknown. Its title and the dated letter of dedication misleadingly imply that the work was intended for publication on 1 January 1832, but when Hogg wrote to his wife on 10

January it was just being printed: 'I have the little manual of prayers and hymns for my children in the press, and will send each of them a copy this week' (see Garden, p. 248). As Hogg had arrived in London on the last day of 1831 he must either have brought copy for the publication with him or composed it within ten days of his arrival. The existence of draft manuscripts for part of the contents of the work (discussed in detail below) may be thought to suggest a longer genesis for it than a mere ten days, but a small booklet consisting partly of reprinted pieces could conceivably have been drafted and rearranged within this limited period. On the other hand it is perhaps all too easy to envisage Hogg, separated from his own children and seeing the seasonal crop of gift-books in the drawing-rooms of the houses where he visited, dashing off a little present for the family at Altrive which might also earn him some useful money during his stay.

By 17 January the printing seems to have been almost finished, for writing that day to his wife Hogg mentioned the imminent departure of a friend from London for Scotland: 'He sails for Scotland to morrow and may possibly bring the children's books with him' (Stirling University Library, MS 25B(8)). However, the copies did not arrive at Altrive until the beginning of the following month. Writing to her husband on 11 February Margaret Hogg reports, 'The children are delighted with your beautiful Prayers & Jas has been learning one, we only got them last week you must bring some more with you to give away'—see Norah Parr, *James Hogg at Home: Being the Domestic Life and Letters of the Ettrick Shepherd* (Dollar: Douglas S. Mack, 1980) p. 103. The precise date of publication in London is unknown, but must have been before 4 February, for a review appeared in *The Athenæum* of that date (p. 78), which also gives the selling-price in describing it as 'this stitched sixpenny trifle'. The number of copies printed is not known. *A Father's New Year's Gift* was published by James Cochrane, also the publisher of Hogg's *Altrive Tales*, the publication of which as the first volume of his collected prose works had been the primary object of Hogg's journey to London. Sales were probably satisfactory since Cochrane was prepared to engage in a proposed 'Young Lady's Sabbath Companion' in 1835, a work which was in the press at the time of Hogg's death—see Introduction, p. xxvii.

A Father's New Year's Gift contained four freshly-written prose prayers and a number of verse hymns, several of which were revised from earlier publications, especially from Hogg's contributions to juvenile annuals. Although there are a number of surviving manuscripts (discussed in detail below in relation to individual items of the work), none of them appears to represent Hogg's final fair-copy used by Cochrane's printers. *A Father's New Year's Gift* is therefore reprinted here from the published pamphlet.

Letter of Dedication (p. 259)

Hogg's letter of dedication for *A Father's New Year's Gift* was clearly ante-dated to suit with the title of the work. A manuscript version has survived in the Beinecke Rare Book & Manuscript Library, Yale University (James Hogg Collection: GEN MSS 61, Box 1, Folder 43) with a similar symbolic dating but a slightly different sentence structure to the published version: this seems to represent a rough version of the copy prepared for the printer. The dedicatory letter is printed from *A Father's New Year's Gift* of 1832 without change.

Prayer for the Sabbath Morning (p. 260)

This prose prayer was first published in *A Father's New Year's Gift*, p. 3. There is a surviving manuscript in NLS, MS 9634, fols 5–6, a paper folded to make a small four-page booklet with the pages numbered 1 to 4 by Hogg. 'Prayer for the Sabbath Morning' occupies page 1 and half of page 2 of this booklet, and it is followed by 'Prayer for the Sabbath Evening' on pages 2, 3, and part of 4. This order is that in which the two prayers appear in the printed pamphlet, and a direction after the opening phrase of the Lord's Prayer at the conclusion of 'Prayer for the Sabbath Morning' '(print in full)', as it is clearly addressed to the printer, would appear to imply that this four-page booklet is Hogg's fair-copy manuscript for these two prayers in *A Father's New Year's Gift*.

Other features of this manuscript, however, suggest it was produced as a self-sufficient manuscript without reference to the other parts of *A Father's New Year's Gift*. The page beginning with 'Prayer for the Sabbath Morning' was numbered 1, even though preceded in the published pamphlet by the title and dedicatory letter: similarly the second half of page 4 is blank rather than continuing with the next item in the published work ('Hymn for Sabbath Morning') and in addition Hogg has signed his name immediately after the conclusion of this second prayer. In general the manuscript is neatly written, but with some deletions and additions in Hogg's hand.

It seems likely that this manuscript represents an intermediate stage in preparing copy for *A Father's New Year's Gift*. After assembling suitable items from his previously-published children's hymns Hogg's next tasks would be to decide what new copy was required to link these into the plan of a manual, and to compose the missing items. Perhaps he originally intended to present the printer with a mixture of printed and manuscript items, but this would be confusing and liable to misinterpretation and wrong ordering, and it seems likely that Hogg then decided to produce a coherent manuscript for the entire work, rendering this manuscript of the two prayers redundant. At all events, no significant textual variation is revealed by a collation of these two prayers as they appear in this manuscript against the published version of these texts in *A Father's New Year's Gift*.

'Prayer for the Sabbath Morning' is therefore reprinted from *A Father's New Year's Gift* without change.

Prayer for the Sabbath Evening (pp. 260–61)

'Prayer for the Sabbath Evening' was first published in *A Father's New Year's Gift*, pp. 4–5. A manuscript version exists on pages 2, 3, and part of 4 of a folded four-page booklet in NLS, MS 9634, fols 5–6. An analysis of this manuscript is given in the textual note to 'Prayer for the Sabbath Morning' above: it appears to represent a transitional phase of production, when Hogg's existing work was complemented by the writing of new items for his children's manual, rather than the final fair-copy manuscript. 'Prayer for the Sabbath Evening' is therefore reprinted from *A Father's New Year's Gift* without change.

Hymn for Sabbath Morning (pp. 261–62)

'Hymn for Sabbath Morning' was first published in *Ackermann's Juvenile Forget Me Not* for 1831, pp. 172–73, and then reprinted in *A Father's New Year's Gift*, pp. 6–7. The two printings agree in substantives but differ in accidentals and are also laid out differently on the page, the earlier printing consisting of an unbroken succession of lines and the later one being divided into four-line stanzas. Despite the fact that the two printings represent one version of 'Hymn for Sabbath Morning' rather than two it seems plain that the one was not directly typeset from the other.

There is also a surviving manuscript of 'Hymn for Sabbath Morning' in the Beinecke Rare Book & Manuscript Library, Yale University (James Hogg Collection, GEN MSS 61, Box 1, Folder 43), which was plainly prepared for *A Father's New Year's Gift*. It occupies part of a paper folded to make a four-page booklet and numbered 3 to 6: in this booklet Hogg wrote 'Hymn for the Close of the Week' (pp. 3–4), 'Hymn for Sabbath Morning' (pp. 5–6), and 'Hymn for General Use' (p. 6) all of which are in *A Father's New Year's Gift*. The Beinecke manuscript shares some of the characteristics of NLS, MS 9634, fols 5–6, and may in fact be a counterpart to it. It also contains a direction to the printer on p. 6, where in the margin and at right-angles to 'Hymn for General Use' Hogg has written 'This Hymn to be the last and to follow the prayers p. 8–9'. This direction would normally imply that the Beinecke manuscript is part of Hogg's fair-copy manuscript for *A Father's New Year's Gift*, but this does not appear to be the case. 'Hymn for General Use' is not the last hymn in the work and it does not immediately follow any of the prose prayers there. Nor is the order of the three items in this manuscript that of the printed pamphlet, in which 'Hymn for the Close of the Week' is on pp. 11–12, 'Hymn for Sabbath Morning' on pp. 6–7, and 'Hymn for General Use' on pp. 13–14. A curious feature of this manuscript is that Hogg signs his full name at the end of the first and second items, a redundant gesture in a manuscript containing items intended for publication together as part of a larger work by Hogg himself. The text of 'Hymn for Sabbath Morning' in the Beinecke manuscript seems to be closer to the printing in *A Father's New Year's Gift* than the one in *Ackermann's Juvenile Forget Me Not* in that it is written in four-line stanzas. It too agrees with *A Father's New Year's Gift* in substantives while differing in accidentals.

The Beinecke manuscript (like the NLS one) appears to represent a transitional stage in the development of *A Father's New Year's Gift*, where Hogg was assembling material for his gift-book but had not yet decided upon the final running-order for it. Although he may have supposed on first writing it that it would serve as copy for the printer he probably prepared another manuscript subsequently with a final and complete version of the contents of the publication in the order in which they appear in the published work. 'Hymn for Sabbath Morning' is therefore given in the present volume from *A Father's New Year's Gift* without change.

Hymn for the Sabbath Evening (p. 262)

'Hymn for the Sabbath Evening' was first published in *A Father's New Year's Gift*, p. 8, and never reprinted in Hogg's lifetime. Hogg's manuscript does not appear to have survived. It is given in the present volume from *A Father's New Year's Gift* with the following emendation:

l. 4 between?] between (*FNYG*)

Morning Prayer for Week Days (pp. 262–63)

'Morning Prayer for Week Days' was first published in *A Father's New Year's Gift*, p. 9, and never reprinted in Hogg's lifetime. Hogg's manuscript does not appear to have survived. It is given in the present volume from *A Father's New Year's Gift* without change.

Evening Prayer for Week Days (p. 263)

'Evening Prayer for Week Days' was first published in *A Father's New Year's Gift*, p. 10, and never reprinted in Hogg's lifetime. Hogg's manuscript does not appear to have survived. It is given in the present volume from *A Father's New Year's Gift* without change.

Hymn for the Close of the Week (pp. 263–65)

These verses were first published as 'A Child's Hymn for the Close of the Week' in Anna Maria Hall's *The Juvenile Forget Me Not* for 1831 (see note above), pp. 78–80, and subsequently as 'Hymn for the Close of the Week' in *A Father's New Year's Gift*, pp. 11–12. The two printings agree in wording except for two small differences as follows:

l. 13 But this I know, (*JFMN*)] I only know (*FNYG*)
l. 18 Has round (*JFMN*)] Hast round (*FNYG*)

The punctuation and spelling of the two printings, normally regarded at the time as the printer's province, also vary somewhat. It seems likely that the second printing was not typeset directly from the first since a manuscript version clearly prepared by Hogg for *A Father's New Year's Gift* exists as part of the Beinecke manuscript discussed in the textual note to 'Hymn for Sabbath Morning' above: this manuscript seems to represent a transitional stage of preparation for *A Father's New Year's Gift* rather than the author's final fair-copy manuscript for the published work.

Since the differences between 'Hymn for the Close of the Week' and 'A Child's Hymn for the Close of the Week' are relatively insignificant it has seemed to the editors preferable to analyse these rather than to give both printings in the present volume, and precedence has been given to the version that appeared in Hogg's own collection of children's prayers and hymns. 'Hymn for the Close of the Week' is printed in the present volume, therefore, from *A Father's New Year's Gift* without change.

Hymn for General Use (pp. 265–66)

These verses were first published as 'A Child's Prayer' in Anna Maria Hall's

The Juvenile Forget Me Not for 1830 (see note above), pp. 114–15, and subsequently as 'Hymn for General Use' in *A Father's New Year's Gift*, pp. 13–14. Apart from the usual differences in capitalisation and punctuation, resulting from the work of two different printers, there are only minor differences between the two versions. The layout of Hogg's lines is the most obvious of these, the earlier printing consisting of four eight-line stanzas and the later printing of eight four-line stanzas. The later version also includes a footnote to 'dear parents' in line 25, thoughtfully stating that 'relations' might be substituted 'if the child has no parents'. Otherwise the only substantive difference is in line 15 where *The Juvenile Forget Me Not* reads 'I bless thee, Lord' and *A Father's New Year's Gift* reads 'I bless the Lord'.

A third version, dated 2 September 1829 and with the last two stanzas omitted, exists as a manuscript entitled 'A Young Girl's Prayer' (NLS, MS 573, fol. 73). This was plainly created by Hogg after his copy had been sent for *The Juvenile Forget Me Not* for 1830 as a presentation holograph and not as a literary manuscript intended for transmission into print, a note, presumably by the recipient (one H. Wilson), stating 'given to me on the same day it was written'.

There are two further manuscript versions of these verses, neither of which represents printer's copy for *A Father's New Year's Gift* of 1832. The first is part of a sheet of rough drafts by Hogg preserved in Stirling University Library, MS 25, Box B (2)): the top of the sheet contains a rough draft of a jingling rhyme to the traditional dance tune of 'Merrily danced the quaker's wife' and headed 'A little girl's song', possibly representing an abandoned intention to create a companion-piece to 'A Boy's Song' for one of the annuals, though it was never refined and published. An untitled version of 'A Child's Prayer' was then drafted underneath to make use of the blank part of the sheet, and when Hogg reached the bottom of the paper he continued to draft by turning it sideways and writing in the wide margin. This manuscript appears to represent the earliest stage in composing 'A Child's Prayer', predating the version published in *The Juvenile Forget Me Not* for 1830.

The second manuscript, headed 'Hymn for general use' is on the final page (p. 6) of the Beinecke manuscript discussed in the textual note to 'Hymn for Sabbath Morning' above, and gives only the first twenty-four lines, laid out in the eight-line stanzas of *The Juvenile Forget Me Not* poem rather than the four-line stanzas of the 1832 pamphlet. It appears to represent an intermediate stage in the preparation of *A Father's New Year's Gift* rather than Hogg's fair-copy manuscript for the printer.

'Hymn for General Use' is therefore taken in the present volume from *A Father's New Year's Gift* without change.

Hymn on the Omnipresence of the Deity (p. 266)

'Hymn on the Omnipresence of the Deity' appeared in *A Father's New Year's Gift*, pp. 15–16, after having had the longest publication history of any item in the collection. Its first appearance was as one of the Covenanting servant Nanny's hymns in *The Brownie of Bodsbeck and Other Tales*, 2 vols (Edinburgh:

Blackwood; London: Murray, 1818), I, 294–95. The hymn was then extracted from this context and slightly revised by Hogg as 'Dweller in Heaven', one of the songs of *A Selection of German Hebrew Melodies*, set to music by the composer W. E. Heather and published around 1817 by the London music-seller C. Christmas (pp. 30–39). When Hogg included a section in his four-volume *Poetical Works (1822)* derived from this publication and headed 'Sacred Melodies', 'Dweller in Heaven' was naturally reprinted there (IV, 217–19): this printing is substantively the same as the one on p. 39 of *A Selection of German Hebrew Melodies*, and so close to it in accidentals as to suggest that the version in the 1822 *Poetical Works* may well have been typeset from Hogg's song-collection.

A similar group of 'Sacred Melodies' including 'Dweller in Heaven' was included in the posthumous editions of Hogg's poetry published by the Glasgow firm of Blackie and Son. Its eminent suitability to a religious gift-book is demonstrated by a subsequent reprinting under the title 'Adoration' in *Harp of Judah; or, Gems of Sacred Poetry*, published by Thomas Nelson in 1868 and it was natural that Hogg should have chosen to include it in his own gift-book.

Several details of 'Hymn on the Omnipresence of the Deity' in *A Father's New Year's Gift* demonstrate that Hogg revised his poem once more for this 1832 publication—in particular the word 'Omniscience' on line 16 had been 'Omnipotence' in all previous versions, while the reading 'adore what through life' on line 30 had previously been 'adore what on earth'. No manuscript for this version appears to have survived, however, and 'Hymn on the Omnipresence of the Deity' is printed in the present volume from *A Father's New Year's Gift* without change.

The Young Lady's Sabbath Companion
Unpublished
Manuscript Fragment (p. 269)

Following the success of *A Father's New Year's Gift*, James Cochrane agreed in June 1835 to publish 'a small religious work' by Hogg, to be called *The Young Lady's Sabbath Companion* (see Introduction, pp. xxvi–xxvii). This project did not come to fruition because of Hogg's death in November 1835, and it appears that all that remains of *The Young Lady's Sabbath Companion* is a manuscript fragment now owned by Professor Tom Richardson. The fragment in question consists of a small single leaf approximately five and a quarter by eight and a quarter inches. Hogg's text is on one side, and on the other is a note by his daughter Mary Gray Hogg (Mrs Garden): 'This is my father's handwriting M G Garden'. The manuscript fragment carries a partial watermark 'ATMAN | Y MILL | 34', the full version of which is almost certainly 'J WHATMAN | TURKEY MILL | 1834'. Clearly, the manuscript must date from either 1834 or 1835, but there is no sign of a precisely similar paper being used by Hogg for letters in either of those years. His letter to James Cochrane of 15 June 1835 offering *The Young Lady's Sabbath Companion* has a watermark 'J WHATMAN | TURKEY MILL | 1835'. The text contains one or two phrases also used in the first pages of 'Sermon XI. Deistical Reformers'—see *Lay Sermons*, ed. Hughes (S/SC, 1997), pp. 108–09, but this seems to be rather a case of Hogg recycling, consciously or unconsciously, than that this manuscript is a draft for that portion of *Lay Sermons*. The present volume reprints without change the text contained in the surviving manuscript fragment of *The Young Lady's Sabbath Companion*.

A Parting Gift

Two poems published

A Parting Gift is one of the pocket-sized gift-books produced by the well-known Victorian printing and publishing firm of Thomas Nelson. Thomas Nelson (1780–1861) was the son of a Stirlingshire farmer and had worked with a London publisher before setting up as a second-hand bookseller in Edinburgh in 1811, and as a publisher and printer from 1825. By 1845, when *A Parting Gift* was published, his sons William (1816–87) and Thomas (1822–92) were both partners in the firm, which was clearly thriving during these years with premises in London as well as Edinburgh. The younger Thomas Nelson made the key publishing invention of the rotary press in 1850, and a New York office was opened in 1854—see the online Scottish Book Trade Index at http://www.nls.uk/catalogues/resources/sbti/index.html (as consulted on 8 September 2004).

A Parting Gift is a modest volume by comparison with the annuals in their heyday, and unlike an annual contains only poetry. It makes no general claim to originality for its contents, which are mostly reprinted pieces by well-known modern classic poets (Ben Jonson, Sheridan, Samuel Johnson, Burns, Scott, and Coleridge) and suitably sentimental verses by more ephemeral writers (L. E. L., Barry Cornwall, Miss Mitford, and Mrs Hemans). In a prefatory address 'To the Reader' dated from Edinburgh on 5 December 1845, the anonymous editor describes it as a gift-book such 'as shall form a pleasing memorial of the giver, wherein affection may recall to remembrance the absent friend', and as a 'Memorial of Friendship'. The title does not include a date, and only the publisher's imprint gives the year of publication as 1846. On each page the verses are boxed within a double-lined frame, but there are no illustrative engravings, apart from an illuminated frontispiece providing a decorative version of the title. The red binding is machine-embossed, with a decorative gilt spine reading 'Affection's Parting Gift' and the pages are also gilt-edged to match. The fact that the title does not include a date suggests that the publisher hoped for an ongoing sale extending over several years, and in this respect it resembles Hogg's own gift-book, *A Father's New Year's Gift* more than annuals such as *Friendship's Offering* or *Forget Me Not*.

The volume includes two items by Hogg, neither of them, obviously, contributed directly by him to a publication produced ten years after his death. Both of them, however, have an indirect connection to Hogg's work for annuals. One, 'An Arabian Song' had first been published, with music by the popular composer Henry Rowley Bishop (1786–1855), in his *Select and Rare Scottish*

Melodies (pp. 30–32). The publishers of this song-book, the London music-publishing firm of Goulding & D'Almaine, were also the publishers of the annual *The Musical Bijou* to which Hogg first contributed at much the same time and it seems likely that Hogg sent the firm a variety of song lyrics from which some were chosen to appear in *Select and Rare Scotish Melodies* and some in the firm's musical annual (see the headnote to *The Musical Bijou* above). When Hogg prepared copy for the printer for his own song-collection, *Songs (1831)*, 'Arabian Song' was included (see NLS, MS 4805, fols 36–37). It was printed from this manuscript on pp. 35–36 of *Songs (1831)*. This volume did not include musical settings, but in a prefatory note Hogg referred the reader to *Select and Rare Scotish Melodies* for Bishop's 'air' (p. 35). These were the only two appearances of 'Arabian Song' in Hogg's lifetime, and except for minor variations in punctuation and spelling ('heavenly' replaces 'heavn'ly' in line 13, for instance), the one is essentially a straightforward reprinting of the other.

The relatively inexpensive Blackwood volume almost certainly had a much wider circulation than Goulding & D'Almaine's music-book, and from there 'Arabian Song' was transmitted to the posthumous collection of Hogg's poetry published by the Glasgow firm of Blackie and Son—see 'Arabian Song', *The Poetical Works of the Ettrick Shepherd*, 5 vols (Glasgow, 1838–40), V, 66.

The song appears as 'An Arabian Song' on p. 247 of *A Parting Gift*, and could have been taken from either *Songs (1831)* or the fifth volume of *The Poetical Works of the Ettrick Shepherd* of 1838–40, since there are one or two minor differences in punctuation between both of these and the text of *A Parting Gift*, almost certainly the result of the work of three different compositors. This simple two-stanza appeal from an eastern lover to his mistress for an evening meeting by a fountain was ideally suited to the gentle and sentimental tone of the Victorian gift-book, but 'An Arabian Song' is not included in the present volume as its appearance in *A Parting Gift* was a reprinting of an earlier Hogg publication.

To Mary (p. 273)

During the early months of 1832 James Hogg was in London for the first and only time in his life. His object was to secure the publication of his *Altrive Tales*, a volume which he hoped would be the start of a collected prose fiction series in emulation of Sir Walter Scott's *magnum opus* edition of the Waverley Novels. For most of his stay Hogg was living with his publisher, James Cochrane of 11, Waterloo Place, and he became intimate with Cochrane's wife and children. Hogg was amused, for example, that when he appeared at church with Cochrane's family a newspaper reporter mistook them for his own wife and children, writing about the error to his son, James Robert Hogg, on 18 January:

> [...] it was only Mrs Cochrane and Miss Cochrane who is the age of Jessie and Alexr who is a year older than Maggy. Mrs Cochrane is a very beautiful lady with black hair and eyes very like your Mamma's

but she is not half so bonny to me. But she is very kind to your Papa indeed so kind that she does not know what to do with me (Hogg Letters Project Papers, University of Stirling)

Hogg left for his home in Scotland by the *United Kingdom* steamship on Sunday, 25 March, and during the last few days of his London visit made a number of small gifts to his friends there. Among them was a little poem to his hostess, Mary Cochrane, headed 'To Mrs James Cochrane' and end-dated 'Waterloo-Place | March 20th 1832'. Hogg's manuscript for this presentation holograph survives in the National Archives of Scotland, GD205/47/17/78(2).

'To Mrs James Cochrane' is substantially a reworking of lines 141–42 and 147–58 of 'A Highland Eclogue', a poem contributed by Hogg to the annual *The Gem* for 1830, and included on pp. 209–13 of the present volume, with an introductory and textual note on pp. 336–37 above. The heroine of Hogg's poem is warned in a dream about the threat to her happiness posed by her forthcoming marriage to a religious sceptic. Acting upon this warning she is responsible for securing both the eventual conversion of her husband and the happiness of their married life together, which is described in these lines as a day which, beginning with threatening omens, yet turns out a fine one before the evening.

Hogg's very personal adaptation of these lines from 'A Highland Eclogue' urges his hostess to work to secure her husband's happiness, and hence her own, in marriage—a significant plea, since during his London visit Hogg had introduced the young John M'Crone to the family, and Mrs Cochrane's subsequent adultery with M'Crone ended the Cochrane marriage in the summer or early autumn of 1834—see Allan Cunningham's letter to Hogg of 15 November 1834, in NLS, MS 2245, fols 249–50. Presumably the marriage was under strain even prior to John M'Crone's intimacy in the family.

The poem appears never to have been published in Hogg's lifetime, and presumably remained in the ownership of its subject and recipient, although Mrs Cochrane disappears from view in the autumn of 1834. It seems clear that, on his discovery of her adultery, James Cochrane repudiated her as his wife, since subsequent letters exchanged between Cochrane and Hogg mention Cochrane's family as consisting of his adolescent daughter and younger children alone. James Hogg died on 21 November 1835. ·

The poem Hogg wrote as a gift for Mary Cochrane reappeared under the title 'To Mary' on pages 248–49 of *A Parting Gift*, published by Thomas Nelson in Edinburgh in 1845. Clearly Hogg himself could not have been responsible for its appearance some ten years after his death. Somehow Mrs Cochrane's gift had passed into the hands of the unnamed editor of the volume who decided to increase his work's attractions by including in it a hitherto-unpublished poem by the well-known Ettrick Shepherd. In order to tailor the poem to his specific requirements the editor removed the original title and end-date, so that the poem in its new context has a general sentimental application rather than referring specifically to the state of the Cochrane marriage in March 1832. Otherwise the version in *A Parting Gift* adds punctuation to Hogg's original, and removes the initial capital from 'Autumn' in line 3. It serves to illustrate how Hogg's work was kept before the public eye in the Victorian period by means of various gift-books and anthologies, and how material originally published in annuals and gift-books could move away from that context and be reintroduced to it subsequently.

As the poem is quite short it is reprinted in the present volume both from Hogg's manuscript and from *A Parting Gift*, without emendation.

Gillian Hughes

Hyphenation List

Various words are hyphenated at the ends of lines in the present edition. The list below indicates those cases in which such hyphens should be retained in making quotations.

p. 10, l. 22 passers-by	p. 82, l. 40 bad-looking
p. 12, l. 39 Drown-cow	p. 102, l. 31 father-in-law
p. 12, l. 40 Hobblequa-moss	p. 111, l. 40 ewe-milking
p. 13, l. 5 Walker-cleugh	p. 112, l. 20 peacock-tailed
p. 14, l. 16 ill-boding	p. 178, l. 24 nettle-earnest
p. 54, l. 14 short-lived	p. 183, l. 21 twa-pund-ten
p. 57, l. 20 Butt-haugh	p. 184, l. 3 five-an-twanty
p. 58, l. 41 hap-wo	p. 184, l. 35 Hope-park-end
p. 60, l. 28 half-stifled	p. 201, l. 3 counting-house
p. 60, l. 41 ill-shaped	p. 203, l. 20 church-yard
p. 65, l. 2 yarn-merchants	p. 221, l. 40 May-lily
p. 78, l. 3 hay-field	p. 223, l. 2 Glen-Luran
p. 81, l. 3 hay-rake	p. 224, l. 4 May-lily
p. 81, l. 10 hay-stack	p. 224, l. 39 Glen-Dual
p. 81, l. 35 cart-shaft	

Explanatory Notes

In the Explanatory Notes which follow, page references are followed by line numbers in brackets in the case of verse items. Thus 4(42) refers to the text of 'Invocation to the Queen of the Fairies' on page 4 at line 42. For prose items page references include a letter enclosed in brackets: (a) indicates that the passage concerned is to be found in the first quarter of the page, while (b) refers to the second quarter, (c) to the third quarter, and (d) to the fourth quarter. Where it seems useful to discuss the meaning of particular phrases this is done in the Notes: single words are dealt with in the Glossary. Quotations from the Bible are from the Authorised King James version that was familiar to Hogg and his contemporaries; in the case of the Psalms, however, reference is given to the metrical *Psalms of David* approved by the Church of Scotland, where this seems apposite. For references to plays by Shakespeare, the edition used has been *The Complete Works: Compact Edition*, ed. by Stanley Wells and Gary Taylor (Oxford: Clarendon Press, 1988). For initial references to other volumes of the Stirling / South Carolina Edition the editor's name is given after the title, with the abbreviation 'S/SC' and date of first publication following in parentheses. References to Sir Walter Scott's fiction are to the *Edinburgh Edition of the Waverley Novels* (EEWN). The National Library of Scotland is abbreviated as NLS. The Notes are greatly indebted to the following standard works: *The Oxford Dictionary of National Biography*, *The Oxford English Dictionary*, and *The Scottish National Dictionary*. In addition, *Ships and Seamen: A Dictionary of British Ships and Seamen*, ed. by Grant Uden and Richard Cooper (Middlesex: Allen Lane, 1980) has been helpful in understanding nautical terms. Other works extensively used in the Notes are referred to by the following abbreviations:

Anecdotes: James Hogg, *Anecdotes of Scott*, ed. by Jill Rubenstein (S/SC, 1999)

Child: *The English and Scottish Popular Ballads*, ed. by Francis James Child, 5 vols (Boston: Houghton Mifflin, 1882–98)

Confessions: James Hogg, *The Private Memoirs and Confessions of a Justified Sinner*, ed. by P. D. Garside (S/SC, 2000)

Garden: Mrs Garden, *Memorials of James Hogg, the Ettrick Shepherd* (Paisley, [n.d.])

Letters I: *The Collected Letters of James Hogg: Volume 1 1800–1819*, ed. by Gillian Hughes, (S/SC, 2004) [In this volume letters are arranged by date, so references to it do not need to specify pages]

'Memoir': James Hogg, 'Memoir of the Author's Life' and 'Reminiscences of Former Days', in *Altrive Tales*, ed. by Gillian Hughes (S/SC, 2003)

ODEP *The Oxford Dictionary of English Proverbs*, ed. by F. P. Wilson, 3rd edn (Oxford: Clarendon Press, 1970)

Poetical Works (1822) *The Poetical Works of James Hogg*, 4 vols (Edinburgh: Constable; London: Hurst, Robinson, 1822)

Queen Hynde James Hogg, *Queen Hynde*, ed. by Suzanne Gilbert and Douglas S. Mack (S/SC, 1998)

Queer Book James Hogg, *A Queer Book,* ed. by P. D. Garside (S/SC, 1995)

The Shepherd's Calendar James Hogg, *The Shepherd's Calendar*, ed. by Douglas S. Mack (S/SC, 1995)

Songs (1831) *Songs by the Ettrick Shepherd* (Edinburgh: Blackwood; London: Cadell, 1831)

The Spy James Hogg, *The Spy*, ed. by Gillian Hughes (S/SC, 2000)

These Explanatory Notes, to which both volume editors have contributed, should be read in conjunction with Gillian Hughes's Introductory and Textual Notes, which provide: information relating to the individual annuals and gift-books to which Hogg contributed; a textual history for each item of text; and a list of any emendations made to the version(s) printed in the present volume. Eight poems contributed by Hogg to the annuals were later included in his collection *A Queer Book* (1832), and these poems have appeared in Peter Garside's S/SC edition of *A Queer Book* (1995): see this volume's Introductory and Textual Notes, p. 283. Where this volume (by Peter Garside's kind permission) reprints his annotation in its Explanatory Notes, this is indicated thus: '(P. G.)'.

Literary Souvenir
Invocation to the Queen of the Fairies
3(1–2) Muse [...] a harp uncouth of olden key in *The Queen's Wake* (1813) Hogg associates his own poetry with the ancient, simple, robust, and non-aristocratic Caledonian harp awarded by Mary, Queen of Scots to 'the Bard of Ettrick' for his performance of his fairy ballad 'Old David' at the wake held by the bards of Scotland to celebrate the return home of their Queen after her years in France. *The Queen's Wake* links 'Old David' with Hogg's own poetry, and (significantly) this poem draws heavily on 'Tam Lin' and 'Thomas Rymer' (Child 39 and 37), traditional oral fairy ballads of Hogg's native Borders. Queen Mary's prize Caledonian harp is discussed by Douglas Mack in the Introduction to the S/SC edition of *The Queen Wake* (2004): see pp. xxv–xxxiii. Interestingly, in *The Shepherd's Calendar* (p. 107) Hogg records that his much-loved maternal grandfather Will Laidlaw of Phaup was the last person in Ettrick 'who heard, saw, and conversed with the fairies, and that not once or twice, but at sundry times and seasons'.

3(3–4) And with her [...] starry sheen Hogg summarises the settings of his long narrative poems: much of *The Queen's Wake* (1813) is set in the Scottish Borders; *Mador of the Moor* (1816) is set in the Highlands ('Grampians'); and *The Pilgrims of the Sun* (1815) takes its protagonist, Mary Lee, through the heavens with a supernatural guide.

3(5–6) With my gray plaid [...] waving wings the second edition of *The Queen's Wake* (1813) was preceded by a publisher's advertisement assuring the public that the poem '*is really and truly the production of* JAMES HOGG, *a common shepherd, bred among the mountains of Ettrick Forest, who went to service when only seven years of age; and since that period has never received any education whatever*'. A grey plaid was the traditional working clothing of 'a common shepherd' of the Scottish Borders.

3(8–9) an air of heaven [...] mellow chords Hogg also refers to the Romantic symbol of the Aeolian harp in the closing lines of *The Queen's Wake*, as Suzanne Gilbert indicates in the S/SC edition of *Queen Hynde* (p. 270). As Gillian Hughes's Introductory and Textual Notes explain, another version of this poem opens Book Sixth of *Queen Hynde*. Several of the following notes are indebted to the S/SC edition of *Queen Hynde*.

4(37) thy halls of the emerald in traditional lore, green is the colour associated with the fairies.

4(42) my loved Muse, my Fairy Queen Hogg once contrasted himself as 'king o' the mountain and fairy school' with Scott as king of the school of chivalry—see *Anecdotes*, p. 61. John Wilson also declared that Hogg was 'the poet laureate of the Court of Faery' in *Blackwood's Edinburgh Magazine*, 4 (1819), 529.

4(48) the bells of her palfrey's flowing mane a feature of fairy processions in the traditional ballads 'Tam Lin' and 'Thomas Rymer' (Child 39 and 37), and in Hogg's 'Old David' in *The Queen's Wake*.

4(52) old Edmund's lay a reference to *The Faerie Queene* of Edmund Spenser.

4(54–55) the Bard of Avon's [...] midnight dream a reference to William Shakespeare's fairy play, *A Midsummer Night's Dream*.

4(56–57) the harp that rang abroad | O'er all the paradise of God a Romantic reading of John Milton's *Paradise Lost*.

4(58) the sons of the morning a phrase deriving from Isaiah 14. 12.

4(61) the land 'twixt heaven and hell fairies traditionally occupy an otherworld distinct from both Heaven and Hell.

5(89) little blackamoor pioneer an allusion to *Hamlet* I. 5. 164–65: 'Well said, old mole. Canst work i' the' earth so fast? | A worthy pioneer'.

5(101) Where the sun never shone, and the wind never blew echoing the account in 'Kilmeny' in *The Queen's Wake*, of a heavenly and fairy world 'Where the rain never fell, and the wind never blew'.

5(105) the star of the western heaven Venus, the particularly bright star also known as 'the morning star'.

6(114) now I have found thee I'll hold thee fast in the ballad of 'Tam Lin' Tam instructs Janet to 'hold me fast, and fear me not'. In many folk narratives holding fast to a supernatural being, or one under supernatural influence, is rewarded.

6(117) I'll call it a Queen this can be read as a reference to *Queen Hynde*: see note on 3 (8–9), above.

Love's Jubilee

6(6) star of love the planet Venus; often called the 'evening star', because it is the first to show at nightfall. (P.G.)

7(37) yon twin stars possibly referring to Castor and Pollux, twin stars in the constellation of Gemini. (P.G.)

8(70) sweet wood-reef *woodruff* is a low growing herb, with clusters of small white flowers and sweet-scented leaves; often, as here, descriptively called 'sweet wood-ruff'. (P.G.)

8(71) wabron leaf the plantain-leaf. Compare John Leyden, 'Scenes of Infancy' (1803): 'The wabret leaf, that by the pathway grew, | The wild-briar rose, of pale and blushful hue'. Leyden in a note observes that 'WABRET, or WABRON, a word of Saxon origin, is the common name for the plantain-leaf in Teviotdale' (*Works* (1858), p. 128, 128n). (P.G.)

8(90) celestial bow the rainbow. (P.G.)

9(109) An eve to dream of—not to tell compare S. T. Coleridge, 'Christabel', Part I, line 253 ('A sight to dream of, not to tell!'). In the *Queer Book* of 1832 this line and its repetition at line 143 are placed in quotation marks, effectively acknowledging the allusion. (P.G.)

The Border Chronicler

10(c) Prince's-street the main fashionable promenade in the New Town of Edinburgh.

10(d) topped boots high boots, often having a contrasting top of white, light-coloured, or brown leather.

10(d) Galashiels grey a coarse grey woollen cloth manufactured at Galashiels in Selkirkshire.

10(d) "the multitude are never wrong." this expression (also used by Hogg in discussing the reception of his poem *Queen Hynde* in his 'Memoir', p. 42) contradicts 'The multitude is always in the wrong', l. 183 of 'Essay on Translated Verse' (1684), by Wentworth Dillon, 4th Earl of Roscommon (*c.* 1633–85).

11(b) an auction room as the original version of this passage was written for John Ballantyne's weekly paper *The Sale-Room* (see Introductory and Textual Notes, p. 287), Hogg was probably envisaging Ballantyne's own premises on South Hanover Street, which joins Princes Street at right angles.

12(a) reested kippers Edinburgh was nicknamed 'Auld Reekie' for its smoky atmosphere, and the countryman implies that its inhabitants have been cured by being smoke-dried like fish.

12(a) the 'Merican war the 1770s saw a general economic downturn in Scotland: the Ayr Bank collapsed in 1772, the American War of Independence broke out in 1775, and the harvest failed in 1782–83: see T. C. Smout, *A History of the Scottish People 1560–1830* (Glasgow: Collins, 1969), p. 229.

12(a) nothing ava like this the years following the end of the Napoleonic Wars in 1815 were also years of agricultural depression.

12(a) the braxy a sheep disease, described by Hogg as 'this universal ravager of the young flocks' in *The Shepherd's Guide* (Edinburgh: Constable; London, Murray, 1807), p. 17.

12(a) Candlemas-day turned out foul Candlemas Day (2 February) is one of the Scottish quarter-days. The Scottish proverb relating to it runs 'If Candlemas day be dry and fair, | The half o' winter's to come and mair; | If Candlemas day be wet and foul; | The half o' winter's gone at Yule' (Colin Walker, *Scottish Proverbs* (Edinburgh: Birlinn, 2000), p. 128). Bad weather on Candlemas Day therefore signifies an early spring.

12(b) a ruined nation this prophet of doom recalls Mr A. B. in Hogg's 'Evil Speaking Ridiculed by an Allegorical Dream'—see *The Spy*, pp. 475–81.

12(d) Charlie Dinmont o' the Waker-cleuch a name clearly inspired by the Dandie Dinmont of Charlieshope of Scott's *Guy Mannering* (1815).

12(d) the original-sin man a description that suggests his Evangelical leanings: man is guilty by reason of original sin and cannot therefore be saved by adherence to the law of God but only by God's grace.

13(a) 'ewie wi' the crooket horn,' John Skinner's poem of that title is a lament for a dead pet sheep and a precursor of Burns's 'The Death and Dying Words of Poor Mailie'—see John Skinner, *Amusements of Leisure Hours; or, Poetical Pieces Chiefly in the Scottish Dialect* (Edinburgh: Cheyne; Aberdeen: Brown, 1809), pp. 63–66. There is presumably a secondary allusion to a drinking horn.

13(a) Dead-for-Cauld a real location: Dead for Cauld is a hill (1879 feet) in Megget-dale. It lies about four miles west of Tibbie Shiels Inn and St Mary's Loch.

13(d) beuk-sworn having taken an oath to tell the truth on the Book, or Bible.

14(b) his arm within mine a common way of promenading with male friends in Edinburgh at the time. George Taylor recollects Hogg's liking for it in a note to his *A Memoir of Robert Surtees, Esq.* (Durham: G. Andrews, 1852), p. 157, recalling his meeting with Surtees in 1819: 'The atmosphere was sultry, of itself enough to make Mr. Surtees, at any time, uncomfortable, and Hogg *would* walk arm in arm with him upon the hot flags in Prince's Street. This custom Surtees always abominated most heartily, but he submitted, for a while, in patience'.

14(c) a tavern, at the east end of Rose-street Rose Street (still famous for its pubs) runs between and parallel to Princes Street and George Street in Edinburgh's New Town.

15(b) the Mathews of the Border the actor Charles Mathews (1776–1835) was celebrated for his comic roles and for his imitations and ventriloquism. Reporting on his first appearance in Edinburgh on 4 April the *Caledonian Mercury* of 6 April 1812 describes his imitations of famous London actors and of his 'personating different characters at the same time, who appear to speak from different points', adding that the 'applauses of the audience, and their merriment [...] were almost continual'.

15(d) checks on human crimes a similar view is expressed by Barnaby in Hogg's story 'The Wool-Gatherer': 'We dinna believe in a' the gomral fantastic bogles an' spirits that fley light-headed fock up an' down the country, but we believe in a' the apparitions that warn o' death, that save life, an' that discover guilt. [...] the bogles, they are a better kind o' spirits, they meddle wi' nane but the guilty; the murderer, an' the mansworn, an' the cheater o' the widow an' the fatherless, they do for *them*'—see *The Brownie of Bodsbeck and Other Tales*, 2 vols (Edinburgh: Blackwood; London: Murray, 1818), II, 89–228 (pp. 140–41).

15(d) ghosts of hapless females prostitution was a daring subject to introduce in a story for one of the annuals.

16(b) made without answerable souls a similar hope is expressed by Hogg in one of his 'Epitaphs on Living Characters'—see *The Spy*, p. 20.

16(c) thy pilgrimage here on earth a phrase originating in Hebrews 11, which describes the lives of the patriarchs as a pilgrimage of faith: 'they were strangers and pilgrims on the earth' (verse 13).

16(c) **saying o' questions** members of a household meeting for religious worship on Sunday would ask each other questions from *The Shorter Catechism* or *The Larger Catechism*, these relating to the seventeenth-century Westminster *Confession of Faith* as the theological bedrock of Scottish Calvinism. Hogg's own household at Altrive continued this traditional practice—see *Confessions*, p. xvi.

16(d) **darkness visible** an echo of Milton's description of Hell in Book I of *Paradise Lost* (see I. 63).

16(d) **Past *twall o'clock!!!*** Charlie's apparition is an Edinburgh watchman.

17(b) **weel-bred minister lads** an allusion to the Moderate party in the Church of Scotland, which had much support among the gentry. The Moderates were opposed to all forms of religious enthusiasm, and were in sympathy with the appeal to reason of the eighteenth-century Scottish Enlightenment. Their opponents the Evangelicals had much support among the people. The Evangelicals placed a high value on traditions inherited from the seventeenth-century Covenanters, and tended to see the teaching of the Moderates (with its stress on reason, gentility, and proper conduct) as a 'cauldrife, insignificant, matter-o'-fact' kind of religion (to quote Charlie's words). The Evangelicals saw faith, repentance, and the redemptive power of Christ as providing the path to salvation, and disapproved of the Moderates' reliance on mere propriety and 'good works'.

17(c) **Hempton market, at Carlisle** Carlisle is the chief English town on the West Border with Scotland. The Carlisle Hempton fairs seem to have been held on Saturdays in October. See, for example, the *Carlisle Journal* for 27 October 1810: 'At Carlisle first Hempton fair, on Saturday last, there was a great number of cattle exposed on the Sands, which met with a dull sale'.

17(d) **the guide's house** not located. There were several fords across the Solway firth. The proper way from England to Scotland was by Gretna which took much longer than crossing the sands at any of the fords, which were however dangerous because of the speed at which the tide came in often with waves three feet high. Evidence of drownings dating back to medieval times can be found in the 'Melrose Chronicle' (referred to by Hogg for other tales), and also in legal arrangements. For example, it seems that by the Border laws of 1219 cattle wrongfully taken by either English or Scots were made to cross the Esk and if they could get more than half-way back to their native country without drowning the men who had reived them were supposed to have made restitution, but if they drowned on the reivers' side of the half-way mark compensation was due. The Annan wath seems to be the ford indicated in Scott's *Redgauntlet* (1824) as the one by which Darsie Latimer was carried into England—see W. T. McIntyre, 'The Fords of the Solway', in the *Cumberland News* of 26 April 1930.

18(a) **the deil's dozen** thirteen, twelve people plus one for the devil to claim. If there are thirteen in a party then one is supposed to die shortly. This may originate in the Lord's Supper where Christ and the disciples made up the number thirteen, but in Norse mythology Loki intruded on a banquet in Valhalla, making the number up to thirteen, and Balder was slain.

18(c) **that's ay some comfort** Hogg attempted to amuse Scott with this piece of selfish folk-wisdom when he was told that a gamekeeper had slandered him to the young Duke of Buccleuch: 'the chap that tauld the lees on me will gang to hell that's aye some comfort'—see *Anecdotes*, p. 74.

18(d) my hogs to a bad market a variation of the proverbial 'He has brought his hogs to a fine market', spoken ironically when a business has gone badly—see *ODEP*, p. 376. Little takes this literally, assuming that the stranger is a dealer in bacon.

18(d)–19(a) the flesh [...] the spirit a familiar religious distinction between the bodily existence of man and his soul, which Little again takes literally as meat and distilled liquor.

19(a) a smuggler the proximity of the Isle of Man to the Solway Firth meant that the smuggling of goods into Scotland was common in the district. Smuggling on the Solway features largely in Scott's *Guy Mannering* (1815) and *Redgauntlet* (1824).

19(a) a strang reekit saur the traditional whiff of demonic brimstone.

19(b) a white horse the opposition of a white horse for a good rider and a black horse for an evil rider persisted into the twentieth-century cowboy film. In Revelation 19. 11 the rider of the white horse is called 'Faithful and True'.

19(c) scoured, at a light gallop, across the tide similarly, in Hogg's *The Three Perils of Man* (1823) the devil, disguised as the Abbot of Melrose, rides across precipices and through the air—see Douglas Gifford's edition (Edinburgh: Scottish Academic Press, 1972), pp. 330–32.

20(a) riding for a broose the race at a country wedding from the church or the bride's house to that of the bridegroom. Hogg gives a graphic account of such a race in the fourth chapter of 'The Shepherd's Calendar', in his *Winter Evening Tales*, 2 vols (Edinburgh: Oliver & Boyd; London: Whittaker, 1820), II, 186–97 (pp. 191–94): see S/SC edition (2002), pp. 397–404 (pp. 400–02).

20(b) the river Eden the Eden flows just north of Carlisle into the Solway Firth.

20(b) the beds of the Esk the course of the river Esk flows mainly in Eskdale in the Scottish county of Dumfriesshire, but it crosses the Border into England a few miles before joining the Solway near Gretna.

20(c) see that you fall not out by the way Joseph, the deliverer of Israel from famine, sent his brothers home from Egypt to their father with the instruction 'See that ye fall not out by the way' (Genesis 45. 24).

20(c) Graitney this was another name for Gretna (see the entry for Gretna in *Ordnance Gazetteer of Scotland: a Survey of Scottish Topography*, ed. by Francis H. Groome, 6 vols (Edinburgh: Jack, 1882–85). If the party had crossed the Solway Firth at the Beds of Esk as they supposed, Gretna would be the first town they would come to on the Scottish side of the Border.

20(c) Annan lies on the Scottish side of the Solway, to the west of Gretna.

20(c) Langtown or Longtown, on the river Esk, lies to the east of Gretna, just over the Border into the English county of Cumberland.

21(a) cauldrife dogmas [...] heartless philosophers another attack on the ideas of the Moderates and of the Scottish Enlightenment as destructive of warm religious feeling: see note on 17(b).

21(a–b) I dinna believe [...] as they may Barnaby of Hogg's story 'The Wool-Gatherer' expresses similar views—see note to 15(d).

21(b) an edition of that story myself as told by Barnaby of 'The Wool-Gatherer', in *The Brownie of Bodsbeck and Other Tales*, 2 vols (Edinburgh:

Blackwood; London: Murray, 1818), II, 89–228 (pp. 142–43).

21(b) **Glen-Tress** Glentress is in Tweeddale, a little to the east of Peebles.

21(c) **Tait [...] suffered muckle for religion's sake** no details relating to the Taits of Glentress have been found in Covenanting histories.

21(c) **Colquhar** not traced.

21(d) **begun the psalm** in 'History of the Life of Duncan Campbell' Hogg explains that family worship typically 'consisted in singing a few stanzas of a psalm, in which all the family joined their voices' with that of the male head of the household, who then 'read a chapter from the bible, going straight on from beginning to end of the scriptures. The prayer concluded the devotions of the evening'—see *The Spy*, p. 504.

22(c) **a moral harangue [...] our ain doings** another gibe at the Enlightenment-influenced Moderate party of the Church of Scotland: see note on 17(b).

22(d) **the enlightened and polished part of the community** an admission of the possible problems involved in transferring traditional tales from the community to which they belong to a genteel, middle-class audience.

Stanzas for Music

23(5) **unblest and unshrieven** the implication is that the child has not undergone baptism, which with the Lord's Supper is one of the two sacraments of Protestant churches. In Hogg's poem *Mador of the Moor* (1816) the fact that Ila Moore's illegitimate child has not been baptised is cause for fear that it may be open to attack from supernatural powers.

23(13) **The moralist's boast** an indication of the scorn directed at the illegitimacy of the dying baby, and also a reference to the Evangelical view of the inadequacy of the teaching of the Moderates: see note on 17(b).

The Bijou
An Aged Widow's Own Words

27(1) **is he gane** Mrs Garden relates that the speaker here is Hogg's mother-in-law Janet Phillips, and that the poem 'is supposed to express her feelings, when left alone after a married life of more than half a century (Garden, pp. 154–55). Peter and Janet Phillips had been living at Hogg's house at Altrive Lake in Yarrow since June 1824 (see Hogg's letter to Blackwood of 28 June 1824 in NLS, MS 4012, fols 184–85), while Hogg and his family inhabited the nearby farmhouse of Mount Benger. According to his gravestone in Ettrick kirkyard Peter Phillips died on 16 May 1827 at the age of seventy-nine. Hogg commented on his death in an undated letter to William Jerdan as follows: 'My father-in-law is removed from this stage of existence since I wrote you,—an excellent old man, reduced from great affluence to a total dependence on me. My frail mother-in-law, with her attendants, are now incorporated with our own family'—see *The Autobiography of William Jerdan*, 4 vols (London: Hall, Virtue, 1852–53), I, 145–47. Janet Phillips died at Mount Benger less than a year after her husband on 4 March 1828 at the age of eighty-five.

27(6) **fifty years and three** this would date the marriage of Peter Phillips and Janet Carruthers roughly to 1774, though no record appears to have survived.

27(9) **mony a braw and boardly son** of the couple's three sons only the third, Walter Phillips, was still alive in 1827. The eldest, John, had died abroad several years earlier after working as a planter in Jamaica and as a Writer to the Signet in Edinburgh—see Norah Parr, *James Hogg at Home: Being the Domestic Life and Letters of the Ettrick Shepherd* (Dollar: Douglas S. Mack, 1980), pp. 16, 31. The death announcement of the second son, Peter, who had been set up by his father as a farmer at the Carse, Kirkcudbright, appeared in the *Dumfries and Galloway Courier* of 25 June 1822: 'At Carse of Kircudbright, on the 19th curt. Mr Peter Phillips, farmer there. Few lived more highly respected, or died more sincerely regretted'.

27(10) daughters in their prime of the couple's three daughters, only the youngest, Hogg's own wife, was still alive in 1827. The eldest daughter, Mary, had married James Gray and died in Edinburgh on 9 November 1806—see the announcement of her death in the *Scots Magazine*, 68 (December 1806), 967. The death announcement of the second daughter, Janet (known as 'Jessie') appeared in the *Dumfries and Galloway Courier* of 19 June 1821: 'At Locherwoods, on the 14th inst. Miss Janet Phillips, after a long illness, which she bore as became a Christian'.

Ane Waefu' Scots Pastoral

28 [footnote] Hogg reported the decimation of lambs during this late snowstorm to William Blackwood in his letter of 3 May 1827 (NLS, MS 4019, fols 189–90): 'my loss on Monday eight days was fully beyond my proportion of lambs, but I lost no old sheep. Every farmer has lost a part perhaps about 100 out of every 1000 is very near the country loss here'.

29(30) August 12 August ('The Glorious Twelfth') was, and is, the first day of grouse-shooting, when Hogg and other sportsmen would head for the moors with their dogs and guns. See, for example, Hogg's letter to Blackwood of 11 August 1827 (NLS, MS 4019, fols 195–96): 'I have been trying all I could to finish "Ane Pastorale of the Rocke" for you but on looking at the ominous date of this you must percieve that it is sticked for the present. The moors! the moors! nothing else can at present be thought of'.

29(33) laverock the sky-lark, a Romantic symbol to Hogg as to a number of other poets because of the male's habit of singing high in the sky to the female in her nest. Hogg's own 'The Skylark' was contributed to *Forget Me Not* for 1828, and appears on p. 39 of the present volume. The bird is also a character in his poem 'Ringan and May'—see *Queer Book*, pp. 106–09.

29(49) curlew's Hogg mingles English and Scots names for birds in this poem: the English curlew is a 'whaup' in Scots.

29(56) thriftless weavers handloom weavers were one of the casualties of the Industrial Revolution, as T. C. Smout explains: 'The weavers began in the 1780s as the most confident and affluent of all groups, and ended up in the 1830s appallingly depressed and pauperised'—see *A History of the Scottish People 1560–1830* (Glasgow: Collins 1969, repr. 1977), pp. 393–402 (p. 393).

Woman

30(3) my mountain lore another allusion to Hogg's self-proclaimed position as 'king o' the mountain and fairy school'—see note to 4(42) above.

30(8–12) (What once I sparingly believed) [...]faithful love? Hogg discusses illegitimate children in a letter to John Aitken of 20 December 1817: 'I have two very lovely daughters who bear my name the one 11 the other

8 years of age the one I am sure is my own the other may be mine for any thing that I know to the contrary': see this letter in *Letters I.* See also Gillian Hughes, 'James Hogg and the "Bastard Brood"', *Studies in Hogg and his World,* 11 (2000), 56–68.

31 (56–58) A being prone [...] moral poet sung see Alexander Pope, 'Epistle II. To a Lady: Of the Characters of Women' in his *Epistles to Several Persons.* In 'A Letter about Men and Women' Hogg referred to Pope's *Essay on Man,* II. 1–2, arguing good-humouredly, 'there is no doubt that the proper study of mankind is WOMAN; and Mr Pope was wrong'—see *Blackwood's Edinburgh Magazine,* 26 (1829), 245–50 (p. 246).

31 (59–60) That men [...] at heart a rake?" from Pope's *Epistles to Several Persons,* 'Epistle II. To a Lady: Of the Characters of Women', ll. 215–16.

Superstition and Grace

33 (14) Lammer law Lammer Law (1773 feet), Lothian, a peak in the Lammermuir Hills, 4 miles South of Gifford. (P.G.)

33 (18) gyre carle supernatural being. (P.G.)

34 (67) Lammer-muir i.e. the hilly moorland country in SE Scotland. (P.G.)

35 (92) Gil-moules name for the Devil. See also note to 'Jocke Taittis Expeditioune till Hell', line 77 [in the S/SC edition of *A Queer Book*]. (P.G.)

36 (137) queen isle of the sea Britain. In describing the banishing of older forms of superstition, this poem overlaps with accounts of the departure of the fairies from Scotland in 'The Origin of the Fairies' and 'The Last Stork' [both from *A Queer Book*]. (P.G.)

Forget Me Not
The Sky Lark

39 (4) Emblem of happiness the sky-lark was associated by a number of Romantic poets with human aspirations and happiness because of the male's habit of singing high in the sky to the female in her nest—see note to 29 (33).

39 (6) O to abide in the desart with thee! writing to an unidentified correspondent on 27 October 1833 Hogg made his identification with the sky-lark plain in the following words: 'The laverock (or skylark) has always been a peculiar favourite of mine, for he was, like myself, an inmate of the wilds, and the companion of my boyhood'—see *Notes and Queries,* fifth series 10 (1878), p. 386.

The Descent of Love

40 (6) best earliest gift of heaven an echo of Adam's address to Eve as 'Heaven's last best gift' in Milton's *Paradise Lost,* V, 19.

40 (18) Which man immortal might have proved the disobedience of Adam and Eve brought death into the world—see Genesis 3. 19.

40 (25–26) Euphrates [...] Arabian lands the river Euphrates is mentioned as one of the four rivers emerging from the Garden of Eden in Genesis 2. 14.

40 (28) the earliest flowers that grew that is in Eden, soon after the creation of the world.

40 (35) By deep remorse and sorrow tossed the ninth book of *Paradise Lost* depicts Adam and Even in bitter mutual accusation after the Fall.

41(55) **young twin roses** in the ballad 'The Douglas Tragedy' (see Child 7B) the rose springing from the lady's grave in St Mary's churchyard in Yarrow intermingles with the briar springing from her lover's grave, signifying the continuation of love after death.

41(67) **Eden's sacred tree** in Genesis 2. 9 the tree of life is 'in the midst of the garden'.

41(74) **nature's queen** 'And Adam called his wife's name Eve; because she was the mother of all living' (Genesis 3. 20).

St. Mary of the Lows

44(10) **hallow'd soil** echoing Walter Scott's lines in the Introduction to the 2nd Canto of *Marmion* (1808): 'Yet still, beneath the hallow'd soil, | The peasant rests him from his toil'. Hogg heard Scott recite his description of St Mary's Loch from the proofs of *Marmion* before its publication (see [S/ SC *Anecdotes*, pp. 54–55]). His own version noticeably extends the social and historical range of those buried in the churchyard. (P.G.)

45(18) **hunted as the osprey's brood** the osprey, which feeds on fish, was hunted down as a pest in country districts. Here Hogg likens its plight to that of the Covenanters when persecuted in the 17th century (P.G.)

45(24) **low graves** the graves of the Covenanters were often marked by very small stones, owing to the circumstances of their burial after summary execution. St Mary's churchyard contains a number of rough slabs without visible inscription, but there is no evidence to connect these with the Covenanters. Several examples, however, can be found in nearby Ettrick churchyard. (P.G.)

45(25) **the last of all the race** Walter Grieve, minister of the reformed presbyterian synod, who died on 7 March 1822 aged 75 years. His son, John Grieve, helped support Hogg in Edinburgh and was one of his closest friends. For details of surviving monuments to the Grieve family, see 'St. Mary's Kirkyard, Yarrow', *Transactions of the Hawick Archaeological Society* (1964), p. 49. (P.G.)

45(41) **forest bowmen** alluding to Ettrick Forest once having been a royal hunting-ground. Compare Hogg's 'Statistics of Selkirkshire': 'The forest of Ettrick continued a hunting station of the kings of Scotland from the days of Alexander the Third to those of Queen Mary Stuart, who was the last sovereign that visited it' (*Prize-Essays and Transactions of the Highland Society of Scotland*, 9(1832), 290). (P.G.)

45(46) **Scotts, and Kerrs, and Pringles** of these leading clan names on the Scottish Border, only that of Scott can be found in St Mary's churchyard. (P.G.)

45(48) **Whose fathers there to death contended** Hogg's 'Mary Scott' (the Fourteenth Bard's song in *The Queen's Wake*) tells of a battle at St Mary's churchyard between a group of Scotts and a group of Pringles and Kerrs. 'Mary Scott' is based on the traditional ballad 'The Gay Goshawk' (Child 96), and the Fourteenth Bard is a portrait of Hogg's friend John Grieve: see note on 45(25). For 'Mary Scott' see Hogg, *The Queen's Wake* (S/SC, 2004), pp. 108–29, 428–31.

46(65) **here lies one** the young woman addressed is probably a fictional creation. (P.G.)

Eastern Apologues

48(a) Sadac a Persian nobleman named Sadak is the protagonist of one of the *Tales of the Genii* by James Ridley (1762). See also Gillian Hughes's essay on 'Hogg, Art, and the Annuals', at pp. l–li.

48(a) Azor the name occurs in the genealogy of Christ in the first chapter of Matthew: 'and Eliakim begat Azor; And Azor begat Sadoc' (see Matthew 1. 13–14).

48(b) Cathema an imaginary place suggestive of Marco Polo's 'Cathay'.

48(b) Persia an ancient kingdom of Asia.

48(b) Amerabia possibly an echo of the 'Amhara' of Samuel Johnson's *Rasselas* (1759), another work about the choice of life. Also, Mount Amara is referred to in Milton's *Paradise Lost* at IV. 281.

48(d) Mahomed the Arabian prophet Muhammad, founder of Islam. The Koran is said to have been communicated to Muhammad at Medina by an angel.

49(c) seraphs a seraph is one of the seraphim, and in medieval angelology the seraphim are the highest of the nine orders of angels. They are described at Isaiah 6. 2–3.

49(c) thrones, principalities, and powers the names of a further three of the nine orders of angels (see previous note). Echoing Colossians 2. 14–15, Milton at *Paradise Lost* X. 184–86 describes Christ's defeat of Satan's fallen angels, 'principalities and powers'.

49(d) from the mouths of Moses, of David, of Isaiah these three major Old Testament figures are seen here as sources of inspired prophetic utterance: David appears in this context as author of the book of Psalms.

49(d) Ismael, son of Berar Ismael's name echoes that of the biblical Ishmael, son of Abraham and the Egyptian woman Hagar, Sarah's servant. Ishmael is regarded as the ancestor of the Arabs. See Genesis chapters 16, 21, and 25, and I Chronicles 1. 29–31.

50(c) Bahara perhaps an echo of the 'Bahurim' of 2 Samuel 16, 17, and 19.

52(c) Abra, my beloved wife Abra is the submissive concubine who later becomes the dictatorial chief consort of Solomon in Matthew Prior's 'Solomon on the Vanity of the World'—see *The Literary Works of Matthew Prior*, ed. by H. Bunker Wright and Monroe K. Spears, 2 vols (Oxford: Clarendon Press, 1959), I, 306–85. The Solomon of Prior's poem is also in pursuit of happiness, and tests if it is to be found in wealth and greatness, gardening and building, music and feasting, and love. He concludes, however, that all are vanity and vexation of spirit.

52(d) silken gauze of Cashmere the name of a province in the Western Himalayas in India, familiar to Hogg's contemporaries for the Cashmere goat whose wool was made into fine and expensive shawls. In a letter to his wife of 2 March 1822 Hogg says, 'I have bought you [...] a very grand cassimere [*sic*] shawl' (NLS, MS 2245, fols 78–79).

53(d) seven days and seven nights a frequently-mentioned time-span in the Bible: see, for example, the seven days and nights of Creation in Genesis 1 and 2.

53(d) Euphrates see note to 40 (25–26).

53(d) Media the area bordering on Persia and corresponding to the northern part of Iraq. Biblical phrases such as 'the power of Persia and Media' (Esther 1. 3) and 'the law of the Medes and Persians, which altereth not'

(Daniel 6. 8) name it in conjunction with Persia.

54(b) the short-lived and fading flowers of the valley: 'And the glorious beauty, which *is* on the head of the fat valley, shall be a fading flower, *and* as the hasty fruit before summer' (Isaiah 28. 4).

54(d) Maxims rules or principles of conduct, given to the unworldly poet by his patron and ruler. It is now Sadac's turn to be the instructor.

55(a) "He hath blasphemed a deliberately-engineered plot reminiscent of the one engineered when 'the chief priests, and elders, and all the council, sought false witness against Jesus, to put him to death; But found none: yea, though many false witnesses came, *yet* found they none. At the last came two false witnesses, And said, this *fellow* said, I am able to destroy the temple of God, and to build it in three days. And the high priest arose, and said unto him, Answerest thou nothing? what *it is which* these witness against thee? But Jesus held his peace. And the high priest answered and said unto him, I adjure thee by the living God, that thou tell us whether thou be the Christ, the Son of God. Jesus saith unto him, Thou hast said: nevertheless I say unto you, Hereafter shall ye see the Son of man sitting on the right hand of power, and coming in the clouds of heaven. Then the high priest rent his clothes, saying, He hath spoken blasphemy; what further need have we of witnesses? behold, now ye have heard his blasphemy' (Matthew 26. 59–65). See also the plot engineered by Jezebel against Naboth so that her husband King Ahab could possess his coveted vineyard in I Kings 21. 1–16.

55(c) our supreme prophet hath taken up the vindication of his own cause compare Romans 12. 19: 'Dearly beloved, avenge not yourselves, but *rather* give place unto wrath: for it is written' Vengeance *is* mine; I will repay, saith the Lord'.

55(d) as a lamb is among young leopards compare Isaiah 11. 6: when the Messiah comes 'The wolf also shall dwell with the lamb, and the leopard shall lie down with the kid; and the calf and the young lion and the fatling together; and a little child shall lead them'.

56(a) the rules of life these are the maxims referred to in the relevant subheading to this part of the tale. Compare I Peter 2. 17, 'Honour all *men*. Love the brotherhood. Fear God. Honour the King'.

56(b) mark of Cain because he has murdered his brother Abel, Cain is condemned by God to the life of a fugitive and a vagabond: 'And the LORD set a mark upon Cain, lest any finding him should kill him' (Genesis 4. 15).

Seeking the Houdy

56(c) Meggat-dale the lands around Megget Water in Peeblesshire. Robin's house is described later in the tale as situated at 'the Craigy-rigg', and Craigierig is located in Megget-dale about two miles upstream from the point at which Megget Water flows into St Mary's Loch.

56(c) bean-glhuine, or, *te the toctor* *bean-ghlùine* is the Gaelic word for 'midwife', while *te the toctor* ('the she doctor') appears to be an example of the way in which the English speech of native Gaelic speakers was conventionally rendered in print in Hogg's period: see Mairi Robinson, 'Modern Literary Scots: Fergusson and After', in *Lowland Scots: Papers Presented to an Edinburgh Conference*, ed. by A. J. Aitken, Association for Scottish Literary

Studies Occasional Papers, 2 (Edinburgh: ASLS, 1973), pp. 38–55 (p. 39).

56(d) a hair halter [...] straw sunks a halter made of animal hair, which would often have wooden branks or side-pieces, was a cheaper alternative to the usual leather bridle and reins. A straw sunks, or cushion, was a similar substitute for a leather saddle.

57(b) killed with a snibbelt perhaps an oral tradition, since no record of this killing has been found.

57(c) Glengaber-foot lies on the Megget Water, just over half a mile downstream from Craigierig.

57(c) Henderland lies on the Megget Water, just under a mile downstream from Glengaber-foot.

57(c) the Sandbed possibly associated with Sundhope, which is situated in the Yarrow valley about seven miles from Henderland.

58(a) Saint Sampson! the cult of Saint Samson (d. 565), one of the Celtic monk-bishops, was chiefly associated with Wales and Brittany—see David Hugh Farmer, *The Oxford Dictionary of Saints* (Oxford: Clarendon Press, 1978), pp. 351–52. In the context of a display of strength it seems more likely here that the Samson of Judges 13–16 is intended, especially as in medieval times it was common for prominent Old Testament characters to be referred to as 'Saint'.

58(c) Capper Cleuch is on the western shore of St Mary's Loch, immediately to the north of the point at which Megget Water flows into the loch.

59(d) imprecations [...] short prayers for preservation expletives such as 'Damn her!' and 'Lord save us!' are often taken literally by spiritual powers in Hogg's writings.

60(c) a being like a woman in Hogg's novel *The Brownie of Bodsbeck* (1818) Walter Laidlaw encounters the supposed apparition of a woman near Megget Water and St Mary's Loch, during a journey by night: see *The Brownie of Bodsbeck*, ed. by Douglas S. Mack (Edinburgh: Scottish Academic Press, 1976), pp. 146–48.

62(b) or a mermaid mermaids appear to have been associated with inland waters as well as the sea. The narrator of 'The History of Duncan Campbell', for example, relates of himself and Duncan as children that 'We loved the fairies and brownies, and even felt a little partiality for the mermaids, on account of their beauty and charming songs; we were a little jealous of the water-kelpies, and always kept aloof from the frightsome pools'—see *The Spy*, p. 491.

62(b) viper o' the pit hell is termed the pit in various psalms, as for instance in Psalm 28. 1.

62(b) beast o' Bashan 'Many bulls have compassed me: strong *bulls* of Bashan have beset me round' (Psalm 22. 12).

64(c) discontinuance of midwifery this statement may be the result of Hogg's own change in status from peasant to middle-class writer. His wife, for example, had gone into Edinburgh to be under the care of a male doctor for the birth of the couple's first child, James Robert Hogg. The birth notice in the *Dumfries and Galloway Courier* of 27 March 1821 reads 'At 6, Park street, on the 18th March, Mrs Hogg, Altrive Lake, of a son'.

A Sea Story

64(d) forty years ago as this story was first published in *Forget Me Not* for

1831, 'forty years ago' suggests the early 1790s. In his account (published 1793) of the parish of Dry'sdale (from Dryfsdale) in Dumfriesshire, the Rev. Thomas Henderson writes that 'every family is a small factory for both linen and woollen cloth': see Sir John Sinclair, *The Statistical Account of Scotland*, 21 vols (Edinburgh: Creech, 1791–99), IX, 418–33 (pp. 418, 428).

64 (d) *muckle wheel* the large hand-turned spinning wheel used for wool, as opposed to the 'wee wheel' that was used for spinning flax.

65 (b) **Clyde** one of the largest Scottish rivers, and a major centre for shipping. In the 1790s larger vessels docked at Greenock or Port Glasgow in the Firth of Clyde, rather than proceeding upstream to Glasgow.

65 (c) **about four feet lang, wi' an auld withered face** this creature bears some resemblance to the eponymous 'Brownie of the Black Haggs', who has 'the form of a boy, but the features of one a hundred years old'—see *The Shepherd's Calendar*, p. 244.

65 (d) **rigging o' the top-gallant** the top was the platform at the head of the lower mast in sailing ships. Above both of these was the top mast that carried the topsails, and above that the top gallant mast carrying the top gallant sails. Men who worked this part of the sails and rigging were known as 'top men' and were generally the best seamen of the crew.

66 (a) **to reef with all expedition** a *reef* is part of a sail that can be taken in, rolled up, and secured by reef points or strips of canvas running horizontally along a square sail. To *reef in* is to shorten an area of sail by one or more reefs.

66 (b) **keel play rusk** the lowest part of the ship is scraped on the sea bed.

66 (c) **the number o' our days fulfilled** an expression of biblical origin—see, for example, Psalm 90. 12 ('teach *us* to number our days'), and Lamentations 4. 18 ('our end is near, our days are fulfilled').

66 (c) **Achan** by secreting valuables in disobedience to God, Achan brings down the divine displeasure on the rest of the company, a situation resolved when he is put to death: see Joshua 7. 18–26.

66 (c) **Jonah** ordered by God to go to Nineveh, Jonah disobeys and takes ship for Tarsish instead, bringing down a storm on the ship which is only calmed when his shipmates cast him overboard (see Jonah 1).

66 (d) **water-kelpie** see note to 62 (b).

67 (a) **winds and waves at his control** a frequently-expressed sign of divine power in both Old and New Testaments, and implicit in the story of Jonah. There may also be a specific allusion to Christ's stilling of the storm, related as evidence of his power in Matthew 8. 26 and Luke 8. 24.

67 (b) **a mixed body of marines and sailors** marines are soldiers trained for naval warfare, while sailors are members of the ship's crew.

68 (c) **Helm-a-lee** the helm is the handle of the rudder, while to go leeward is to head in the opposite direction from the way the wind is blowing.

68 (c) **put about ship, and lay-to** change the ship's course and go in another direction.

69 (d) **new appellation was unfortunate** Duncan and the narrator of his story in 'The History of Duncan Campbell' are also more afraid of a ghost than the devil. 'We hated the devil most heartily, but we were not much afraid of him—but a ghost! oh dreadful!'—see *The Spy*, p. 491.

71 (a) **the body of a young woman** a similar incident was reported in *The Times* of 4 November 1824: 'This morning (Saturday) the corpse of a woman

was discovered in a box, like a package of goods, in the *Eclipse* steamboat by a watchman on board of the boat, by means of a disagreeable smell issuing from the box. It was sent from Dublin by the stage-coach to Belfast, and directed to a Mr. Jones, Edinburgh'. This item was repeated in Scottish newspapers such as the *Glasgow Chronicle* later in the month.

71(c) in the flesh a biblical expression used, for example in Romans 7 and 8.

71(c) men and angels perhaps an allusion to I Corinthians 4. 5, where the Lord 'will bring to light the hidden things of darkness', verse 9 continuing 'we are made a spectacle unto the world, and to angels, and to men'.

A Love Ballad

71(1) postman the first of a series of images joining natural sounds to human activity, the beetle's note sounding like the post-horn sounded from a mail coach.

71(5) harper rail presumably the landrail or corncrake rather than the water-rail is intended, as line 19 places him 'among the corn'.

71(6) uncouth strain the corncrake is known for its characteristic rasping cry.

71(8) his last Amen see note to 21(d) for an account of the traditional family worship undertaken before the members of a Scottish household went to bed. The prayers formed the concluding part of the devotion.

73(62) Beyond what angels can enjoy a similar idea is expressed in 'The Descent of Love', l. 12.

73(72) elysian dream happy or delightful, from the Elysian fields which are the abode of the blessed in Greek mythology, and also mentioned as Elysium in Milton's *Comus*.

Maggy o' Buccleuch

73 AIR–Days of Yore printed as the tune to 'The Flower of Amochrie' in R. A. Smith, *The Scotish Minstrel*, 6 vols (Edinburgh: Purdie, 1820–24), V, 72.

73(3) beauty's rural queen there may be an element of compliment in this song to the family of Hogg's patrons, the Dukes of Buccleuch. When this song was subsequently set to music by Edward J. Nielson it was dedicated to the young Duchess of Buccleuch, although her name was Charlotte rather than Margaret. Hogg's song 'The Stuarts of Appin', published during his London visit of 1832, was dedicated to Lady Margaret Scott (1811–46) and her sisters. Lady Margaret (whose brother was Walter, 5th Duke of Buccleuch) was unmarried at the time the *Forget Me Not* for 1832 was published.

73(6) Yarrow braes Bowhill, the residence of the Dukes of Buccleuch, is situated near the confluence of Yarrow Water and Ettrick Water.

74(15) wild bee wad like to sip perhaps the association of bee and honeyed lip derives from Suckling's well-known description in his 'Ballad. Upon a Wedding' of a full lower lip being as if 'some bee had stung it newly'.

74(17) cauldrife north Hogg makes an imaginary journey to the frozen polar regions in 'The p and the q' published in *Blackwood's Edinburgh Magazine*, 26 (1829), 693–95, and also in 'The Surpassing Adventures of Allan Gordon', published in his posthumous *Tales and Sketches by the Ettrick Shepherd*, 6 vols (Glasgow: Blackie, 1836–37), I, 241–316.

74(19) As far as reels the rowin earth another hyperbolic statement, presumably meant to embrace the limits that the rolling earth traverses through space.

74(20) the burning line the equator, separating the northern from the southern hemisphere. Hogg himself never travelled outside Britain except in imagination, though his Jock M'Pherson of 'The p and the q' does circumnavigate the globe.

The Battle of the Boyne

74 [title] the Battle of the Boyne was fought around and across the river Boyne in Ireland in the summer of 1690, when William of Orange and the Protestant army defeated the forces of the Roman Catholic James VII and II, who fled and afterwards escaped to France. Agitation over Catholic emancipation (a debate on whether or not to grant Roman Catholics the same civil rights as Protestants, resolved by Peel's 1829 Catholic Relief Act) would make this famous battle topical at the time Hogg's dramatic scene was written and published (see Introductory and Textual Notes). The battle is still commemorated in Northern Ireland as a Protestant triumph over the forces of Roman Catholicism.

74 [note] Reverend George Walker George Walker (1618–90) was educated at the University of Glasgow, and appointed to two parishes in County Londonderry in 1669, before moving to Donaghmore near Dungannon in 1674. At the close of 1688 Londonderry was besieged by the adherents of James VII and II and, after helping to organise military resistance in the area, Walker became joint governor of the town on 19 April 1689 after the defection of the acting governor Robert Lundy. Walker, as well as being a clergyman, was then a colonel in command of a regiment of nine hundred men. He managed to keep the peace between the Presbyterians and Episcopalians in his regiment and to hold out until the town was relieved on 28 July. He was then sent to England to represent Londonderry, bearing a loyal address to King William. In Scotland he was given a hero's welcome and presented with the freedom of the cities of Glasgow and Edinburgh, while in London he received a hero's welcome and the new king expressed an intention of making him Bishop of Londonderry. The House of Commons supported his claim for two thousand pounds for those widowed and orphaned during the siege, and he received an honorary doctorate from Cambridge before his return to Ireland—for further details see the article by Piers Wauchope in the *Oxford DNB*. Walker died at the crossing of the river Boyne on 1 July 1690, and was buried on the battle-field. In 1828 a statue of him atop a pillar was erected at Derry.

74 [note] account of that notable siege probably Walker's own *A True Account of the Siege of Londonderry* published in London in 1689, and soon translated into both German and Dutch. This was supplemented by Walker's defence of his account against criticism, published in the same year.

74 [note] an account of his Life this has not been traced, nor does Philip Dwyer mention it in his *The Siege of Londonderry in 1689 as Set Forth in the Literary Remains of Colonel the Rev. George Walker* (London: E. Stock, 1893), though this reprints Walker's 'True Account of the Siege' and 'A Vindication of the true Account', in addition to 'A Letter on the Treachery of Lundy', 'Other Official Letters', and 'Sermons, Prayers, and Speeches during the Siege'.

74 [direction] there is no reference in Philip Dwyer's *The Siege of Derry in 1689* to John, Walker's eldest son, being present at the Battle of the Boyne, though other sons named Robert and George served alongside their father at the siege of Derry. In his 'Vindication' (Dwyer, p. 79) Walker stated that he has left 'four sons' in active service.

75 (9) confessor? a joke about the auricular confession of the Roman Catholic church.

75 (15) chaff before the wind in a printed sermon entitled 'The Christian Champion; or, A Second Sermon Preached to the Besieged Protestant Soldiers in Londonderry [...] before a Vigorous Sally against the French and Irish Enemies', dated 30 July 1689, Walker had written 'Let not our foes affright us, nor any fears attend us, for God will give the victory to them that serve Him and make their enemies fly before them, like chaff before the wind'—see Dwyer, pp. 97–103 (p. 98).

75 (16–19) tyrant's arm [...] where is he now? James VII and II fled to France after the Battle of the Boyne and never returned to Britain. He died in Paris in 1701.

75 (27) the good cause a phrase adopted by both Protestants and Catholics from the seventeenth century onwards. In this case Walker clearly intends to indicate his support for the Protestant succession.

75 (29) five bold brothers it is uncertain how many sons Walker had—see note on 74 [direction].

75 (33) if such a thing as after-life there be there appears to be nothing to suggest that Walker would have voiced the kind of death-bed doubting Hogg ascribes to him here. His monumental inscription at the church of Donoghmore, dating from 1703, ends 'But his fame shall be more durable than Rock, | Nor shall future ages less than the present admire a Soldier so pious and a Minister so intrepid' (Dwyer, p. 237).

76 (63) from Adam the first man, from whose transgression suffering and death entered the world—see Genesis 3. 17–19.

76 (84) those in office presumably a reference to Robert Lundy, the faithless governor of Londonderry.

76 (88) light ineffable Christ is described in I Timothy 6. 16 as 'dwelling in the light which no man can approach unto', while in Milton's *Paradise Lost* (III. 136, 137), 'the blessed spirits elect' are suffused as God speaks with a 'sense of new joy ineffable'.

77 (95) that mystic bond the link between God and man was viewed as a series of covenants or agreements, with Noah, with Moses, and then through the atonement of Christ's death as a voluntary sacrifice for man's transgressions.

77 (97) that awful bourn an allusion to *Hamlet*, III. 1. 81–82.

77 (99) valves used here in the archaic sense of a pair of folding doors.

77 (101) deodand literally a thing to be given to God, and in this case another reference to Christ's atonement.

77 (103) Sun of the soul! Christ was prefigured for Christians in the 'Sun of righteousness [...] with healing in his wings' of Malachi 4. 2.

77 (103) bright polar star of hope! the pole star, used by sailors in navigation because it indicates the north, also signifies a guiding principle of any description.

77 (111) a gulf profound the threat of the unfathomed abyss is presented in

John Martin's painting *Sadac in Search of the Waters of Oblivion* (1812), and in Hogg's own *The Private Memoirs and Confessions of a Justified Sinner* (see *Confessions*, pp. 110 and 165).

77(122–23) spring, | Opened in David's house a reference to the prophecy of Zacharias on seeing the infant Christ. He declared that God has 'raised up an horn of salvation for us in the house of his servant David', and that through 'the tender mercy of our God [...] the dayspring from on high hath visited us' (Luke 1. 68–79). See also the genealogy of Christ set out in the first chapter of Matthew.

Scottish Haymakers

78(a) Wilkie the Scottish painter David Wilkie (1785–1841). Hogg's interest in Wilkie is discussed in Gillian Hughes's essay on 'Hogg, Art, and the Annuals', at pp. xliii, xlviii.

78(c) Mr. Terry, the player the actor Daniel Terry (1780?–1829) was a friend of Sir Walter Scott, and made frequent appearances at the Edinburgh theatre from 1809 onwards. His second wife, Elizabeth Nasmyth, was the daughter of the painter Alexander Nasmyth.

78(c) the two celebrated Naesmiths Alexander Nasmyth (1758–1840) and his eldest son Patrick ('Peter') (1787–1831), both of whom were celebrated painters. See Gillian Hughes's essay on 'Hogg, Art, and the Annuals', at pp. xlii–xliv, xlvii–xlviii.

78(c) Monsieur Alexandre the French ventriloquist Alexandre Vattemar was known in Edinburgh by his stage-name of 'Monsieur Alexandre'. During April and May 1824 he gave a number of performances at the Caledonian Theatre at the head of Leith Walk in Edinburgh to packed houses. Both *The Rogueries of Nicholas; or, The Adventures of a Ventriloquist* and *Devil Upon Sticks; or, Asmodeus in London* seem to have been one-man plays in which Alexandre played every part in the drama, keeping the characters distinct by means of disguise and his acting ability as well as his ventriloquism. The advertisement for his first Edinburgh performance in the *Caledonian Mercury* of 15 April 1824 describes him as 'celebrated and distinguished on the Continent' and as having appeared 'with signal approbation before crowded audiences for nearly One Hundred and Fifty Nights, in London'. There are reviews of his two plays in the *Caledonian Mercury* for 21 April and 13 May 1824 respectively. The first of these describes him as 'about 27 years of age; his personal appearance is handsome, and his countenance pleasing and interesting'. Poetical tributes to M. Alexandre from Sir Walter Scott and from Sir John Sinclair were printed in the *Caledonian Mercury* of 29 April and 20 May respectively. For further details of Alexandre's Edinburgh visit see R. P. Gillies, *Memoirs of a Literary Veteran*, 3 vols (London: Bentley, 1851), III, 98–100.

78(c) Grieve and Scott Henry Scott and John Grieve were partners in a hatter's business on the North Bridge in Edinburgh. Grieve (1781–1836) was the son of Walter Grieve, who had been minister of the Reformed Presbyterian Church in Dunfermline but then retired to farm in Ettrick. Walter Grieve is discussed in ll. 25–40 of 'St. Mary of the Lows', an earlier contribution by Hogg to *Forget Me Not*: see p. 45 and note on 45(25). John Grieve and Henry Scott had been particularly generous in their financial and other support to Hogg on his arrival in Edinburgh in February 1810– see 'Memoir', p. 27.

78(c) "The Hunter's Tryste," this inn is still in existence (present address 97 Oxgangs Road, Edinburgh) on the road between Fairmilehead and Colinton. In Hogg's day it was a resort of the Six-Feet Club, of which he became honorary laureate. The Club, founded in 1826 as the guard of honour to the Hereditary Lord High Constable of Scotland, was formed for 'the practice and promotion of the National Games of Scotland, and of Gymnastics in general'. Of its three General Meetings each year, two took place at the Hunters' Tryst, in May and in November—see *Summary of the Rules and Regulations of the Six-Feet Club* (Edinburgh: printed by J. Johnstone, 1829).

78(c) the hills of Braid the Braid Hills lie among the southern outskirts of modern Edinburgh, but their surroundings were more rural in Hogg's day. Fairmilehead and Colinton (see previous note) lie a little further to the south.

78(d) the castle Edinburgh Castle, prominent on its rock at the heart of the city, lies to the north of the Braid Hills

79 [Illustration] the engraving for which Hogg wrote his 'Scottish Haymakers' was taken from a painting by the Scottish artist William Kidd (1790–1863), known for his Scottish genre scenes influenced by the work of David Wilkie (1785–1841) and Alexander Carse (*fl.* 1812–20). Titles such as *The Highland Reel* (1842), *The Cotter's Saturday Night* (1845) and *The Jolly Beggars* (1846) reveal the closeness of his art to Scottish writing. He first exhibited at the Royal Academy in 1817, and subsequently also at the British Institution and the Society of British Artists, and in 1849 was elected an honorary member of the Royal Scottish Academy. His popular paintings were frequently engraved—see Christopher Wood, *Dictionary of British Art: Volume IV Victorian Painters 1. The Text* (Woodbridge, Suffolk: Antique Collectors Club, 1995), p. 294, and also Duncan Macmillan *Scottish Art 1460–2000* (Edinburgh: Mainstream, 2000), pp. 183–84. The illustration to 'Katie Cheyne' in the present volume is also taken from Kidd's work. The engraver James Mitchell (1791–1852) was employed to produce engravings for several annuals, including *Literary Souvenir, The Gem*, and *The Keepsake* besides working on illustrations for the *magnum opus* edition of Scott's Waverley Novels (1829–33). The engraving of Wilkie's *The Dorty Bairn* in the present volume is also Mitchell's work.

81(b) my uncultivated judgment, which can only discern what is accordant with nature by looking on nature itself a suggestion, perhaps, that Hogg's own art does not rely on deception (like Alexandre's), but tries to tell it like it is. Hogg likewise expresses his sense of the basis of the value of his own art when, at the conclusion of Book First of his poem *Queen Hynde*, he addresses his imagined reader, the 'Maid of Dunedin':

> Let those who list, the garden chuse,
> Where flowers are regular and profuse;
> Come thou to dell and lonely lea,
> And cull the mountain gems with me;
> And sweeter blooms may be thine own,
> By nature's hand at random sown;
> And sweeter strains may touch thy heart
> Than are producible by art.

A similar point is likewise made at the conclusion of the first 'Circle' of

Peril First in *The Three Perils of Woman*: see *Queen Hynde* (S/SC, 1998), pp. 31, 253 (note on 31(1080–86)); and *The Three Perils of Woman* (S/SC, 1995), pp. 25, 441 (note on 25(b)). See also Hogg's poem 'To Miss M. A. C—e' (pp. 203–05 in the present volume) and the introductory and textual note to that poem (pp. 335–36).

81(c) the ladies of the family Alexander Nasmyth had six daughters: Jane (born 1778); Barbara (born 1790); Margaret (born 1791); Elizabeth (born 1793); Anne (born 1798); and Charlotte (born 1804). All of them were known as artists and entered paintings in exhibitions in Edinburgh, London, and Manchester, besides helping their father with the art classes he held at his home at 47 York Place, Edinburgh.

81(d) a child among the hay the *Caledonian Mercury* of 21 April 1824 describes a scene in *The Rogueries of Nicholas* where there is a brawl among an assortment of domestic animals: an 'old woman alternately scolding at the brutes, and soothing an infant whom their noise has set a squalling, present a scene at once noisy, ludicrous, and diverting'. William Bewick's account of M. Alexandre's visit to Abbotsford stresses how deceptive his performances could be: he pretended to saw the dining-table, and when Scott tried to persuade his wife that the table was not really injured she is supposed to have replied, 'Impossible, what! don't I hear the shavings come off and drop down?"—see *Life and Letters of William Bewick*, ed. by Thomas Landseer, 2 vols (London: Hurst & Blackett, 1871), I, 248.

81(d) Peter was rather deaf this seems to have been the consequence of an illness contracted by sleeping in a damp bed when he was about seventeen years old—see the article by J. M. Gray (revised by Mungo Campbell) on Patrick Nasmyth in the *Oxford DNB*.

83(b) On the stage M. Alexandre gave performances at the Caledonian Theatre on 19, 21, 24, 26, 28 April and 1, 3, 5, 12 and 15 May 1824—see the advertisements in the *Caledonian Mercury* of 15 April and 3 and 6 May 1824. Hogg's letter to William Blackwood written from Mount Benger in Yarrow on 28 June 1824 (NLS, MS 4012, fols 184–85) suggests that he had paid a visit to Edinburgh during the preceding weeks.

83(c) a bottle in its review of *Devil upon Sticks* the *Caledonian Mercury* of 13 May 1824 refers to 'the joke of the Devil in the bottle'.

84(a) the chimney in its review of *The Rogueries of Nicholas* the *Caledonian Mercury* of 21 April 1824 mentions that Nicholas held 'discourse with the officer, who has taken refuge up the chimney to avoid discovery'.

84(b) Mr. Trotter's plantations Alexander Trotter of Dreghorn was the largest landowner in the parish of Colinton, then on the outskirts of Edinburgh. The Rev. Lewis Balfour in his account of the parish ('Drawn up November 1838, Revised October 1839') says that his residence of Dreghorn Castle was built at the beginning of the century, and 'is embosomed among trees, some of which are stately beeches belonging to the olden times, but the greater proportion have been planted by the present proprietor, and are in a very thriving condition'—see *New Statistical Account of Scotland*, 15 vols (Edinburgh: Blackwood, 1845), I, 107–33 (pp. 115–16, 120).

84(c) his death Patrick Nasmyth seems never to have been very robust: besides his deafness he injured his right arm in his youth and had learned to paint left-handed. His death on 17 August 1831 seems to have been the result of a chill, following influenza, caught while out sketching by the Thames near London.

The Lord of Balloch

84 [title] when the original version of 'The Lord of Balloch' was published in the *Edinburgh Literary Journal* as 'A Ballad from the Gaelic' (see Introductory and Textual Notes) Hogg provided a note which states: 'The scene of this ancient and horrible legend seems to have been in the country of the Grants, whose chief may have been the Lord of Balloch'—see *Edinburgh Literary Journal*, 10 July 1830, p. 30. Hogg may perhaps have associated the name 'Balloch' with a Grant chieftain because of the family of the Grants of Ballindaloch, several of whom were notable soldiers—see William Anderson, *The Scottish Nation*, 3 vols (Edinburgh: Fullarton, 1865), II, 362. A soldierly Grant of Ballindaloch features in 'The Adventures of Colonel Peter Aston', in *Tales of the Wars of Montrose*, ed. by Gillian Hughes (S/SC, 1996), pp. 109–37.

84 (1–6) The eagle [...] links of Spey the bird's flight takes it from Ben Nevis (the highest mountain in Britain and a natural haunt of eagles) over the Grampian mountains to Badenoch and Strathspey, the districts through which the river Spey runs to the Moray coast in north-east Scotland.

85 (15) Lochdorbin's men Lochindorb (Gaelic for 'the lake of trouble') is 'in the parish of Cromdale, on the Spey' as Hogg's note (p. 87) says. Grantown-on-Spey and the ancient Grant stronghold of Castle Grant lie about six miles to the south-east of Lochindorb. On an island in Lochindorb are the ruins of a castle thought to have been built by Edward I of England ('the Hammer of the Scots') on the site of a hunting-lodge belonging to the Comyns, Lords of Badenoch. John Comyn, Lord of Badenoch (*d.* 1306) was an ally of Edward I and an opponent of the Scottish hero-king Robert I (the Bruce): famously, John Comyn was killed by Bruce at Dumfries in 1306. Lochindorb was later the base of Alexander Stewart (*c.* 1345–1405), the notorious Wolf of Badenoch (see note on 87 (97)). All in all, Lochindorb would have thoroughly negative connotations for Hogg.

85 (16) Gordons of the glen the Gordons were one of the major families of north-east Scotland. Eric Simpson quotes the traditional rhyme 'The Gordon, the gool [the corn marigold], and the hoodie craw, | Were the three worst ills that Moray e'er saw'—see *Banff, Moray and Nairn* (Edinburgh: John Donald, 1992), p. 33.

87 (91–93) twenty serfs [...] hung by the neck Castle Grant (see note on 85 (15)) still has on view a 'Lochindorb hanging beam', from which prisoners and sheep-stealers were frequently hanged.

87 (97) Lochdorbin's brutal chief no historical figure precisely fits Hogg's description, but Lochdorbin's most famous brutal chief was Alexander Stewart (*c.*1343–1405), Lord of Badenoch and Earl of Buchan. He was the fourth son of Robert II and his mistress (and later wife) Elizabeth Mure, commemorated by Hogg as Ila Moore in his poem, *Mador of the Moor* (1816). With Lochindorb as his stronghold he used his position as king's justiciar for the north in the late fourteenth and early fifteenth centuries to terrorise and waste much of north-east Scotland, and was known as the Wolf of Badenoch from his heraldic crest. He is the subject of Sir Thomas Dick Lauder's historical romance *The Wolfe of Badenoch* (1827).

87(108) castle a ruin unto this day in his note to 'A Ballad from the Gaelic' in the *Edinburgh Literary Journal*, 10 July 1830, p. 30 Hogg stated: 'there is an ancient castle, or rather garrison, of great strength and magnificence, called Lochindorb. It is situated on an island. Its walls are twenty feet thick and it covers fully an acre of ground. It has a spacious entrance of hewn stone, and strong watch-towers at each corner. The inhabitants of the district can give no account of it, but say it was the residence of a great cateran chief, who was put down by the Earl of Moray and the Laird of Grant. Another account is, that he and his followers were surprised, and cut off to a man, by the Laird of Grant. It is not improbable that this cateran chief may have been one of King Edward's officers'. Hogg's elision of historical events in his note here mirrors that of the poem, where he conflates different lairds of Lochindorb into one powerful and awesome 'cateran chief'.

87(116) Buchan a district of north-east Scotland.

87(116) Bogie a river of Aberdeenshire in north-east Scotland.

The Anniversary
The Carle of Invertime

91(4) Gudeman of Invertime *Gudeman* was sometimes applied specifically to the keeper of a jail (e.g. 'the Gudeman of the Tolbuith'). *Inver*, as a prefix in place names, usually means a confluence of streams or the mouth of a river: hence 'Inver Time', at the junction or gateway of time. (P.G.)

93(78) true Faith, sweet Charity the speaker is Hope, so the passage echoes I Corinthians 13. 13 ('And now abideth faith, hope, charity, these three; but the greatest of these is charity'). (P.G.)

95(166) vale of death Psalm 23. 4. (P.G.)

The Cameronian Preacher's Tale

96 [title] Cameronian the Cameronians were the followers of a young Dutch-trained field preacher called Richard Cameron, who on 20 June 1680 made a public declaration at the cross of Sanquhar renouncing their allegiance to Charles II and his government and declaring war on him and his brother and heir the Duke of York (later James VII and II). Cameron himself was killed by Royalist soldiers in a skirmish at Airds Moss about a month later, while his successors Donald Cargill and James Renwick were executed in 1681 and 1688 respectively. When, after the 'Glorious Revolution', William II and III established a national Presbyterian Church of Scotland, the Cameronians scorned what they termed this Erastian establishment, and in due course went on to set up the Reformed Presbyterian Church, which claimed to be the true Kirk of the Covenants. As heirs of the Covenanters, the Cameronians continued the tradition of field-preaching established during the reigns of Charles II and James VII and II.

96(b) my children a traditional preacher's address, stemming perhaps from I Thessalonians 2. 11, 'As ye know how we exhorted and comforted and charged every one of you, as a father *doth* his children'.

96(b) days and hours are numbered compare Daniel 5. 26: 'God hath numbered thy kingdom, and finished it'.

96(b) preached [...] profited compare Hebrews 4. 2: 'the word preached did not profit them, not being mixed with faith in them that heard *it*'.

96(c) our latter days compare Daniel 2. 28 ('what shall be in the latter days'), and Daniel 10. 14 ('what shall befall thy people in the latter days').

96(c) lay it up in your hearts compare Luke 2. 19: 'But Mary kept all these things, and pondered *them* in her heart'.

96(d) as with a cloud compare Job 22. 13: 'And thou sayest, How doth God know? can he judge through the dark cloud?'.

96(d) Dryfe Water flows into the River Annan near Lockerbie, Dumfries-shire.

97(b) the fair of Longtown Longtown is on the River Esk, just over the Border into Cumberland. The 1829 *Gazetteer of Cumberland and Westmorland* (repr. Beckermet, Cumbria: Michael Moon, 1976), states that 'The ancient market day is Thursday, but a market is also held on Monday, principally for *bacon* and *butter*, in which articles a great trade is carried on here. A *Horse Fair* is held on the Thursday before Whitsuntide; a *Cattle Fair* on the Thursday before September 30th; and *Races* in the last week of April' (p. 405).

98(b) "Revenge is mine, saith the Lord," see Romans 12. 19 ('Vengeance is mine; I will repay, saith the Lord').

99(a) Pennieland lies to the east of Dryfe Water.

100(a) a fool and no prophet perhaps an allusion to the denunciation of the times in Hosea 9. 7: 'the prophet *is* a fool'.

101(b) his tent was pitched in biblical terms, the place where a patriarch was living—see, for example, Genesis 12. 8, 13. 12, and 26. 17.

101(b) my text probably from Amos 3.6: 'Shall a trumpet be blown in the city, and the people not be afraid? shall there be evil in a city, and the LORD hath not done *it* ?'

103(c) sorely troubled compare Psalm 71. 20: 'great and sore troubles'.

104(a) your days be long in the land the promise made in Exodus 20. 12 to those who honour their parents.

104(c) a quiet friend by this term Macmillan intended Johnstone who being dead can make no noise, but the brothel-keeper Janet interprets it as a reference to her discretion in keeping Macmillan's stays with her a secret from his relations and co-religionists.

104(d) a freer kirk perhaps the Scottish Episcopal Church, which was linked by Hogg with the Royalist gentry of the south of Scotland.

104(d) send you awa to the mountains the implication is probably that Janet will call for Royalist soldiers, a serious threat to a Cameronian preacher in the 1680s but not in the 1760s.

105(c) a corse candle [...] a corse light that is, a corpse candle, a softly-burning light seen over a grave, believed to appear as an omen of death.

105(c) elf candle a spark or flash of light, thought to be of supernatural origin.

106(a) 'Clavers and his Highlandmen' this song is probably the one given as 'Song XVII. The Battle of Killiecrankie' in the first series of Hogg's *Jacobite Relics of Scotland* (S/SC, 2002), pp. 28–29, which begins 'Clavers and his Highlandmen | Came down upon the raw, man'. The implication is perhaps that the piper is a Jacobite.

106(b) wandering streamers the *aurora borealis*, or northern lights, are bands of light seen in high latitudes.

106(d) souls made perfect that is, those justified through the Covenant of Grace and so fitted for Heaven—see Hebrews 12. 23, for example, where

'God the Judge of all' is accompanied by 'the spirits of just men made perfect'.

106(d) Grahame John Grahame of Claverhouse, first Viscount Dundee (1649?–89), known in the south of Scotland as 'bloody Clavers' (see note on 106(a)) for his persecution of the Covenanters in the reigns of Charles II and James VII and II. He is an important character in Hogg's *The Brownie of Bodsbeck* (1818) and in Scott's *The Tale of Old Mortality* (1816).

106(d) Grierson Sir Robert Grierson of Lag, in Dumfriesshire 1655?–1733), another persecutor of the Covenanters, with a reputation for enjoying the torture of his prisoners and of mocking Covenanting beliefs in his drunken revels.

107(a) appeared to me [...] with a sorrowful look presumably the apparition of a murdered victim, whether in a dream or as a ghost, is intended to promote discovery of the missing corpse. In his notes to 'The Pedlar' Hogg says 'it is a received opinion, that, if the body, or bones, or any part of a murdered person is found, the ghost is then at rest, and that it leaves mankind to find out the rest'—see *The Mountain Bard* (Edinburgh: Constable; London: Murray, 1807), p. 31.

107(a) consolation to the widow and the fatherless Psalm 146. 9 praises God because 'he relieveth the fatherless and the widow'.

107(a) the hour is come a phrase perhaps deriving from Matthew 26. 45 ('behold, the hour is at hand').

107(d) the embalming nature of the morass Hogg knew of several preserved corpses being recovered from peat-bogs. A note to 'The Pedlar', for example, instances the discovery made by a couple cutting peats at Craighope-head of 'a man's head [...] with long auburn hair, and so fresh that every feature was distinguishable'—see *The Mountain Bard* (1807), p. 31. His best-known fictional exploration of this idea occurs in *The Private Memoirs and Confessions of a Justified Sinner*.

108(b) good John Farley here Hogg first identifies the narrator as John Fairley (1729–1806), a well-known historical figure known both to himself and the *Anniversary*'s editor, Allan Cunningham. Fairley had been ordained Cameronian minister to the widely-scattered congregation in the south of Scotland at Leadhills on 21 December 1763, his ministry lasting for forty-three years. He would make a fifteen- or sixteen-week tour of the district for which he was responsible, preaching and examining the people in the tenets of their faith. Matthew Hutchinson describes him, in *The Reformed Presbyterian Church in Scotland: Its Origin and History 1680–1876* (Paisley: J. and R. Parlane, 1893), as 'quick and irritable in temper' with 'a power of sarcasm which those who provoked him did not easily forget' (pp. 221–23). On one occasion, denouncing bishops who did not preach, he declared that the Bishop of Bangor was worse than Balaam's ass which at least spoke once to rebuke the prophet's madness. His eloquence attracted large numbers of hearers to his sermons, although some would leave before the conclusion when exposition of doctrine sometimes turned into flyting, or personal application. 'He had a wonderful gift in prayer' Hutchinson adds, 'sometimes most touchingly pathetic, and again rousing the heart by sublime utterances' (p. 223). He lived firstly at Thirton House near Douglas, and then at Howgill, Newtonhead, and died on 18 April 1806. Allan Cunningham gave his own portrait of Fairley in 'Recollections. No. I–The

Cameronians', *Blackwood's Edinburgh Magazine*, 6 (1819), 169–74.

108(b) a man whom I knew and loved Hogg had presumably known Fairley shortly before his death on 18 April 1806: at this time Hogg was serving as a shepherd to a Mr. Harkness of Mitchellslacks farm in Closeburn parish. There was a notable settlement of Covenanters at Quarrelwood in the nearby parish of Kirkmahoe, while the Harkness family themselves were celebrated Covenanters. William McDowall in his *History of the Burgh of Dumfries*, 2nd edn (Edinburgh: A. and C. Black, 1873), pp. 466–67 mentions that in 1684 Clavers apprehended Thomas Harkness of Mitchelslacks, who was later executed in Edinburgh. His brother James was also taken, but escaped from Canongate Jail and lived to old age at his farmhouse of Locherben, a farm which was leased by Hogg in 1807.

Katie Cheyne

109 [Illustration] engraved from a painting by the Scottish artist William Kidd (1790–1863)–for further details see note to 79 [Illustration]. Nothing is known of the engraver, whose name is given as J. Shury. This illustration was first published with 'Katie Cheyne' in *The Bouquet* for 1832: see the present volume's Introductory and Textual Notes, at pp. 308–09.

111(b) simplicity, saith the proverb perhaps an allusion to Proverbs 1. 22: 'How long, ye simple ones, will ye love simplicity? and the scorners delight in their scorning, and fools hate knowledge?'

111(b) as the daft sang says this has not been identified.

112(a) some Cameronian sermon see note to 96 [title].

112(a) the Lammas fair Lammas is 1 August, one of the Scottish Quarter Days: the fair may possibly be the Lammas fair of Lockerbie–see the account of the parish of Dryfesdale in the *New Statistical Account of Scotland*, 15 vols (Edinburgh: Blackwood, 1845), II, 451–59 (p. 458).

112(b) all who run will read 'He that runs may read' (*ODEP*, pp. 689–90).

112(c) look low [...] lift little compare 'I will never lout so low and lift so little' (*ODEP*, p. 488).

113(b) the spell of pen and ink a written promise of marriage could give rise to a lawsuit for breach of promise, or even (in conjunction with consummation) itself constitute a marriage in Scottish law.

113(c) hap step and loup Hogg described the contest of hop-step-and-leap in his 'Anecdotes of the Pastoral Life. No II', *Blackwood's Edinburgh Magazine*, 1 (1817), 143–47 (p. 144): 'It consists of three succeeding bounds, all with the same race; and as the exertion is greater, and of longer continuance, they can judge with more precision the exact capability of the several competitors. I measured the ground, and found the greatest distance effected in this way to be forty-six feet'.

113(d) unpressed curd the product of the first stage of cheese-making. The curds are then compressed and matured into cheese.

115(a) my thumb on't a bargain is confirmed by the parties concerned licking their thumbs and pressing them together.

115(b) no a' made up frae the pan and spoon something more in him than his food, i.e. is more than usually clever.

116(a) like a mill shelling a reference to the removal of the husk from grain such as oats.

118(b) whaups and craneberries wild and boggy ground would be the best-suited to an abundance of curlews and cranberries.

118(d) the tenth of Nehemiah the chapter begins with a long list of Hebrew names of those who signed the covenant, and is a difficult chapter, therefore, to read aloud.

119(b) Queensberry, as Criffil, as Skiddaw-fell Queensberry is a high hill in Dumfriesshire, Criffell one in Kirkcudbrightshire, and Skiddaw one in Cumberland. These names suggest that Hogg is setting his tale near Cunningham's native district in south-west Scotland.

119(c) galloway nag a small, sturdy type of horse, named after the Galloway district of south-west Scotland.

119(c) penny wedding a wedding at which the guests contributed money or food towards the entertainment, any surplus being a gift to the couple concerned.

119(c) a dropping year dropping in this sense means to let fall in birth—a year which is a good one for births among flocks of sheep.

119(d) grope a dizen of trouts fishing with the hands rather than with a rod and line. Hogg describes the process as 'gumping' or 'guddling' in 'The Wool-Gatherer'—see *The Brownie of Bodsbeck and Other Tales*, 2 vols (Edinburgh: Blackwood; London: Murray, 1818), II, 89–228 (pp. 169–70).

Friendship's Offering
Auld Joe Nicholson's Bonny Nannie

123(1) day-lily a lily, the flower of which lasts for one day: a genus of the liliaceous plants, *hemerocallis*, with large yellow or orange flowers.

Ballad

124(1) Now lock my chamber door the poem takes the form of a speech by Mary Gray, the niece of Hogg's wife and daughter to his old friend James Gray. She had recently been staying at Mount Benger, and had been jilted—for details see Introductory and Textual Notes, pp. 311–12.

124(1) father Hogg is generalising the situation, as Mary's father, James Gray, was in fact in India when she was jilted.

124(3) my step-mother Mary Gray's own mother, Mary Phillips, had died on 9 November 1806, and her father had married Mary Peacock on 25 October 1808—for further information see *The Spy*, pp. 562, 564. Mrs Gray was also in India when Mary Gray was jilted.

124(25) Farewell, ye banks a reference to the rural Mount Benger farm, where Mary Gray had been staying with Hogg and his family. There is perhaps an allusion to Burns's well-known song 'The Banks o' Doon', which also takes the voice of a forsaken girl.

125(31) the opening gates of day a reference to the renewed life of heaven after the sleep of death: Milton's *Paradise Lost*, VI. 4 describes how Morn 'unbarred the gates of light'.

Verses to a Beloved Young Friend

125 [title] the poem is addressed to Mary Gray, and like 'Ballad' in *Friendship's Offering* concerns her suffering over her broken engagement—for further details see Introductory and Textual Notes, pp. 312–13.

125(1) the last look Mary Gray's last look at Mount Benger before departing for Edinburgh and, ultimately, India, but also Hogg's last look at his young relation.

125(16) Child of a darkling world Hogg's parting from Mary presages the parting from all his loved ones in death.

126(31) Indus the river flowing south, through what is now Pakistan, from Kashmir to the sea.

126(38) My love shall be as it hath been the gentlest of reminders to the sorrowing girl of the comfort available in the faithful affection of her relations. According to Hogg's letter to Allan Cunningham of 18 October 1829 Mary appears to have married a Mr Robert Money ('a young English gentleman in the Company's civil service being their resident at the court of Catch') soon after her arrival in India (Beinecke Rare Book & Manuscript Library, Yale University, James Hogg Collection, GEN MSS 61, Box 1, Folder 7).

The Minstrel Boy

126 [title] there is a reference here to Edwin, the minstrel of James Beattie's influential long poem *The Minstrel* (Book I, 1771; Book II, 1774).

126(16) my loved Fairy Queen see Introductory and Textual Notes, pp. 285–86 (on 'Invocation to the Queen of the Fairies').

126(18) son of Apollo Apollo is the classical god of music and poetry, whose instrument is the lyre. He is represented in this role in Virgil's *Eclogues*, in which of course shepherds are prominent.

127 [Illustration] Hogg's poem was originally published with, and was written to match, this illustration from a painting by Charles Robert Leslie (1794–1859), born in London but of American parentage and upbringing. He studied art in London and was a close friend of the painter John Constable (1776–1837), as well as being acquainted with many literary men such as Coleridge, Scott and Washington Irving. In the autumn of 1824 he visited Abbotsford 'for the purpose of painting a portrait of Sir Walter Scott for Mr. Ticknor of Boston', carrying with him from John Murray to Scott 'a mourning ring, which had been left to him by Lord Byron'—see Charles Robert Leslie, *Autobiographical Recollections*, ed. by Tom Taylor, 2 vols (London: Murray, 1860), I, 83–85. It is not known whether or not he met Hogg on this occasion. Leslie was subsequently employed to illustrate Scott's *magnum opus* edition of the Waverley Novels, and many of his most popular paintings, such as *Sir Roger de Coverley Going to Church*, were of literary subjects. Nothing is known of the engraver of this picture, named as 'A. Duncan'.

129(39) days that are past and gone Hogg gives a less idealised account of his childhood service in 'Memoir', pp. 12–15, which also mentions his running races against himself.

130(74) This high resolve not to be beat Hogg's brother William recollected: 'In the play-ground [...] he was every day entering into competitions which gave me uneasiness, as I knew he had no chance with his competitors in racing, wrestling, etc. They were frequently far above his age, and above his strength, yet his frequent defeats did not discourage him'—see Garden, p. 14.

131(105) its slave Hogg's Ettrick Shepherd persona was characterised by susceptibility to the fair sex. His account of his childhood referred to in the note to 129(39) includes a passage added in 1832 describing how he fell in love for the first time at the age of eight.

A Scots Luve Sang

131 [title] in *Songs (1831)* Hogg states that this and another song, 'Love Letter', 'were both written in 1811, forming parts of humorous letters to the young lady who afterwards became my wife' (p. 193).

131(6) man maun hae this teazing crony a jocular reference to Genesis 2. 18: 'And the Lord God said, *It is* not good that man should be alone; I will make him an help meet for him'.

131(13–14) my tunefu' pegs [...] mountain strains a reference to the bardic persona of Hogg's early publications *The Mountain Bard* (1807) and *The Forest Minstrel* (1810).

131(15–16) Megs | Wi' glossy een sae dark an' wily Hogg's earliest extant letter to Margaret Phillips, of 27 July 1811, was written after her return from James Gray's house in Edinburgh to her Dumfriesshire home, and in it Hogg wishes that he would find her at Gray's house on his visit that evening, quoting the phrase 'and I would watch thy witching smile and glossy een sae dark and wiley': see this letter in *Letters I*.

132(21) harp waves on the willow a jocular allusion to Psalm 137. 2 ('We hanged our harps upon the willows in the midst thereof'). This equates Hogg's separation from Margaret in Edinburgh to the ancient Israelites' captivity in Babylon.

The Fords of Callum

132 [title] the place-name 'Fords of Callum' has not been identified, but references later in the story indicate a location on Kinnel Water in Annandale in south-west Scotland. 'The Fords of Callum' may have been a name current at the time Hogg's tale is set but which did not survive after Kinnel Water was bridged. The Rev. Robert Colvin states that 'the first bridge over the Kinnel at St Anns, near Raehills, was built in the year 1782, rebuilt in 1795, and considerably widened and improved in 1817'—see the *New Statistical Account of Scotland*, 15 vols (Edinburgh: Blackwood, 1845), IV, 164–65.

132(c) 'at open doors the dogs come ben' a proverbial expression—see *ODEP*, p. 599 ('At open doors dogs come in').

132(d) cousin-german a first cousin, the child of a sibling of one's father or mother.

133(c) Lockerbie tryste probably the Lammas fair at Lockerbie in Dumfriesshire—see note to 112(a) above. In his account of the parish of Dryfesdale in the *New Statistical Account of Scotland*, 15 vols (Edinburgh: Blackwood, 1845), the Rev. David B. Douie explains that 'When the border raids had so far ceased as to allow a slight intercourse between the Scot and the southern, our sheep farmers assembled here every year, to meet with English dealers. This they called a tryst; but, as Lockerbie increased in population [...] the fair became a greater object of importance [...]' (II, 458). There is also the possibility, however, that one of the hiring markets for servants is alluded to here, of which Douie says, 'The hiring market for servants for the summer half-year is in April. For the winter half-year, the one fourteen days after Michaelmas. To these two markets an immense concourse of people assemble from all parts of Annandale' (note on p. 458).

134(a) speak o' the deil an' he'll appear see 'Talk of the devil, and he is sure to appear' (*ODEP*, p. 804). The proverb is also listed in 'A Collection of Scots Proverbs' in *The Works of Allan Ramsay: Vol.V*, ed. by Alexander M. Kinghorn and Alexander Law (Edinburgh: Scottish Text Society, 1972), pp. 63–129 (p. 108).

134(c) the folk o' Sodom and Gomorrah the biblical cities of the plain, which were destroyed by God because of the wickedness of their inhabit-ants—see Genesis 19. Sodom means 'burning' and Gomorrah 'a rebellious people'.

135(d) to look for a body here (as often in Scots speech) *body* is used to mean 'a human being', 'a person'.

136(b) Nithsdale a district to the west of Annandale.

136(b) Queensberry a mountain that lies between Annandale and Nithsdale.

136(c) Duff's Kinnel a rivulet in the north-west part of Annandale. It joins Kinnel Water a little above Raehills.

136(c) Dr. Johnstone then living in Moffat the town of Moffat is in Annandale. The Rev. Alexander Johnstone in his account of the parish of Moffat (dated January 1834) relates that 'An heiress of Johnstone of Corhead having married Dr George Milligan, minister of Moffat, their son Dr George Milligan Johnstone, M.D. became distinguished in his profession; he analyzed the mineral waters'—see the *New Statistical Account of Scotland*, 15 vols (Edin-burgh: Blackwood, 1845), IV, 102–23 (pp. 112–13).

137(b) Wat looked so ill Wat's illness and death are the consequence of his having seen Annie's wraith (which her mother has only heard but not seen). David Proudfoot in Hogg's story 'Tibby Johnston's Wraith' explains that 'Wraiths are of twa kinds, you see. They appear always immediately before death, or immediately after it. [...] Now, when the wraith appears after death, that's the soul o' the deceased, that gets liberty to appear to the ane of a' its acquaintances that is the soonest to follow it; and it does that just afore it leaves this world for the last time [...]'—see *Winter Evening Tales* (S/SC, 2002), p. 505.

137(c) carrying the head this implies that the stranger was acting as Annie's father, and is perhaps indeed her father.

137(d) the late Duke of Q— William Douglas, 4th Duke of Queensberry (1724–1810) succeeded to the title in 1778. He was nicknamed 'Old Q', and known for his gambling and dissipated life-style, to pay for which he cut down trees on his Drumlanrig estate near Thornhill in Nithsdale. Hogg had lived in the vicinity between 1805 and 1809.

A Bard's Address to his Youngest Daughter

138(2) Harriet Harriet Sidney Hogg was the fourth child of Hogg's marriage to Margaret Phillips, born on 18 December 1829 (Yarrow OPR).

138(15) like Maggy o'er her book Margaret Laidlaw Hogg, named after Hogg's mother, was the third child of Hogg's marriage, born on 18 Janu-ary 1825 (Yarrow OPR), and presumably just learning to read.

139(36) Let little children come to me Jesus's words, 'Suffer the little chil-dren to come unto me', as given in Mark 10. 14 and Luke 18. 16. (P.G.)

139(41–44) Thy very name [...] extremity Harriet was named after Harriet,

Duchess of Buccleuch (1773–1814), daughter of 1st Viscount Sydney. Hogg is apparently alluding to her dying wish that he should receive the farm at Altrive Lake. The Duke's letter of gift of 26 January 1815, however, points to a general influence on the Duchess's part rather than to any specific death-bed request (NLS, MS 2245, fol. 13). (P.G.)

139(46) all I honour and revere the manuscript version of this poem continues here with allusions to other family members, notably Harriet's two grandmothers and her other two siblings—see *A Queer Book*, ed. by P. D. Garside (S/SC, 1995), pp. 144–46 (notes on pp. 251–53). Hogg may perhaps have thought these more appropriate for family circulation than for publication.

Musical Bijou
The Harp of Ossian

143 [title] during the 1760s, James Macpherson (1736–96) published what he claimed were his translations of Gaelic poems by the third-century Highland warrior-bard Ossian. Macpherson's *Ossian* texts were much admired and were widely influential, but their authenticity was questioned by writers such as Dr Samuel Johnson. Scholars now believe that they are imaginative recreations of traditional Gaelic poems and tales—see Fiona Stafford, 'Introduction', in *The Poems of Ossian and Related Works*, ed. by Howard Gaskill (Edinburgh: Edinburgh University Press, 1996), pp. v–xxi. Hogg himself drew on Macpherson's *Ossian* in his own Scottish epic *Queen Hynde* (1824).

143(1) Old Harp of the Highlands the mysterious sounding of Ossian's harp is a fateful and atmospheric prelude to epic conflict in Book Second of *Queen Hynde*: 'And well they knew, the omen drear | Boded of danger death and weir' (S/SC, 1998), p. 42.

143(12) They fight, but they fight not for Scotia or me after the Union of Parliaments of 1707, Scottish soldiers formed part of the British army. Recruitment was particularly vigorous in the Highlands. 'Beginning on a small scale during the Seven Years War (1756–63) and increasing during the American War of Independence, recruitment multiplied to extraordinary levels during the Napoleonic Wars when, on one estimate, the Highlands supplied around 74,000 men for regiments of the line, the Militia, Fencibles, and Volunteers out of a total regional population of about 300,000'—see T. M. Devine, *The Scottish Nation 1700–2000* (London: Allen Lane, 1999), pp. 184–85.

143(14) our old mortal foe England.

143(20) voices of strangers the English language, with which the post-Union British state intended to supplant the Gaelic language of Ossian.

143(22) eye of the free a reference to a traditional Scottish claim that Scotland had long remained unconquered, whereas England had been conquered first by the Romans and then by the Normans. This claim is celebrated in the opening lines of Book First of *Queen Hynde*.

144–48 [music] musical settings of verse by noted writers was the most distinctive feature of the *Musical Bijou*, though (naturally enough when engraving was so labour-intensive) not every poem was so distinguished. 'The Harp of Ossian' was arranged for a single voice with a basic piano accompaniment designed to be well within the capabilities of amateur drawing-room performers. For information on the composer, Henry Rowley Bishop (1786–1855), see the Introductory and Textual Notes, p. 317.

My Emma, My Darling

149(1) from winter's domain [...] city again upper-class families in Hogg's day would spend the autumn on their country estates and come into London or Edinburgh for winter social events.

150–53 [music] Henry Rowley Bishop set Hogg's song for single voice with piano accompaniment in the same way as he had for 'The Harp of Ossian'– see note to 144–48 [music].

O Weel Befa' the Guileless Heart

154 AIR–The Wauking o' the Fauld this tune had been published in the first volume of James Johnson's *Scots Musical Museum* in 1771, and may most easily be consulted in the facsimile edition introduced and edited by Donald Low (Aldershot: Scolar Press, 1991), I, 88.

154(7) blooming asphodel a genus of liliaceous plants with very handsome flowers, which was said to cover the Elysian fields. Hogg links the flower with purity through the lily, completely ignoring its mythological association with death.

Fairy Songs

155 [direction] in naming the singer as Queen of the Fairies Hogg may intend an allusion to Titania, wife of Oberon, in *A Midsummer Night's Dream*. The later Victorian obsession with fairies is already discernible at this time. Weber's *Oberon* was produced in London in 1826, while Henry Rowley Bishop (1786–1855), the composer who had set Hogg's 'The Harp of Ossian' and 'My Emma, My Darling' to music for the *Musical Bijou* for 1829, had composed music for Covent Garden productions entitled *Midsummer Night's Dream* in 1816, and *The Gnome King* in 1819.

155(10) polar way perhaps an indication that the fairies are travelling northwards guided by the Pole Star.

155(12–13) Over tree | Over lea a parallel to the 'Over hill, over dale' of *A Midsummer Night's Dream*, II. 1. 2–5.

155(24) the morning star the harbinger of dawn.

156(32) the first star perhaps Venus, known as the evening star–see *A Queer Book*, ed. by P. D. Garside (S/SC, 1995), p. 260.

156(32) the window of heaven compare Genesis 7. 11 ('the windows of heaven were opened').

156(33) palace of light the details that follow (of a throne, columns and precious stones) recall the description of the heavenly city in Revelation 21. 11–25, a passage that had earlier informed Hogg's description of the dwelling-place of God in his narrative poem, *The Pilgrims of the Sun* (Edinburgh: Blackwood; London: Murray, 1815), pp. 44–46.

156(38) middle sky a phrase which may indicate the position of the fairies between earth and heaven, just as the phrase 'middle earth' denotes the earthly world between heaven and hell.

156(39) the spheres this relates to the Ptolemaic system of cosmology, in which nine spheres carried the stars and planets.

156(42) the end of our days a suggestion that the immortality of a super-

natural being in time is counteracted by its lack of a soul at the Last Judge-
ment, an idea given expression by Hogg in 'The Mermaid'—see *Poetical
Works (1822)*, II, 231–37. The traditional ballad 'Tam Lin' (Child 39) also
mentions that every seven years the fairies pay a teind to hell in the form
of one of their number.

The Amulet
A Lay of the Martyrs

161(3) **Wanlock-head** in Upper Nithsdale, about 5 miles NE of Sanquhar;
Wanlockhead was a busy lead-mining community in the 19th century. (P.G.)

161(4) **Louther brae** the Lowther Hills range between Dumfriesshire and
Lanarkshire; Green Lowther (2403 feet) and Lowther Hill (2377 feet), the
two highest points, overlook the village of Wanlockhead from the SE.
(P.G.)

161(13) **Enterkin** the Enterkin Burn runs for about six miles from a point
close to Wanlockhead, entering the River Nith at Enterkinfoot; it was once
used as a route between Dumfries and Edinburgh. For the Enterkin Pass
Rescue in 1684, see introductory comments above [at Introductory and
Textual Notes, pp. 323–24]. (P.G.)

161(14–15) **dens o' the Ballybough [...] howes o' the Ganna linn** neither
place name has been identified, but the kind of hiding-place indicated matches
Wodrow's account of Graham of Claverhouse's visit to the region in the
aftermath of the Enterkin Pass Rescue: 'Wonderful were the preservations
of the persecuted about this time. The soldiers frequently got their clothes
and cloaks, and yet missed themselves. They would have gone by the
mouths of the caves and dens in which they were lurking, and the dogs
would snook and smell about the stones under which they hid, and yet
they remained undiscovered' (*History of the Sufferings of the Church of Scotland*,
4 vols (Glasgow, 1836–38), IV, 174). (P.G.)

163(68) **say how I liked him now** echoing the words allegedly spoken by
Graham of Claverhouse to the wife of John Brown after her husband's
summary execution: 'Claverhouse said to his Wife, What thinkest thou of
thy Husband now, Woman? She said, I thought ever much good of him,
and as much now as ever' (Patrick Walker, *Some Remarkable Passages in the
Life and Death of Mr. Alexander Peden* (1724), p. 75). (P.G.)

165(133) **the popish duke** either the Duke of Lauderdale (1616–1682),
Secretary of Scottish Affairs from 1660 to 1680; or the Duke of York, who
took up residence at the Palace of Holyroodhouse in November 1679,
briefly acting as Royal Commissioner in Scotland before his accession as
James VII and II in 1685. The cupidity of Hogg's 'duke' best fits Lauderdale;
'popish', on the other hand, more obviously relates to the Duke of York, a
professed Roman Catholic, who installed a Catholic chapel at Holyrood.
(P.G.)

165(145) **down the bow** probably the Nether Bow, Edinburgh's eastern
entrance. The journey envisaged appears to be up the Canongate from
Holyrood, through the Netherbow Port (gate), and down to the
Grassmarket—the place of execution—at the foot of the Castle. (P.G.)

166(187) **right hand hang beside his cheek** compare Wodrow's account of
the execution of the preachers John Kid and John King in 1679: 'Their
heads were cut off, and their right hands, and affixed upon the Netherbow-

port of Edinburgh' (*History of the Church of Scotland*. III, 136). The practice of displaying both the heads and hands of executed Covenanters features in two influential novels of Hogg's period, Scott's *Tale of Old Mortality* (1816) and John Galt's *Ringan Gilhaize* (1823). (P.G.)

167 (227) never yet laid that burden on echoing Psalm 55. 22 ('Cast thy burden upon the Lord, and he shall sustain thee'). (P.G.)

A Tale of Pentland

168 [title] the Pentlands are a broken range of hills about sixteen miles long, stretching from 3 miles south-west of Edinburgh almost into Lanarkshire. The Covenanters' Rising of 1666 (known as the Pentland Rising because it ended at Rullion Green in the Pentland Hills) was directed against Charles II's church settlement in Scotland at the Restoration, when episcopacy and lay patronage were re-established and many ministers who refused to accept the new settlement were deposed. Many congregations remained loyal to their deposed ministers and the Presbyterian Covenants, but their clandestine meetings or conventicles were outlawed. On 13 November 1666 a scuffle between Royalist soldiers and conventiclers took place at Dalry. The victorious conventiclers then captured Sir James Turner at his headquarters in Dumfries and proceeded from there towards Edinburgh. Their small and hastily formed force was eventually dispersed by a superior Royalist force under Sir Thomas Dalyell at Rullion Green on 28 November. An example was made of those conventiclers (now termed Covenanters, after their ceremony of renewal of the Covenants at Lanark) who were taken prisoner, with some thirty-six executed, and many others transported to places like Barbados.

168(a) WOODROW the Rev. Robert Wodrow (1679–1734) was the major historian and apologist for the Scottish Covenanting resistance in his *The History of the Sufferings of the Church of Scotland from the Restauration to the Revolution*, 2 vols (Edinburgh: James Watson, 1721–22). This had recently been edited by the Rev. Robert Burns and republished in Glasgow in four volumes (1828–30). Wodrow was an important source for Hogg in tales: see the Introductory and Textual Notes on 'A Lay of the Martyrs'. The story of 'A Tale of Pentland', however, does not appear to be in Wodrow.

168(a) Mr. John Haliday no historical original has been identified.

168(b) Gabriel Johnstone no historical original has been identified.

168(b) the sufferings of the church of Scotland an allusion to the title of Wodrow's history—see note to 168(a).

168(d) reformed religion the Scottish Reformation dates from 1560 when the parliament, repudiating the pope's authority, forbade the celebration of mass, and approved a Protestant Confession of Faith.

169(a) West Linton a village in Peeblesshire, situated at the point where the River Lyre emerges from the Pentland Hills and near an important drove road linking the Borders with the central lowlands of Scotland.

169(b) Biggar an historic burgh in Lanarkshire between Lanark and Peebles.

169(b) Craigengaur a hill of 1700 feet near where the counties of Lanark, Midlothian, and Peebles meet, sixteen miles south-west of Edinburgh.

169(c) hinds' feet an expression deriving from Psalm 18. 33: 'He maketh my feet like hinds' *feet*, and setteth me upon my high places'. The Covenanters' published apologia for the Pentland Rising was called *Napthali*, from Genesis 49. 21 ('Napthali *is* a hind let loose'). The subsequent Covenanting apologia of the Cameronian historian Alexander Shiels is entitled *A Hind Let Loose* (1687).

169(d) **Mr. Livingston** the Scottish Covenanting minister John Livingston (1603–1672) was deposed and banished in 1662 for refusing the oath of allegiance to Charles II. He was exiled to Rotterdam in April 1663, never returning to Scotland. He gave his last communion sermon on 12 October 1662 in his parish church of Ancrum in Roxburghshire. As well as having this historical figure in mind when choosing the name of this story's Covenanting minister, Hogg may have been thinking of I Peter 2. 4–5, a well-known passage in which Christians are urged to come to Christ: 'To whom coming, *as unto* a living stone, disallowed indeed of men, but chosen of God, *and* precious, Ye also, as lively stones, are built up a spiritual house, an holy priesthood, to offer up spiritual sacrifices, acceptable to God by Jesus Christ'.

169(d) **Slipperfield** moor-land in the north-east of the parish of Linton in north-west Peeblesshire.

169(d) **milk of redeeming grace** another reference to I Peter 2: 'As new-born babes, desire the sincere milk of the word, that ye may grow thereby: If so be ye have tasted that the Lord *is* gracious' (verses 2–3).

170(a) **the penalty of their lives** conventicles were regarded as hotbeds of sedition even before the Pentland Rising, but afterwards involvement in conventicles was treason, a capital offence.

170(b) **William Rankin** no historical original has been identified.

171(a) **new act of council** following the Pentland Rising the Scottish Privy Council adopted a series of measures to attempt to control Scottish support for Presbyterianism. The Clanking Act of 1670 made preaching at conventicles a capital offence, while in 1669 and again in 1672 an attempt was made to gain control over deposed ministers by offering them a series of indulgencies that allowed them to function officially but with severe restrictions.

171(b) **slouch bonnets** hats pulled down to conceal the face.

171(b) **General Drummond** Lieutenant-General William Drummond (1617?–88) had been a comrade of the persecutor Thomas Dalyell in the Russian service, but returned to England to serve Charles II in 1665, and in January 1666 was appointed Major-General of the king's forces in Scotland. He was supposed (with Dalyell) to have introduced torture by the thumbscrew from Russia into Scotland. He was appointed Lieutenant-General of the king's forces in Scotland on the accession of James VII and II in 1685.

171(c) **Mr. Livingston, and other eleven** Livingston (see note to 169(d)) was summoned along with other nonconforming ministers to appear before the Privy Council on 11 December 1662 'for turbulency and sedition'. He was required to take the oath of allegiance to the king, and when he refused was subsequently banished.

171(c) **examined before the council** there is a record of Livingston's trial in the *Register of the Privy Council of Scotland*, ed. and abridged by P. Hume Brown, third series, 16 vols (Edinburgh: H. M. General Register House, 1908–70), I, 302–03.

171(c) **Mr. John Lindsay, from Edinburgh** the *Register of the Privy Council of*

Scotland, third series, II, 241 notes a decision of December 1666: 'The Lords of his Majesties Privy Concill doe hereby superseid the execution of the sentence of death pronunced against [...] John Lindsey untill the first Councill day of January nixt and untill the Councill give further order theranent'. In March 1667 the Council granted him 'liberty furth of the tolbuith of Edinburgh to come to a chalmer in the toune upon sufficient caution, under the payne of tuo hundreth lib. sterling, that he shall re-enter prisoner againe when requyred and that he shall at no tyme be seen upon the streets, whilk caution he hath found accordingly' (II, 278). There is no mention of his eventual fate.

171(d) extracts from his sermons [...] produced against him on his trial this is not recorded in the *Register of the Privy Council of Scotland*.

171(d) His text see Genesis 6. 5 ('And GOD saw that the wickedness of man *was* great in the earth, and *that* every imagination of the thoughts of his heart *was* only evil continually'), part of a passage where God intends to destroy mankind for their wickedness but resolves to spare Noah as a good and just man. Hogg's inexact quotation is probably from memory.

172(c) king's advocate the chief law-officer of the crown in Scotland, who had full discretion over criminal prosecutions and also advised the government on Scottish legal affairs. In 1666 the King's Advocate was Sir John Nisbet (1609?–87), who had held the position since October 1664. After the Pentland Rising, on 15 August 1667 he proposed that fifty persons concerned in it should be tried in their absence, which was agreed, and those persons finally sentenced to death. Nisbet was raised to the bar as Lord Dirleton.

172(d) executed [...] on the 14th of December the date of the executions of those convicted of involvement in the Pentland Rising—see Wodrow, *The History of the Sufferings of the Church of Scotland*, ed. by Robert Burns, 4 vols (Glasgow, 1828), II, 50. For the fate of John Lindsay see note to 171(c) above.

173(a) Privy Council [...] Gilmour Sir John Gilmour (*d.* 1671) was an advocate with connections among the Royalist party. In February 1661 (after the Court of Session was re-established at the Restoration) he was appointed Lord President, and was also a member of the Privy Council. There he refused to vote for the execution of those taken prisoner at the Pentland Rising to whom quarter had been granted, but he agreed with the Court of Session that sentences of forfeiture could be pronounced against accused persons in their absence if they had been duly summoned to appear. He resigned as a judge in December 1670 because of ill health and died the following year.

173(b) Tolbooth jail the Edinburgh city prison, situated on the High Street in Parliament Square in front of St Giles Cathedral. It was demolished in 1817 when the new jail was built on Calton Hill. In Hogg's day it was famous as a setting used by Scott in *The Heart of Midlothian* (1818).

174(d) Captain Robert Gilmour appears to be Hogg's invention.

174(d) Mr. Welch John Welsh (?1624–81), a great-grandson of John Knox. Like Livingston, and along with a third of the Presbyterian clergy of Scotland, he was ejected from his parish (Kirkpatrick-Irongray in Dumfriesshire) for not conforming to episcopacy. Between 1662 and 1679 he preached at field conventicles and in barns and houses throughout Scotland, in Perth and Fife as well as in the south-west. He was involved in the three major Covenanting skirmishes, at Pentland, Drumclog, and Bothwell Bridge, at the last of which he urged moderation. He escaped to London after Bothwell Bridge and was never captured.

175(a) **Gilmerton** this village lies a mile south of Liberton, and is now in the south-eastern suburbs of Edinburgh.

176(c) **the righteous avenger of blood** in the Old Testament (see, for example Joshua 20. 3) the 'avenger of blood' was the next-of-kin of a slain person who had the duty and the right to avenge his killing. The expression is also used by Hogg in *Confessions*, p. 105.

176(c) **the Lord [...] into our hands!** see Judges 16. 24 ('Our god hath delivered into our hands our enemy'), which relates to the capture of Samson by the Philistines.

177(a) **thy blood be upon thine own head** 'Thy blood *be* upon thy head' was part of David's response to the slayer of Saul in II Samuel 1. 16.

177(d) **maxims o' our blessed Saviour** an explicit reference to the forgiveness of enemies advocated in Christ's Sermon on the Mount. See Matthew 5. 44, 'Love your enemies, bless them that curse you, do good to them that hate you, and pray for them which despitefully use you, and persecute you'.

178(c) **like is an ill mark** proverbial: see 'A Collection of Scots Proverbs' in *The Works of Allan Ramsay: Vol. V*, ed. by Alexander M. Kinghorn and Alexander Law (Edinburgh: Scottish Text Society, 1972), pp. 63–129 (p. 97). Hogg also uses this proverb in *Confessions*, p. 47.

[Three Sketches:] The Dorty Wean

180 **[Illustration]** an engraving of Wilkie's painting *The Dorty Bairn* (1818) was sent to Hogg by S. C. Hall on 25 June 1829 with a request to him to write accompanying letterpress—see Introductory and Textual Notes, pp. 325–30. Further information about the painter David Wilkie (1785–1841) is given in the note to 78(a) above, and about the engraver James Mitchell in the note to 79 [Illustration].

181(d) **my shepherd's house in Benger-Hope** Hogg had taken from the Duke of Buccleuch a nine-year lease of the farm of Mount Benger in Yarrow, beginning at Whitsunday 1821.

[Three Sketches:] The History of an Auld Naig

183 **[title]** there is no specific Wilkie painting with this title, but the scene described is characteristic of Wilkie's early work. Gillian Hughes writes: 'While there is no Wilkie picture corresponding exactly to Hogg's sketch here Duncan Macmillan remarks that in Wilkie's painting *Pitlessie Fair* there is a group of figures to the right haggling in similar terms over a cow (not a horse) the potential customer examining its teeth with great scepticism. *Pitlessie Fair* was painted in 1804, and put on exhibition in Edinburgh in 1821 at the Institution for the Promotion of the Fine Arts, where Hogg may have seen it' (see *Studies in Hogg and his World*, 2 (1991), p. 108). Wilkie's *Pitlessie Fair* may now be seen at the National Gallery of Scotland in Edinburgh, and it is reproduced in this volume in the Introductory and Textual Notes.

183(a) **St. Boswell's fair** this fair, held on 18 July at St Boswells near Melrose in Roxburghshire, was one of the largest in Scotland and a major event in the farming calendar.

183(d) **Gerse Merkat o' Edinbrough** regular stock-markets were held in Edinburgh's Grassmarket. The premises of John Taylor, the printer of Hogg's *Scottish Pastorals* (1801) are described in the *Edinburgh and Leith Directory to July 1801* as 'opposite Buchts', or sheepfolds—see *Scottish Pastorals*, ed. by Elaine Petrie (Stirling: Stirling University Press, 1988), p. xii.

183(d) **Newbiggings** Stuart Harris says that 'Newbygging (Old Town) was a name in use in the neighbourhood of the future GRASSMARKET in 1363'— see *The Place Names of Edinburgh: Their Origins and History* (Edinburgh: Gordon Wright, 1996), p. 457.

184(c) **Meadow Park** the Meadows is to the south of the Old Town of Edinburgh, on the site of the former south loch.

184(d) **Hope-park-end** the Meadows was also known as Hope Park from the name of its eighteenth-century developer, Thomas Hope of Rankeillor. Harris comments on the way in which even after housing developments in the area 'a section of Causeyside was known as HOPE PARK END'—see Harris, *The Place Names of Edinburgh*, p. 342.

[Three Sketches:] David Wilkie

185(a) **in Yarrow** for details of Hogg's introduction to Wilkie in Yarrow see the Introductory and Textual Notes on 'Three Sketches', pp. 325–30.

185(a) **scenes out of his native country** Wilkie went abroad in 1826 visiting Italy, Switzerland, and Spain. He was particularly impressed by Spanish painting, which was a major influence on his later style and his modern history paintings like *The Defence of Saragossa* (1828).

185(b) **Mr Wm Murray** William Henry Murray (1790–1852), the younger brother of Henry Siddons's widow, who took over the management of Edinburgh's Theatre Royal on the death of his brother-in-law in 1815. Hogg comments unfavourably on his acting as a young man in *The Spy* (see pp. 134, 591), but he later did well with comic and character parts as well as being a successful theatre manager.

185(b) **a small piece** Wilkie's *A Scene from 'The Gentle Shepherd'* was painted for Sir Robert Liston in 1823. It was engraved, but Hogg may have seen the original painting when it was shown in an exhibition of the Institution for the Promotion of the Fine Arts in Scotland in Edinburgh in 1824. The original painting is not on public display but there are almost identical versions painted by Wilkie in the National Gallery of Scotland and the Aberdeen Art Gallery—see the catalogue by H. A. D. Miles and David Blayney Brown to the exhibition *Sir David Wilkie of Scotland (1785–1841)* (Raleigh, North Carolina: 1987), p. 196.

185(c) **scene from Allan Ramsay's Gentle Shepherd** Wilkie's painting illustrates a scene related by the disappointed lover Roger to his friend Patie, in Allan Ramsay's *The Gentle Shepherd: A Pastoral Comedy*, I. 1. 91–94.

A Cameronian Ballad

186(15) **Earlston** either the Covenanter William Gordon of Earlstoun (1614–1679), or his son, Alexander Gordon of Earlstoun (1650–1726). The death of William Earlstoun at Bothwell Bridge is described by Wodrow in the following terms: 'that excellent person, William Gordon of Earlston, who was coming up to the western forces, was killed by the English dragoons, who behaved but very cowardly at the bridge. [...] And, as if the death of so good a man had not been expiation enough for this crime, his lady had her jointure seized, her house spoiled, and many horses and cattle taken from her' (*History of the Church of Scotland*, 4 vols (Glasgow, 1836–38), III, 108). Alexander, who was at the battle and escaped his pursuers by dressing in women's clothes, is identified by Walter Scott as the 'brave Earlstoun' of the Covenanting ballad 'The Battle of Bothwell Bridge', published in his *Minstrelsy of the Scottish Border* (1802–03), perhaps from the recitation of Hogg's mother (see Elaine Petrie, 'James Hogg: A Study in the Transition from Folk Tradition to Literature' (unpublished doctoral thesis, University of Stirling, 1980), p. 305). Alexander's wife, Janet (d. 1696), shared much of her husband's imprisonment after his eventual capture. Earlstoun Castle is about 2 miles N of St John's Town of Dalry, Kirkcudbrightshire, in SW Scotland. (P.G.)

188(94) best o' this warld's breed i.e. the best of those who are not the people of the Covenant. (P.G.)

188(95) your liefu lane all by yourself; solitary. (P.G.)

189(119) the water o' Clyde i.e. from the River Clyde, over which the Royalist forces forced their passage to secure victory at Bothwell Bridge. (P.G.)

A Hymn to the Redeemer

191(7) the star of the east one of several allusions in this poem to the Nativity story—see Matthew 2. 2.

191(12) Prince of peace one of the titles of the Messiah in Isaiah 9. 6.

191(15) the hungry with bread the feeding of the five thousand is one of the miracles of Christ, related in Matthew 14. 15–21.

191(16) raised from the grave the mouldering dead Lazarus had been in his grave for four days when revivified by Jesus—see John 11. 11–44.

191(17) walked on the waves another of the miracles of Christ, related in Matthew 14. 25–31.

191(18) cried to thy Father an allusion to Christ's words during his agony in Gethsemane: 'Abba, Father, all things are possible unto thee; take away this cup from me: nevertheless not what I will, but what thou wilt' (Mark 14. 36).

191(21) thy last breath an allusion to Christ's saying on the cross, 'Father, forgive them; for they know not what they do' (Luke 23. 34).

191(22) by man that man might live Christ's atonement in his death is seen by Paul as cancelling out the doom of death incurred by Adam's transgression—see especially 1 Corinthians 15. 21 ('For since by man came death, by man came also the resurrection of the dead').

191(23) death and the grave [...] victory this continues the reference to the Pauline discussion of death in the previous line—see 1 Corinthians 15. 55 ('O death, where is thy sting? O grave, where is thy victory?').

191(30) chariot of heaven in Psalm 104. 3 God 'maketh the clouds his chariot'.

191(31) the gates of light an allusion to the heavenly city of Revelation 21. 25: 'And the gates of it shall not be shut at all by day: for there shall be no night there'.

192(37) **on the right hand of our God** an image deriving from the account of Christ's ascension in Mark 16. 19: 'So then after the Lord had spoken unto them, he was received up into heaven, and sat on the right hand of God'.

192(41) **spirits in floods of light are swimming** light in the Bible is holy and associated with God—see for example John 8. 12 ('I am the light of the world'), and 1 John 1. 5 ('God is light').

192(43) **waters of life** see Revelation 7. 17: 'For the Lamb [...] shall lead them unto living fountains of waters: and God shall wipe away all tears from their eyes'.

192(44) **crowns of glory** an image of the faithful Christian's reward: see for example Paul's distinction between a corruptible and an incorruptible crown in 1 Corinthians 9. 25. The 'crown of life' is mentioned in Revelation 2. 10.

192(52) **our help, our stay, our shield** in Psalm 115. 11 those who fear God will find him 'their help and their shield'.

192(59) **Bow down thy heavens** perhaps an echo of David's 'Bow down thine ear, O Lord' (Psalm 86. 1).

192(60) **come in the cloud, in the flame, or the thunder** images found in the depiction of Christ's second coming and final victory in the book of Revelation—see for example Revelation 1. 7, 14 and 10. 4.

Morning Hymn

192(4) **Heal the heart long broke** compare Luke 4. 18, where Jesus announces God 'hath sent me to heal the broken-hearted'.

193(17) **slumber'st not nor sleepest** an allusion to Psalm 121. 4 ('he that keepeth Israel shall neither slumber nor sleep').

The Judgment of Idumea

193 **[title]** Idumea (deriving from the Hebrew 'Edom', meaning red) is a region of southern Palestine, bordering Judaea. It was the name given to Esau who sold his birthright to his brother Jacob for a mess of pottage—see Genesis 25. 30–34. According to the transcription of the poem probably made by Hogg's brother William or a member of his family (see Introductory and Textual Notes, pp. 333–34) the inspiration for the poem was a recent and highly popular theological work by Alexander Keith (1791–1880), *Evidence of the Truth of the Christian Religion Derived from the Literal Fulfilment of Prophecy: Particularly as Illustrated by the History of the Jews and by the Discoveries of Recent Travellers* (1828), which attempted to demonstrate how Old Testament prophecy had been fulfilled using the evidence of travellers in the near East and recent archeological discoveries. In his Introduction to the work Keith argues that 'The fulfilment of prophecy forms part of the evidence of Christianity'—see the third edition (Edinburgh: Waugh & Innes, 1828), p. 13. Chapter V, 'Prophecies Concerning the Land of Judea and Circumjacent Countries', contains a section on Idumea on pp. 172–220, comparing accounts of present-day travellers and natives of the district with Isaiah 34. 5, 10–17 and other scriptural texts.

193 **Versified** this poem is effectively Isaiah 34 turned into verse. Compare, for instance, the first four lines with Isaiah 34. 1: 'Come near, ye nations, to hear; and hearken, ye people: let the earth hear, and all that is therein; the world, and all things that come forth of it'.

193(2) list to the words Isaiah and other prophets announced God's sentence of complete destruction upon the Edomites, traditional enemies of Israel, for their invasion of Judah.

193(5) Bozrah the ancient capital of Edom.

194(31–32) Avenger | of Israel God is frequently praised in the Old Testament for his vindication of oppressed Israel shown in the punishment of the oppressor—see, for example, Judges 5. 2 ('Praise ye the LORD for the avenging of Israel').

194(32) the land of the stranger the Gentiles, distinguished as alien from Israel as God's chosen people.

194(47) lamia a female demon who devours children, and not found in Isaiah 34. Keats's 1820 poem of that name recounts how a bride was recognised as a serpent or lamia, and vanished in an instant.

195(55) toad and the adder Keith stresses that the ruins of the city of Petra in Idumea are 'abounding with a variety of lizards and vipers'—see *Evidence of the Truth of the Christian Religion*, 3rd ed., p. 212.

195(60) A beacon of terror for ever and ever according to Keith 'if the history itself correspond with the prediction, then the evidence which the prophecies import, is a sign and a wonder to every age'—see *Evidence of the Truth of the Christian Religion*, 3rd ed., p. 9.

Letter to the Ettrick Shepherd

195(c) the hand of the Lord a biblical phrase for affliction, as used for example in Ezekiel 6. 14 ('So will I stretch out my hand upon them, and make the land desolate').

196(a) for Mr. Blackwood Hogg's Ettrick Shepherd persona was prominently featured in the masculine world of *Blackwood's Edinburgh Magazine* during the 1820s.

196(a) your friend Sir C. Sharpe's advice Sir Cuthbert Sharp (1781–1849) was born at Sunderland, and settled at Hartlepool where he studied local antiquities and published his *History of Hartlepool* in 1816. His name is presumably introduced here to establish a generalised north-east of England setting for the tale.

197(b) Beckwith Common not identified as a location.

198(b) *stone-chatter* the stonechat is a small bird which inhabits heaths and commons in Britain and Europe and gets its name from its alarm call, which is supposed to sound like two pebbles striking together.

198(d) a deed of such enormity part of the moral instruction imparted by juvenile annuals was kindness to animals. The conclusion to Miss Dagley's story 'The Pet Donkey' in the *Juvenile Forget Me Not* for 1834 (pp. 163–84), for example, is that 'The secret is this—good usage brings forth good dispositions; and many a poor animal that is characterised as obstinate or vicious, would never have become so but from *ill treatment*' (p. 184).

199(c) a sparrow cannot fall to the ground an allusion to Matthew 10. 29: 'Are not two sparrows sold for a farthing? and one of them shall not fall on the ground without your Father'.

201(a) the service for a bed of sickness the Book of Common Prayer contains 'The Order for the Visitation of the Sick', but this is a service for a priest to conduct and not a lay person. However, it includes several printed prayers, including 'A Prayer for a sick person, when there appeareth small hope of recovery' and as this is a very touching prayer it may be what Hogg envisages Alice reading.

201(c) **the island of Tobago** Tobago, in the West Indies, was a sugar colony in the eighteenth century. After changing hands several times between Britain and France, it was ceded to Britain for the last time in 1814.

202(d) **the banks were exterminated** agricultural prices and rents had risen rapidly during the French Revolutionary and Napoleonic Wars, but the peace of 1815 initiated a period of severe agricultural depression. In the 1820s rash speculation in joint-stock companies created an unstable financial climate, leading eventually to the collapse of the stock market at the end of 1825 when Hogg's friend and patron Sir Walter Scott was ruined.

203(c) **some of the juvenile periodicals** this tale was originally composed by Hogg for Anna Maria Hall's *Juvenile Forget Me Not* rather than the *Amulet*, edited by her husband, Samuel Carter Hall—see the Introductory and Textual Notes.

203(c) **ALICE BRAND** Hogg had previously used this name as that of a female letter-writer in No. 7 of *The Spy* (pp. 64–66).

To Miss M. A. C——e

203(4) **please myself alone** an earlier version of these lines had been published by Hogg as the conclusion to Book First of his epic poem *Queen Hynde* (see Introductory and Textual Notes, pp. 335–36), lines which Suzanne Gilbert and Douglas Mack have interpreted as 'a declaration of independence from the limitations imposed by fashionable Edinburgh's perception of the Ettrick Shepherd's proper role'—see *Queen Hynde*, p. xiii. Mr and Mrs Hall edited two of the most stringently-censored annuals in the *Amulet* and the *Juvenile Forget Me Not*, making this an apt and ironic item for Hogg to send to them. Several other notes to this poem are also indebted to those of Gilbert and Mack to the S/SC edition of *Queen Hynde*.

204(21) **Wing the thin air or starry sheen** an allusion to Hogg's poem *The Pilgrims of the Sun* (1815), in which Mary Lee is escorted on a tour of the cosmos by her spiritual guide Cela.

204(22) **the child upon the green** since the line also occurs in *Queen Hynde* (1825) it cannot be a reference to Hogg's works for juvenile annuals such as the *Juvenile Forget Me Not*, edited by the wife of S. C. Hall, editor of the *Amulet*. Hogg had, however, written other accounts of childhood experience, notably 'The History of Duncan Campbell' which was first published in *The Spy* and was later popular as a chapbook.

204(23) **the sea-maid's coral dome** perhaps an allusion to Hogg's ballad 'The Goode Manne of Allowa', in which a sea-maid takes an auld man on a horse ride into the Firth of Forth and enriches him with the treasure from a sunken wreck (*Queer Book*, pp. 54–68).

204(24) **fairy's visionary home** the most famous of Hogg's poems about fairyland is the 'Kilmeny' of *The Queen's Wake* (1813).

204(25) **Sail on the whirlwind or the storm** perhaps an allusion to *Queen Hynde* itself, where in Book Third Columba and his monks, together with the disguised Prince Eiden, encounter fierce storms on their voyage around the west coast of Scotland.

204(26) **trifle with the maiden's form** Hogg's reputation stood high as a composer of love-lyrics.

204(27) raise up spirits of the hill probably a general allusion to Hogg's proficiency in the supernatural, although more specifically *The Royal Jubilee*, written for the visit of George IV to Scotland in August 1822, is set on Arthur's Seat, an extinct volcano overlooking Edinburgh's Holyrood Palace, and consists of songs and disputes by various spirits representing different aspects of Scotland.

204(30) Nature's [...] child an allusion to Hogg's status as peasant poet, implying closeness to the sources of inspiration as well as lack of cultivation. His pen-name of the Ettrick Shepherd and his seal displaying a harp with the motto 'Naturae Donum' consciously echoed Burns's persona of the Heaven-taught Ploughman.

205(51) nightingale the bird of the night as opposed to the lark of day (see *Romeo and Juliet*, III. 5. 1–2), and also the Philomela ('lover of song'), from the girl in Greek myth who was turned by the gods into a nightingale. For Hogg's fellow-feeling for the lark as an inhabitant of the wilderness see the note to 39(6) above.

The Gem
A Highland Eclogue

209(2) Mary of Moy Moy is about 8 miles SE of Inverness, and Moy Hall was the seat of Mackintosh, Chief of the Clan Chattan. It was here that an attempt was made by government forces to capture Prince Charles Edward, a few weeks before the battle of Culloden in 1746; this was foiled by the suspicions of Lady Anne Mackintosh and the intervention of a handful of Jacobites led by the Moy blacksmith. In *The Three Perils of Woman* (1823), Lady Mackintosh features as Lady Balmillo and the blacksmith becomes Peter Gow, one of Hogg's central characters. For Hogg's use of Mary as a name for his young heroines, see Douglas S. Mack, 'Hogg and the Blessed Virgin Mary', *Studies in Hogg and his World*, 3 (1992), 68–75. (P.G.)

209(26) Allan of Borlan-dale Borlan-dale has not been identified, though there is a similarity to Borrodale, in the Western Highlands, where Charles Edward first landed on the mainland of Scotland, leaving again from the same place in 1746. The name of Allan of Borlan-dale also echoes that of the young Highlander, Diarmid M'Ion of Boroland, the main male romantic figure in the first two volumes of *The Three Perils of Woman*. (P.G.)

211(76) Sky the Island of Skye, in the Inner Hebrides. (P.G.)

212(115) schedule-deed gerent a *deed* in Scots law refers to a formal written instrument setting out the terms and conditions of an agreement, while in Hogg's day *schedule* normally referred to a deed recounting an action of legal significance; *gerent* is not a term of legal significance, and one suspects that Hogg is largely improvising his legal terminology. (P.G.)

213(154) the dark and the bright indicative of the lights and shadows of Scottish life, which Hogg had made his theme in *The Three Perils of Woman*. (P.G.)

The Remembrance
The Two Valleys

218(a) Luran in Gaelic *Luran* is a male rather than a female word, meaning 'pretty youth or boy; beloved, smart, gallant'. The place is imaginary.

218(c) Dual in Gaelic *Dual* signifies 'hereditary disposition; birthright; bias of character', which clearly could be interpreted as good or bad. The place is imaginary.

218(d) respect and deference to every sort of religion compare Hogg's poem 'To the Right Honourable Lady Anne Scott of Buccleuch': 'As flowers which vary in their dyes, | We all shall bloom in Paradise'—see *The Brownie of Bodsbeck and Other Tales*, 2 vols (Edinburgh: Blackwood; London: Murray, 1818), I, i–xiii (p. v). Lady Anne was an Episcopalian, while Hogg was a Presbyterian

218(d) a different religion in an earlier, incomplete manuscript version of this tale in NLS, MS 1709, fols 65–66, Hogg explicitly refers to the children of Dual as 'papists' who followed 'the modes of Catholic worship', while the children of Luran adhere to 'the protestant faith as proffessed [*sic*] by the Church of England'. For a full discussion of the different versions of the tale and a text of the manuscript one, see Janette Currie, 'Two Early Versions of Tales from Literary Annuals', *Studies in Hogg and his World*, 11 (2000), 87–121.

219(b) evil genii [...] power over them the idea that God's protection can be withdrawn because of sin is also expressed by an elderly shepherd in Hogg's tale 'Mr Adamson of Laverhope': 'It appears to me that sin' he roupit out yon poor but honest family yesterday, the Lord has ta'en his guiding arm from about him'—see *The Shepherd's Calendar*, pp. 38–56 (p. 45).

219(d) a beautiful little lady, dressed in green satin traditionally, green is the colour worn by fairies.

220(a) primitive language of the country Gaelic, a surviving rather than dominant language of Scotland by Hogg's day. It had been brought to the west coast of Scotland from Ireland between the third and fifth centuries.

220(a) What is in a name? a phrase famously employed in *Romeo and Juliet*, II. 1. 85, which is also a story about a divided community.

220(b) perfume of Paradise here, as in Hogg's celebrated poem 'Kilmeny' from *The Queen's Wake* (1813), there seems to be an implied link between Heaven and the fairy world: however, the fairies of the folk tradition also had a capacity for mischief-making.

221(a) the looks of innocence and purity more specifically, virginity is supposed to tame wild beasts. The unicorn was said to lie down at a virgin's feet, but Hogg may be thinking in this context of Edmund Spenser's Una, a virgin who signifies the true religion. In Book I of *The Fairie Queen* she meets and is protected by a lion.

221(d) a peeled wand a young branch stripped of its bark and used as an instrument of correction.

222(d) the injunctions of his Saviour as given in Luke 6. 27–35, a series beginning with 'Love your enemies', something the Glen-Luran people do by their gifts to the Glen-Dual boys at the end of the story.

223(a) St. Cyprian's day 16 September in the Roman Calendar, although wrongly given as 26 September in the Book of Common Prayer—see David Hugh Farmer, *The Oxford Dictionary of Saints* (Oxford: Clarendon Press, 1978; repr. 1980), p. 98.

223(d) a fairy ring circles of dark green grass often found in meadows: actually caused by nitrogen produced by fungi, they were popularly supposed to have marked the site of fairy dances.

224(b) braying resembled [...] crying of a herd of lubberly boys when the Borderers in Hogg's *The Three Perils of Man* are transformed into cattle, glimpses of their true human nature show through their metamorphosis in the same way—see *The Three Perils of Man*, ed. by Douglas Gifford (Edinburgh: Scottish Academic Press, 1972), pp. 346, 348.

224(d) the village pastor the use of 'pastor' (and subsequently 'minister') instead of 'priest' indicates the Protestantism of Glen-Luran.

225(a) the book of all books, the book of life the Bible, especially the New Testament. The phrase 'book of life' is used particularly in Revelation to signify the record of those who are saved—see, for example, Revelation 3. 5.

225(b) around the truly virtuous [...] the wicked can never remove echoes ideas expressed in Psalm 125.

The Covenanter's Scaffold Song

225 [title] both ultra and moderate Covenanters' last testimonies and scaffold speeches were written, or transcribed and recorded by hearers, and some were later published in both Church of Scotland and Cameronian histories such as the Rev. Robert Wodrow's *The History of the Sufferings of the Church of Scotland from the Restauration to the Revolution*, 2 vols (Edinburgh: James Watson, 1721–22) and *A Cloud of Witnesses for the Prerogative of Jesus Christ; or, The Last Speeches and Testimonies of Those Who Have Suffered for the Truth in Scotland since 1680* (1714). The first Covenanting scaffold speeches were published in *Naphtali; or, The Wrestlings of the Church of Scotland for the Kingdom of Jesus Christ, from the Reformation of Religion unto the Year 1667*, a Covenanting apologia written by John Stewart and John Stirling after the battle of Pentland in 1666. The very moving and sincere speech of Hugh McKail, a young probationer, was used thereafter as the exemplum for the majority of Covenanting testimonies. In this song Hogg draws much of the detail from the description of McKail's scaffold speech and from his closing exhortation:

> At the place of execution, Mr. M'Kail having addressed to the people a speech and testimony, which he had previously written and subscribed, sung part of the 31st Psalm, after which he prayed with great power and fervency. "[...] And now I leave off to speak any more to creatures, and begin my intercourse with God, which shall never be broken off. Farewell father and mother, friends and relations—farewell the world and all delights—farewell meat and drink—farewell sun, moon, and stars—welcome God and Father—welcome sweet Jesus Christ, the Mediator of the new covenant,—welcome blessed spirit of grace, and God of all consolation—welcome glory—welcome eternal life, and welcome death." (Robert Wodrow, *The History of the Sufferings of the Church of Scotland, from the Restoration to the Revolution*, 4 vols (Glasgow: Blackie & Son, 1836–39), II, 58–59).

In *The Private Memoirs and Confessions of a Justified Sinner* (1824) Robert Wringhim's last words represent a corrupted form of these Covenanting scaffold speeches and last testimonies: see *Confessions*, pp. 165, 248.

225(4) crown of glory named in I Peter 5. 4 as one of the rewards of the faithful Christian: 'And when the chief Shepherd shall appear, ye shall receive a crown of glory that fadeth not away'.

226(19) To the Lamb our song shall be a reference to the heavenly worship of Jesus, the Lamb of God, as described in Revelation 5.

The May Flower
Song

229(4) my young May in a footnote to the third stanza of Canto II of his poem *Mador of the Moor* Hogg writes: 'A May, in old Scottish ballads and romances, denotes a young lady, or a maiden somewhat above the lower class': see *Mador of the Moor*, ed. by James E. Barcus (S/SC, 2005), p. 34.

Juvenile Annuals
Ackermann's Juvenile Forget Me Not
Dramas of Infancy. No. 1. What is Sin?

234(b) What is Sin? [...] transgression of the law of God this is question and reply number 14, as contained in *The Shorter Catechism* of the Church of Scotland (see note on 16(c)). This question and reply are derived from I John 3. 4: 'Whosoever committeth sin transgresseth also the law: for sin is the transgression of the law'.

234(d) God chooses the greater part of his elect from among the poor and the indigent echoing James 2. 5: 'Hath not God chosen the poor of this world rich in faith, and heirs of the kingdom which he hath promised to them that love him?'.

235(b) my good book the Bible, or perhaps *The Shorter Catechism*.

235(b) born to sin, and can do nothing of ourselves but sin echoing I John 1. 8: 'If we say that we have no sin, we deceive ourselves, and the truth is not in us'.

235(b) like sin itself matching the proverbial expession 'as ugly as sin' (*ODEP*, p. 853).

235(c) Do you never break the Sabbath? an action contradicting the fourth commandment in Exodus 20. 8–10.

235(d) do you not sometimes tell lies reply number 77 of *The Shorter Catechism* says: 'The ninth Commandment requireth the maintaining and promoting of truth between man and man, and of our own, and of our neighbours good names, especially in witness-bearing'.

Dramas of Infancy. No. 2. What is Death?

236 [title] question 37 of *The Shorter Catechism* asks 'What benefits do believers receive from Christ, at death?', the corresponding answer being: 'The souls of believers are at their death made perfect in holiness, and do immediately passe into glory, and their bodies being still united to Christ, do rest in their graves, till the resurrection'.

236(d) I have seen his picture for an example of the kind of print Hogg alludes to here see 'The Messenger of Mortality; or a dialogue between DEATH and the LADY', reproduced in Sheila O'Connell, *The Popular Print in England 1550–1850* (London: British Museum, 1999), p. 199.

237(c) Cain the first shedder of human blood Cain, the son of Adam, slew his brother Abel, thus committing the first murder—see Genesis 4. 8.

237(d) the soveriegn of the Grave [...] life see Revelation 6. 8: 'behold a pale horse: and his name that sat on him was Death, and Hell followed with him. And power was given unto them over the fourth part of the earth, to kill with sword, and with hunger, and with death, and with the beasts of the earth'.

237(d) Yet no man needs to be afraid of Death [...] him compare Psalm 68. 20: '*He that is* our God *is* the God of salvation; and unto GOD the Lord *belong* the issues from death'.

237(d)–238(a) God made man at first pure [...] all have sinned compare Romans 5. 12: 'Wherefore, as by one man sin entered into the world, and death by sin; and so death passed upon all men, for that all have sinned'.

238(a) These our bodies [...] and the grave compare I Peter 1. 24: 'For all flesh *is* as grass, and all the glory of man as the flower of grass. The grass withereth, and the flower thereof falleth away'.

238(a–b) But Jesus Christ [...] Eternity compare I Corinthians 15. 55–57: 'O death, where *is* thy sting? O grave, where *is* thy victory? The sting of death *is* sin; and the strength of sin *is* the law. But thanks *be* to God, which giveth us the victory through our Lord Jesus Christ'.

The Poachers

241(a) little Benjy 'Little Benjie' (Benjamin Coultherd) features in Scott's *Redgauntlet* (1824), where he is described as having been 'convicted of snaring partridges' and other acts of poaching—see *Redgauntlet*, ed. by G. A. M. Wood and David Hewitt, EEWN 17 (Edinburgh: Edinburgh University Press, 1997), p. 50.

241(a) Sprinkell Springkell is a mansion in Kirkconnel, Dumfriesshire. In his account of the parish of Kirkpatrick-Fleming (dated February 1834) the Rev. Thomas Landells describes the mansion as follows: 'In the north-west part of the parish stands the mansion-house of Springkell, which was erected in 1734, in the Grecian style of architecture, about 200 or 300 yards to the eastward of the place where the old family residence and village of Kirkconnel stood. The present mansion-house, the seat of Sir Patrick Maxwell, Bart. was greatly enlarged about sixteen years ago, by the addition of a handsome wing to the east, and a corresponding one to the west end. The building is remarkably elegant, and the surrounding grounds are tastefully laid out'—see *The New Statistical Account of Scotland*, 15 vols (Edinburgh: Blackwood, 1845), IV, 274–88 (p. 280).

241(a) gird a cog encircle a barrel or tub with hoops.

241(a) his master, the baronet Sir John Shaw Heron Maxwell, 4th Baronet of Springkell (1772–1830) succeeded his father, Sir William Maxwell, Bart. on his death in March 1804. He was M.P. for the burghs of Dumfries and Sanquhar in 1806, when Hogg was living in Dumfriesshire, entered the army, and became a Lieutenant-General. On his death he was succeeded by his son, Sir Patrick Maxwell, 5th Baronet—see William Fraser, *Memoirs of the Maxwells of Pollok*, 3 vols (Edinburgh: privately printed, 1863–75), I, 448–49.

241(b) It is the leading principle [...] no mercy Hogg did not have a high regard for gamekeepers. In his essay 'On the Changes in the Habits, Amusements, and Condition of the Scottish Peasantry' he described them as 'the most vexatious, insolent, and insignificant persons in the whole world'—see *Quarterly Journal of Agriculture*, 3 (1831–32), 256–63 (p. 261). In this essay Hogg compares the situation in his youth where the odd countryman 'shot a hare by moonlight' with the contemporary situation, marked by a recent rise in poaching gangs and the 'deficient' game laws that were hurriedly brought out to curb them.

241(b) sold [...] by public auction Hogg himself had recently suffered the indignity of a roup or warrant sale, at the expiry of his nine-year lease of Mount Benger farm in Yarrow. Writing to Blackwood on 26 May 1830 (NLS, MS 4036, fols 102–03) Hogg announced: 'The confusion and the sale are over and here I am crept into my little cot again several hundreds of pounds minus nothing. The sale was accounted a good one and proportioned with the times was certainly so most articles giving their value and some above it. [...] I have committed the winding up of my affairs to a committee of friends (farmers) who have undertaken to make a private settlement and after all with young Buccleuch's lenience there will be but little loss'.

241(d) Benoni a name meaning 'son of my sorrow'. The biblical Benjamin, to whom it relates, was the son of Jacob and Rachel (who died in giving birth to him)—see Genesis 35. 18.

242(c) transmitted to London R. B. Thornhill, in *The Shooting Directory* of 1804, stated that 'little reliance can be placed on the expectation of a reduction in the number of poachers, sanctioned and supported as they are by thousands in the metropolis'—see Harry Hopkins, *The Long Affray: The Poaching Wars in Britain 1716–1914* (London: Secker & Warburg, 1985), p. 82. George Crabbe also commented on the practice in his *Tales of the Hall* of 1820: 'The well-known shops received a large supply | That those who could not kill at least might buy'—see Hopkins, p. 87.

242(c) black cocks according to Hogg's essay in the *Quarterly Journal of Agriculture* (see note to 241(b)) it was the introduction of black-cocks into the Scottish Borders that increased the incidence of poaching in the region.

242(d) plantation in his account of Kirkpatrick-Fleming parish Mr Alexander Monilaws stated: 'There are in the neighbourhood of Springkell, woods and plantations of considerable extent, all in a very thriving condition, which have been mostly planted since the year 1762, by the present proprietor'—see *The Statistical Account of Scotland 1791–1799*, ed. by Sir John Sinclair, re-ed. by Donald Withrington and Ian R. Grant, 20 vols (Wakefield: EP Publishing, 1973–83), IV (1978), 312–41 (pp. 334–35).

243(c) constables at the beginning of the nineteenth century there was no organised police force in either Scotland or England. Constables worked part-time as required and usually followed a trade or occupation. They were 'officer[s] appointed by the Justices of the Peace in the country, and by the magistrates in burghs'. The Justices of the Peace 'at their quarter sessions' appointed 'two constables at least for every parish, and more, according to their discretion'. On taking up their appointment constables swore an oath to keep the 'King's Peace'. They were directed to conduct themselves 'with lenity, temper, and moderation, though, at the same time, with firmness and courage'. Constables reacted to requests for services; usually they were called upon by the written or verbal authority of the

Justices of the Peace, but they could also act on behalf of 'private persons' on cases involving insolvency and poinding—see George Tait, *A Summary of the Powers and Duties of a Constable in Scotland in Public and Private Cases and of these of a Private Person in Criminal Cases*, 3rd edn (Edinburgh: Anderson; London: Longman, 1815), and George Tait, *A Summary of the Powers and Duties of a Justice of the Peace in Scotland* (Edinburgh: Anderson; London: Longman, 1815). In 1829 Robert Peel's Metropolitan Police Bill passed both Houses of Parliament and led to the re-organisation and re-structuring of the London police into a professional force which, in turn, led to a nation-wide police force. Scotland followed a different course in organising its police force, but at the time when 'The Poachers' was written the reform of policing and the nature of authority were topical issues—see David Philips and Robert D. Storch, *Policing Provincial England 1829–1856: The Politics of Reform* (London: Leicester University Press, 1999).

244(a) game bird the Night Poaching Act of 1828 defined game as including hares, pheasants, partridges, grouse, heath or grouse moor game, black game and bustards—see Gerald H. Gordon, *The Criminal Law of Scotland*, 2nd edn (Edinburgh: W. Green & Son, 1978), p. 1101.

244(a) Johnnie Cope Sir John Cope was the leader of the Hanoverian forces that were routed by the Jacobites at Prestonpans in 1745. He is the subject of a satirical Jacobite song entitled 'Johny Cope are ye wauking yet', included by Hogg in his *Jacobite Relics: Second Series* (S/SC, 2003), pp. 111–15. Hogg's accounts of the Duke of Buccleuch's rumbustious rendering of this song at a 'great festival' that took place at Bowhill are given in *Anecdotes*, pp. 5–6, 45.

246(d) Sir John's Sir John Shaw Heron Maxwell, 4th Baronet of Springkell— see note to 241(a).

246(d) Annandale the middle one of three divisions of Dumfriesshire.

246(d) Cannobie a Border village and parish of Eskdale, in south-east Dumfriesshire.

248(c) Kirtonholm the reference may be to the Teviotdale parish of Kirkton (sometimes called Kirton), which is situated near Hawick. A *holm* is a stretch of low-lying level ground on the banks of a river or stream. The poet John Leyden (1775–1811) spent his childhood at Kirton, and began his education at the parish school there.

248(d) Mr. Beattie John Beattie was the name of the Ettrick parish schoolmaster, whose daughter Mary Hogg's brother William had married on 28 December 1798 (Yarrow OPR). The two John Beatties, father and son, had been schoolmasters in Ettrick for over a hundred years.

248(d)–249(a) school [...] college the normal course of education in Scotland for ministers was a general arts course at one of the four universities, followed by theological training.

249(b) 12th of August the first day of grouse-shooting after the close season—see note to 29(30).

249(c) Shepherd of Ettrick Hogg's letter of 11 August 1829, replying to John Wilson's invitation to pay him a visit at Elleray in the Lake District, reveals the extent of Hogg's enthusiasm for the shooting season: 'I never thought you had been so unconscionable as to desire a sportsman on the 11th or even the 13th of August to leave Ettrick Forest for the bare scraggy hills of Westmoreland! Ettrick Forest where the Black cocks and white

cocks brown cocks and gray cocks, ducks, plovers peaseweeps and whilly-
whaups are as thick as the flocks that cover her mountains and come to the
hills of Westmoreland that can nourish nothing better than a castrel or
stone-chat' (NLS, MS 3278, fols 66–67)

249(c) **Minister of Shootinglees** a place-name on the Buccleuch estate in
Yarrow parish, presumably known to Hogg and adopted into this tale
because of its appropriate sound as the parish of a shooting minister—see
the section on 'Catslack, Blackgrain, Shootinglees, and Glengaber' in T.
Craig-Brown, *The History of Selkirkshire*, 2 vols (Edinburgh: David Douglas,
1886), I, 390.

Play Up my Love

250(17) **Music has power to still the waves** an allusion perhaps to the
opening lines of Congreve's tragedy *The Mourning Bride* (1697): 'Music hath
charms to soothe a savage breast. | To soften rocks, or bend a knotted oak'.

251 **[Illustration]** an engraving of 'The Shepherd Boy's Song' had been sent
to Hogg by Shoberl, with a request for verses to accompany it—see Introductory and Textual Notes, p. 346. The painter Henry Warren (1794–
1879) in his early youth was drawn to a career as a musician and also
began to train as a sculptor before training as a painter at the Royal Academy in 1818. He worked primarily in water-colour, and he was president
of the New Society of Painters in Water-Colours from 1839 to 1879. He
designed illustrations to a number of literary works, including Lockhart's
Spanish Ballads, Wordsworth's *Pastoral Poems*, and Moore's *Paradise and the
Peri*—see *Bryan's Dictionary of Painters and Engravers*, rev. edn, ed. by George C.
Williamson, 5 vols (London, 1903–05), V, 336. Nothing is known about
the engraver, whose name is given as 'H. Rolle'.

Gift-Books

The Casket

The Admonition

255(38) **young Jamie o' the Glen** there is perhaps a suggestion here that in
this poem Hogg is re-imagining his own youthful love adventures from
another perspective. Looking back to that period of his life in his 'Memoir',
he writes: 'For several years my compositions consisted wholly of songs
and ballads made up for the lasses to sing in chorus; and a proud man I
was when I first heard the rosy nymphs chaunting my uncouth strains, and
jeering me by the still dear appellation of "Jamie the poeter"' (p. 17).

A Father's New Year's Gift

Dedicatory Letter

259(b) **MY DEAREST CHILDREN** Hogg and his wife, Margaret Phillips,
had four children: James Robert Hogg (born 18 March 1821); Janet Phillips
Hogg (born 23 April 1823); Margaret Laidlaw Hogg (born 18 January
1825); Harriet Sidney Hogg (born 18 December 1827); and Mary Gray
Hogg (born 21 August 1831)—see Yarrow OPR.

259(b) **hear you recite them** Peter Garside notes Hogg's religious training of his children as including memorisation of *The Shorter Catechism* (see *Confessions*, p. xvi, and note on 16(c), above). Hymns and prayers would presumably also be committed to heart.

259(b) on my return to his home at Altrive in Yarrow from London, where Hogg was staying at the time *A Father's New Year's Gift* was published.

Prayer for the Sabbath Morning

260 [title] prayer is defined by *The Shorter Catechism* as 'an offering up of our desires unto God, for things agreeable to his will, in the Name of Christ, with confession of our sins, and thankful acknowledgment of his mercies'. Each of the four prayers in *A Father's New Year's Gift* is in accordance with this definition.

260(a) offending see James 3. 2: 'For in many things we offend all'.

260(a) the footstool of thy grace compare Psalm 99. 5: 'Exalt ye the LORD our God, and worship at his footstool'.

260(a) bountiful benefactor compare Psalm 13. 6: 'I will sing unto the LORD, because he hath dealt bountifully with me'.

260(b) newness of life Paul argues in Romans 6. 4 that as Christ was raised from the dead, so the redeemed Christian 'should walk in newness of life'.

260(b) their God and their guide perhaps a common formula in prayers. In Hogg's story of 'The History of Duncan Campbell' Duncan as a child, trying to imitate his master's evening prayers, can only remember one sentence, 'O Lord, be thou our God, our guide, and our guard unto death, and through death'–see *The Spy*, pp. 505–06.

260(c) Our Father [...] *Amen The Shorter Catechism* teaches, 'The whole word of God is of use to direct us in prayer; but the speciall rule of direction is, that form of Prayer which Christ taught his Disciples, commonly called the *Lords Prayer*'. See also Matthew 6. 9–13.

Prayer for the Sabbath Evening

260(d) light that is inaccessible [...] eye can penetrate an allusion to God taken from the description of the divine nature of Jesus in I Timothy 6. 15–16 ('the King of kings, and Lord of lords; Who only hath immortality, dwelling in the light which no man can approach unto; whom no man hath seen, nor can see').

260(d) my guilty and polluted self this phrase reflects Scottish Calvinism's strong sense of the corruption of Fallen human nature.

260(d)–261(a) Take me under the shadow of the wings see Psalms 17. 8 and 63. 7, in which David rejoices under 'the shadow of thy wings'.

261(a) imputed righteousness from James 2. 23: 'Abraham believed God, and it was imputed unto him for righteousness'.

261(a) my soul shall magnify the Lord [...] God my Saviour echoes the opening words of the Magnificat, Mary's song of thanksgiving in Luke 1. 46–55.

261(a) blotted out of the book of thy remembrance the image of a written record of God-fearing people is a feature of both Old and New Testaments. The prophet Malachi describes 'a book of remembrance' written before God to note those 'that feared the LORD, and that thought upon his name'–see Malachi 3. 16. Similarly, in Psalm 69. 28 David asks that his enemies' names be 'blotted out of the book of the living, and not be written with the righteous', while Revelation 22. 19 gives a warning to those who disregard the prophecy ('God shall take away his part out of the book of life').

261(a) dark and silent watches of the night echoes the Scottish Metrical Psalms: 'And when on thee I meditate | in watches of the night' (63. 6).

261(a) my mouth may be filled with thy praises compare Psalm 34. 1: 'I will bless the LORD at all times: his praise *shall* continually *be in* my mouth'.

261(a) ties of the covenant of grace a major theme of Hebrews 8 and 9 is the replacement of the old covenant between God and Moses (known as 'the Covenant of Works') by a new one ('the Covenant of Grace') based on Christ's atonement.

261(b) mercies [...] both special and common benefits from God specific to oneself (special mercies), and benefits from God to humanity in general (mercies in common).

261(b) thy unspeakable gift 'Thanks *be* unto God for his unspeakable gift' (II Corinthians 9. 15).

Hymn for Sabbath Morning

261 [title] Sunday, the Christian Sabbath, is the first day of the week, and the day of Christ's resurrection.

261(5–8) this world [...] day form'd and the night points to the creation story in Genesis 1: 'And God called the light Day, and the darkness he called Night. And the evening and the morning were the first day' (Genesis 1. 5).

261(11–12) A second time to glorious light | It rose, by grace renew'd the reference is to Christ's resurrection. We read in Matthew 28. 1–3: 'as it began to dawn toward the first *day* of the week, came Mary Magdalene and the other Mary to see the sepulchre. And, behold, there was a great earthquake: for the angel of the Lord descended from heaven, and came and rolled back the stone from the door, and sat upon it. His countenance was like lightning, and his raiment white as snow'.

261(20) rainbow of the soul the rainbow was a sign of God's covenant with Noah that the earth would never be destroyed by flood—see Genesis 9. 11–13.

262(26) Dawn o'er the eastern sea in Hogg's tale 'Mary Burnet', Mary's old father thinks she will be restored to them from the east 'because a' our blessings come frae that airt' (*The Shepherd's Calendar*, p. 221).

Hymn for the Sabbath Evening

262(4) Without a veil between an image perhaps drawn from II Corinthians 3. 13–16, where Moses's seeing God through a veil is contrasted with the more perfect perception of the Christian.

Morning Prayer for Week Days

262(d) made the outgoings of the evening and morning to rejoice over me 'thou makest the outgoings of the morning and evening to rejoice' (Psalm 65. 8).

262(d) a new creature created in Christ Jesus unto good works the faithful act of belief in Christ's atonement was depicted as the imaginary shedding of the believer's old self and the taking on of a new and Christian personality, and an outward physical sign of belief was the performance of good works. See Ephesians 2. 10: 'For we are his workmanship, created in Christ Jesus unto good works, which God hath before ordained that we should walk in them'.

262(d) May his precious blood blot out all my sins the New Testament sacrifice of Christ was the atonement for the sin of all mankind: see Acts 3. 19.

263(a) in thy fear it is a biblical commonplace that those who worship God do so with an equal measure of fear and praise. See, for example, Psalm 112. 1: 'Praise ye the LORD. Blessed *is* the man *that* feareth the LORD, *that* delighteth greatly in his commandments'.

Evening Prayer for Week Days

263(b) Thou watchest over thy people [...] followers of that which is good echoes ideas expressed in Psalm 91.

Hymn for the Close of the Week

263(1) thy footstool a reference to Psalm 99. 5: 'Exalt ye the LORD our God, and worship at his footstool; *for* he *is* holy'.

263-64 (9-12) Whether thy way [...] waves deform a recollection perhaps of Psalm 107. 25: 'For he commandeth, and raiseth the stormy wind, which lifteth up the waves thereof'.

264(23) angel of thy presence the phrase 'angel of his presence' occurs in Isaiah 63. 9.

264(44) riches of thy grace a reference to Ephesians 2. 7: 'That in the ages to come he might shew the exceeding riches of his grace in *his* kindness toward us through Christ Jesus'.

Hymn for General Use

265(16) Gospel of thy grace referring to Paul's words in Acts 20. 24: 'the ministry, which I have received of the Lord Jesus, to testify the gospel of the grace of God'.

265(22) dust to dust declines from God's curse on Adam in Genesis 3. 19: 'for dust thou art, and unto dust shalt thou return'.

265(23-24) beyond the sun [...] glory shines an allusion to the New Jerusalem of Revelation: 'And the city had no need of the sun, neither of the moon, to shine in it: for the glory of God did lighten it, and the Lamb *is* the light thereof' (21. 23). See also Hogg's depiction of the tent of God beyond the sun in Part II of *The Pilgrims of the Sun* (Edinburgh: Blackwood; London: Murray, 1815), pp. 44–46.

Hymn on the Omnipresence of the Deity

266(8) This knowledge [...] too high! Hogg's 'Hymn' draws extensively on Psalm 139, and this specific passage derives from Psalm 139. 6: '*Such* knowledge *is* too wonderful for me; it is high, I cannot *attain* to it'.

266(11) The light and the darkness [...] same Psalm 139. 12 states that 'the darkness and the light *are* both alike *to thee*'.

266(17-19) Or mount I [...] parts of the sea '*If* I take the wings of the morning, *and* dwell in the uttermost parts of the sea' (Psalm 139. 9).

266(21-22) scale I the cloud [...] shadows of hell 'If I ascend up into heaven, thou *art* there: if I make my bed in hell, behold, thou *art there*' (Psalm 139. 8).

To Mrs James Cochrane

273 [title] Mrs Cochrane is discussed in the Textual and Introductory Note to this poem.

273(14) **Waterloo-place** the Cochrane family lived at 11 Waterloo Place in London.

Glossary

This Glossary is intended only as a brief guide to Hogg's less familiar vocabulary. For words from poems that also appeared in Hogg's *A Queer Book*, it is greatly indebted to the Glossary in Peter Garside's edition of that collection (S/SC, 1995). It is also greatly indebted to those great standard works, the *Oxford English Dictionary* and the *Scottish National Dictionary*, as well as to *The Concise Scots Dictionary*, ed. by Mairi Robinson (Aberdeen: Aberdeen University Press, 1985), and *The Scots Dialect Dictionary*, ed. by Alexander Warrack (New Lanark: Waverley Books, 2000). Readers requiring more information are advised to refer to these works. In a number of places Hogg uses phrases and idioms which require further explanation: these cases are discussed in the Explanatory Notes rather than in this Glossary.

aboon: above

adventine: perhaps a nonce word from 'adventitious'

ae: one

air-springs: perhaps 'air vents'

aneath: beneath

anent: concerning, about

angel: a divine messenger

annealed: kindled, burnt, or baked

apologue: a moral fable, an allegorical story that conveys a useful lesson

apothegm: a pithy saying, giving an important truth in a few words

arglebargaining: disputing, haggling

asklent: aslant

astonied: as if turned to stone; stunned, numbed or paralysed

athraw: awry

athwart: across; from one side to the other, often obliquely

ava: at all, of all

awis: perhaps from 'awys', to think seriously

awthegither: altogether, nothing but

aye: ever, always

ayont: beyond

ayril: meaning uncertain, but possibly signifying a musical air

bairn: a child

barmings: yeast formed on a fermenting liquor

Bawtie: a common name for a dog

beck: a bow, or gesture of respect

bedgown: a kind of jacket worn by working women

behadden: beholden, obliged, in duty bound to do something

ben: inwards, towards the best room in the house: the best and most inward room

ben-end: the part of the house containing the *ben*

beuk-sworn: on oath, having sworn on the bible

big: to build

binge: to bow humbly or servilely

bire: a cowshed

bittle: a kitchen tool for bruising barley, mashing potatoes, &c.

black-cock: the male of the black grouse

blaeberries: bilberries

blatter: a blow, or a loud rattling noise like hail

blink, blynke: a glance, a gleam, a moment

blithe: joyous, cheerful, in good spirits

blithemeat: food given to people at the time of a birth, a thanksgiving feast at the birth of a child

blithesome: cheerful, merry

boardly: burly, stalwart, or rough

bode: a bid or offer; an invitation

body: a human being, a person

bogles: an ugly or terrifying ghost; a phantom, or bugbear

bog-stalker: an idle, lounging, stupid fellow

boon: gracious, benign, bounteous

bosky: covered with bushes or undergrowth; wild, unfrequented

bountith: a bounty, a gift

bourne: destination, goal

brae: a hill, a bank

branks: a type of bridle with wooden side-pieces

braw: handsome; of fine physique

brawly: finely

braxy: a fatal intestinal disease of sheep

bree: the brow

brent: smooth, unwrinkled

brock: the badger; also used contemptuously of a person

brockit: streaked; having a white stripe down the face, like a badger

broose: a race at a country wedding

bught: a fold for sheep or cattle

bumb'd: played or sung music, badly

cairn: a pyramid of rough stones, raised either as a memorial or as marking a boundary

callant: a boy, or youth

Cameronian: a member of the Reformed Presbyterian Church

cannie: cautious, careful, astute; lucky, well-omened

capperkyle: the wood-grouse

carded: prepared wool for spinning by combing the fibres parallel to one another

carle: a man, a fellow; an old man

cation: a legal term for one who stands security

cauldrife: cold in manner, lacking cheerfulness; lacking religious zeal

chack: catch; snap the teeth

chambering: indulging in lewdness

cheip: to chirp

cherub: one of the second order of angels; also used for a beautiful and innocent child

cherubim: the plural of *cherub*

chimla: chimney; also used to signify the hearth or fireside

chump: perhaps 'to chomp'

clars: perhaps a verb derived from to 'clarion'

clash: an impact, a downpour (of something soft or moist)

claverin: idle or foolish talking

clinked: moved quickly or hurriedly

clippit: shaved or pared: figuratively, like a clipped coin

closers: arguments which end or close a dispute

clough: a ravine or gorge; a cliff

clout: a rag or piece of cloth

cludds: clouds

coal-cawer: coal-crier, i.e. a coal-seller

cockamers: meaning uncertain

coft: bought, purchased

cog: a wooden container made of staves

companion-door: entrance to the master's cabin; door beneath a skylight admitting light to a lower deck or cabin

compend: an abbreviation or shortening or embodiment in miniature

cope: a covering like a vault

correi: a hollow on the side of a mountain

cousin-german: first cousin, the child of a parental sibling

couthie: sociable, sympathetic, comfortable, snug, pleasant

cover: woods, undergrowth and bushes that serve to shelter game

cowes: surpasses, outdoes

craik: to croak; utter a harsh cry (of birds)

crane-berries: cranberries

crouse: bold, confident, self-satisfied

daddit: struck heavily

daffin: fun, foolish behaviour

darn: to hide or conceal oneself

day-lily: a type of lily, the flower of which lasts only for a day, of the genus *Hemerocallis*

Deil ma care!: no matter, for all that

deils: devils

den: a narrow valley or ravine

deodand: a thing to be given to God; see also note on 77(101)

dern: dark, dreary, desolate; to hide

dights: wipes or rubs clean

dike: a boundary wall of stones or turf

dink: neat, finely-dressed, trim and dainty

dinted: indented, having marks made by blows or pressure

dirl: to tingle, to vibrate

disk: dusk

division: the length of pavement between two roads which intersect it

dole: grief, pain

donjon: an archaic form of 'dungeon'; great tower or keep of a castle

dool: grief, distress

douce: sedate, sober, respectable; neat, tidy, pleasant, comfortable

doure: sullen, humourless, dull

douss: see *douce* above

dow: dove

downa: to be unable to

downae: am unwilling to

dowrer: harder, more severe

dowy: sad, dismal

draught: the action of displacing so much water; the depth of water which a ship draws

dreigh: long, wearisome

dress: to trim, or prepare in a proper manner

drouth: thirst

dung (down): cast or driven down

dwam: a swoon or fainting-fit

ee: eye

ee-bree: eyebrow, eyelash

een: eyes

eggler: a hawker who collects eggs from outlying farms and villages for sale at local markets

eiry: fear-inspiring, weird, strange

eiry: the nest of a bird of prey, such a building high in the air

eldern: elderly

eldrich: resembling elves; weird, unearthly, strange

euphonies: pleasant musical sounds

ewe-gowan: the common daisy

fack: really, indeed, as sure (as)

fadge: a loaf of bread

farrand (with *auld):* of a certain disposition, or temperament

fauld: a sheepfold; to fold, to enclose

faured (well- or *ill-):* appearance, aspect or look

fay: a fairy

feal-dike: a field wall, built or covered with sods

feared: afraid

feck: the majority, the greater part

fere: a companion, a mate; a dwarf

fit: foot

fizenless: spiritless, lacking energy or substance

flam: a counterfeit, mockery, or deception

flaught: to weave, to intertwine

fleeching: coaxing, cajoling, or flattering

flexile: yielding, tractable, easily bending

flummery: mere compliment, trifling, empty nonsense

flyting: scolding, or chiding

foggie: an old-fashioned fellow; a garrison soldier

forbye: besides, in addition to

forecastle: a short raised deck at the forepart of the ship

foreflown: meaning not identified

franked: directed by an M.P. or other privileged person, so the recipient would not have to pay postage

fremit: strange, foreign, unfamiliar

gair: a strip of green grass on a hillside

Galashiels (grey): a coarse, grey woollen cloth manufactured at Galashiels in Selkirkshire

gar: to make or cause something to be done

gate: way or path, sometimes figurative

gauze: a thin, transparent fabric

gaye, gayan: very, considerably

gaye and: considerably, rather

gee'd (up): turned up

gerse: grass, pasture for animals

gin: if, whether

gird: encircle, fasten with a band or bands

girn: snarl, grin, grimace

glede: a kite, or other bird of prey

gleg: keen, quick in perception, alert

gleid: a spark, a glimmer

glisk: a glimpse or glance

gloaming: dusk, evening twilight

gloff: a shock, a scare

glyde: an old, worn-out horse

gomeral: a fool, a stupid person

goodman: a husband; the male head of a household

goud: gold

gowan: the daisy

gowd: gold

gowk: the cuckoo; a fool or simpleton

grained: groaned

grat: wept

greet, greeting: weep, weeping

groo: shrink or shudder in horror or terror

gudeman: see under 'goodman'

guerdon: a reward or recompense

gully (knife): a large knife

gunnel: the upper edge of a ship's side; the timber extending round the top side of the hull

gyes: masquerades

gyre: see note on 33(18)

gysand: dry, shrivelled

hack: a horse for ordinary riding as opposed to hunting; often used contemptuously of a sorry jade

haffets: the temples, or side-locks of hair

hags: a hollow of marshy ground in a moor; a channel from which peat has been cut

hallan: an inner wall or partition between the door and the fireplace, or between the living-room and the byre of a cottage

hallanshaker: a beggar, vagabond, or tramp

hantle: a considerable quantity, a great deal

hap, happing: to cover, or covering, so as to conceal or shelter

hap-shackle: a hobble for tethering a horse

harling: dragging or scraping

harns: brains, intelligence

haud: to go on, to continue

haurning: toasting, or baking on a girdle

haw: the fruit of the hawthorn

headsteel: head-stall, the headpiece of a bridle

heeze: a heave, a hitch up

hempie, hempy: a rogue, someone deserving to be hanged; used jocularly for an unruly young girl

hind: behind

hind: a farm-servant; a youth; a peasant

hinder end: the back part of anything

hing: to hang

hizzy: a disparaging term for a woman, a frivolous woman

hoolie: go carefully, be cautious

horse-couper: a horse-dealer

houdy: a midwife
hough: the thigh
hove: rose up
howe: a hollow, a cavity
howlet: the owl

ilka: each; every
ineffable: that which cannot be expressed in words
intercommuned: denounced in letters of intercommuning, i.e. outlawed or proscribed

jalouse: suspect, be suspicious of
jib-sail: a triangular stay-sail, stretching from the outer edge of the jib-boom to the fore-top-mast head

kail-yard: a kitchen garden
kebbuck: a whole cheese
kelpie: a water demon
ken: to know
kerling: an old woman; a witch
kie: cows
kimmers: intimate female friends, gossips
kirn: a churn
knowe: a knoll, the rounded top of an eminence
kythe: to show, to display; to appear

lacker: shiny, as if lacquered
lane: solitary, on one's own
lang-nebbit: long-nosed, polysyllabic
lapper: half-melted snow
lave: the rest, the remainder
laverock: the skylark
lea: a meadow; open grassland
ledges: small pieces of timber placed athwartships under the decks of a ship between the beams
leel: loyal, chaste, pure, constant in love
leglins: milk-pails
liefu: solitary
lift: the sky, the heavens
limmer: term of abuse for a woman

ling: to swing along
links: the land enclosed by the loops and windings of a stream or river
linn: a deep, narrow gorge; a waterfall; a tumbling burn in a gorge
lippen: to trust, depend upon
locker: to curl
lootching: bending the body
losel: a scoundrel, a loafer
lowe: a flame; by transference, in a rage
lown: a rogue, a rascal
lubber: a lout, a clumsy stupid fellow
luff: to bring the head of the ship nearer to the wind
lugs: the ears
lumb: the chimney or flue of a fireplace

maen: a moan
mailen: a tenant farm
mair: mair
marled: marbled, mottled
marl-pits: clay-pits, used metaphorically for the earth
matin: a morning or daybreak performance, from the name of one of the canonical offices of the breviary
maun: must
mavis: the song-thrush
mazed: perplexed, bewildered, confused
meat: food in general, for people or animals
meikle: much
minent: a minute
minim: a musical note, half the value of a semibreve
misrid: tangled, involved, confused
mockrife: scornful, mocking
moor-bink: a moorland bank
moor-cock: the male of the red grouse
moote: to moult; to decay slowly
morn (with the): tomorrow, the

following morning or day

moss: a bog, or moorland

moteley: variegated, or parti-coloured

mountebank: an impudent charlatan, who might mount a bench or stage before his audience

muckle: much, a great deal of; the bigger of two

mumping: nibble, twitching the lips like a rabbit

muslin: delicately woven cotton or linen fabric—perhaps white by association

muth: oppressed or exhausted by heat

neeve: the fist

nettle-earnest: in dead earnest

niddelty-noddelty: perhaps from *nid-nod*, 'to nod repeatedly'

noisome: offensive, harmful

off loof: offhand, extempore

onyx: a quartz consisting of plane layers of different colours

orient: the region of the heavens in which the sun rises

oughts: anything

ouphe: an elf's child, a fairy changeling: the earlier form of 'oaf'

palfrey: a small saddle-horse for ladies

pall: a canopy, especially the dark cloth spread over a coffin

partricks: partridges

pawkie, pawky: characterised by a sly, quiet wit

pease-weep: the lapwing

pickle: a small amount

piece: a piece of bread, a snack given to children or workers

pioneer: an excavator or miner

plaister: a plaster, or dressing for a wound

plenishing: goods, necessary equipment

quags: marshy or boggy spots, especially those covered with a layer of turf which shakes when walked on

quean: a girl or young woman

quid: a piece of tobacco, to be held in the mouth and chewed

rail: a woman's short-sleeved mantle, a bodice

rath: early; eager

reavers: plunderers, robbers

rede: advise, counsel, warn

reef: to reduce the extent of sail by taking in and rolling up part of it

reek: smoke

reekit: smoked, or sooty

reested: cured or smoked

reirdit: roared, made a loud noise

remede: remedy, redress

resting-chair: a long chair, shaped like a settle

revert: a return

rhame: a phrase or remark repeated over and over again

riggin: the ropes or chains used to support the masts and to work the sails of a ship

rivin: tearing up, lacerating, ripping

rokelay: a kind of short cloak

roost: rust

roundelay: a short simple song with a refrain

round-house: a cabin or set of cabins on the after-part of the quarter-deck of a ship

rowan: the mountain ash, which has bright red berries

rowed, rowing: rolled, rolling

ruing: repenting, regretting

ruggin: tugging, pulling

rusk: see note on 66(b)

sackless: innocent, inoffensive

sair: sore; severely, very much

sand-lark: the ringed plover; the sand-piper

sark: a shirt

saur: a smell, particularly an evil or sickening one

screeds: a shrill or screeching noise

seraphic: pertaining to the seraphim

seraphs: the highest of the nine orders of angels, supposedly distinguished by the fervour of love

shakedown: a bed made of straw loosely disposed on the floor

sharping-stane: a whetstone

shaw: a wood, a thicket

shelling: the act removing husks

shieling: a roughly-made hut, a shepherd's house

shilfu': the chaffinch

shot-stern: shooting-stars

shrouds: a pair of ropes leading from the head of a ship's mast and serving to relieve it from lateral strain

sic: such

sickan: such, of such a kind

side-langled: (of an animal), hobbled, having the foreleg and hindleg tied to prevent straying

siller: silver coin, money in general

skairs: scours

skempy: scamp-like

skreeds: see *screeds*

skreeving: gliding along, speeding on smoothly

slack: to be backward or dilatory

smeddum: spirit, energy

smirl: a snigger, a sneering or mocking laugh

snappit: caught

snibbelt: a small piece of wood at the end of a tether, slipped through an eye at the other end to fasten it

snirls: nostrils

snirting: snorting, breathing sharply through the nose

snood: a ribbon for tying hair

snore, snored: to snort, snorted

soke: a ploughshare

solan: the solan-goose, or gannet

sonsie: attractive, comely, buxom

sowp: a large amount of liquid, a soaking

spaining: weaning

spang: a sudden movement, a jerk or bound

sparry: of a lustre resembling that of spar

speer, speir: to ask a question, to make inquiries

split (new): absolutely new, as new as split wood

spring: a lively tune

spring: to cause a bird to rise from cover

spunk: spirit, mettle, courage, pluck

stabled: secured, established

starns: stars

steek, steeked: close(d), fasten(ed)

stite: to stagger or stumble; to walk clumsily

stown: stolen

striffles: meaning not identified

sturt: trouble, disquiet

sugh: the sound of the wind, or of a deep sigh

sumph: a simpleton, a slow-witted person

sun-fawn: dappled by the passage of clouds overhead in sunlight

sunks: straw pads or cushions slung across a horse to act as a saddle

swairf: to swoon or fall into a stupor

swan-shot: a large size of shot, used for shooting swans

swathe: the space covered by a sweep of a mower's scythe; the grass fallen on the ground after being so cut

swaw: to swing, to sway

swoof: to make a rustling or murmuring sound

syne: since (*sin syne*, since then)

tabernacle: a shrine, from the Old Testament tent containing the Ark of the Covenant

teemfu': prolific or fertile

teen: harm or injury suffered; affliction

term: one of four days in the year when rents are due and leases begin and end: Candlemas, Whitsunday, Lammas, and Martinmas

terrene: of the nature of the earth, earthly

theeket: thatched

thole: to endure, to suffer

thow: a thaw, melting with the heat

thrapple: the throat or windpipe

thrawn: thrown

thumbikins: a thumbscrew

timmer: wooden, made of wood

titties: sisters

tod: a fox

toom: empty

top-gallant: a sail at the head of the topmast of a ship

touts: trumpets, makes a noise like a horn

touzle: a struggle or contest

towzling: a rough romp with a person of the opposite sex

trials: the examination of a probationer by a presbytery before he is licensed as a preacher

trow: to feel sure, to believe

tryste: a market or fair, though not one fixed by charter

twa-pun-ten: costing two pounds and ten shillings, fifty shillings (£2.50)

uncannie: unlucky, inauspicious; mysterious, ominous

unco: remarkable, extraordinary, notable; unknown, strange, unusual

unshrieven: not absolved; someone who has not made a confession and received absolution

unyirthly: unearthly, supernatural

upmade: pleased, elated

valves: see note on 77 (99)

wae: woe; grieved, sorrowful

waefu': woeful, afflicted with distress

wale: the pick, the thing chosen as the best

wappit: waved violently, was moved to and fro

wareless: unwary, incautious

warp: the threads which are tautly extended lengthwise in a loom

waste: ruined, unoccupied, empty

waste: uncultivated and uninhabited or sparsely-inhabited land

watch coat: a thick jacket like the one a sailor would wear aboard ship during his watch

water-kelpie: a water-demon

waukin, wauking: waking; keeping watch over

waw: wail; the sound made by a cat or a child in distress

wean: a child, especially a young one

weary fa': a curse or imprecation

weft: the threads that go sideways in a loom, interlaced and at right angles to the warp threads

whaups: curlews

wheen: a few of, a small number of

whew: to whistle

whig, whigamore: names for a Covenanter

whiles: sometimes

whitty-whattying: shilly-shallying; a *whittie-whattier* is a person who employs every means to gain his or her end

win: make or find one's way

winna: will not, shall not

wis: to know

wit (with *get*): learn, find out, become aware of

witch-bell: the harebell, *Campanula rotundifolia*

won: to dwell

wood-betony: the woodland plant *stachys* or *betonica officinalis*, which has medicinal properties *woodbine:* a climbing and twining plant, usually *convulvulus* but sometimes honeysuckle

wraith: an apparition of a living person taken as an omen of that person's death; a ghost or apparition of a dead person

wudd: mad, demented, insane

yammer: howl, grumble, complain, raise a din

yaud: an old mare or horse; a contemptuous term for a woman

yawl: a ship's boat, usually having four or six oars

yerk, yerking: whip, strike, beat

ye's, yese: you shall

yill: ale, beer

yird: earth

yool: to howl, to wail

yorlin: the yellowhammer